Databric Lakehouse Platform Cookbook

100+ recipes for building a scalable
and secure Databricks Lakehouse

Dr. Alan L. Dennis

www.bpbonline.com

First published: 2024

Published by BPB Online
WeWork
119 Marylebone Road
London NW1 5PU

UK | UAE | INDIA | SINGAPORE

ISBN 978-93-55519-566

www.bpbonline.com

Dedicated to

My loving and supportive wife,

Kim

Foreword

There is no denying that data is the lifeblood of industry. Everyone understands that businesses that harness their data well, will thrive while the ones that do not, will fall by the wayside. Choosing the correct platform for your data estate is, perhaps, the most critical decision a business can make. The second most important factor is, of course, to hire the right team to build on this chosen platform.

2023 has shown us that GenAI is the future and I am convinced that there is only one data platform that is natively suited for the demands that GenAI will impose on the data estates of the future: the Lakehouse built on Databricks. Over the last 10 years, Databricks has transformed itself from a niche Spark-focused shop to a visionary organization building a holistic data platform that can support Analytics, Data Integration (a fancier term for ETL or ELT) and AI/ML: including the now white-hot GenAI use cases. While a lot of competing data platforms and data clouds make similar claims, there is only one platform, that is, Databricks: that has been doing cloud-native, multi-language data processing at scale: for 10 years now.

I consider myself fortunate that I discovered and fell in love with Apache Spark in 2014 and then got a chance to join Databricks in 2019. I am truly grateful that I got to pick the brains of some of the smartest minds in the universe during that time. The author of this book, Dr. Alan Dennis, is one such individual and it is my honor to count him as a friend and a business partner.

Whether you are a seasoned data professional or someone looking to unlock the potential of data in your organization, this book is your key to a data revolution. Databricks and the Lakehouse paradigm offer a fresh perspective on data management, and this book is your guide to mastering it. Alan's recipe-driven approach to teaching is perfect for the real world: it will enable you to deliver results quickly in the immediate term: and will help you connect the dots and build a strong foundation for self-learning over the longer term. The context-setting sections give you a quick history of features and approaches over the years. It will help you appreciate how the platform has evolved and most importantly, help you avoid old pitfalls and anti-patterns.

Apache Spark, Databricks and Lakehouse have transformed my life for the better: and it is my sincere hope and best wishes that you, the reader, have a similar fulfilling experience. Onward!

Subramanian Iyer
Principal, Speedboat Professional Services
Award-winning Architect and Certified Instructor on Databricks and Lakehouse
Ex-Brickster (2019-2023) and Spark fanboy since 2014

About the Author

Dr. Alan L. Dennis has been writing software for over 30 years. His experiences range from being one of the first employees at a startup to leading a team of over twenty developers. He has held titles such as Programmer, Architect, Chief Technical Officer, and member of technical staff. He has worked for many Fortune 50 companies, with a wide range of industry experience.

He holds a Doctorate in Computer Science with a concentration in Big Data Analytics, a Master's in Computer Science with specialization in Artificial Intelligence, and a Bachelor's of Business Administration with focus on Computer Information Systems. He teaches graduate classes at several universities and is a Databricks Certified Trainer.

About the Reviewers

❖ **Jay Kalathia** is an experienced Senior Software Engineer, with over two decades of experience in designing, developing, and optimizing cloud-based solutions on the Azure platform. He has a diverse background with proficiency in various programming languages such as Python, C#, JavaScript, and more. Jay is skilled in building infrastructure as code, developing CI/CD pipelines on Azure DevOps, and working on cloud-native solutions and tools including Azure, AWS, AKS, Kubernetes, and Terraform. Additionally, he has extensive experience with Azure Databricks and other cloud-based Big Data solutions. Jay is also a learner; from taking courses to completing certifications to stay up to date with latest technology trends.

❖ **Mahesh Das** is a Technology Evangelist and a Databricks Certified Data Science Professional. He is currently focused on the development of cloud-native solutions for ingesting and refining data from various sources using Azure Cloud, Databricks, Azure Data Factory, and Terraform scripts. Mahesh is actively engaged in projects implementing Large Language Models for diverse applications and remains a dedicated learner in the field of Machine Learning and Artificial Intelligence. With over 18 years of experience, he has contributed to numerous significant IT transformation projects for Fortune 500 clients across a range of industries, including Manufacturing, FMCG, oil and gas, Managed Print Services, and metals and mining. Mahesh possesses additional skills in AWS Cloud and SAP Master Data Governance, covering various functional domains such as sales and distribution, finance, and manufacturing. He is not only an avid reader of cutting-edge AI technologies but also serves as a technical reviewer for books within the same domain.

Acknowledgement

Many people have had a hand in this book. First, I would like to thank my parents for always supporting and encouraging me. They taught me to figure out how things work and, ideally, put them back together again afterward. My mother passed before this book could be completed. She will be missed, but her Heavenly Father called, and she went. I would also like to thank my wife Kim, for supporting and encouraging me and understanding when I disappear for weeks on end.

I would like to thank Jay, and Mahesh for their input to the book. They provided valuable feedback throughout the process. I would also like to thank Subramanian for his kind words in the foreword.

Lastly, I am incredibly thankful for you, gentle reader. I wrote this for you and I hope you find value in it. There is something for everyone in this book, let me know what you find.

Preface

It is commonly understood that valuable insights can be found in an organization's data. One way to extract that value is to construct a Data Lakehouse. This book helps you create a Lakehouse on the Databricks Platform. It is the culmination of decades of data processing design and implementation.

It is not easy to create a data ecosystem. There are many competing priorities and technical challenges. This book walks you through the process, providing hands-on examples. We organize those steps into recipes. This keeps the author from waxing on about theory and helps the reader find the information needed in a given situation. We cover the theory behind the approaches used and guide the reader to avoid common pitfalls.

We start with the basics, such as explaining what a Databricks Lakehouse is, why we need them, and what value it brings. We move on to applying the concepts in practice. Part of the reason for constructing a Data Lakehouse is to enable users to access its data. We then discuss the various personas that benefit from a Databricks Lakehouse.

While we start with the fundamentals, we rapidly move on to more advanced topics. A good understanding of SQL, Python, Spark, and cloud computing would benefit the reader but is not required.

Chapter 1: Introduction to Databricks Lakehouse – This chapter provides a brief history of Big Data, Spark, and Databricks. It introduces the reader to the community edition of Databricks as a starting point for using Databricks. We discuss why we construct a Lakehouse and present the overall architecture. We provide clear definitions for each of the layers of a Databricks Lakehouse. We discuss design considerations and compare Lakehouses to other data technologies.

Chapter 2: Setting-up a Databricks Workspace – This chapter presents the information necessary to provision and effectively use a Databricks environment. This includes examining core Databricks concepts, service tier selection, and cloud selection considerations. Deployment details are examined, including those with long-lasting implications. Access control and other configurations are discussed, along with the types of clusters and performance levels.

Chapter 3: Connecting to Storage – This chapter covers the approaches and tradeoffs to connect to storage. The Databricks File System is discussed in detail as it is an important element of the Lakehouse platform. The background of the file system is reviewed, and various ways of connecting to storage are explored. The approaches to Lakehouse design are presented, with recommendations on how to organize a Lakehouse. Recommendations are provided regarding the documentation of allowed operations. Recipes containing various examples of connecting to Azure storage systems are provided.

Chapter 4: Creating Delta Tables – This chapter describes how to construct a Delta Lake, including a discussion of managed and external tables. Guidance is provided to help decide which type of table to create. Examples are provided of creating tables using SQL and the Spark API. Core concepts such as secrete scopes are discussed, along with example of creating tables from AWS S3, GCP buckets, and Azure ADLS.

Chapter 5: Data Profiling and Modeling in the Lakehouse – This chapter examines two of the more important activities when constructing a Data Lakehouse. Various ways of performing profiling are examined, including Databricks' native Data Profile feature. Discussion of the Databricks Describe and Summary features are included, along with analysis at scale using ydata_profiling.

Chapter 6: Extracting from Source and Loading to Bronze – This chapter covers the first step in refining data. A discussion is presented regarding using the raw zone or skipping it and going from source to bronze. Several ways of incrementally ingesting data are presented, which is essential for a high-performance Databricks Lakehouse. These methods include self-managed watermarks, Auto Loader, Delta Live Tables, and streaming data.

Chapter 7: Transforming to Create Silver – This chapter continues the refinement journey, picking up data at the Bronze layer and moving it to Silver. Both incremental and full refinement are discussed. Several approaches to processing are discussed, including the importance of data quality rules and expectations. Common Silver-to-Silver operations are discussed, including denormalization, JSON exploding, and projection reshaping.

Chapter 8: Transforming to Create Gold for Business Purposes – This chapter continues the discussion of refining data, with the goal of answering business questions. Gold tables are built to answer a specific question. The sources for Gold tables are discussed, with implementations in PySpark and Delta Live Tables. As Gold tables are optimized for consumption, a brief discussion of support-related operations such as vacuuming and optimizing tables is present.

Chapter 9: Machine Learning and Data Science – Data scientists are common users of the Databricks Lakehouse. We examine using Machine Learning in Databricks, and the use of AutoML. Next, we discuss MLflow, and the importance it plays in deploying models to production. Lastly, we briefly discuss the Databricks feature store.

Chapter 10: SQL Analysis – SQL is one of the most widely known languages. We discuss the SQL Analysis features built into Databricks, including Databricks SQL. We show how to create and manage a SQL Warehouse. We discuss the usage of the SQL Editor and use it to write common queries. We create dashboards and alerts using those queries. We close with a discussion of cost and performance considerations.

Chapter 11: Graph Analysis – There are many ways to perform analysis; one way is to use mathematical graph algorithms. We discuss the nature of graphs and when using graph algorithms is appropriate. We discuss GraphX and GraphFrames, along with the operations they enable and associated algorithms. Lastly, we discuss reading data from Neo4J's AuraDB from Databricks.

Chapter 12: Visualizations – There are many ways to present data; visualizations can be very powerful. We discuss visualization best practices and how to create a Databricks dashboard. We also discuss native visualization support within a Databricks notebook. We conclude the chapter by discussing the use of Power BI with Databricks.

Chapter 13: Governance – Without proper governance, a Databricks Lakehouse will not be successful. We discuss the role of data governance and the use of Databricks' Unity Catalog. We walk through the installation and usage of Unity Catalog and review the major benefits. We discuss the steps to install and use Azure Purview in combination with Unity Catalog.

Chapter 14: Operations – This chapter covers the steps necessary to keep a Lakehouse working effectively, including source code management and orchestration. Preventive scheduled maintenance can help avoid unacceptable processing time and outages. We also discuss how to manage and maintain visibility of costs.

Chapter 15: Tips, Tricks, Troubleshooting, and Best Practices – This final chapter contains important elements that did not make it into other parts of the book. We revisit ingesting data, by ingesting relational data. Discuss performance optimizations such as using pools. We discuss how to orchestrate notebooks. Lastly, we conclude with a discussion of best practices and guiding principles.

Code Bundle and Coloured Images

Please follow the link to download the
Code Bundle and the *Coloured Images* of the book:

https://rebrand.ly/llidt00

The code bundle for the book is also hosted on GitHub at
https://github.com/bpbpublications/Databricks-Lakehouse-Platform-Cookbook.
In case there's an update to the code, it will be updated on the existing GitHub repository.

We have code bundles from our rich catalogue of books and videos available at **https://github.com/bpbpublications**. Check them out!

Errata

We take immense pride in our work at BPB Publications and follow best practices to ensure the accuracy of our content to provide with an indulging reading experience to our subscribers. Our readers are our mirrors, and we use their inputs to reflect and improve upon human errors, if any, that may have occurred during the publishing processes involved. To let us maintain the quality and help us reach out to any readers who might be having difficulties due to any unforeseen errors, please write to us at :

errata@bpbonline.com

Your support, suggestions and feedbacks are highly appreciated by the BPB Publications' Family.

Did you know that BPB offers eBook versions of every book published, with PDF and ePub files available? You can upgrade to the eBook version at www.bpbonline.com and as a print book customer, you are entitled to a discount on the eBook copy. Get in touch with us at :

business@bpbonline.com for more details.

At **www.bpbonline.com**, you can also read a collection of free technical articles, sign up for a range of free newsletters, and receive exclusive discounts and offers on BPB books and eBooks.

Piracy

If you come across any illegal copies of our works in any form on the internet, we would be grateful if you would provide us with the location address or website name. Please contact us at **business@bpbonline.com** with a link to the material.

If you are interested in becoming an author

If there is a topic that you have expertise in, and you are interested in either writing or contributing to a book, please visit **www.bpbonline.com**. We have worked with thousands of developers and tech professionals, just like you, to help them share their insights with the global tech community. You can make a general application, apply for a specific hot topic that we are recruiting an author for, or submit your own idea.

Reviews

Please leave a review. Once you have read and used this book, why not leave a review on the site that you purchased it from? Potential readers can then see and use your unbiased opinion to make purchase decisions. We at BPB can understand what you think about our products, and our authors can see your feedback on their book. Thank you!

For more information about BPB, please visit **www.bpbonline.com**.

Join our book's Discord space

Join the book's Discord Workspace for Latest updates, Offers, Tech happenings around the world, New Release and Sessions with the Authors:

https://discord.bpbonline.com

Table of Contents

CHAPTER 1
Introduction to Databricks Lakehouse

Introduction

Welcome to our journey of learning and mastering the Databricks Lakehouse Platform. This is a hands-on book. While we will cover each topic's theoretical and technical foundations, you will have code to help you learn how to build a Lakehouse and succeed using Databricks.

Structure

In this chapter, we will cover the following topics:

- Background
- Brief history of Big Data, Spark, and Databricks
- Databricks community edition
- Data Lakehouse value proposition
- Lakehouse architecture
- Design considerations
- Lakehouse compared to other data technologies

Objectives

This chapter introduces nomenclature commonly used when discussing the Databricks Lakehouse Platform. By the end of the chapter, you should be able to describe a typical Lakehouse configuration and understand the architectural components and the value proposition of the lakehouse architecture.

Background

It is often important to understand a phenomenon's history that influenced its creation, and Data Lakehouse is no exception. We start with a brief history of Big Data, Spark, and Databricks. We briefly discuss the Databricks community edition and perform our first analysis in Databricks. We close this section by discussing the value proposition that drives the adoption of Data lakehouse, particularly Databricks Lakehouse.

Brief history of Big Data, Spark, and Databricks

When looking at how things came to be, we often discuss supporting and challenging forces. In the case of Big Data, several forces were driving its adoption. One key supporting force was the shift of the Internet from companies and government entities sharing information with their customers to users of platforms creating content in social media. Companies also learned that online sales had many advantages over traditional outlets, including lower operating costs. This shift generated vast amounts of data that previously was minimal. Online retailers learned that examining those log files could give insights into their customers that previously was not possible. The desire to process this information, which was too large to process with traditional file-processing approaches, led to the creation of a new set of technologies. Big Data was used to label these distributed, software-based fault-tolerant algorithms and technologies.

One of the early success stories of Big Data was Hadoop. Hadoop is a collection of open-source projects related to processing large, fast, or variant data. An early processing approach in Hadoop was called MapReduce. MapReduce was a framework that simplified the process of creating distributed solutions. Before Big Data frameworks like MapReduce, software developers coordinated activities between various workers attempting to work together to solve a problem. Often, one or more of those workers would become unavailable. The software developer's job was to determine how to address this and many other challenges. With MapReduce, a developer was tasked with writing a few functions called by a framework to simplify the process. While MapReduce was a significant advancement, it was limited by its original design and purpose. MapReduce was focused on processing large or numerous files. Due to this design goal, it failed to support iteration and relied heavily on disk drives.

Spark was developed to address many of these challenges. Spark is a computational solution that relies on other technologies for storage. It also favors processing data in memory, resulting in significant performance improvements over MapReduce. Spark also enabled iteration during processing. These advancements lead to its rapid adoption and increasing popularity. Many of the creators of Spark formed Databricks in 2013. Databricks is a cloud company supporting the major cloud vendors. In 2017 Azure Databricks was announced. This partnership was notable because of the high integration between Azure and Databricks.

A data lakehouse is an architecture that combines the best elements of data lakes to address data warehousing needs. It is an open standards-based set of technologies. A key distinction of data lakehouse from data lakes is that it uses a schema and **Atomic, Consistent, Isolated, and Durable** (**ACID**) transactions. Lakehouses allow updates to a record, while data lakes treat data as immutable. In Databricks, Spark is the computational engine supporting all lakehouse processing, and Delta Lake is the storage format used to enable ACID transactions and schemas. Delta Lake is based on the Parquet format, with transaction logs in **JavaScript Object Notation** (**JSON**) to journal interactions with data. A Delta Lake exists on top of data lakes and cloud storage containers.

Databricks community edition

Databricks understands that learning technology is essential for its adoption. Databricks offers a community edition of its platform to enable learning and smaller workloads. The community edition offers limited functionality compared to the enterprise-class versions available on AWS, Azure, and **Google Cloud Platform** (**GCP**). The community edition has several restrictions, including little computational power and lacks automation capabilities via an API. To learn more about the Databricks community edition, go to **https://docs. databricks.com/getting-started/community-edition.html**.

Recipe 1: Signing up for the Databricks community edition

To sign up for the Databricks community edition, go to **https://www.databricks.com/try-databricks** and fill out the form, as shown in *Figure 1.1*. You will be asked for your name, email, company, and job title:

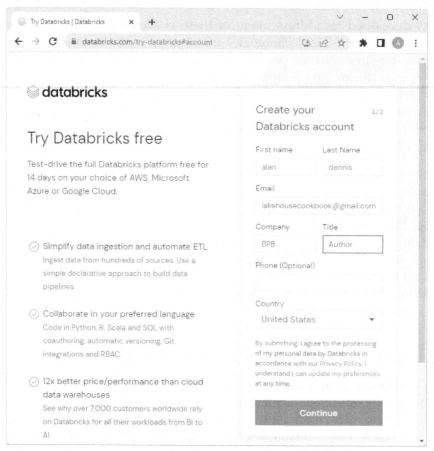

Figure 1.1: Sign-up for Databricks Community Edition

After clicking **Continue**, you are presented with a page asking you to choose your cloud provider, as shown in *Figure 1.2*. Under the section that refers to not having a cloud account, there is a link titled **Get Started** with Community Edition. It is relatively small and easy to miss, but it is how to sign up for the free community edition.

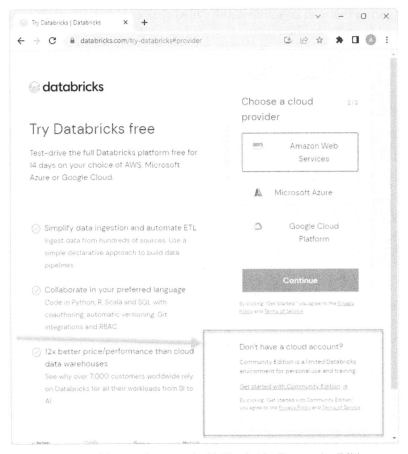

Figure 1.2: *Select getting started with Databricks Community Edition*

After clicking the link, you will likely be asked to prove you are a human by solving a simple puzzle. After solving the puzzle, you will be redirected to a page asking you to confirm your email address. Check your email and click the link in the body to confirm receipt of the email message. You are then asked to provide a password for logging into the tool. After supplying a password, you will be redirected to the Databricks community edition home page.

Recipe 2: Creating a notebook in the Databricks Community edition

The areas of the community edition Databricks workspace are similar to that of the enterprise-class cloud-hosted versions, as shown in *Figure 1.3*. The layout is organized with left navigation that can be expanded by hovering over it and a panel containing the commonly used features on the right:

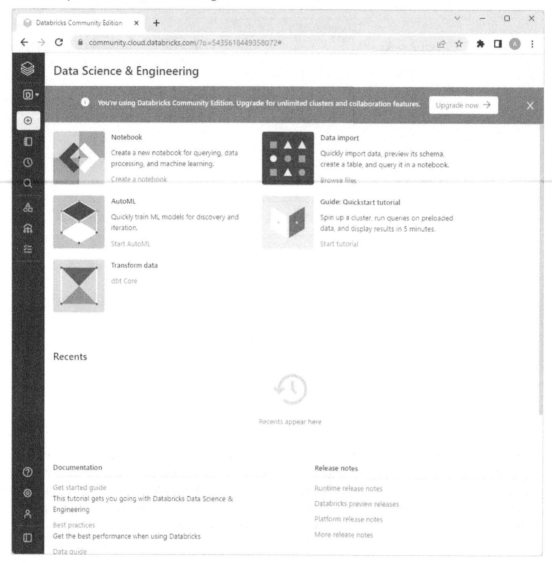

Figure 1.3: *Databricks Community Edition landing page*

Note that the interface will likely change as Databricks continues to innovate and expand its offerings. Regardless of changes, creating a new notebook and importing data will remain available. To write our first query, click on **Create a Notebook**.

The notebook paradigm has become a popular programming construct. It allows the mixing of comments, code, and results into a single experience. It also enables line-by-line execution, facilitating bug detection and data exploration. Notebooks are made up of cells, and a cell can contain source code or comments as a markdown. Notebooks in Databricks also have a default language. A powerful feature of Databricks is that each cell within a notebook need not be in the default language. We can have a single notebook with cells containing different languages, such as Python, R, SQL, or Scala.

Recipe 3: Changing a notebook's default language

To switch the default language of a notebook, click the chevron next to the language located to the right of the notebook's title at the top of the page, as shown in *Figure 1.4*:

Figure 1.4: *Default language of a Databricks Notebook*

For example, we change the notebook's default language to SQL. The first time you switch the language, you will see a prompt confirming that you want to change the language. After switching the language, we need to add some SQL that creates a table using a dataset available in all Databricks installations. Setting the default language for a notebook saves time, as each cell is already set to be the desired language. The language you use will depend on the situation. Python is a popular choice for analytics, partly because of its readability and the availability of many programming examples.

Recipe 4: Create a table from CSV using SQL

This example is based on the Databricks quick start at **https://docs.databricks.com/ getting-started/quick-start.html**. Once the SQL is in place, as shown in *Figure 1.5*, the next step is to execute it, which requires a cluster. When you click the **Run All** button, you will receive a notification that you must attach to a cluster. In this case, we want to **Create**, **Attach**, and **Run** on a cluster with the default name **My Cluster**. It will take some time to provision your cluster. Once created, you usually only need to restart the cluster before doing analysis once per session. Databricks community edition deactivates clusters after two hours of inactivity. Refer to the following *Figure 1.5*:

Figure 1.5: *Creating a Table from a CSV file*

The SQL we have entered checks to see if a table exists named **diamonds**. If it does, it will be dropped. Next, a table is created with that name using a **Comma Separated Value (CSV)** file located within the Databricks example datasets. We can tell that the CSV includes a header in the file's first row.

Recipe 5: Query a table using SQL

Once a table exists, a common thing to do is examine its contents using a **SELECT** statement, as shown in *Figure 1.6*:

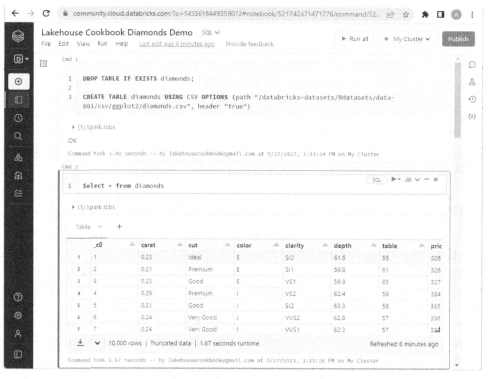

Figure 1.6: *Query Table using SQL*

Notice that the SQL is like SQL you might have written in other database systems.

Recipe 6: Examine a table's structure

When working with data, we often want to know the data types within the table. Formally, we refer to this as the **Data Definition Language** (**DDL**). To see the columns and their datatype, we use the **DESCRIBE** statement, as shown in *Figure 1.7*:

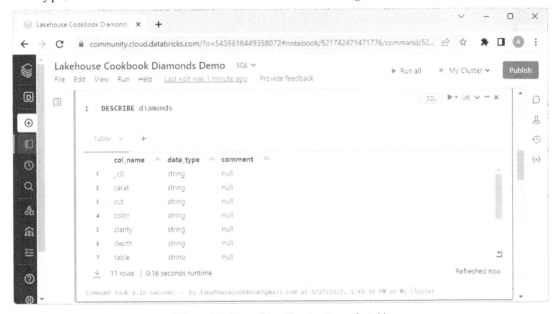

Figure 1.7: Describing the structure of a table

Notice that everything in the table is a string. This is a characteristic of CSV files. While there are several ways to address this challenge, one of the simplest is to tell Databricks to infer the table schema during load.

Recipe 7: Use infer schema on CSV in SQL

Many file formats include schemas natively. However, CSV is not one of those formats. Since knowing a schema is often essential, we want to determine it as soon as possible. Schema inference involves sampling a file or set of files' contents to discover the data types of the various attributes. The process is not perfect, but often it is good enough. Another solution is to describe the schema manually or to convert it to the desired schema after initial loading. To use schema inference is as easy as adding the infer schema option with a value of true to our **CREATE TABLE** statement, as shown in *Figure 1.8*:

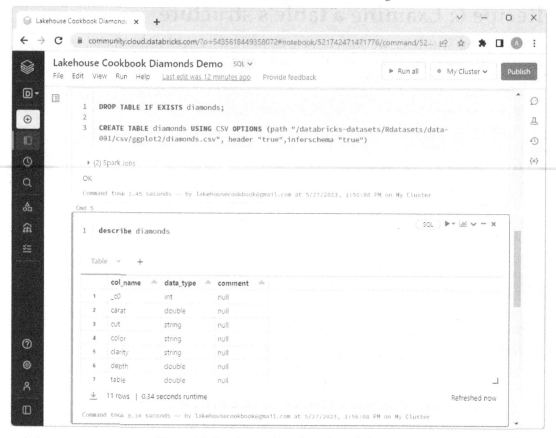

Figure 1.8: *Creating a table using schema inference*

After recreating the table using schema inference, notice that there are columns with a double data type. This data type change allows us to do some aggregation and other simple descriptive analyses.

Recipe 8: Compute mean in group by in SQL

A frequent problem we often encounter involves knowing the largest mean value of things of a certain type. For example, what clarity of diamonds has the highest average price? To answer this question, we use the **GROUP BY** statement followed by an **ORDER BY**, as shown in *Figure 1.9*. Since we want the highest value first, we use the **DESC** keyword to order values descending:

Figure 1.9: Group by with mean

Recipe 9: Importing a notebook

One useful thing is to be able to import a notebook in Databricks. There are several supported formats, including importing **Jupyter Notebooks (IPYNB),** scripts in various languages, and **Databricks Archives (DBC)**. There are several ways to import a notebook. If you have a notebook open, from the **File** menu, select **Import Notebook**, as shown in *Figure 1.10*:

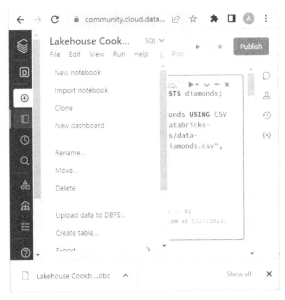

Figure 1.10: Import notebook

You are then presented with the choice of dropping a file in an area of the screen or browsing a file by clicking the browse link. Refer to the following *Figure 1.11*:

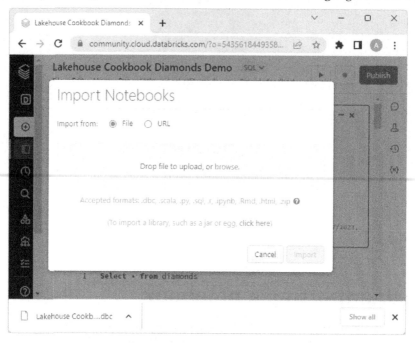

Figure 1.11: *Select file to import*

Regardless of the method, it will be available in your workspace after selecting the file.

Recipe 10: Exporting a notebook in Databricks Community Edition

Exporting from Databricks can be done at a notebook, folder, or workspace level. When viewing a notebook, export is available under the **File** menu. Selecting the DBC archive will produce a self-contained file that can be imported into a different Databricks workspace. Exporting a notebook as a source file (such as a SQL script) or as HTML is also possible. Often HTML exports are useful in sharing information with others, such as when an error is encountered.

To export a workspace, open the **Workspace** area using the left navigation. Click the chevron next to **Workspace** and select Export, as shown in *Figure 1.12*. Again, you have the choice of format:

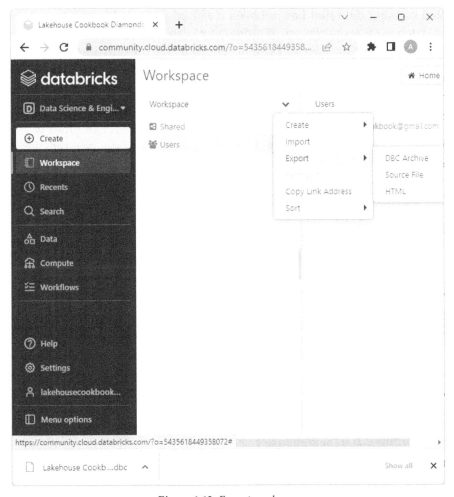

Figure 1.12: Export workspace

Data Lakehouse value proposition

Data lakes revolutionized data analysis. However, there were several challenges associated with data lakes. Data lakes removed many of the barriers to consolidating data, and without proper data governance controls, this became a problem. Multiple copies of the same data often enter a data lake in different locations. This was problematic because of the increased costs of redundant storage and because multiple copies introduced the potential for inconsistencies. This means that when choosing which copy to use, a considerable amount of research was needed to determine the lineage of each copy.

Other challenges relate to the fundamental characteristics of a data lake. With data lakes, we load data into the lake and then clean and refine it as the data is needed to address business problems or questions. This iterative refinement approach introduces the potential of using data that has not been cleansed while believing it has been. While approaches such as zones (or layers of refinement) were introduced to address this issue, they often relied on the data's location in the lake as it was the only indicator of the quality of the data. To address these challenges, many organizations utilize data catalogs to record the quality of data sets.

Another challenge with data lakes is that data is often stored in files that do not natively support schemas. While this flexibility is useful, the data format can differ when dealing with each dataset. To use the data, one must first determine the dataset's location in a complex directory structure and then determine the file format in which the data is stored. Next, the user must determine the schema of the data. This operation can be difficult with formats that support complex data storage, such as JSON.

Data warehouses have different challenges. When data is in a data warehouse, it has been through extensive processing before its being made available. Data warehouses are highly governed and, in turn, highly rigid. This characteristic is designed to ensure that the information within the data warehouse is correct and can be used to make business decisions. The consequence of this approach is that changes to data warehouses are difficult and highly governed.

A data lakehouse addresses these challenges by layering schemas and constraints on top of a data lake. Data are organized into zones with unambiguous names. When a data item is part of a zone, such as Silver, that designation has a clear and consistent implication. Additionally, a lakehouse combines structured, semi-structured, and unstructured data. This single location for data enables users with different goals to use the same data store. Historically, it was very challenging for a data scientist or a machine learning practitioner to utilize data within a data warehouse.

A fundamental improvement a data lakehouse offers over data warehouses and lakes is that Lakehouses have a single processing path. Rather than separate flows of data into different paths based on their refresh rate, data is processed in a single flow. Ideally, data is processed incrementally. If the data must be accessed quickly, incremental processing may occur continuously, leveraging the micro-batch element of spark structured streaming. This approach allows flexibility in scheduling the data flow so that the proper cadence can be assigned based on business requirements. This means the return on investment of processing data can consider the cost of the processing frequency and the business value derived based on that processing.

Lakehouse architecture

Often it is helpful to look at technology from an architectural perspective. Databricks Lakehouse is built upon several existing technologies. These technologies and concepts include the separation of computation from storage, data lakes, Delta Lake, and a computation engine. We will go over each and discuss the reasons they are included.

Separation of computing and storage

Long ago, Hadoop and MapReduce utilized a cluster to perform operations. As networking technology was limited, the data being processed was stored on the same nodes that were doing the processing. This architectural decision addressed several performance problems but required the cluster to be active to access the data it housed. One thing that Spark enabled (and even required) was the separation of compute resources from storage. This change enabled lower-cost access to data when viewing the data was all that was required. Separation also enables changing the cluster size for business reasons, such as lowering processing time or cost.

Data lake

Data lakes gained popularity in part due to the prominence of the **Hadoop Distributed File System** (**HDFS**). They made it easy to store data in a distributed, relatively low-cost way. Data lakes are also agnostic to the format of the data they store. This means that unstructured data, such as a video file, could be stored along with a Parquet file containing information about that video file. This flexibility enables storing data in multiple formats in a centralized location. This essentially tore down the silos that had plagued the field of data engineering and processing for decades.

Delta Lake

Delta Lake is a relatively new addition to the data field, and Databricks created Delta in 2019. Rather than keeping it proprietary, Databricks open-sourced the project, enabling an open and collaborative approach. Numerous organizations have contributed to the project, including Microsoft, Apple, Amazon, and IBM.

Delta Lake brings several key features to the lakehouse. First, it enables ACID transactions. This means that we do not have to worry about partial updates. An operation will succeed or fail but not leave values in an intermediate state. This feature implies that operations should include a mechanism to retry, as there is a chance they may fail. Time travel is another key feature of Delta. Time travel allows considering values at a point in time. This also gives us a versioned history, similar to system-managed temporal tables in relational databases. Examining the history of a table shows transactions that impacted that table. It is also possible to revert to a previous version. This is useful if an update occurred to the table that should not have, such as a bad data load. Several maintenance features are also important to lakehouses. For example, we can *OPTIMIZE* a table, which rewrites the underlying Parquet files to an optimal file size organized in a configurable way. This operation can have a significant impact on the performance of a lakehouse.

Computational engine

In the Databricks Lakehouse platform, Spark is the computational engine. There are two types of Spark engines in use in Databricks. The traditional Scala-based engine is similar to the open-source Spark implementation, with some proprietary changes to improve performance, security, and so on. Alternatively, **Photon** is a C++ re-implementation of the Spark APIs. For certain workloads, Photon is an order of magnitude faster. In other words, it is ten times as fast as the Scala implementation. While there is a higher cost to use Photon, the reduced execution time offsets that cost, resulting in a lower cost of operation. When starting in the lakehouse, minimal knowledge of Spark is acceptable. Over time, you will likely learn more about its internal workings.

Design considerations

While lakehouse brings a new set of technologies to the data ecosystems, we will not see improvement if we do not adjust how we use those technologies. Historically, extraction from a source system to a data lake followed a particular pattern. For example, if a project needed a table from a **Customer Relationship Management** (**CRM**) system and one table from an **Enterprise Resource Planning** (**ERP**) system, those tables would be loaded in a structure close to each other. Often, the name of the project would be the containing folder. This section discusses an alternative approach where data is ingested into a location relative to the source system. We discuss the zones in the lakehouse architecture and provide a clear definition of each. Lastly, we discuss security considerations.

Extraction and storage by system

Extracting data and organizing it by the system have several benefits. Often, the effort to extract data from a single file or table is the same as extracting all the data for a given system, especially when using a metadata-driven extraction system. Additionally, when the source system organizes data, it is much easier to locate as its data travels through the various zones.

Compared to project-based locations, there is virtually no chance of data duplication, as the system's name uniquely identifies it. This reduces the change for data drift and different record locations and removes unnecessary extraction and storage costs. This mindset shift also enables organizations to bring data that is not required into the lakehouse, enabling lower friction efforts later. The extraction frequency can be adjusted based on the volume of data and its useful lifetime.

Zones and their definitions

The lakehouse platform relies on the Medallion Architecture, with a few clarifications. The Medallion architecture relies on zones with specific and well-defined names. Source, bronze, silver, and gold have specific characteristics and uses.

Source

Data starts in a source system. Examples of source systems include relational databases, file-based storage systems, and event streams. Data stored in this location is stored in the format of the system it resides in or by the process that placed it there. Data in this zone is of mixed veracity, as not all source systems are equal in their level of governance.

Bronze

The first zone in the lakehouse architecture is the bronze zone. The bronze, silver, and gold zones are stored in the Delta Lake format. This consolidation of formats reduces the challenges of cross-zone interactions. There is likely data duplication in the bronze zone, especially when the source system is transactional. Each time a value is extracted from a source system, it is inserted into the bronze table. Ideally, data inserted into Bronze has a unique identifier and a means of determining the latest update. However, in practice, we encounter data lacking these characteristics. In that case, the choice is to have a full data load.

When doing a full load into the bronze, there are two choices. The first is to maintain all versions of the data and differentiate the sets of information using Delta capabilities, such as **Change Data Feed (CDF).** The alternative is to replace the table's contents, essentially deleting the records in the bronze table and then inserting the current version. Cost often decides the choice, especially if the table is large. Ideally, all insertions into bronze are incremental, meaning only changes or new records are added.

The primary goal of using the bronze zone is to simplify the process of populating the silver zone. Bronze is generally appended only, and we do not merge into bronze but rather insert new copies of data as it is extracted from the source systems. This means that over time the bronze zone will continue to grow. Likely, organizations will implement data retention policies to ensure the growth of bronze does not become cost prohibitive.

Silver

The silver zone contains data that businesses use, to make decisions. The data in the silver zone has data quality rules applied to it before ingestion. The data in the silver zone has the duplicates removed by merging based on a unique identifier in order to ensure the most recent value is used. If the data does not have a unique identifier and a way of ordering the data, then the contents of a silver table must be replaced in entirety, similar to the approach used in the bronze zone. Ideally, incrementally merging into the silver zone should be performed as it reduces cost and latency.

Gold

While a business can use silver tables to answer questions, they are not created to answer specific questions. Rather, data is processed with the expectation that it will be used to derive a table intended to answer a specific question. Gold tables are created through aggregation, filtering, joining, and other data engineering activities to satisfy a specific business objective, such as supporting a report or dashboard. Gold tables are optimized for reading and often are highly turned.

Lakehouse compared to other data technologies

People learning about the lakehouse architecture often come from different backgrounds. Many people moving to the lakehouse architecture have been data engineers for years. Comparing and contrasting lakehouse with a historical approach often helps one understand the concepts.

Extract load transform and extract transform load

A lakehouse typically uses an extract load transform pattern. The idea is that data is extracted from a source system, loaded into the lakehouse, and then incrementally refined. This contrasts traditional data warehouse workloads, where considerable effort goes into transforming data before insertion into a table. One advantage of an ELT approach is that data can be made available to those who wish to use it before it has transformed. For example, individuals skilled in the art, such as data scientists, can use data in the bronze zone before it has been cleansed to Silver as they know its data quality.

Additionally, not all data needs to be refined to Silver. As mentioned earlier in this chapter, there is often a very low incremental effort to extract a source system's data elements compared to a single data element. One way to approach this can be to extract data to the bronze layer, then refine it to silver when there is a need and funding, to perform that operation.

Compared to traditional data lake approaches

Traditional data lakes often utilize zones or levels of refinement. The names of these zones vary but often include things like raw, enriched, and curated or landing, curated, application, sandbox, and temporary. A key distinction that a lakehouse brings is a clear and consistent nomenclature. When a lakehouse professional refers to a silver table, their meaning is not ambiguous. They are describing a table that can be used by the business to answer a question but that does not exist for a specific question. Additionally, having both silver and gold available for consumption by the business avoids creating identical tables in different regions just to satisfy the methodology.

Other naming conventions include ingestion, distillation, processing, and insights. While the intent is noble, organizations often end up with many zones or regions that are challenging to differentiate. Also, many of these processing approaches fail to focus on incremental ingestion and refinement. One of the benefits of the lakehouse architecture utilizing the medallion architecture is that it is relatively simple to understand and avoids large numbers of hops from zone to zone.

Differences from Lambda architecture

One approach used in cloud computing is referred to as the Lambda architecture. In Lambda, there are typically two paths of processing. One typically focuses on fast processing, usually a stream processing technology. The other is a batch processing pattern, where a relatively long process operates on large amounts of data. The idea is to perform analytics quickly for situations where time is critical while taking longer for processing that is not time sensitive. One challenge with this approach is that the value computed by the faster path often differs from the value produced by the slower path. Additionally, the technologies utilized for each path often differ, causing duplicate implementations of the same logic in different technologies or programming languages.

A lakehouse addresses this challenge by relying on Spark's ability to run the same code within a micro-batch as within a long-running process. Additionally, a lakehouse has a bias toward incremental processing. This design choice separates the processing life cycle (batch or stream) from the implementation approach. A unit of work can be scheduled to run continuously or in a more traditional batch processing cycle. A single path lowers the overall development and maintenance effort and the need to uphold values.

Conclusion

In this chapter, we discussed the concept of a Data lakehouse. A brief history of big data, Spark, and Databricks was presented, and the Databricks community edition was used to create a table from a CSV file and perform analytics. The lakehouse architecture and design considerations were discussed, and the approach was compared to other traditional data processing approaches.

In the next chapter, we will provision Databricks in each cloud provider and discuss the configuration and architectural considerations.

Points to remember

There are several key concepts to take away from this chapter. First, Databricks is a cloud-hosted version of Spark.

It is the computation engine for the lakehouse architecture.

- The lakehouse is built on top of data lakes and brings governance through standardization in format (Delta) and the ability to make changes with ACID transactions.

- Lakehouse's business value is reducing the time to insight and lowering operations costs.

CHAPTER 2
Setting-up a Databricks Workspace

Introduction

Creating a Databricks workspace is one of the most important steps in a Lakehouse journey. If things are misconfigured, it can cause rework and impact delivery schedules. The chapter covers creating a Databricks environment in each of the major cloud providers.

Structure

In this chapter, we will cover the following topics:

- Core Databricks concepts
- Pick your cloud
- Deployment details
- Initial configuration

Objectives

By the end of this chapter, you should be able to recommend which cloud provider to use for a Databricks workspace. You will understand the concepts of a Databricks workspace and functionality that is cloud provider specific. Most importantly, will also be able to create a Databricks workspace and configure it.

Core Databricks concepts

To create a Databricks workspace, it is important to understand some foundational concepts. Databricks offers different tiers of their service. We will discuss the tiers and supply guidance on which one to use. We will also go over some of the workloads that people use Databricks for. We will also briefly discuss the cloud providers and offer advice on selecting a cloud.

Databricks service tiers

Before selecting a cloud provider, we need to discuss the different service tiers Databricks offers. This is because the first thing you will do when signing up for Databricks is to pick the service tier and associated pricing plan. There are two tiers of Databricks, standard and premium. As the names imply, the standard is the entry-level offering and costs less than the premium offering, and it also has fewer features. *Figure 2.1* contains a flowchart to help you decide which tier you require. Keep in mind that you can always switch from standard to premium as you meet the needs that are not satisfied. Generally, starting with the standard is the best practice, as most organizations and individuals are cost-conscious:

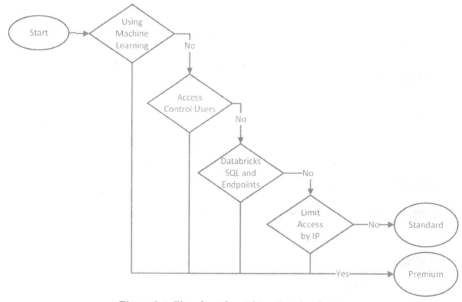

Figure 2.1: Flowchart for picking Databricks tier

To make an informed decision, we will need to discuss these features, in part to determine if they are required.

Brief introduction of Databricks features

Databricks has grown to include many features. We will discuss the features related to the platform tier. This is by no means an exhaustive list but rather an introduction.

Machine Learning

Machine Learning (**ML**) is a broad term for solving problems using numerical computing. It has its own computation requirements, often leveraging **Graphical Processing Units** (**GPU**) and other high-performance technologies. In the standard tier, there is limited support for ML and accelerated runtimes. A Databricks runtime is the packaging of versions of the software that Databricks uses, namely Spark and related technologies.

Notebook access control

For larger teams, it may be important to restrict who can see certain notebooks. One way to do that is to use Databricks access control. Databricks access control enables restricting operations users can perform on things such as notebooks, folders, clusters, and so on. **Access control lists** (**ACLs**) are used to implement the security model. This is a premium feature that becomes more important as the number of individuals with access to Databricks increases.

Databricks SQL and endpoints

Databricks SQL is a feature of Databricks intended to support **Business Intelligence** (**BI**), visualization, and SQL analytics. Databricks SQL relies on Photon to deliver performance. Often, we need to connect to Databricks as though it were a relational database. This is done using SQL endpoints. This feature may be required to access data housed in Databricks SQL that is consumed by business intelligence tools, such as Microsoft Power BI.

Internet protocol addresses access control

Often, it is desired to limit access to the Databricks workspace. Historically, that involved creating a virtual network peering Databricks' network to use it. A newer feature allows for **Internet Protocol** (**IP**) access control address filtering to control access to the Databricks workspace.

Databricks pricing model

Databricks uses a **Databricks Unit** (**DBU**) for tracking usage and, in turn, costing. DBUs are converted to currency during the billing process. The conversion may be impacted by pre-purchased commitments and other factors. A DBU is a way of tracking how much a customer is using Databricks. The various functions are billed at differing levels. When constructing a cluster, the DBUs per hour are an important consideration.

Pick your cloud

Often the cloud provider you will use will be dictated by your organization. It is said that data has gravity. By saying that data has gravity, we are saying that once an organization starts putting data into a particular cloud provider, it will become increasingly difficult to switch to a different provider. Over time, that preference often becomes a standard, as there is often a cost saving in having all data and processing within a single cloud provider. If you work at a larger company, they likely have a preferred cloud provider. As an individual making the decision, you can pick the cloud that you are the most familiar with.

AWS

Amazon Web Service (AWS) is a popular cloud provider. Databricks launched was launched in 2015 on AWS. To create a Databricks workspace, search for Databricks on the console homepage. You will be presented with a description of the product along with a button to view the purchasing options, as shown in *Figure 2.2*:

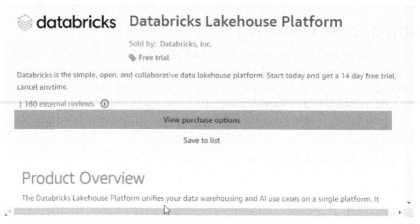

Figure 2.2: Databricks purchase overview

You will then be presented with a purchase option that outlines the conversion from DBS to currency, as shown in *Figure 2.3*. Clicking on the **View purchase options** brings up a page with the available subscriptions listed:

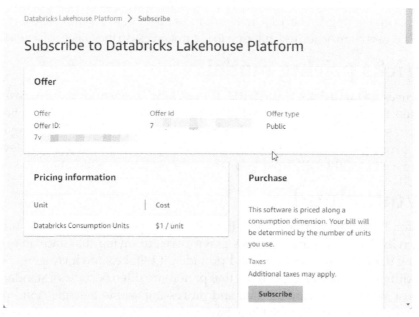

Figure 2.3: Subscribing to Databricks Lakehouse platform

Clicking on subscribe brings up a prompt to set up your Databricks account, as shown in *Figure 2.4*:

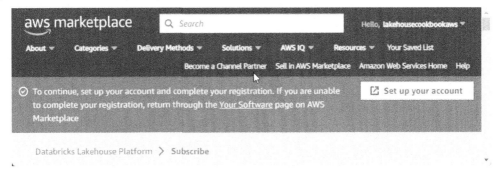

Figure 2.4: *Setting account*

Once the Databricks account page loads, you will be prompted for contact information, such as your email address, name, and company name, as shown in *Figure 2.5*:

Figure 2.5: *Databricks signup screen*

After clicking **Sign up**, you should receive an email with a link to verify your email and complete the setup. Clicking the link shows a screen to set your password, as shown in *Figure 2.6*:

Figure 2.6: Setting Databricks password

AWS on Databricks includes an additional tier potion, **Enterprise**. The enterprise tier includes IP filtering and user-supplied keys for encryption. Generally, we start with the standard tier and upgrade as required. Select the desired subscription plan and click continue, as shown in *Figure 2.7*:

Figure 2.7: Select AWS Databricks subscription plan

After selecting the subscript plan, the next step is to create a workspace. During the process, Databricks shares a diagram that shows the relationship between accounts, workspaces, and tools. Clicking the Getting Started button brings you to a confirmation screen where you are asked to ensure you have an AWS account. You will need to know the password to the Databricks account and be ready to name the workspace. *Figure 2.8* shows the form. Click **Start** quickstart to continue the process:

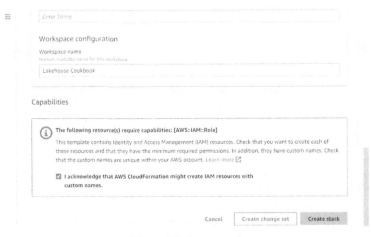

Figure 2.8: Namespace Details

Next, you are presented with a screen to create the stack, as shown in *Figure 2.9*. This screen lets you review the information you previously provided. You acknowledge that the AWS CloudFormation might create IAM resources. When you are sure everything is correct, click the **Create stack** button:

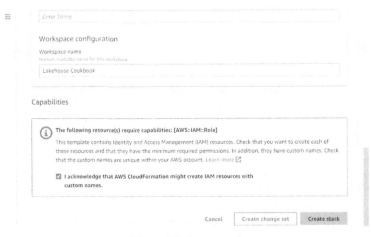

Figure 2.9: Create stack

After clicking the **Create stack** button, AWS starts the process of deploying the assets. You can monitor the progress as the resources are provisioned. Once the workspace is provisioned, you can access it by going to **https://accounts.cloud.databricks.com/ workspaces,** as shown in *Figure 2.10*:

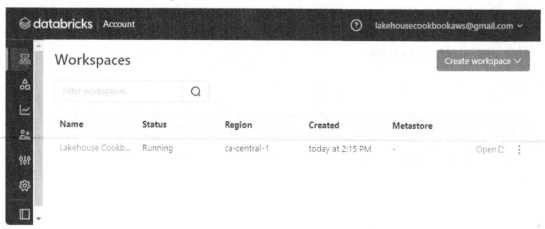

Figure 2.10: *Databricks AWS workspace after create*

Clicking on **Open** brings up the Databricks workspace's interface. You will likely be prompted for your credential. When the workspace opens for the first time, it asks you to select a personalized experience. These choices are based on personas that commonly use Databricks. For our purposes, the **Building Data Pipelines** choice is the best choice.

Azure

Creating an Azure Databricks workspace starts by searching for Azure Databricks in the marketplace. An Azure subscription is necessary to create Azure Databricks. Subscriptions are billing constructs and contain a collection of resources organized into groups. It is usually a good idea to create a new resource group when creating a Databricks workspace. Several resources are created automatically, and placing those resources in a new resource group simplifies cleanup. Azure uses a wizard-based approach to capturing the information necessary to create a new workspace. The first page is shown in *Figure 2.11*:

Create an Azure Databricks workspace ⋯ ✕

Basics   Networking   Encryption   Tags   Review + create

Project Details

Select the subscription to manage deployed resources and costs. Use resource groups like folders to organize and manage all your resources.

Subscription * ○   Lakehouse Cookbook   ∨

Resource group * ○   (New) LakehouseCookbook   ∨
                               Create new

Instance Details

Workspace name *   LakehouseCookbook

Region *   South Central US   ∨

Pricing Tier * ○   Trial (Premium - 14-Days Free DBUs)   ∨

                        Standard (Apache Spark, Secure with Azure AD)

                        Premium (+ Role-based access controls)

                        Trial (Premium - 14-Days Free DBUs)

Review + create   < Previous   Next : Networking >

Figure 2.11: *First step in creating Azure Databricks*

At this point, you could click **Review + create**, but it is good to visit each of the pages of the creation wizard. The next screen contains networking-related questions, as shown in *Figure 2.12*. The first option controls if the Databricks workspace is available on the public internet. The second option controls if you want to deploy Databricks to an existing virtual network:

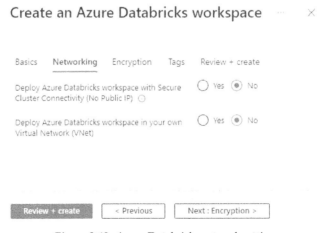

Create an Azure Databricks workspace ⋯ ✕

Basics   **Networking**   Encryption   Tags   Review + create

Deploy Azure Databricks workspace with Secure Cluster Connectivity (No Public IP) ○   ○ Yes ◉ No

Deploy Azure Databricks workspace in your own Virtual Network (VNet)   ○ Yes ◉ No

Review + create   < Previous   Next : Encryption >

Figure 2.12: *Azure Databricks network settings*

Clicking **Next** brings up the Encryption page. The options on this page are influenced by the Databricks subscription plan. Encrypting data with a customer-supplied key requires the premium tier. Additionally, encrypting the platform-encrypted data with a custom key also requires the premium plan. Note that everything is encrypted in Databricks; the question is who has control of the keys that are used. Some customers feel it is more secure to use their own keys. *Figure 2.13* shows the encryption options:

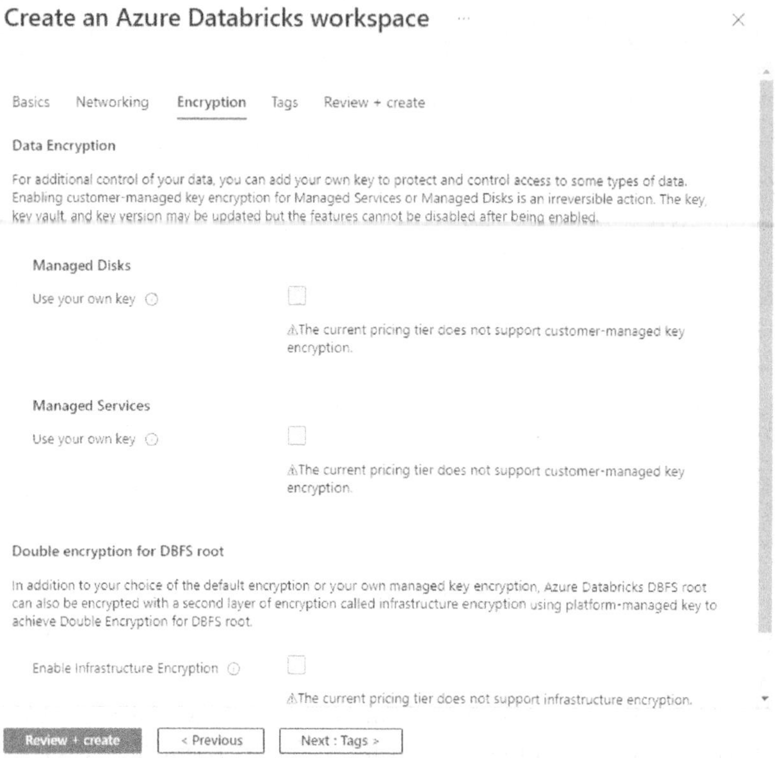

Create an Azure Databricks workspace   ···   ✕

Basics   Networking   **Encryption**   Tags   Review + create

Data Encryption

For additional control of your data, you can add your own key to protect and control access to some types of data. Enabling customer-managed key encryption for Managed Services or Managed Disks is an irreversible action. The key, key vault, and key version may be updated but the features cannot be disabled after being enabled.

Managed Disks

Use your own key ○   ☐

⚠ The current pricing tier does not support customer-managed key encryption.

Managed Services

Use your own key ○   ☐

⚠ The current pricing tier does not support customer-managed key encryption.

Double encryption for DBFS root

In addition to your choice of the default encryption or your own managed key encryption, Azure Databricks DBFS root can also be encrypted with a second layer of encryption called infrastructure encryption using platform-managed key to achieve Double Encryption for DBFS root.

Enable Infrastructure Encryption ○   ☐

⚠ The current pricing tier does not support infrastructure encryption.

[Review + create]   [< Previous]   [Next : Tags >]

Figure 2.13: *Azure Databricks encryption options*

The final tab contains a form for adding tags to the Databricks workspace. Tags are useful for tracking expenses. *Figure 2.14* shows the form used to add tags to the Azure Databricks Service:

Create an Azure Databricks workspace   ···   ✕

Basics   Networking   Encryption   **Tags**   Review + create

Name ○   Value ○   Resource

[   ] : [   ]   Azure Databricks Service

[Review + create]   [< Previous]

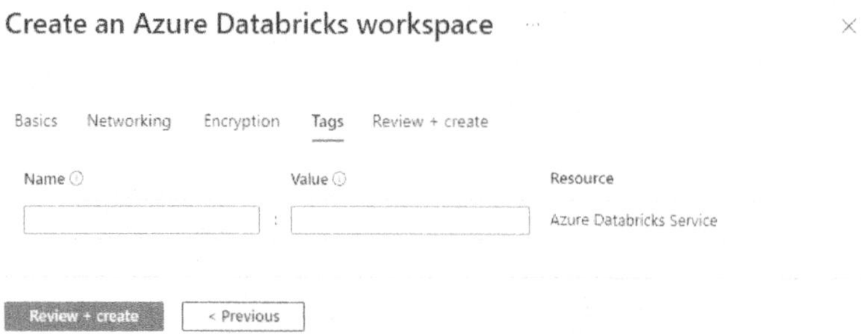

Figure 2.14: *Azure Databricks tags*

The final step is to review the information you supplied and start the provisioning process. *Figure 2.15* shows the information we entered. You also have the option of downloading the template that will be used during creation. We will revisit this topic in *Chapter 15, Tips, Tricks, Troubleshooting, and Best Practices.* Clicking **Create** starts the provisioning process. Please refer to the following *Figure 2.15*:

Figure 2.15: *Creating Azure Databricks workspace*

During deployment, the screen is updated as resources are created. Once complete, a link is supplied, allowing you to visit the resource.

Google Cloud Platform

Google Cloud Platform (GCP) is the latest addition of Databricks cloud providers. Creating a GCP Databricks workspace requires a GCP account. After you have provisioned an account, you will need to create a project to house the Databricks workspace. Once you have an account and a project, you are ready to create a Databricks workspace. If working within an organization, contact your Google billing manager to ensure you follow the proper processes.

There are several ways to get to the screen to create a Databricks workspace. An easy way is to search for Databricks using the search box at the top of the GCP console page at **https://console.cloud.google.com/**, as shown in *Figure 2.16*:

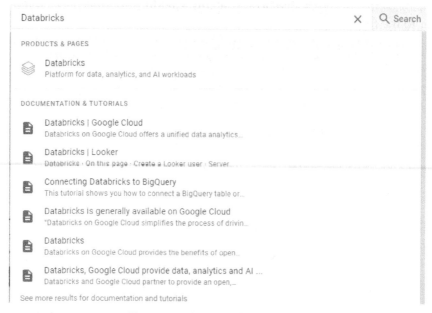

Figure 2.16: *Searching for Databricks*

You are then presented with a screen where you may be able to start a free trial or subscribe to the Databricks offering. If you use the free trial, you will have the option to switch it later. Next, you will need to accept the terms of the licensing agreement. After accepting the license agreement, you will see a screen informing you that the request for your Databricks workspace has been sent, as shown in *Figure 2.17*:

Figure 2.17: *Submitted Databricks request*

Clicking the signup link takes you to a Databricks account page. You may be prompted for a company name and asked to sign in with your Google account, as shown in *Figure 2.18*:

Figure 2.18: *Prompted for company name in Databricks*

The sign-in process requires you to select your Google account. You should end up on an account page prompting you to select your subscription plan, which determines your service tier, as previously discussed, at **https://accounts.gcp.databricks.com/subscription-plan-select**. The choices are standard and premium, as shown in *Figure 2.19*. Keep in mind that Databricks SQL is an interactive experience intended for SQL analysis. It is not the same as running SQL statements in a Databricks notebook. Please refer to the following *Figure 2.19*:

Select a subscription plan

	Most popular
Standard	**Premium**
Basic platform for your data analytics and ML workloads	Cloud native security and autoscaling
✖ Databricks SQL	✔ Databricks SQL
✖ IP access list	✔ IP access list
✖ Role based access control	✔ Role based access control
Select Standard	Selected

Your 14-day free trial starts when you click Continue. Thereafter, you will be charged at the list rates.

Continue

By clicking continue you agree to Databricks terms and conditions.

If your company has an existing contract with Databricks, please talk to your company contact before creating a Databricks environment so that any negotiated discounts are applied.

Figure 2.19: *Select subscription plan*

Based on your needs, select the subscription plan, and click **Continue**. You will then land on a page to create a workspace, as shown in *Figure 2.20*:

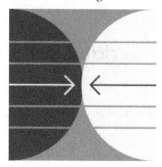

Workspaces

Your workspace is the environment for doing work in Databricks. Create one to get started.

Create workspace

Figure 2.20: GCP Create Workspace Starting Screen

After selecting Create workspace, you are prompted for the name of the workspace, the region you want to use, and the cloud project identifier to use. The workspace name should identify the intended purpose of the workspace. It could be related to a part of the organization or based on workload. For example, a workspace might be called Predict if its primary purpose was to run ML models that focus on prediction. A more general name is better, as workloads often change over time. A region is a physical location where resources are housed. You can think of it as a data center. When selecting regions, it is important to keep resources in the same region unless there is a reason to do otherwise. The final information required is the Google Cloud project identifier. You can locate the ID on the home page of the Google console, as shown in *Figure 2.21*:

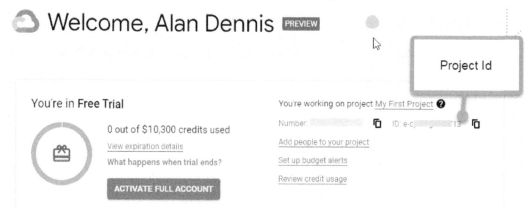

Figure 2.21: GCP create workspace

Once you have located the project id, enter it, along with the **Workspace name** and **Region** in the form, and click **Save**, as shown in *Figure 2.22*:

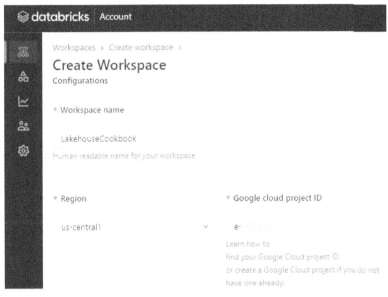

***Figure 2.22:** GCP create workspace*

Next, you will select your Google account and consent to access Databricks' requests. After reviewing the access being requested, click **Continue**. You will see a screen indicating that the workspace is being provisioned. Once it finishes, congratulations, you have just created your GCP Databricks workspace.

Once the provisioning is complete, you can open the workspace by clicking **Open Workspace**, as shown in *Figure 2.23*:

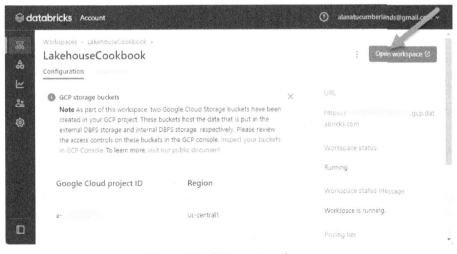

***Figure 2.23:** GCP create workspace*

Once the workspace opens, the user experience is the same for all cloud providers. Going forward, only features of flow that differ by a cloud provider will be discussed.

Deployment details

During deployment, there are sometimes challenges, often related to organizational policies. This section discusses those challenges related to networking and provisioning Databricks.

Public availability

During installation, we must decide if Databricks should be accessible from the internet. The reason this is done is to reduce vulnerability. The idea is that if the service is not accessible, there is less chance of someone compromising it.

Secure Cluster Connectivity is a Databricks option to restrict access to the cluster nodes. It allows a simple way of restricting access to the cluster nodes. The idea is that the cluster nodes will not have a public **Internet Protocol (IP)** address, and ports will be closed. The node within the cluster establishes a connection to the control plane over port 443. This connection allows the control plan to communicate with the workers while having the cluster highly secured. In Databricks, the control plan is the set of operations and systems that control the execution. Alternatively, the data plan is the operations and systems concerned with interacting with data stores.

Network size

When provisioning Databricks, it is important to ensure the number of available IP addresses is sufficient for the expected workloads. Network size is expressed using Classless **Inter-Domain Routing (CIDR)** blocks. The basic idea of a CIDR block is to express the range of IP addresses that can be specified within a subnet, and, in turn, how many devices can be assigned addresses. If too small of a block is assigned, it will limit the number of nodes within that workspace, introducing a limitation that is challenging to remove. CIDR blocks are expressed using notation such as **/16** or **/24**. The larger the number, the fewer IP address that can be assigned. For example, a block of **/24** corresponds to 256 IP addresses.

Network peering

It is often desirable to use virtual networks to restrict access to resources. For example, it is a common practice to place database servers on a virtual network that is not easily accessible. Databricks can be configured to peer with networks to allow access to resources. Network peering is also called VNet injection. The reason to do it is to gain access to resources, such as data storage systems.

Initial configuration

Once a Databricks workspace has been provisioned, we need to configure and govern it. Many of these features require the premium tier.

Access control

Access control requires a premium-tier workspace. Access control enables your users of the Databricks workspace to control who can view, run, or edit their notebooks. Within the Databricks workspace, one of the folders is the **Users** folder, as shown in *Figure 2.24*:

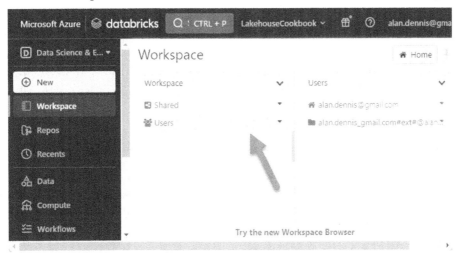

Figure 2.24: Users folder in the workspace

By enabling the access control feature in the workspace, each folder under the **Users** folder becomes private to that user. When users select permissions for their folder, they can configure an access control list, as shown in *Figure 2.25*:

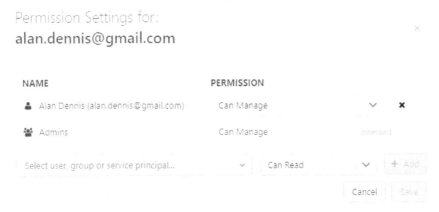

Figure 2.25: User's Permission Settings

As the number of users within a workspace grows, the need for securing each user's items becomes more important.

Cluster types

There are two types of clusters in Databricks. Each cluster type is intended to address a specific need. We will discuss how to create a cluster, discussing the way the cluster is used, and if it is a single node or a traditional multimode cluster.

All purpose

All-purpose clusters are, as the name implies, meant to be used in various situations. A cluster in Databricks is a set of resources and configurations that run various workloads, such as analytics, data engineering, data science experiments, and stream processing. General purpose clusters are usually used in an interactive fashion, where a user issues commands that are evaluated and results displayed. A key characteristic of an all-purpose cluster is that it can be created by a user interactively.

Job clusters

Job clusters are created to execute a job. If you look at the job compute section of the Databricks workspace, you will notice no option to create a new cluster. Rather job clusters are created during the execution of a job based on the configuration that is specified for that job.

Cluster creation details

Creating a cluster is an important activity. It is one of the first things you will do. We will go over most of the configuration choices.

Single or multiple nodes

When creating a cluster, the first choice to answer is if the cluster has a single node or multiple nodes. Historically, spark clusters used a driver node and at least one worker node. However, there are times a single node cluster is more appropriate. This is sometimes called a pseudo-distributed cluster. A single-node cluster is often used for simple workloads.

Access mode

Clusters are often used in different ways. Often a cluster is used by a single user. When the single-user option is selected as the access mode, a user is assigned as the user to access resources.

The shared option allows multiple users to use the same cluster. However, when accessing resources, either table access control must be enabled or passthrough authentication (if available). The idea is to allow users to share the same cluster but interact with data using their identity. An alternative to this approach is to use single-user access mode, with autoscaling enabled, and pools to reduce the time to start or resize each user's cluster.

The no-isolation shared access mode allows multiple users to share a cluster. When this option is selected, you will likely want to enable admin protection for no isolation clusters. This option should not be considered if sensitive data, such as that containing personally identifying information, is being processed.

Choosing performance level

Databricks creates packages of Spark and supporting technologies into versioned runtimes. Changing runtimes has the potential to introduce defects. When selecting a runtime, you pick the highest version runtime that has the **Long-term Support** (**LTS**) text on it. There are exceptions to this approach, such as a higher versioned runtime has a required feature or addresses a known defect.

The Photon acceleration checkbox controls what Spark framework evaluates your code. Photon is considerably faster than Scala-based Spark; however, as of this writing, there are some Spark functions that have not been implemented in Photon. Also, given Photon has a higher cost, experimentation may be necessary to see if it offers sufficient performance improvements to justify the high cost.

Autoscaling adjusts the size of a multiple-node cluster based on load. When a cluster is utilized beyond a certain level, additional nodes are added. Additionally, when the cluster utilization drops below a threshold, nodes are removed from the cluster. This reduces the number of DBUs that are being used. The downside of autoscaling is that it impacts the execution when it occurs. There will be pauses in the processing nodes that are added or removed. Utilizing compute pools can help with this, which we will discuss later.

Automatic termination shuts down the cluster after a period of inactivity. This results in significant savings. However, if the time span is too small, users of the cluster will have to wait for it to be restarted. Often, a setting of 30 minutes works well.

Tags are a way of tracking expenses. During cluster creation, you can assign tags to a cluster. Tags are a name-value pair. Often organizations have a tagging structure to enable business functions such as chargebacks.

The advanced options section contains settings that are not typically used. Things such as Spark configuration, logging settings, and scripts to run when the cluster starts are set here. If you are using Azure Databricks and have the premium tier, you can enable passthrough authentication, which takes the identity of the current users and passes it to various cloud services, such as storage accounts, to gain access to those resources as the current user.

Conclusion

This chapter covered the process of creating a Databricks workspace. We covered the core concepts needed to choose your cloud provider and select the correct service tier. We walked through the steps to provision a workspace in AWS, GCP, and Azure. We discussed some deployment details that can be problematic and finished with a discussion of creating clusters. In the next chapter, we will discuss how to connect to cloud storage providers from Databricks and provide an overview of how to design a Lakehouse implementation.

CHAPTER 3

Connecting to Storage

Introduction

A Lakehouse exists on top of a cloud storage system. Connection to a storage system has long-lasting implications. It also requires forethought and design. Hands-on examples of using various storage systems from Azure Databricks are presented. In subsequent chapters, examples using AWS's and GCP's Databricks will be presented.

Structure

In this chapter, we will cover the following topics:

- Databricks file system
- Lakehouse design
- Azure
- Blob storage

Objectives

By the end of this chapter, you will have a better understanding of how to connect to storage accounts and how to design for a Lakehouse implementation. You will have hands-on examples of how to interact with key systems within the Azure platform and concepts related to Databricks in general.

Databricks file system

Most operating systems have a file system to manage interaction with files. We have already talked about **Hadoop Distributed File System (HDFS)**. **Databricks File System (DBFS)** is like HDFS in many ways. Both are distributed file systems with a Unix-like way of interacting with files. This means that HDFS and BFS were created to deal with files stored across multiple places. The file system of Unix inspires both file systems and, in turn, Linux file systems. DBFS is a layer of abstraction on top of the cloud storage systems it supports. This means that when interacting with the files in Databricks, the experience is similar regardless of the cloud provider or service used. DBFS is important because it is how we access data, regardless of where it is stored.

Using mount points

One approach to interacting with cloud storage systems is to utilize a mount. A mount looks like a directory but references a location on a remote storage system. Mount points are easy to interact with files but should be used cautiously. There are security considerations that we will discuss later related to using mounts. Security information is associated with the location being mounted when creating a mount. This makes it much simpler to interact with a storage location and provides a uniform way of interacting with remote storage locations.

Recipe 11: Using the DBFS file browser

DBFS is an important part of the Databricks Lakehouse platform. One feature Databricks added is a DBFS File Browser. It may be turned off by default; if so, go to **Admin Settings**, located under the menu with your email address in the upper right corner of the workspace, as shown in *Figure 3.1*:

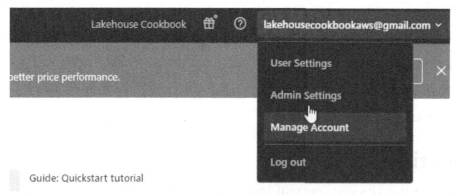

Figure 3.1: Manage account

Clicking **Admin Settings** brings up a tabbed page. One of the tabs is **Workspace** settings; click that tab. Scroll down until you see the **Advanced** section, as shown in *Figure 3.2*:

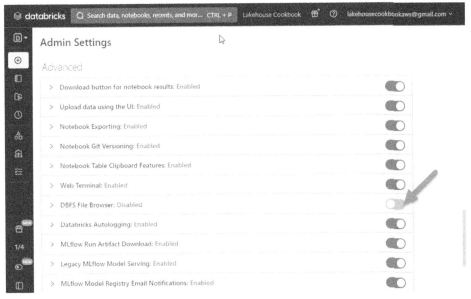

Figure 3.2: *Advanced section of Admin Settings*

Clicking the switch turns on the DBFS File Browser and indicates that you must refresh the page for the change to occur. *Figure 3.3* is an image showing DBFS File Browser having been enabled:

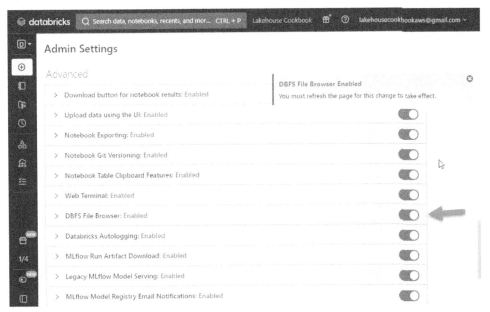

Figure 3.3: *DBFS file browser enabled*

After enabling DBFS File Browser and refreshing the page in the browser, click on **Data** in the left navigation. You will see a button labeled **Browse DBFS** near the top of the page, as shown in *Figure 3.4*:

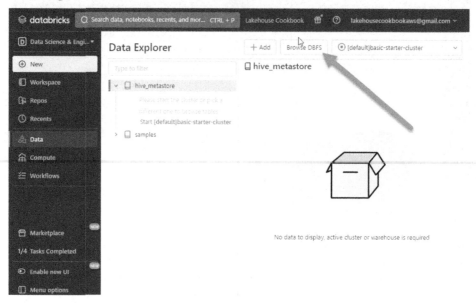

Figure 3.4: *Browser DBFS button*

Clicking the **Browse DBFS** button opens the DBFS browser, as shown in *Figure 3.5*. When working in DBFS, FileStore is a location to store data internally to DBFS. When you upload data and create a table, that information is stored within the FileStore directory structure.

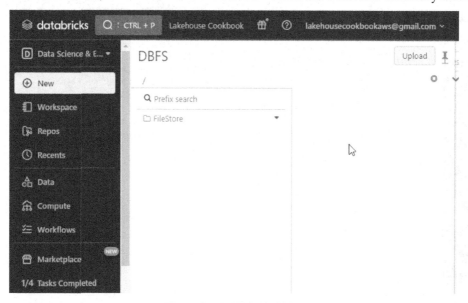

Figure 3.5: *DBFS root folder*

We will return to a discussion of DBFS Explorer later. For now, understand that it is a graphical way of exploring a limited portion of the contents of DBFS.

Recipe 12: Using Databricks' web terminal

Most operating systems have a console or command window. Databricks offers a console that is accessible using a web browser. It is generally turned on by default, but if not, you enable it on the same screen that we turned on DBFS file browser. Once enabled, you access the web terminal by going to the Compute section of the Databricks workspace. You will need a cluster to interact with the web terminal, but it need not be powerful. In this example, we created a single node cluster with a smaller configuration, as shown in *Figure 3.6*:

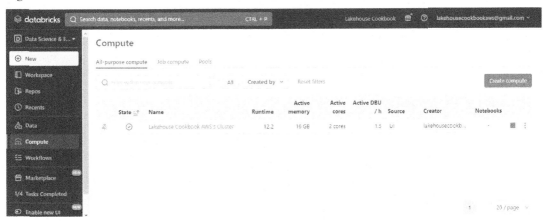

Figure 3.6: Cluster list

Select the cluster by clicking on its name. This will bring up the cluster details. When you see the screen, click on the **Apps** tab, as shown in *Figure 3.7*:

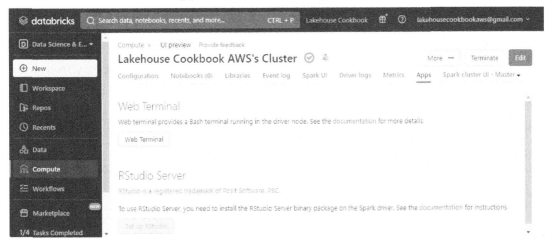

Figure 3.7: Cluster applications

Clicking the **Web Terminal** button brings up the terminal in a new browser tab, as shown in *Figure 3.8*. Terminals are a good way to learn about Databricks' internals:

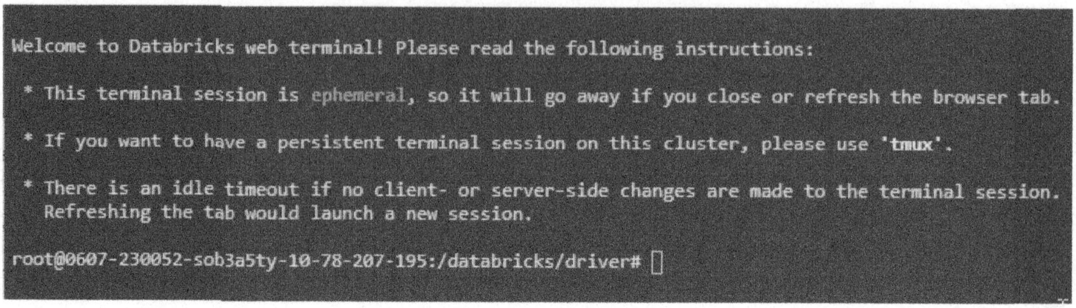

```
Welcome to Databricks web terminal! Please read the following instructions:

 * This terminal session is ephemeral, so it will go away if you close or refresh the browser tab.

 * If you want to have a persistent terminal session on this cluster, please use 'tmux'.

 * There is an idle timeout if no client- or server-side changes are made to the terminal session.
   Refreshing the tab would launch a new session.

root@0607-230052-sob3a5ty-10-78-207-195:/databricks/driver# []
```

Figure 3.8: Web terminal opening screen

To see the same folder as we saw in the DBFS File Browser, we issue the following command:

```
ls -la /dbfs
```

The file listing in *Figure 3.9* shows that the DBFS file browser filters several folders from view, such as the Databricks datasets:

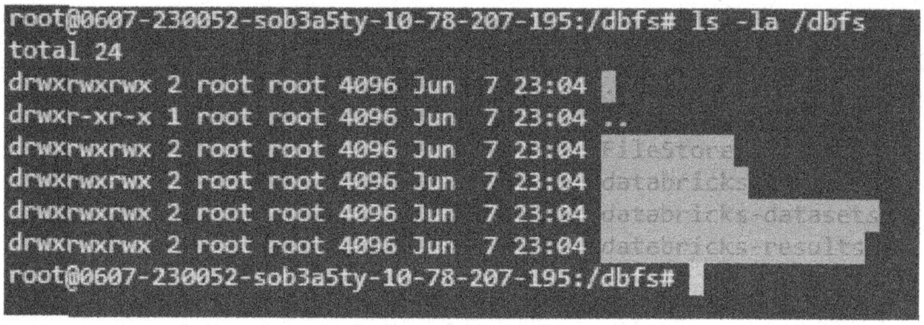

```
root@0607-230052-sob3a5ty-10-78-207-195:/dbfs# ls -la /dbfs
total 24
drwxrwxrwx 2 root root 4096 Jun  7 23:04 ▓
drwxr-xr-x 1 root root 4096 Jun  7 23:04 ..
drwxrwxrwx 2 root root 4096 Jun  7 23:04 FileStore
drwxrwxrwx 2 root root 4096 Jun  7 23:04 databricks
drwxrwxrwx 2 root root 4096 Jun  7 23:04 databricks-datasets
drwxrwxrwx 2 root root 4096 Jun  7 23:04 databricks-results
root@0607-230052-sob3a5ty-10-78-207-195:/dbfs# ▓
```

Figure 3.9: Listing of the dbfs folder

Recipe 13: Using Databricks Utilities' file system methods

Databricks utilities (dbutils) simplify interaction with Databricks workspaces from code. File system operations are one of those things that dbutils simplifies. In Python and Scala, issuing the command:

```
dbutils.fs.help()
```

Display help about the file system methods, as shown in *Figure 3.10*:

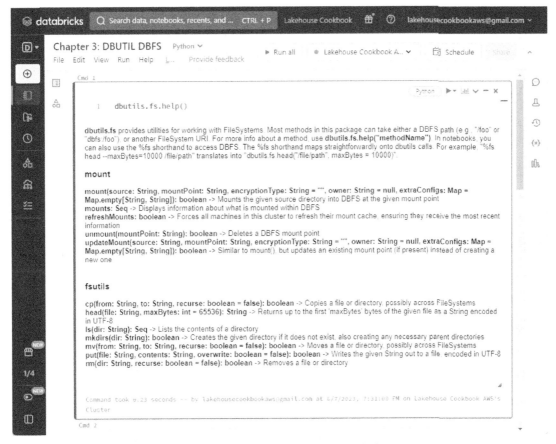

Figure 3.10: *Help about dbutils.fs methods*

We will use **dbutils** often during this chapter. For now, we will look at the root of the folder structure. Notice that the contents of the root folder are the same as that returned by the web terminal, as shown in *Figure 3.11*:

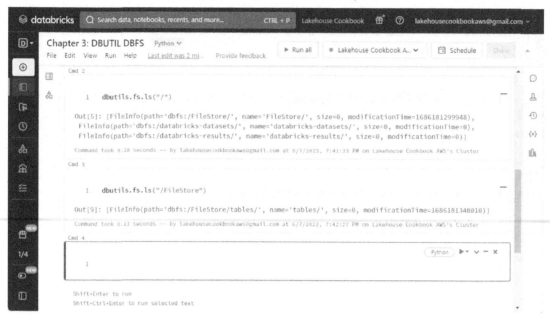

Figure 3.11: Listing the root DBFS directory

The importance of DBFS

DBFS underpins all analytical work in a Databricks workspace. It is a technology that is so successful at its job that it become invisible. Without it, interacting with data would be very challenging. Utilizing DBFS, we can create hierarchies of folders. The way we create those folders is very important. In the next section, we discuss designing for the lakehouse and provide some guidance on organizing data to minimize confusion and follow the principles of a data lakehouse.

Lakehouse design

All-important building efforts begin with design. Before building a house, we develop blueprints that tell the builders how to build the house. Similarly, when building a Data lakehouse, we start with a design. The recommendations presented here are by no means exhaustive. However, they demonstrate several approaches and provide a starting point for creating your design.

Source to Silver

Data intended to reside in a lakehouse often comes directly from a source system. This is not true if you are performing a migration or modernization. In that case, you are laying a lakehouse on top of an existing data solution. But we usually start populating a lakehouse from a source system.

Typically, we do not use managed tables in a lakehouse. Rather, we use external tables often housed in a cloud storage account accessible outside of Databricks. There are several reasons for this decision, but the primary is that it allows more flexibility when dealing with the files that contain the data exposed as a table in the lakehouse.

As a refresher, Databricks has two types of tables, managed and external. External tables are also called unmanaged tables. When dealing with managed tables, we must track the table's name and location. Before listing the tables and locations, the way the data will be stored must be agreed to. A good starting point is to define flow based on source systems, as shown in *Figure 3.12*:

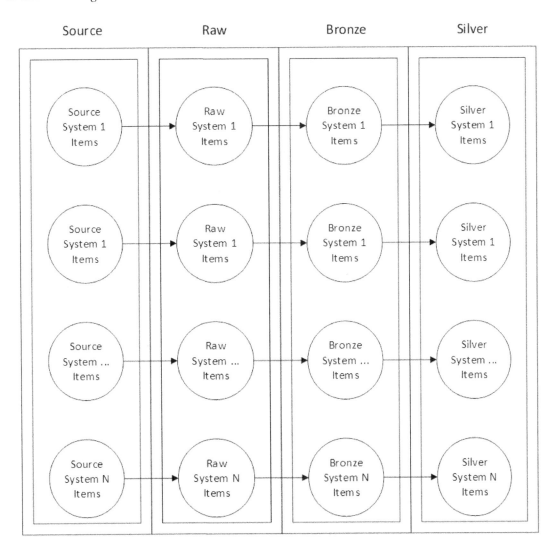

Figure 3.12: *Data flow across lakehouse layers*

Including raw

One area that is not always clear is if the raw layer should be used. It can be argued that the contents of the raw layer are identical to those of the bronze layer. Our approach is to include items coming from file-based systems in the raw zone in their native format. Data from relational or other enterprise-class systems typically skip the raw layer and land directly into bronze. The reason for the distinction is that there is a possibility that the process of standardizing files in different formats to Delta for inclusion into bronze may have an issue. Also, sometimes it is difficult to retrieve historical versions of files to determine the most recent values for all records.

While it is not a cutting-edge technology, Excel (or an equivalent) is a good job choice for tracking information related to lakehouse design. After the design is completed, other approaches would be better, but during the initial stages, we often must track what work should be performed and where things should be placed. As mentioned, unmanaged Delta tables have both a name and a location. Both must be tracked, as shown in the work aid in *Table 3.1*:

Source		Raw	Bronze		Silver			Gold		
Name	Table Folder	Folder	Folder	Table Name	Type	Folder	Table	Type	Folder	Table

Table 3.1: Sheet for tracking items during lakehouse design

Table 3.1 is available as an Excel spreadsheet. As mentioned, this is not an exhaustive list of items to track but a starting point. For example, you likely will want to denote the type of ingestion, such as full or incremental. Additionally, the data update rate within the data items is important when designing ingestion processes. If a table is only updated once a week, there is no value in refreshing the lakehouse more frequently.

The document allowed operations crossing layers

Each team member must understand what changes can be performed when crossing into a given layer. This must be documented early in a project to ensure consistency. This need not be a lengthy document; it could be contained in a PowerPoint presentation. An example presentation is included on the companion website. The presentation should include coverage of each of the types of operations that occur.

Source to raw

When ingesting from a file-based system, the format of the source system should not change. The files are copied with as few changes as possible. If the source system item is being ingested in full, we simply replicate the source item's file name in a location relative to the source system under the raw layer of the lake. The output folder should be time-sliced if the source system is incremental, meaning that files contain only changes or additions. Most likely, the source system is also time-sliced. A time-sliced path is a path that is constructed based on the time of the file's creation that contains the file at the lowest level, as shown in *Figure 3.13*:

Figure 3.13: Time-Sliced JSON file

The preceding example is an image of Azure Storage Explorer looking at a JSON file created on the first of January 2022 at three minutes past midnight. The data source under the raw layer organizes the folder structure. We can verify this is the case by examining the file's properties, as shown in *Figure 3.14*:

Figure 3.14: Details of a time-sliced file

Notice that the file was created on 1/1/2022, and that date and times are in Zulu format.

To restate and empathize, when ingesting data from a source to the raw layer, the contents should not change. The only allowed change is to rename the file to ensure uniqueness and to enable selection based on when it was ingested.

It is worth noting that the name of the file contains slashes. In cloud storage systems, a directory structure is often simulated by naming the file to contain slashes. These filenames are rendered such that they appear within a folder structure but are in a single location. As you can see in *Figure 3.14*, the file's name contains slashes, and there is no reference to a folder other than the data container.

Source to bronze

When interacting with Delta tables (bronze, silver, and gold layers), we need to be concerned with the Delta files' location and how they are written. This means we need not create time-sliced paths. We provide Delta with what we want to be written, and Delta decides how to write it.

When retrieving information from enterprise-class systems, like relational databases, we usually prefer to ingest directly into the bronze tier. Changes to the name of the data asset should be minimized other than to provide uniqueness or to indicate its source system. It is common to include the layer's name in the item's name, often by prefixing it with **bronze** or equivalent. Columns should not be removed, but data types can be adjusted to be Delta-compatible.

There may be cases where a column that includes tracking information may be added. If this is done, it should be clear that the column is not part of the source system. One approach is to prefix with a standard string, such as "**SystemAdded_**" or the like. Avoid starting a column name with an underscore, as it will likely cause issues later in the processing.

Raw to bronze

If files have landed in the raw layer, we will need to convert them from their native format to Delta. This often requires figuring out the format of the files. Autoloader is a feature of Databricks that is very useful for this task. We will discuss Autoloader in depth in *Chapter 6, Extracting from Source and Loading to Bronze*. As with the source to Bronze, it is acceptable to add columns for tracking purposes.

Schemas are a way to ensure that the contents of a column are what they should be. When transforming data in the raw layer, apply the most appropriate data type to each column. Ideally, that is also the most constraining data type as well. However, it is proper to consider the data type in the source system (if available) and use it for guidance. Avoid leaving all columns as strings.

The idea of a bronze item is that it has the history of a given item. This means it will have duplicates if the source system item has changed. These duplicates allow us to examine an item's values over time based on the retention policy for each data asset. Because of the value of the history, replace a table rather than delete it. We will discuss this topic in *Chapter 4, Creating Delta Tables*.

Often, source data may contain a column that contains complex data. This is common in JSON and AVRO file formats from **Internet of Things (IoT)** devices. Do not expand those nested data fields during entry into the bronze layer. Rather, leave it as it is, possibly defining their nature clearly in the column's schema information.

Bronze to silver

Silver items are fit for business use. This means that any data duplication in the bronze layer has been handled by merging into the silver layer. Merge has a specific meaning in this context. If an item exists, it is updated; otherwise, it is added. This process requires a key or unique identifier to find the existing item in the silver layer. We must also determine the most recent record to apply the most current values to the silver layer. Ideally, this watermark column is tracked in the source system, likely with a name like "**modifiedon**." If it is not, then we may rely on change data capture in the Delta silver table.

We should not remove items when merging into Silver. As we converted data types when loading silver, we should not need to change the data type of a silver item. As with adding to bronze, we may need to add a tracking column to a silver table. One use case where these tracking columns become important is when we are figuring out the time it takes for an update to flow from the source system to the corresponding silver tables. In that scenario, columns like "**SystemGeneratedEnterBronze**" and "**SystemGeneratedEnterSilver**" may be needed.

It is a good idea to avoid deleting data from the silver layer. Instead, a soft-delete approach is preferred. In this pattern, we add a column to indicate if a record has been removed and, ideally, when it was removed. In most data systems, removing records can be problematic as there may be foreign key dependencies to consider.

It is important to apply business rules to data to ensure it is fit for use in the silver layer. We do this by ensuring that data that does not meet an organization's expectations are not in the silver layer. One way to do this is to use **Delta Live Tables (DLT)**, which support expectations as a clause associated with a table and the consequence of not satisfying that clause. For example, a field might be expected not to be null. If a null field is encountered, the expectation will designate what should happen, such as filtering it from the table's content.

Silver to silver

Silver tables are fit for use but not created for a certain use case, as gold tables are. Often transformations are required to convert from a silver table to a structure that can enable the construction of a gold table. This operation might be done using intermediate views or may require tables for performance reasons. Same layer transformations are often done to combine two tables together, such as data enrichment and denormalization. We often see cases where a field containing a type is used as a foreign key in a lookup table. It is common to combine these tables during a silver-to-silver refinement.

Since we are populating a new table, it is important to include expectations and constraints. This ensures that we do not have invalid information contained in a silver table. Additionally, we want to be sure that if columns are removed, then we do not lose the uniqueness of a given record.

It is expected that the shape of the data will change significantly during these operations. As we build tables that we think we will need for future work. We often join tables together. It is unlikely that all columns will be wanted after joining a table. Also, as we have not pruned unneeded columns during the bronze-to-silver refinement, we may use same-layer refinements to produce a core set of tables holding the most valuable columns.

Silver to gold and gold to gold

Recall that gold tables are created to address a specific business need. For example, a Gold table may be needed to contain the data present in a dashboard. We construct these tables by joining, aggregating, filtering, or combining data engineering activities on silver tables. It is important to include constraints and expectations on the output to ensure the data is of the highest quality. Typically, the shape of the table is driven by the requirements of the business function. Creating a gold table may combine working from the top-down (starting with the gold table) and bottom-up (starting with source data).

A variation of the silver-to-gold pattern is when one of the source tables is already a gold table. This might be done for convenience, as a table holds most of the required information, or as part of an aggregation activity. In this case, we would continue to use expectations and constraints. The shape of the table would also be driven by the business requirements.

Recipes 14: Using the Lakehouse layer presentation

On the companion website, you will find a PowerPoint presentation containing the information presented in the previous section. It is a good idea to socialize the information before setting up a meeting to go through it. Also, it should be presented as a starting point for establishing your organization's approach to a lakehouse. The idea is to keep the content concise, as seen in *Figure 3.15*:

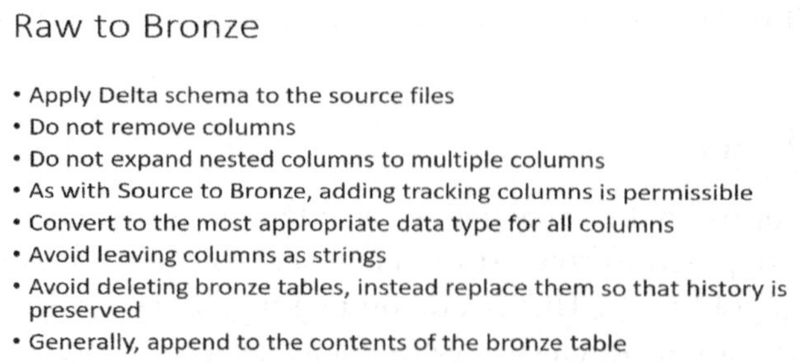

Raw to Bronze

- Apply Delta schema to the source files
- Do not remove columns
- Do not expand nested columns to multiple columns
- As with Source to Bronze, adding tracking columns is permissible
- Convert to the most appropriate data type for all columns
- Avoid leaving columns as strings
- Avoid deleting bronze tables, instead replace them so that history is preserved
- Generally, append to the contents of the bronze table

Figure 3.15: Slide from lakehouse layer operations presentation

Azure

Azure supports multiple storage systems. Two of the most popular are Azure Blob Storage and **Azure Data Lake Storage Gen2 (ADLS Gen2)**. ADLS Gen2 is built on top of Azure Blob Storage. The process of interacting with each is similar, but ADLS Gen2 supports a hierarchical file system and fine-grained access control.

ADLS Gen2

Microsoft created ADLS Gen2 to replace Azure Data Lake Gen1. They did this by combining the best elements of Gen1 with existing capabilities associated with Azure Blob Storage. Gen1 had several limitations, including higher costs and limited availability. By using Azure Blob storage, these issues were addressed.

ADLS Gen2 supports Hadoop-compatible access. This means that existing Hadoop implementations could migrate to ADLS Gen2, often reducing their cost and increasing access and availability. The hierarchical directory structure can be combined with **Access Control Lists (ACLs)** to govern the type of access groups and individuals have to data assets. This enables storing sensitive information, such as **Personal Identifiable Information (PII),** and controlling access to those with a business need. One way this is performed is using credential passthrough.

Credential passthrough

Historically, operations from Big Data systems relied on service accounts. This design choice meant that if an individual had access to the system, they likely had unlimited access to the data it accessed. One thing that Databricks and Microsoft developed was a way to pass the identity and rights of a user from Databricks to ADLS Gen2. This means that the access associated with the identity using Databricks could be used to determine access in ADLS Gen2.

From a management perspective, it is usually better to manage access based on group membership rather than granting a person access. This is a security best practice and is helpful when the individual switches roles or leaves the company. It also helps organizations to think of how a person's role is enabling their access.

ADLS Gen2 supports **Azure Role-Based Access Control (Azure RBAC)** and **Portable Operating System Interface (POSIX)**-like ACLs. Items in a POSIX-based file system have two kinds of permissions: access and default. The access permission governs access to a particular item, while default permissions are used when creating a new item. It is important to understand that permissions do not cascade as they do in some file systems. Changing permission on a parent does not change permissions on its children. This characteristic means we need to get the default permissions correct before adding things to ADLS Gen2.

Recipe 15: Creating a storage account for ADLS Gen2

As with most Azure resources, we start by searching for the service we want to create. In this case, search for Azure Storage Account. Ensure that the service you are creating is from Microsoft and is an Azure Service, as shown in *Figure 3.16*:

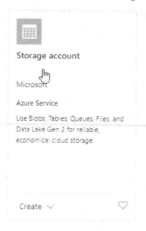

Figure 3.16: *Azure Storage account*

After clicking **Create**, select the right Subscription and Resource group. Then provide an appropriate name. Note that the name must be all lowercase letters and can contain numbers, as shown in *Figure 3.17*:

Figure 3.17: *Storage account name, subscription, and resource group*

Click the **Next** button and ensure you select Enable hierarchical namespace, as shown in
Figure 3.18:

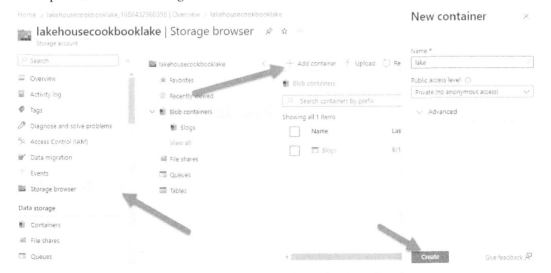

Figure 3.18: *Enable hierarchical namespace*

Complete the service creation, ensuring you select the proper values for your organization
and specific need. Enabling the hierarchical namespace is a crucial step. If you do not do
so during creation, it can be enabled after the fact.

Recipe 16: Creating a container and setting ACLs

Once the deployment of the storage account has finished, you can navigate to that item.
Typically, the first thing you do is create a new container on the newly created storage
account. You can use the Azure Storage Explorer application or the Storage browser in the
Azure portal, as shown in *Figure 3.19*:

Figure 3.19: *Creating a container using Azure Portal*

Once you have created the container, the next step is to set the ACL on it. To do this, right-click on the container name and select **Manage ACL**, as shown in *Figure 3.20*:

Figure 3.20: Manage ACL

Clicking Manage ACL opens a screen for controlling access and default permissions for the selected item. Clicking the Add principal link allows you to search for and select identities which you want to configure an access ACL for, as shown in *Figure 3.21*:

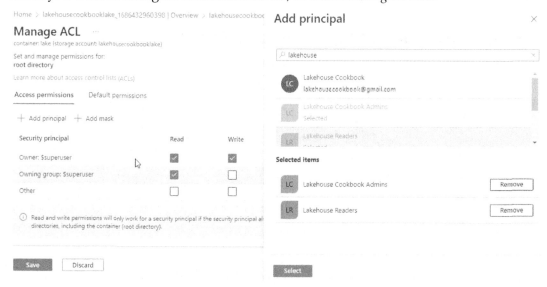

Figure 3.21: Select principal during Manage ACL access

Once you have found and selected the principals you wish to have access, the next step is to set the permissions for each. Note that this controls who can see the item you are setting it on. We need to set the default so that those permissions are applied when items are created inside the container. Select the access for each identity, as shown in *Figure 3.22*:

Figure 3.22: Set access for each identity

Repeat this process for the defaults for the container, as shown in *Figure 3.23*. This ensures that when an item is created within the container, the permissions set in the default will be applied. Execute permission is required on folders to enable traversal. It does not affect files.

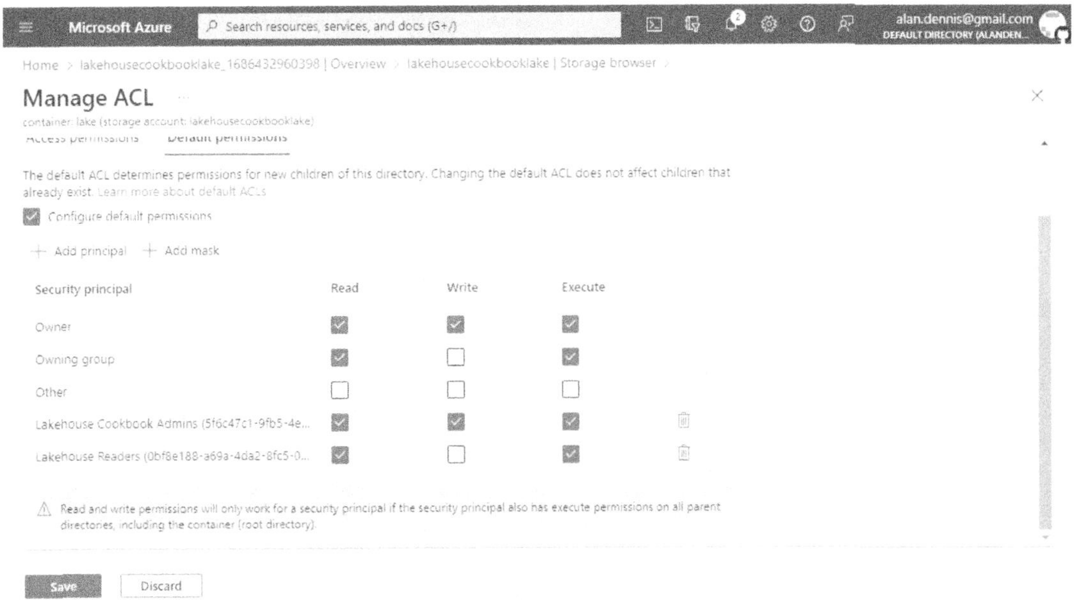

Figure 3.23: Default permission on the container

We have now created a container on our storage account and set both the access and default permissions. In my example, both Lakehouse Cookbook Admins and Lakehouse Readers are Azure Active Directory groups. As previously discussed, this allows us to manage membership in the group rather than granting each user permission. Additionally, granting access rights after data has populated in a hierarchical filesystem is difficult, as the change must be made to each item within the system.

Recipe 17: Using Passthrough authentication

Once a storage account with a container has been created, the next step is to access it from within Databricks. Note that Databricks considers this method legacy but given that there is an additional cost when using Unity, it is presented for completeness.

The first step is to create a cluster that supports passthrough authentication. In the past, this was called a high-concurrency cluster. Today, it can be found by selecting the Power User Computer policy and expanding the **Advanced options** area, as shown in *Figure 3.24*:

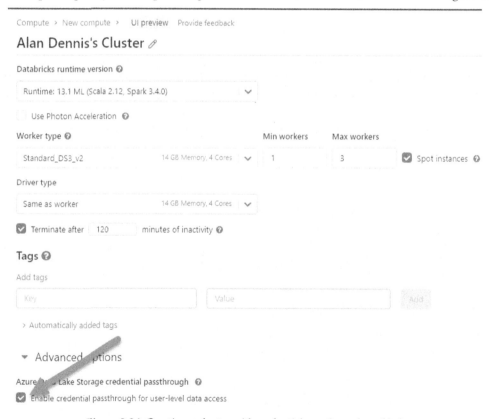

Figure 3.24: Creating a cluster with credential passthrough enabled

Once you have created the cluster, start it. We need a notebook and some data. We uploaded a CSV file downloaded from **https://data.gov.in/catalog/estimates-egg-production**

in a folder named raw in the data lake we just created. To access it, we use a specially constructed **Uniform Resource Identifier (URI)**. The URI is of the form:

`abfss://<container-name>@<storage-account-name>.dfs.core.windows.net`

Where container-name is the container/file system of interest on the storage-account-name you are trying to read. **ABFSS** is the scheme identifier, which stands for **Azure Blob File System Secure**. The final S forces the Hadoop client to use **Transport Layer Security (TLS)**. To learn more about ADLS Gen2 URIs, visit **https://learn.microsoft.com/en-us/azure/storage/blobs/data-lake-storage-introduction-abfs-uri**. We can use the URI to access files relative to the container specific, as shown in *Figure 3.25*:

Cmd 2

```
1   fileName = 'raw/Animal_Husbandry_TABLE_14_2012-13.csv'
2   containerName = 'lake'
3   storageAccountName = 'lakehousecookbooklake'
4   fullUrl = 'abfss://' + containerName + '@' + storageAccountName + '.dfs.core.windows.net/' + fileName
5   display(spark.read.format("csv").load(fullUrl))
```

Table ∨   +

	_c0	_c1	_c2	_c3	_c4	_c5	_c6
1	S. No.	States/UTs	2008-09	2009-10	2010-11	2011-12	2012-13
2	1	Andhra Pradesh	183446.36	193958.45	201277.09	212103.27	222973.83
3	2	Arunachal Pradesh	360.5	380.15	407.42	419	438.69
4	3	Assam	4658.93	4671.22	4707.31	4705	4709.58
5	4	Bihar	10740.43	11001.77	7446.08	7552	8371.86
6	5	Chhattisgarh	9737.92	10520.01	12454.34	12984.44	13704.06
7	6	Goa	148.61	148	149	149.45	457.87

↓ 37 rows | 0.67 seconds runtime

Figure 3.25: Reading a CSV from Databricks using passthrough authentication

We can see that the results are not ideal, as the first row in the CSV appears to be a header. Changing the code slightly tells Spark to treat the first row as a header, as shown in *Figure 3.26*:

Cmd 3

```
1   display(spark.read.format("csv").option("header","true").load(fullUrl))
```

▸ (2) Spark Jobs

Table ∨   +

	S. No.	States/UTs	2008-09	2009-10	2010-11	2011-12	2012-13
1	1	Andhra Pradesh	183446.36	193958.45	201277.09	212103.27	222973.83
2	2	Arunachal Pradesh	360.5	380.15	407.42	419	438.69
3	3	Assam	4658.93	4671.22	4707.31	4705	4709.58
4	4	Bihar	10740.43	11001.77	7446.08	7552	8371.86
5	5	Chhattisgarh	9737.92	10520.01	12454.34	12984.44	13704.06
6	6	Goa	148.61	148	149	149.45	457.87
7	7	Gujarat	12675.35	12761.98	13269.23	14269.19	14558.39

↓ 36 rows | 0.77 seconds runtime

Figure 3.26: Reading a CSV from ADLS Gen2 with a header

We have successfully accessed an ADLS Gen2 account using Azure Databricks credential passthrough.

Key vault and secret scope

Since the following sections rely on storing sensitive information, we should discuss the use of secret scopes and key vaults in Azure. Azure Key Vault is a service for storing keys, secrets, and certificates within Azure. It is similar to password vaults that you might have used personally. Rather than having secret information in your Databricks notebooks, the idea is to put them someplace secure and then authenticate to the Key Vault and retrieve secrets when needed.

Creating a key vault is simple enough. We can skip over the details here. Basically, search for the key vault and ensure that the service is from Microsoft. Click **Create** and give it a meaningful name and select your pricing tier. The standard tier is usually sufficient. Ensure you select a region that is the same as the other region you use. After you have created it, note the URI for the vault, as you will need it when linking a secret scope to it in Databricks.

Recipe 18: Link a key vault to a secret scope

After you create your key vault, note the URI. We link Databricks' secret scope to Azure Key Vault by going to **https://<databricks-instance># secrets/createScope**. Typically, you can take everything to the right of and including the pound sign and put it on the end of your Databricks URL, which typically has a **?o=** after azuredatabricks.net. When you get the URL correct, you will see a screen asking for the Scope Name, DNS Name, and Resource ID, as shown in *Figure 3.27*:

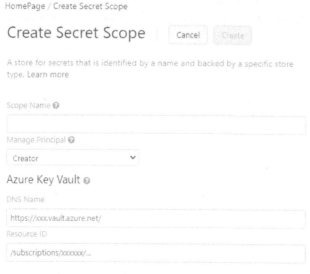

Figure 3.27: Databricks Create Secret Scope

The scope name is up to you. It should be something easy to remember, and you should write it down in an easy-to-find location. It is difficult to retrieve later. The other values you need are located on the **Properties** tab of the Key Vault, as shown in *Figure 3.28*:

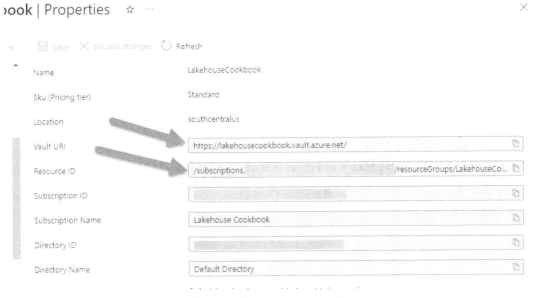

Figure 3.28: Key Vault properties

Once you have found the Vault URI and Resource ID, enter them in the Secret Scope screen, as shown in *Figure 3.29*:

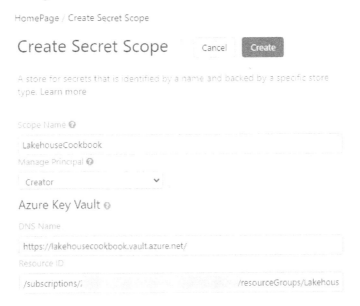

Figure 3.29: Populated Create Secret Scope

Click **Create** to complete the process.

The next step is to use the secret scope and retrieve a secret. This is done by using **dbutils.secret.get**, as shown in *Figure 3.30*:

```
Cmd 1

1   secret = dbutils.secrets.get("LakehouseCookbook","SuperSecret")
2   print(secret)

[REDACTED]
```

Figure 3.30: *Getting a secret using dbutils*

Recipe 19: Displaying a redacted value

Notice that the response indicates the value has been redacted. This is for security reasons. One way to bypass this is to treat the response as an array of characters, as shown in *Figure 3.31*:

```
Cmd 2

1   clear = ""
2   for c in secret:
3       clear += c + " "
4   print(clear)

L a k e h o u s e
```

Figure 3.31: *Displaying a redacted value*

This approach is useful during development, but ensure you are not exposing sensitive values in production. We now have a place to save our sensitive information, which will be important in later sections.

Blob storage

Blob storage is a low-cost storage solution on Azure. As ADLS Gen2 is built on top of it, they are similar. The primary difference is the absence of a hierarchical directory structure with POSIX and Hadoop compatibility. Both can be used to store structured and unstructured data. Both can be accessed using credential passthrough, account keys, service principle, and **Shared Access Signatures (SAS)** tokens.

Recipe 20: Account keys

Note that using account keys is the least desirable way of accessing storage accounts mainly because it is not easy to manage and less granular to control. The first step (after having created your storage account or gaining access) is to find the Storage account name and access keys. Scroll down in the left navigation until you see the Access keys. Click it and copy the keys into your clipboard by clicking Show and then the copy icon, as shown in *Figure 3.32*:

Tip: You will likely need to grant Storage Blob Data Contributor and Storage Queue Data Contributor rights to your Databricks workspace within your Azure Storage Account.

Figure 3.32: Storage account access key

Next, go to Azure Key Vault and add a new secret named storage-account-access-key or whatever is appropriate in your situation. The main thing is that it should match the code in your notebook that retrieves the secret. We can then use code very similar to that used in the passthrough authentication example to display the contents of a file, as shown in *Figure 3.33*:

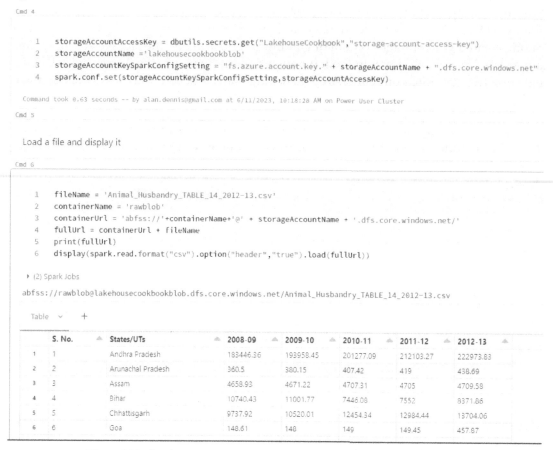

```
Cmd 4

1    storageAccountAccessKey = dbutils.secrets.get("LakehouseCookbook","storage-account-access-key")
2    storageAccountName ='lakehousecookbookblob'
3    storageAccountKeySparkConfigSetting = "fs.azure.account.key." + storageAccountName + ".dfs.core.windows.net"
4    spark.conf.set(storageAccountKeySparkConfigSetting,storageAccountAccessKey)

Command took 0.63 seconds -- by alan.dennis@gmail.com at 6/11/2023, 10:18:28 AM on Power User Cluster

Cmd 5

Load a file and display it

Cmd 6

1    fileName = 'Animal_Husbandry_TABLE_14_2012-13.csv'
2    containerName = 'rawblob'
3    containerUrl = 'abfss://'+containerName+'@' + storageAccountName + '.dfs.core.windows.net/'
4    fullUrl = containerUrl + fileName
5    print(fullUrl)
6    display(spark.read.format("csv").option("header","true").load(fullUrl))

▸ (2) Spark Jobs

abfss://rawblob@lakehousecookbookblob.dfs.core.windows.net/Animal_Husbandry_TABLE_14_2012-13.csv
```

Table ˅ +

S. No.		States/UTs	2008-09	2009-10	2010-11	2011-12	2012-13
1	1	Andhra Pradesh	183446.36	193958.45	201277.09	212103.27	222973.83
2	2	Arunachal Pradesh	360.5	380.15	407.42	419	438.69
3	3	Assam	4658.93	4671.22	4707.31	4705	4709.58
4	4	Bihar	10740.43	11001.77	7446.08	7552	8371.86
5	5	Chhattisgarh	9737.92	10520.01	12454.34	12984.44	13704.06
6	6	Goa	148.61	148	149	149.45	457.87

Figure 3.33: *Get the secret account key, set the configuration, and display the file*

We have loaded a copy of the file we used in our discussion of passthrough authentication. As mentioned, using account keys is discouraged. Next, we will discuss two commonly used and accepted approaches.

Recipe 21: Service principle

Databricks recommends using **Open Authorization 2 (OAuth 2)** to access Azure Storage accounts. Developers often refer to this as the App Registration method, as creating an application registration is required. Not surprisingly, the process starts by creating an application registration in your Azure Active Directory, as shown in *Figure 3.34*:

Figure 3.34: *Create an app registration*

Once the application registration page loads, set the name to something appropriate for your situation, as shown in *Figure 3.35*:

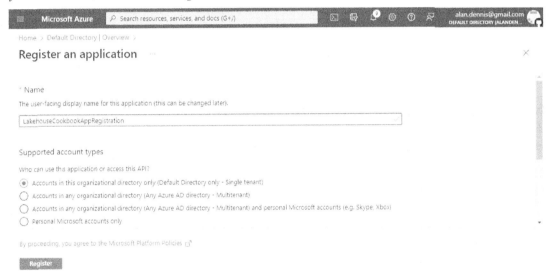

Figure 3.35: *Set application name*

Once the registration has been completed, you are presented with a page containing information that will need to be added to the key vault. The two values of interest on this page are Application and Directory **ID**, as shown in *Figure 3.36*:

Figure 3.36: *Application details*

The names of the secrets in the key vault need to match the names in your code. In this example, applicationId is the secret name for the Application ID, and directoryId is the secret for the Directory ID, as shown in *Figure 3.37*:

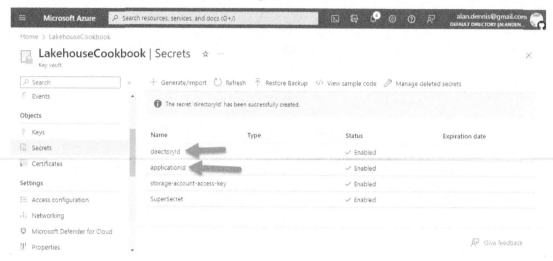

Figure 3.37: Secrets application and directory ID

We have most of the values we need. Next, we need to create an application secret. We do this by clicking on **Certificates and Secrets** located in the application registration left navigation and then clicking on New client Secret, as shown in *Figure 3.38*:

Figure 3.38: Adding an application secret

After the secret has been created, copy its value, as shown in *Figure 3.39*, and add it to the key vault:

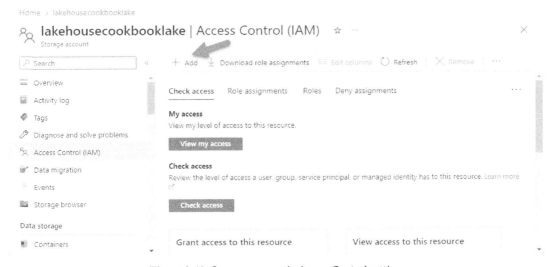

Description	Expires	Value ⓘ	Copied	ecret ID
Databricks Access to Storage A...	6/10/2025	BRtO5pUPW... 🗋	2c	4-8d... 🗋 🗑

Figure 3.39: *Copy application secret*

We now have all the secrets required to access the storage account from Databricks, but we have not granted the newly created App Registration permissions access to the storage account. To access the storage account, the App Registration must have **Storage Blob Data Contributor** rights and others, depending on your organization's configuration. To add the role, get to **Access Control (IAM)** on the storage account by clicking on the left navigation item of the same name, as shown in *Figure 3.40*:

Figure 3.40: *Storage account's Access Control settings*

Once the screen comes up, enter the role name in the search box, select the matching record in the list, then click **Next**, as shown in *Figure 3:41*:

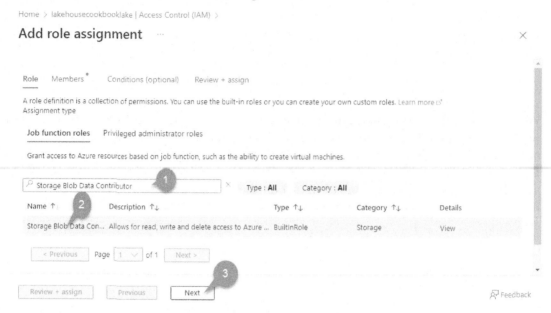

Figure 3.41: *Search for the role and select*

Next, you need to select the **App Registration** principal by clicking **Select Members**, as shown in *Figure 3.42*:

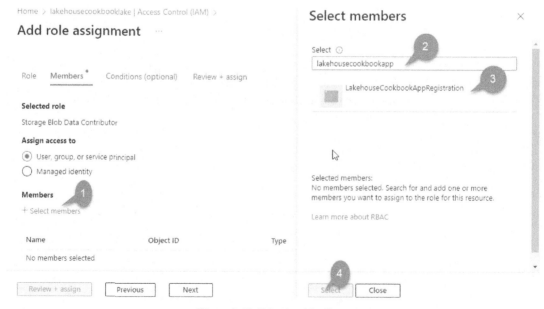

Figure 3.42: *Selecting Members*

After selecting, click the **Review** and **Assign** button to finish the assignment process. You will see a confirmation message that the role has been assigned to the identity. Now it is time to use a Databricks notebook to read a file from the storage account using the App Registration. The code is similar to that for using account keys but contains more values. The first thing we do is create a variable with the name of the storage account and the secret scope to use, as seen in the following code in lines 1 and 2:

```
1.  storageAccountName ='lakehousecookbookblob'
2.  secretScope = "LakehouseCookbook"
3.  # Get Secrets
4.  applicationId =dbutils.secrets.
    get(scope=secretScope,key="applicationId")
5.  directoryId =dbutils.secrets.get(scope=secretScope,key="directoryId")
6.  service_credential = dbutils.secrets.
    get(scope=secretScope,key="serviceCredentialKey")
7.  # Keys
8.  authType = "fs.azure.account.auth.type." + storageAccountName+ ".
    dfs.core.windows.net"
9.  oauthProviderType ="fs.azure.account.oauth.provider.
    type." + storageAccountName+ ".dfs.core.windows.net"
10. oauthClientId = "fs.azure.account.oauth2.client.
    id." + storageAccountName+ ".dfs.core.windows.net"
11. oauthSecret= "fs.azure.account.oauth2.client.
    secret." + storageAccountName+ ".dfs.core.windows.net"
12. oauthEndpoint = "fs.azure.account.oauth2.client.
    endpoint." + storageAccountName+ ".dfs.core.windows.net"
13. # Set Spark Config
14. spark.conf.set(authType, "OAuth")
15. spark.conf.set(oauthProviderType, "org.apache.hadoop.fs.azurebfs.
    oauth2.ClientCredsTokenProvider")
16. spark.conf.set(oauthClientId, applicationId)
17. spark.conf.set(oauthSecret, service_credential)
18. spark.conf.set(oauthEndpoint, "https://login.microsoftonline.
    com/" + directoryId + "/oauth2/token")
```

Next, we retrieve the secret values we previously set on lines 4, 5, and 6. The following lines could be much shorter, but they have been broken into easier-to-read parts. Line 8 sets a variable with the values required to specify the authentication type, which we set on line 14 to OAuth. Lines 9 through 12 set variables with the values that are required for lines

15 to 18. Once we have set the authentication method and required values, we are ready to read a file, as shown in *Figure 3.43*:

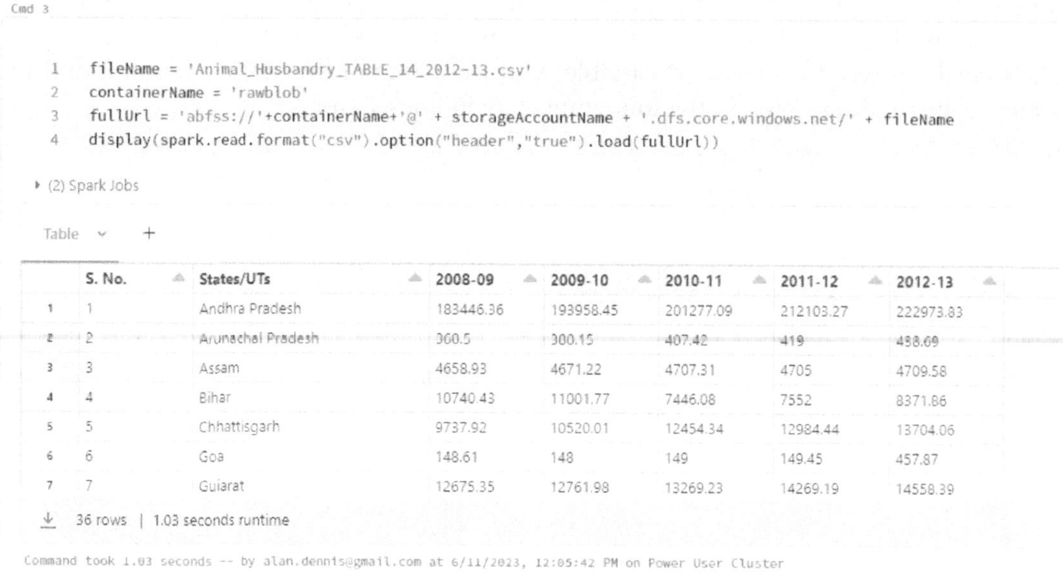

```
Cmd 3

1    fileName = 'Animal_Husbandry_TABLE_14_2012-13.csv'
2    containerName = 'rawblob'
3    fullUrl = 'abfss://'+containerName+'@' + storageAccountName + '.dfs.core.windows.net/' + fileName
4    display(spark.read.format("csv").option("header","true").load(fullUrl))
```

▶ (2) Spark Jobs

Table ⌄   +

	S. No.	States/UTs	2008-09	2009-10	2010-11	2011-12	2012-13
1	1	Andhra Pradesh	183446.36	193958.45	201277.09	212103.27	222973.83
2	2	Arunachal Pradesh	360.5	300.15	407.42	419	488.69
3	3	Assam	4658.93	4671.22	4707.31	4705	4709.58
4	4	Bihar	10740.43	11001.77	7446.08	7552	8371.86
5	5	Chhattisgarh	9737.92	10520.01	12454.34	12984.44	13704.06
6	6	Goa	148.61	148	149	149.45	457.87
7	7	Gujarat	12675.35	12761.98	13269.23	14269.19	14558.39

↓   36 rows | 1.03 seconds runtime

Command took 1.03 seconds -- by alan.dennis@gmail.com at 6/11/2023, 12:05:42 PM on Power User Cluster

Figure 3.43: *Reading a CSV using app registration*

Notice that the code is virtually identical to *Figure 3.25* and *Figure 3.26*. The main difference is the authentication and authorization mechanism. The code will also be similar to that in the coming section using shared access signatures to access Azure Storage.

Recipe 22: Shared access signatures

SAS is a special URI that allows access to Azure Storage. It is more secure than using storage account keys, in part because it is more fine-grained. The term SAS and SAS token are often used interchangeably. To create a SAS token for a storage account, navigate to that account and select Shared access signature from the left navigation. Then select the desired permission and expiration, as shown in *Figure 3.44*:

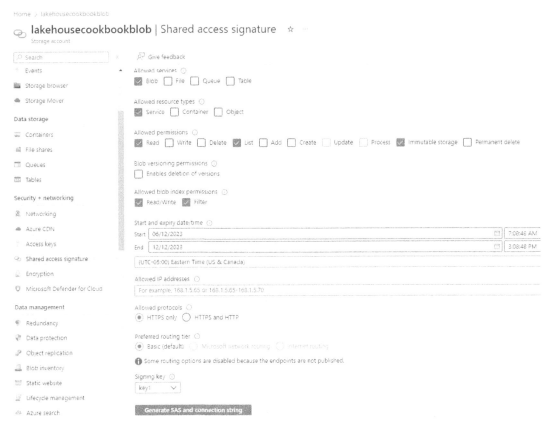

Figure 3.44: *Selecting SAS permissions*

In this case, we have granted read access at a service level to all blobs for six months. We did not restrict **Internet Protocol (IP)** addresses but did require a secure connection. Clicking the button at the bottom of the page causes text boxes to appear containing the SAS token in various formats, as shown in *Figure 3.45*:

Signing key ⓘ

| key1 ∨ |

Generate SAS and connection string

Connection string

BlobEndpoint=https://lakehousecookbookblob.blob.core.windows.net/;QueueEndpoint=https://lakehousecookbookblob.queue.core.windov

SAS token ⓘ

?sv=2022-11-02&ss=b&srt=s&sp=rlitf&se=2023-12-12T20:08:48Z&st=2023-06-12T11:08:48Z&spr=https&sig=B6s9rKEPgFU9RkBz3z7CkUt

Blob service SAS URL

https://lakehousecookbookblob.blob.core.windows.net/?sv=2022-11-02&ss=b&srt=s&sp=rlitf&se=2023-12-12T20:08:48Z&st=2023-06-12T

Figure 3.45: *SAS Connection string, token, and service URL*

Once you have the SAS token, the next step is to add it as a secret to the Key Vault using a name that matches the name in your Databricks notebook. In this case, the name being used is **lakehouseBlobSasTokenKey**, as shown in *Figure 3.46*:

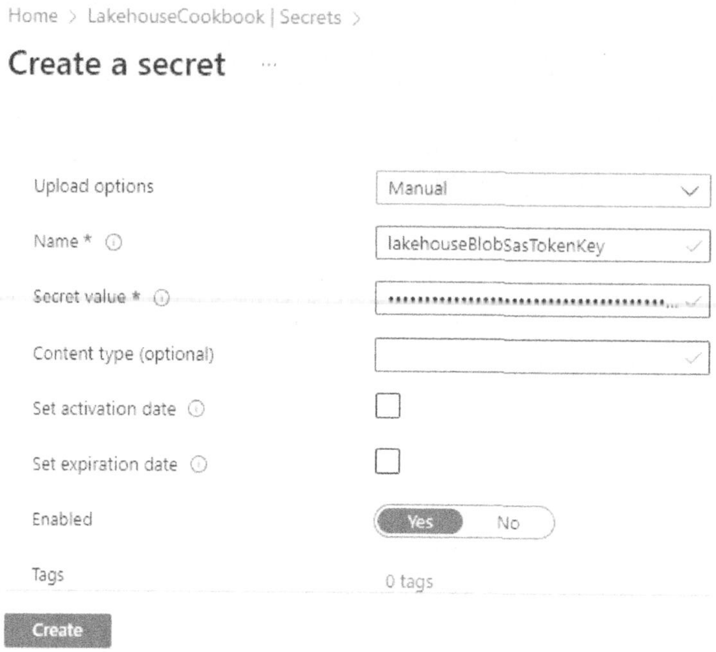

Figure 3.46: Adding SAS token to Key Vault

Once we have added the token to the key vault, the next step is to use it in a Databricks notebook. We use a slightly different format with this example, in part to show the use of format strings, as shown in *Figure 3.47*. A format string allows you to include a variable in the string inside of braces:

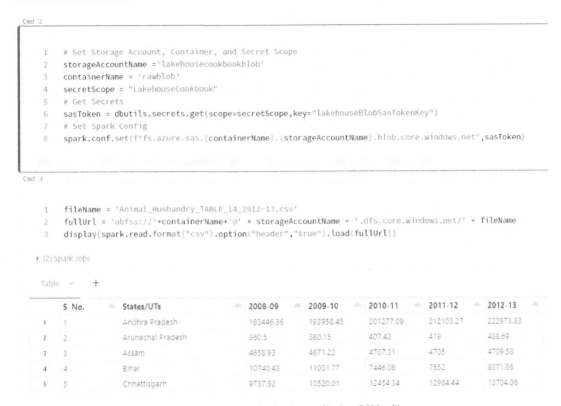

```
Cmd 2

1    # Set Storage Account, Container, and Secret Scope
2    storageAccountName ='lakehousecookbookblob'
3    containerName = 'rawblob'
4    secretScope = "LakehouseCookbook"
5    # Get Secrets
6    sasToken = dbutils.secrets.get(scope=secretScope,key="lakehouseBlobSasTokenKey")
7    # Set Spark Config
8    spark.conf.set(f"fs.azure.sas.{containerName}.{storageAccountName}.blob.core.windows.net",sasToken)
```

```
Cmd 3

1    fileName = 'Animal_Husbandry_TABLE_14_2012-13.csv'
2    fullUrl = 'abfss://'+containerName+'@' + storageAccountName + '.dfs.core.windows.net/' + fileName
3    display(spark.read.format("csv").option("header","true").load(fullUrl))
```

▸ (2) Spark Jobs

Table ∨   +

	S. No.	States/UTs	2008-09	2009-10	2010-11	2011-12	2012-13
1	1	Andhra Pradesh	183446.36	193958.45	201277.09	212103.27	222973.83
2	2	Arunachal Pradesh	360.5	380.15	407.42	419	438.69
3	3	Assam	4658.93	4671.22	4707.31	4705	4709.58
4	4	Bihar	10740.43	11001.77	7446.08	7552	8371.86
5	5	Chhattisgarh	9737.92	10520.01	12454.34	12984.44	13704.06

Figure 3.47: *Using SAS token to display CSV a file*

In *Figure 3.47*, line six retrieves the value for the token from the key vault via the secret scope. Line eight sets the Spark configuration to use the SAS token. The lines in command cell three are virtually the same as shown in the previous examples. The advantage SAS tokens bring over the other approaches (except for pass-through authentication) is a higher degree of control and granularity.

Conclusion

This chapter discussed how to design a lakehouse and the underlying data lake. We discussed the importance of socializing and agreeing to standards related to layers within a lakehouse and allowed operations when moving data from one layer to another.

In the next chapter, we build on the material we learnt in this chapter. We create Delta tables using the storage to which we can now connect. We also revisit connecting to storage for S3 and GCP.

CHAPTER 4
Creating Delta Tables

Introduction

Delta tables are the heart of a Lakehouse. Delta is a critical enabling technology that makes the Lakehouse possible. We will briefly discuss the types of Delta tables and then move onto creating them. Next, we will discuss data exploration and profiling of data in Delta tables. We will close the chapter by discussing and presenting common **Structured Query Language (SQL)** queries and operations often associated with interview coding exercises.

Structure

In this chapter, we will cover the following topics:

- Delta Lake
- Creating managed Delta tables
- Creating unmanaged tables

Objectives

By the end of this chapter, you should be able to create managed and unmanaged Delta tables in GCP, AWS, and Azure. You will be able to compare managed and unmanaged tables. Lastly, you will also have a good understanding of how to access external storage in GCP and AWS.

Delta Lake

Delta is open-source software that extends the functionality of the Parquet file format to include the functionality necessary to construct a Lakehouse. As previously discussed, that functionality includes **Atomic, Consistent, Isolated, and Durable (ACID)** transactions. Additionally, Delta enables optimization and high-performance filtering. ACID transactions are essential in a Lakehouse, as the paradigm relies on updated tables as changes are detected. Delta is the standard table format in Databricks. There are two types of Delta tables, **managed** and **unmanaged**. Unmanaged tables are sometimes called external tables, as the data is stored in an external location. We will discuss managed and unmanaged tables and present a work aid to help you decide which to use.

Managed and unmanaged tables

The primary difference between managed and unmanaged tables is that data is stored external to the Databricks workspace when using an unmanaged table. To do this, we tell Databricks a location to store data during the table creation process. One of the advantages of managed tables is that Delta manages the location of the data, while an unmanaged table requires the table creator to manage the location. When a managed table is dropped, the schema metadata and the data are deleted. Only the schema metadata is deleted when an unmanaged table is dropped, leaving the data intact.

Unmanaged Delta tables can be accessed by systems other than Databricks. This makes them more available to the organization. Assuming the system can read the Delta format, all required is access to the location where the data is stored. A growing number of systems can read Delta format without using Databricks. Generally, you will likely use unmanaged tables when working on an enterprise-class project. The next section will share a flowchart to help you decide where to store your Delta data.

Deciding table type

Deciding where to store Delta table data is important in creating a Lakehouse. Many factors go into this decision, as shown in *Figure 4.1*:

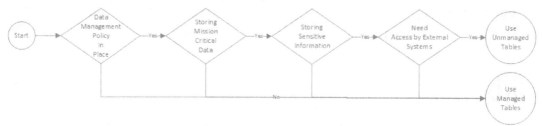

Figure 4.1: Flowchart to decide between managed and unmanaged tables

You may have other factors you wish to consider. Feel free to extend the flowchart or alter it based on your needs. Some people believe that managed tables may be faster than unmanaged tables. That determination would require significant testing, resulting in minimal differences in performance.

A mature data policy should be in place when using unmanaged tables. It should be clear where a table is stored, based on the layer of refinement, where it came from, and why it exists. The additional step required to delete data when dropping the table is important for storing mission-critical data. If using advanced storage systems, such as Azure Data Lake Gen2 with a POSIX file system, sensitive information can be managed securely. Lastly, a growing number of libraries and tools are available to access files stored in Delta format. If it is desirable to allow such access, unmanaged tables are a better choice than managed. Now that we have discussed how to decide on the type of table to create, we can move on to creating them.

Schema and database

Databricks uses the concept of a schema to organize tables. For convenience, Databricks uses the word database as an alias for a schema. To see what schemas/databases exist in a workspace, we use the **SHOW SCHEMAS** command, as shown in *Figure 4.2*:

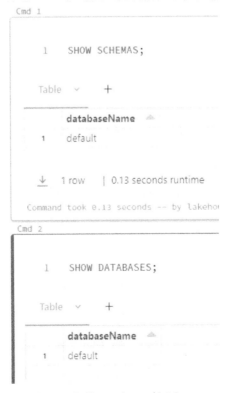

Figure 4.2: Show schemas/databases

Notice that the results are the same. Going forward, we will use the word schema over the word database, as it more accurately reflects the nature of the construct. To create a schema, we use the **CREATE SCHEMA** command, as shown in *Figure 4.3*:

Figure 4.3: *Create and describe a schema*

The command **DESCRIBE SCHEMA EXTENDED** can be used to learn the details of a schema, such as any associated comments and where the schema is stored. Once we have created a schema, the next step is to select it for use and see if there are any tables in it, as shown in *Figure 4.4*:

Cmd 5

```
1    USE LakehouseCookbook;
```

OK

Command took 0.29 seconds -- by lakehousecookbookaws@gmail.com at 6/15/2023, 5:27:47 PM on Lakehouse Cookbook AWS's Cluster

Cmd 6

```
1    SHOW TABLES;
```

Query returned no results

Figure 4.4: *Select a schema and show tables*

Not surprisingly, there are no tables in our newly created schema.

Creating managed Delta tables

Creating Delta tables is one of the most common activities during Lakehouse construction. We will discuss the various ways to create Delta tables and provide examples using various languages and cloud providers. We will also discuss some common pitfalls and touch on setting important Delta table options.

Ways to create

We can create Delta tables using the Databricks workspace to upload files, SQL, the Spark **Application Programming Interface** (**API**), and **Delta Live Tables** (**DLT**). The method depends on the situation and is often influenced by organization standards and best practices.

Recipe 23: Upload data using Databricks workspace

The simplest way to create tables is to add data by uploading a file. This approach is popular enough that Databricks added a link to this function on the **Workspace** homepage, as shown in *Figure 4.5*:

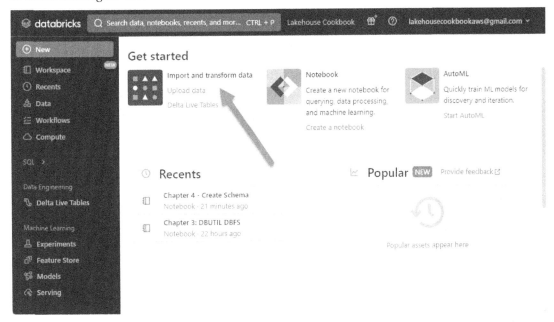

Figure 4.5: *Data import link*

There are many sources of data on the Internet. For this example, we will use the Places: County Data 2020 release dataset available at **https://catalog.data.gov/dataset/places-county-data-gis-friendly-format-2020-release-4ae28**. After downloading the CSV file, we can import it into Databricks by clicking the **Upload data** link. You will then see a screen asking you to drop a file onto a rectangle or **browse** your local file system, as shown in *Figure 4.6:*

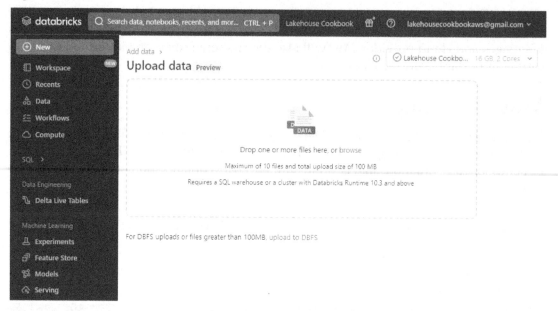

Figure 4.6: Upload data screen

The file uploaded must be in a supported format. If your data is in an archive file, such as a ZIP, you must expand it before uploading. After browsing or dropping your CSV file, you will see a status update as **Databricks uploads** and imports the file, as shown in *Figure 4.7:*

Figure 4.7: Upload data progress

Once Databricks completes the import, you will see a data preview, including the names of the columns, as shown in *Figure 4.8*:

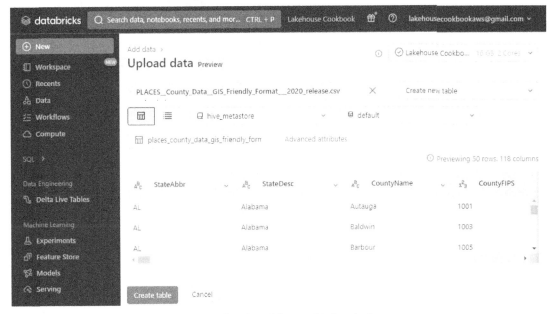

Figure 4.8: *Preview of data and inferred schema*

We now have the option to create a table. Clicking **Create table** causes the table to be created and shows a spinning image, as shown in *Figure 4.9*:

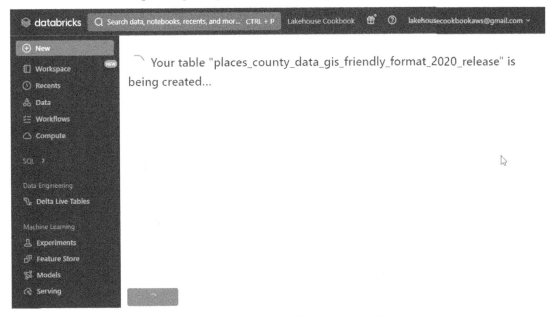

Figure 4.9: *Progress screen during table creation*

Once the process completes, you will be returned to the **Data Explorer** screen. Congratulations, you have just created a Delta table! If you expand the default folder under `hive_metastore`, you will see the newly created table. Clicking the table brings up a view where you can look at columns in the table, see sample data, view the table details, and examine the table history, as shown in *Figure 4.10*:

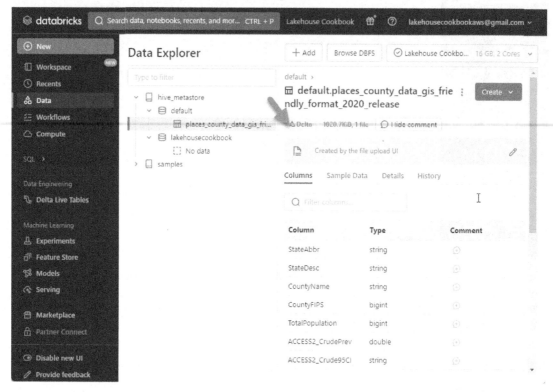

Figure 4.10: *Table created through the workspace user interface*

Notice that the table is in Delta format, as indicated by the small arrow in *Figure 4.10*. If you click the **Create** button, you can create a notebook. The notebook created has **Python** selected as the default language and includes one cell with the **%sql** magic string at the start, making it an SQL cell. Running the notebook shows the contents of the recently created table, as shown in *Figure 4.11*:

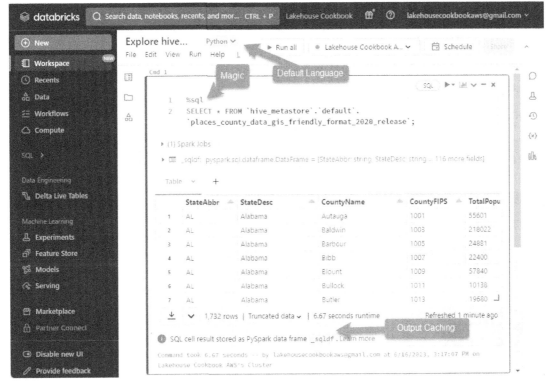

Figure 4.11: Contents of the table

Notice that the results of the **SELECT** statement are available in a DataFrame named **_ sqldf.** This is a feature available in Databricks runtimes 13 and higher. Each time we execute a Python cell, the output is saved in this variable. To keep the value for future use, we want to save it to a variable, as shown in *Figure 4.12*:

Figure 4.12: Saving the Python output

This is one way to create a DataFrame from an SQL statement. There are other ways to do this, which are more explicit. For example, suppose you needed to know the number of counties in each state. To do this, we use a SQL statement like:

```
SELECT StateDesc,count(*) COUNT FROM places_county_data_gis_friendly_
format_2020_release

GROUP BY StateDesc ORDER BY StateDesc.
```

This statement returns the state description and counts for each state. Using **group-by** and **order-by** clauses is common when doing data aggregation and summation. To save the results of this statement, we can use the Spark APIs **sql** function, as shown in *Figure: 4.13*:

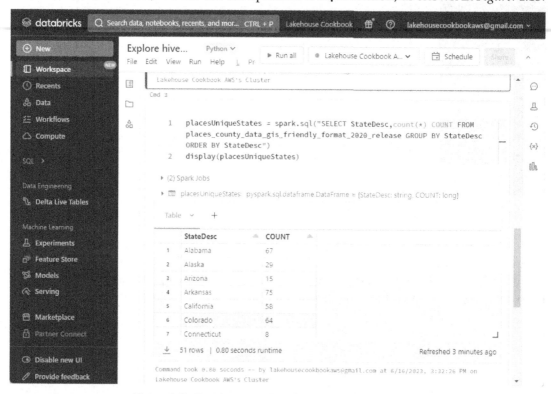

Figure 4.13: Creating a new DataFrame from SQL statement

We will discuss the SQL method in the following section. Notice that the Databricks **User Interface (UI)** color highlights SQL reserved words, such as **SELECT, FROM**, and **GROUP BY**. This formatting is applied even when the words are inside a Python string.

We have created a table using the Databricks UI. While this approach works for smaller files, it has many limitations. In the following sections, we will discuss alternative ways of creating and manipulating Delta tables.

SQL

SQL is a popular language. The language has been around for over 40 years. Databricks' SQL is similar to **American National Standards Institute (ANSI)** SQL. To learn more about Databricks' SQL, consult with the SQL language reference at **https://docs.databricks.com/ sql/language-manual/index.html**. If you scroll down in the SQL language manual, you will see a DDL statement section. This list includes the statements used to **create**, **modify**, or **delete** database objects. Database objects include tables, views, and other database elements. The language manual shows you how the statements must be structured. This syntax helps you while creating database objects. We will explore these statements in depth and supply examples of creating managed and unmanaged tables.

Recipe 24: Reading the SQL language reference

Programming language can be complex. There are generally multiple variations of a command. Usually, there are multiple mutually exclusive options for a particular clause. Language specifications tell you what is syntactically correct. These specifications can be a bit overwhelming, as seen in *Figure 4.14*:

Syntax

```
{ { [CREATE OR] REPLACE TABLE | CREATE [EXTERNAL] TABLE [ IF NOT EXISTS ] }
  table_name
  [ table_specification ]
  [ USING data_source ]
  [ table_clauses ]
  [ AS query ] }

table_specification
  ( { column_identifier column_type [ NOT NULL ]
      [ GENERATED ALWAYS AS ( expr ) |
        GENERATED { ALWAYS | BY DEFAULT } AS IDENTITY [ ( [ START WITH start ] [ INCREMENT BY step ] ) ] |
        DEFAULT default_expression ]
      [ COMMENT column_comment ]
      [ column_constraint ] } [, ...]
      [ , table_constraint ] [...] )

table_clauses
  { OPTIONS clause |
    PARTITIONED BY clause |
    clustered_by_clause |
    LOCATION path [ WITH ( CREDENTIAL credential_name ) ] |
    COMMENT table_comment |
    TBLPROPERTIES clause } [...]

clustered_by_clause
  { CLUSTERED BY ( cluster_column [, ...] )
    [ SORTED BY ( { sort_column [ ASC | DESC ] } [, ...] ) ]
    INTO num_buckets BUCKETS }
```

***Figure 4.14**: Create table specification*

These statements aim to say exactly how you can construct a series of valid clauses and express what you are trying to accomplish. Reading the first line of the specification, we can see two choices when creating a table, separated by a pipe character. Expanding the optional; clauses, your choices are **[CREATE OR] REPLACE TABLE** and **CREATE [EXTERNAL] TABLE [IF NOT EXISTS]**. In the first statement **OR REPLACE** is optional. In the second, **EXTERNAL** and **IF NOT EXISTS** are optional. To create an unmanaged table, you would use the **EXTERNAL** keyword. We will create a managed table in our case, so we will not use **EXTERNAL**. The **OR REPLACE** clause is important. Databricks recommends using it over dropping a table and recreating it, as it allows the history of the table to be preserved. So far, we will be using **CREATE OR REPLACE**.

The next part of the statement is the table name. Table names are used when referencing the table, such as seeing what records are in it or adding records. There is a specification over what characters can be used in the name of a table. On the SQL Language reference page, if you scroll down, you will see the **table_name** section, which is a hyperlink to the rules governing table names located at **https://docs.databricks.com/sql/language-manual/sql-ref-names.html#table-name**. A table name comprises an optional **schema_name** followed by a **table_identifier** and optional **temporatl_spec**, as shown in *Figure 4.15*:

Table name

Identifies a table object. The table can be *qualified* with a schema name or *unqualified* using a simple identifier.

Syntax

🖺 Copy

```
{ [ schema_name . ] table_identifier [ temporal_spec ] |
  { file_format | `file_format` } . `path_to_table` [ temporal_spec ] [ credential_spec ] }

temporal_spec
{
  @ timestamp_encoding |
  @V version |
  [ FOR ] { SYSTEM_TIMESTAMP | TIMESTAMP } AS OF timestamp_expression |
  [ FOR ] { SYSTEM_VERSION | VERSION } AS OF version
}

credential_spec
  WITH ( CREDENTIAL credential_name )
```

Parameters

- **schema_name**: A qualified or unqualified schema name that contains the table.

- **table_identifier**: An identifier that specifies the name of the table or table_alias.

Figure 4.15: Table name specification

As we have discussed, a schema is a way of organizing related tables. In Databricks, schema and database are the same. A **table_identifier** is an identifier. The rules for creating identifiers can be found by clicking on **table_identifiers** in the **Parameters** section of the table names section, which is located at **https://docs.databricks.com/sql/ language-manual/sql-ref-identifiers.html**. The regular expression for regular identifiers is letters, digits, or underscores, as shown in *Figure 4.16:*

For our example, the name we use will be **MyFirstLakehouseTable**. Next, we need to reexamine the **CREATE TABLE** specification. The elements have relationships, as shown in *Figure 4.17:*

```
{ { [CREATE OR] REPLACE TABLE | CREATE [EXTERNAL] TABLE [ IF NOT EXISTS ] }
  table_name
  [ table_specification ]
  [ USING data_source ]
  [ table_clauses ]
  [ AS query ] }

table_specification
  ( { column_identifier column_type [ NOT NULL ]
    [ GENERATED ALWAYS AS ( expr ) |
      GENERATED { ALWAYS | BY DEFAULT } AS IDENTITY [ ( [ START WITH start ] [ INCREMENT BY step ] ) ] |
      DEFAULT default_expression ]
    [ COMMENT column_comment ]
    [ column_constraint ] } [, ...]
  [ , table_constraint ] [...] )

table_clauses
  { OPTIONS clause |
    PARTITIONED BY clause |
    clustered_by_clause |
    LOCATION path [ WITH ( CREDENTIAL credential_name ) ] |
    COMMENT table_comment |
    TBLPROPERTIES clause } [...]

clustered_by_clause
  { CLUSTERED BY ( cluster_column [, ...] )
    [ SORTED BY ( { sort_column [ ASC | DESC ] } [, ...] ) ]
    INTO num_buckets BUCKETS }
```

Figure 4.17: Annotated create table specification

The next element in the specification after **table_name** is an optional table specification. In this case, we want to create a set of columns in our table. If we wanted to add table clauses, we examined the options in the **table_clauses** section. The **table_clauses** section references the **clustered_by_clause** section. We are now ready to create the table.

Recipe 25: Creating a table with SQL

Now, we can finish our create statement, as shown in *Figure 4.18:*

Figure 4.18: Create table SQL

In this example, we created a table named **MyFirstLakehouseTable** in the **lakehousecookbook** schema we created earlier. We also examine the table using the **DESCRIBE EXTENDED** command. Notice the table has two columns, named id and name, with data types of integers, and string, respectively.

Recipe 26: Creating a table with SQL using AS

We have talked about creating an empty table using the **CREATE** statement. A common pattern is to create a new table based on the results of a **SELECT** statement. For example, you might want the distinct values in one table available in another, as shown in *Figure 4.19*:

Figure 4.19: *Creating a table using the AS clause*

Note that the line under the **C** in **CREATE** is an indentation indicator, not a pipe character. The **DISTINCT** clause ensures there are no duplicates in the results. Since we are ignoring the id column, we will have a table containing all the names in the other table at the point the command was issued. If a new record is added to the source table, it does not reflect in the derived table. It is common to use **OR REPLACE** clause on the statement and periodically re-execute the command.

We have discussed ways of creating tables using SQL. Another way to create tables is to use the Spark API.

Spark API

Spark uses DataFrames to represent tabular data. Generally, we populate DataFrames from data sources like files, databases, and event streams. For our example, we will create synthetic data using random selection.

Recipe 27: Creating a table using Spark API and random data

The Spark API can be accessed from multiple programming languages. Python is a popular language partly because of its simplicity and readability. Databricks uses PySpark, a Python API for Spark. In Databricks, that distinction fades, and you only think of calling Spark operation using the spark object, as shown in *Figure 4.20*:

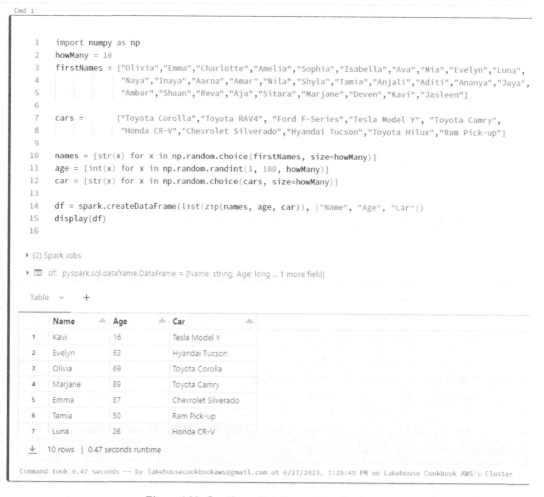

Figure 4.20: Creating a DataFrame using Python

In the first cell, we import **NumPy** in line 1. Next, we define two arrays containing popular first names and car models. Next, we create arrays of size **howMany** containing randomly selected values. Line 14 is where we interact with Spark. The command **createDataFrame** converts arrays of objects to a Spark DataFrame. Line 15 invokes the **display** method, which produces the output at the bottom. We now have a DataFrame; the next step is to save it as a table. We do this using the **write** and **saveAsTable**, as shown in *Figure 4.21*:

Cmd 2

```
1    df.write.format("delta").mode("overwrite").saveAsTable("lakehousecookbook.NameAgeCars")
```

▸ (4) Spark Jobs

Command took 5.28 seconds -- by lakehousecookbookaws@gmail.com at 6/17/2023, 7:51:19 PM on Lakehouse Cookbook AWS

Cmd 3

```
1    %sql SELECT * from lakehousecookbook.NameAgeCars;
```

▸ (2) Spark Jobs

▸ 🔲 _sqldf: pyspark.sql.dataframe.DataFrame = [Name: string, Age: long ... 1 more field]

Table ∨   +

	Name	Age	Car
1	Kavi	16	Tesla Model Y
2	Evelyn	63	Hyandai Tucson
3	Olivia	69	Toyota Corolla
4	Marjane	89	Toyota Camry
5	Emma	87	Chevrolet Silverado
6	Tamia	50	Ram Pick-up
7	Luna	26	Honda CR-V

↓   10 rows | 5.43 seconds runtime

Figure 4.21: *Saving DataFrame as a table*

There are several parts of the written statement we need to discuss. Notice we pass **"delta"** in as the value for format. This is not needed if you are using a recent Databricks runtime. The default table format was switched to Delta in runtime 8.0. The **mode** parameter has two options, **overwrite** and **append**. As the names imply, **overwrite** replaces the values in the table in its entirety, while **append** adds the values to the table, leaving the earlier values in place. When working with bronze tables, we will typically append records. The last part of the instruction is **saveAsTable**. Using the supplied parameters, it creates a table in the Databricks hive metadata store. In this case, we include the schema and table name.

Recipe 28: Examining table history

In Recipe 25, we used a DataFrame to create a table. The statements used were a little longer than needed to explain what is being done when creating a table. We can simplify the code, as shown in *Figure 4.22*:

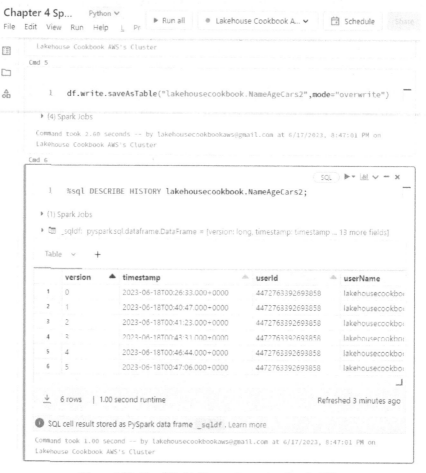

Figure 4.22: Simplified table creation using Spark API

Notice that we moved the mode option into the **saveAsTable** and accepted **Delta** as the default format. The values in tables change over time.

Delta supports time travel operations. This lets us examine the contents of a table at a point in time. The default retention period is 30 days but can be changed based on business needs. Understand that if it is set to be large, there will be an associated increase in storage consumption. One way to look at a table's history is to use the **DESCRIBE HISTORY** command, as shown in *Figure 4.21* in the sixth command cell. We can see that this table has six versions. Using Python, we can select a version using the option **timestampAsOf** or **versionAsOf** depending on if we are using a date and time or if we are using a version number, as shown in *Figure 4.23*:

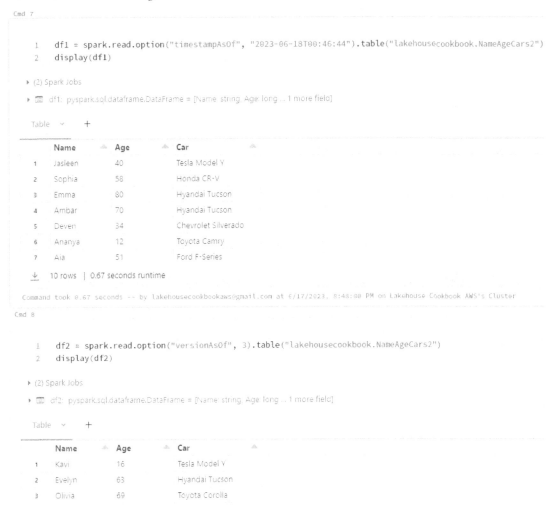

Figure 4.23: Table history using Python

Notice the results differ between the two versions selected. We can also do this in SQL using **TIMESTAMP AS OF** and **VERSION AS OF** clauses in a **SELECT** statement, as shown in *Figure 4.24*. In this example, we add the **LIMIT** keyword to limit the results to three items. Notice that we use the **%sql** magic string to indicate that we want a SQL cell in a Python notebook. A key concept to consider is that crossing the language barrier in a notebook always involves a table, view, or temporary table. Attempting to access a Python variable from an SQL block will result in an error. Please refer to the image below:

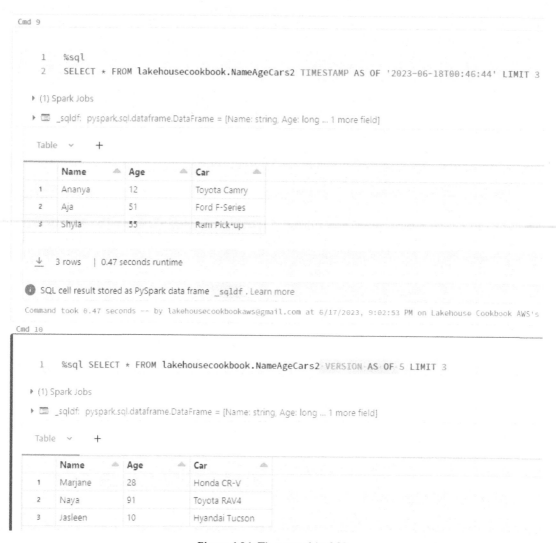

Figure 4.24: *Time travel in SQL*

We have created several managed tables in this section. We will now look at the concept of managed tables more deeply in the next section.

Managed tables details

As discussed previously, when using managed tables, we allow Delta to decide where the data associated with the table is stored. This makes creating managed Delta tables quite easy, as no linkage to an external storage system is required. As discussed in the previous section, there are two common ways to create Delta tables: SQL's **Data Definition Language (DDL)** statements and the Spark API from a language such as Python.

Recipe 29: Managed Delta table details

We have used **DESCRIBE** and **DESCRIBE DETAIL** previously; we will now dig into the details of the results of those commands. **DESCRIBE** returns the metadata about a table. This includes the column names, data types, and any comments, as shown in *Figure 4.25*:

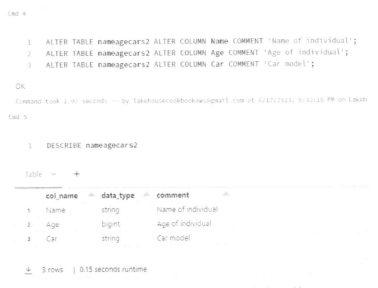

Figure 4.25: *Describe Table results*

In this case, we have three columns of type string, big integer, and string, respectively. Notice none of the columns have a description. Adding a description to a column is a good idea, especially if that column might confuse the data's consumers. Ideally, you should add your comments during creation. If that is difficult (as in the case of saving a DataFrame to a table), you can use the **ALTER TABLE** command to add comments, as shown in *Figure 4.26*:

Figure 4.26: *Adding comments to an existing table*

We can also see more about the table's information using the **DESCRIBE DETAIL** command. This shows us information about the table's format, a description if present, when it was created, and when it was last modified. The output also shows us detailed information, such as the number of partitions, the number of files, and the size of those files in bytes, along with other detailed information, as shown in *Figure 4.27*:

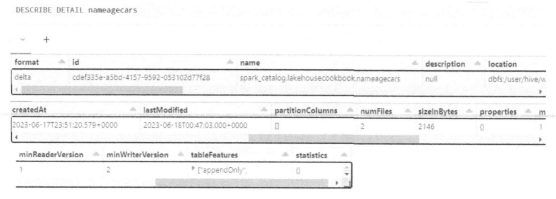

Figure 4.27: Results of the describe detail command

Because of the width of the results, multiple images are used to show the different columns. One column of interest is location. The files for the table are stored under the **hive warehouse**, as shown in *Figure 4.28*:

Figure 4.28: Location of managed table

As we discussed, this is one of the key differences between managed and unmanaged tables. Another way to see this information is by using the **DESCRIBE EXTENDED** command, as shown in *Figure 4.29*:

Figure 4.29: *DESCRIBE EXTENDED results*

Note that the information from the previous commands is consolidated into a single view. The location is easier to see in this format, and looking at row 13 is a way to see that this is a managed table since it is stored in a managed location.

Recipe 30: Using Data Explorer to see table details

The Databricks UI contains a great deal of information. The key information we are concerned with are located on the **Details** tab in the Data Explorer, as shown in *Figure 4.30*:

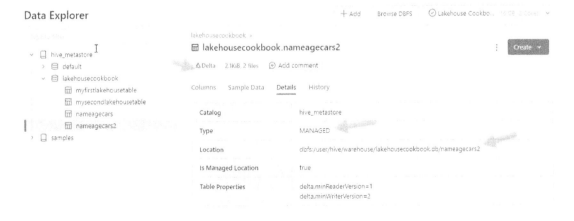

Figure 4.30: *Data Explorer's Details tab*

We can tell at a glance that this is a Delta table. We can also see it is managed and see where the files are being stored. This is a useful tool when determining the type of table, you are working with.

We have worked with managed tables to this point. It is time to transition to unmanaged tables. Unmanaged tables are often used by organizations that want explicit control of where their data is stored.

Creating unmanaged tables

Managed tables require access to a storage mechanism. That means you may need to provision one and determine the mechanism to connect to it before creating external tables. We will work through creating external tables on each of the cloud providers of Databricks.

Recipe 31: Using Databricks CLI to create a secret scope

In *Chapter 3, Connecting to Storage,* we discussed connecting Databricks to Azure storage. In this section, we will discuss enabling access to S3 from Databricks. There are many ways to connect to S3. For simplicity, we will use access keys. Once you have created an access key, you need a place to save it in Databricks. Since this information is sensitive, we will store the values using a Databricks secret scope. To create a secret scope in Databricks on S3, you need to use the Databricks CLI. To do this, you need an installation of Python 3. Once you have Python 3 installed, issue the command `pip install databricks-cli` at a Python prompt, as shown in *Figure 4.31:*

Figure 4.31: Installing Databricks CLI in Python

Once installed, you need to configure access to your Databricks instance. To do so, you will need a Databricks access token. To create an access token, click on your **email address** in the upper right corner and select **User Settings** from the dropdown. On the User Settings screen, click on **Access tokens**, as shown in *Figure 4.32*:

User Settings

Account & password   **Access tokens**   Git integration   Editor settings   Email preferences   Language settings

Personal access tokens can be used for secure authentication to the Databricks API instead of passwords.

[Generate new token]

Comment	Creation	Expiration	
Databricks CLI	2023-06-18 09:16:26 EDT	2024-06-17 09:16:26 EDT	🗑

Figure 4.32: *Databricks access tokens*

Click on **Generate new token**. You will be asked for a comment and lifetime for your token. Once you supply them and click the **Generate** button, you will see a screen displaying your newly created token. Copy this value to a safe place, as you will not have a way to access it after the fact, as shown in *Figure 4.33*:

Generate New Token

Your token has been created successfully.

dapi996   550e8fd0f48   📋

⚠ Make sure to copy the token now. You won't be able to see it again.

[Done]

Figure 4.33: *Newly created access token*

We now have an access token and can configure Databricks CLI to interact with our AWS Databricks workspace. We return to our Python prompt and issue the command **databricks configure --token**. You will be prompted for the Databricks host and the access token. Ensure that you do not include the trailing slash in the Databricks host. Once you have entered the Databricks address and the token, you can test your configuration using the command **databricks fs ls dbfs:/**, as shown in *Figure 4.34*:

```
(PythonAndR) D:\book>databricks configure --token
Databricks Host (should begin with https://): https://dbc-3b97d12a-b3e3.cloud.databricks.com
Token:

(PythonAndR) D:\book>databricks fs ls dbfs:/
FileStore
databricks-datasets
databricks-results
user
```

Figure 4.34: *Configuring and testing Databricks CLI*

Now that we have the Databricks CLI, we can create the secret scope to store our key information. To create a secret scope in AWS Databricks, use the command:

```
databricks secrets create-scope --scope LakehouseCookbook --initial-manage-principal users
```

Which creates a secret scope named **LakehouseCookbook** and grants all users' access. If you are doing this in a production environment, you may want to revisit this approach and require the premium version of Databricks. Now that you have created the secret scope, the next step is to save the IAM access key and secret. You do this by using the commands:

```
databricks secrets put --scope LakehouseCookbook --key S3AccessKey
--string-value <Your access key>
```

```
databricks secrets put --scope LakehouseCookbook --key S3AccessSecret
--string-value <Your secret access key>
```

This creates the secrets and makes them available in a Databricks notebook. The output of these three commands is shown in *Figure 4.35:*

```
(PythonAndR) D:\book>databricks secrets create-scope --scope LakehouseCookbook --initial-manage-principal users

(PythonAndR) D:\book>databricks secrets put --scope LakehouseCookbook --key S3AccessKey --string-value AKI.        /C
TWQ

(PythonAndR) D:\book>databricks secrets put --scope LakehouseCookbook --key S3AccessSecret --string-value V4mH       ı8
                        ıp8B
```

Figure 4.35: Creating a Databricks secret scope and adding secrets using the CLI

Now that we have secrets, we can switch to Databricks and access them. To do this, we use the **dbutils.secrets.get** method, as shown in *Figure 4.36*. We use the string concatenation trick we discussed previously to view the returned values.

Figure 4.36: Accessing Databricks secret scope values

Now that we have our access key and secret, we can move on to access S3 from AWS Databricks.

Recipe 32: Accessing S3 from Databricks on AWS

The first step is to retrieve the values from the secret scope. Once you have them, the secret key must be encoded before use, using the command **urllib.parse.quote**, as shown in *Figure 4.37*. When things are correctly configured, you can list the bucket's contents.

```
Cmd 1

1   import urllib
2   s3AccessKey = dbutils.secrets.get(scope="LakehouseCookbook", key="S3AccessKey")
3   s3AccessSecret = dbutils.secrets.get(scope="LakehouseCookbook", key="S3AccessSecret")
4   encodedSecretKey = urllib.parse.quote(string=s3AccessSecret, safe="")
5   bucketName = "lakehousecookbook"
6   S3Url = "s3n://{0}:{1}@{2}".format(s3AccessKey,encodedSecretKey,bucketName)
7   dbutils.fs.ls(S3Url)

Out[4]:  [FileInfo(path='s3n://[REDACTED]:V4mHdGVf0WRZh8ZaTM%2FOF9haJwmIkJyINC249p8B@lakehousecookbook/Lakehouse/', name='Lakeho
use/', size=0, modificationTime=1687098243540),
 FileInfo(path='s3n://[REDACTED]:V4mHdGVf0WRZh8ZaTM%2FOF9haJwmIkJyINC249p8B@lakehousecookbook/Source/', name='Source/', size=0,
modificationTime=1687098243540)]

Command took 0.25 seconds -- by lakehousecookbookaws@gmail.com at 6/18/2023, 10:24:03 AM on Lakehouse Cookbook AWS's Cluster
```

Figure 4.37: Listing the contents of an S3 bucket

We have now accessed the S3 bucket from Databricks. Several approaches can be used with the access key and secret approach. One is to use a mount point. Databricks no longer recommends the use of mount points. One reason is that they may allow users to access information they should not have access to. Unity catalog brings better options, which we will discuss in *Chapter 13, Governance*. For simplicity, we will use the mount point approach and use that mount to create external tables in the following sections. To create a mount point, we use the **dbutils.fs.mount** function, as shown in *Figure 4.38*:

```
Cmd 3

1   mountName = "LakehouseCookbook"
2   dbutils.fs.mount(f"s3a://{s3AccessKey}:{encodedSecretKey}@{bucketName}", f"/mnt/{mountName}")
3   display(dbutils.fs.ls(f"/mnt/{mountName}"))

▸ (2) Spark Jobs

Table  ∨   +
```

	path	name	size	modificationTime
1	dbfs:/mnt/LakehouseCookbook/Lakehouse/	Lakehouse/	0	1687100058385
2	dbfs:/mnt/LakehouseCookbook/Source/	Source/	0	1687100058385

Figure 4.38: Creating an S3 mount point

Notice in the code, we use two different ways of adding values to strings. In *Figure 4.37*, we use the format function of a string, as seen on line 6. In *Figure 4.38*, we use the format string approach, which has an **f** prefix, as shown in lines 2 and 3. For more on format strings, see **https://docs.python.org/3/tutorial/inputoutput.html**. Now that we can access storage, we can create an external table using SQL.

Recipe 33: Creating an external Delta table in SQL on AWS

A common pattern is to create a view and then create a table from it. To start the process, we read a CSV file from the source folder of the **LakehouseCookbook** mount we created in Recipe 30 and used it to create a temporary view named **ViewAnimalHusbandry**, as shown in *Figure 4.39*:

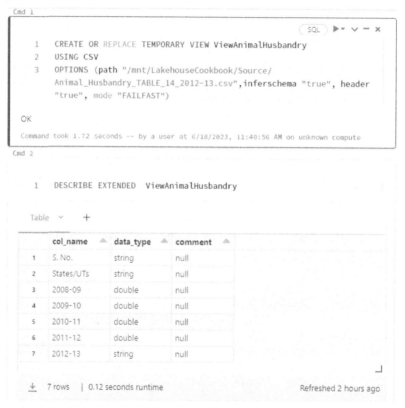

Figure 4.39: Creating a temporary view from a CSV

Notice that **DESCRIBE   EXTENDED** does not include storage information because **ViewAnimalHusbandry** is a view. We can use the view to create a Delta table, as in Recipe 26.

Before creating the table, we need to ensure a location for it. Ideally, this directory would be based on the source system the file was extracted from or placed in a folder indicating how it was acquired, such as the name of the organization that created it. For this example, we will use the estimates of egg production CSV we used in *Chapter 3, Connecting to Storage*, which we acquired from **https://data.gov.in/catalog/estimates-egg-production**. To help keep our lake organized, we will use this path **/mnt/LakehouseCookbook/Lakehouse/Bronze/DataGovIn/EstimatesEggProduction**. The folder Bronze is used to indicate this is a bronze item. That means it has no business rules applied to it and should be treated with caution during analytics. To ensure the folders exist in our S3 bucket, we use **dbutils.fs.mkdirs** to create the folders. As shown in *Figure 4.40*:

```
Cmd 4

1   %python
2   dbutils.fs.mkdirs("/mnt/LakehouseCookbook/Lakehouse/Bronze")
3   dbutils.fs.mkdirs("/mnt/LakehouseCookbook/Lakehouse/Bronze/DataGovIn")
4   dbutils.fs.mkdirs("/mnt/LakehouseCookbook/Lakehouse/Bronze/DataGovIn/EstimatesEggProduction")

Out[5]: True
Command took 0.42 seconds -- by lakehousecookbookaws@gmail.com at 6/18/2023, 11:54:18 AM on Lakehouse Cookbook AWS's Cluster
```

Figure 4.40: *Creating directories for bronze table*

Now that we have a place to put our table, we can start constructing our SQL statement to create the unmanaged table. If we specify a location during the construction of that SQL, Databricks knows the table is unmanaged.

For this example, we have a problem with the names of the columns. We need to do some column name cleanup. Notice that the names in *Figure 4.39* include spaces, slashes, and the minus sign. These are problematic in Delta tables. We rename those columns by using the **AS** keyword in SQL. Note that the keyword **AS** is optional but adds readability to the code. Also, note that SQL is not case-sensitive. This means that we could use lowercase for the SQL keywords. It is better to make them upper case to make the code easier to understand. As you can see in *Figure 4.41*, readability is important:

```
Cmd 5

1    CREATE OR REPLACE TABLE lakehousecookbook.BronzeAnimalHusbandry
2    LOCATION "/mnt/LakehouseCookbook/Lakehouse/Bronze/DataGovIn/EstimatesEggProduction/AnimalHusbandry"
3    COMMENT "Bronze version of AnimalHusbandry"
4    as SELECT `s. no.`    AS sno,
5            `states/uts` AS statesuts,
6            2008-09      AS 2008_09,
7            2009-10      AS 2009_10,
8            2010-11      AS 2010_11,
9            2011-12      AS 2011_12,
10           2012-13      AS 2012_13
11   FROM    viewanimalhusbandry

▶ (4) Spark Jobs

Query returned no results

Command took 4.71 seconds -- by lakehousecookbookaws@gmail.com at 6/18/2023, 11:58:18 AM on Lakehouse Cookbook AWS's Cluster
```

Figure 4.41: *Creating a Delta table from a view with column name cleanup*

Notice that lines 4 through 10 include the **AS** keyword. You will receive an error if you attempt to create the Delta table without doing this mapping. Also, we use the backtick (` ` `) character to reference column names with spaces or slashes. We can now examine the table using the **DESCRIBE EXTENDED** command, as shown in *Figure 4.42*:

Figure 4.42: *Description of the recently created table*

We can see that this is a managed table because the **Type** on line 13 is **EXTERNAL**. We can also see the **Location** on line 15 uses our **LakehouseCookbook** mount point. We can now move on to creating a table using Python in Databricks.

Recipe 34: Creating an external table in PySpark on AWS

We have seen how to create an unmanaged table using SQL on AWS. Now we shift to creating a table using the Spark API with Python. We do not have as much to do since we created folders in Recipe 31 and know that we need to map the column names, as shown in *Figure 4.43*:

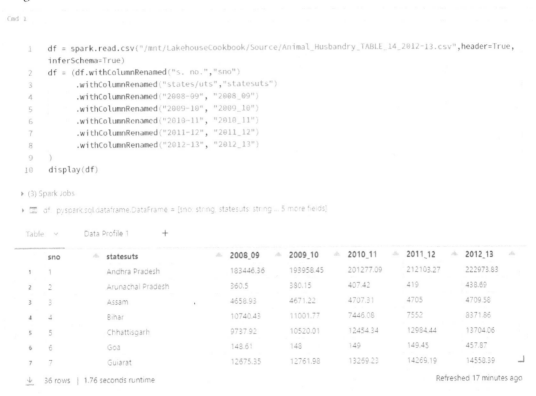

Figure 4.43: Creating a DataFrame with names changed

Notice that we created a DataFrame from the same CSV file as *Recipe 31*. Instead of creating a temporary view, we change the names of the troublesome columns using the **withColumnRenamed** function. Next, we save the DataFrame as a table with the name **BronzeAnimalHusbandryFromPy**, as shown in *Figure 4.44*:

Figure 4.44: *Creating a Table from a DataFrame*

We have now created unmanaged AWS tables using SQL and the Spark API with Python. We will not shift to using Azure Databricks.

Recipe 35: Creating an external Delta table in SQL on Azure

Since we discussed connecting to Azure storage from Databricks in *Chapter 3, Connecting to Storage*, and creating an external table is easy. Since we set up passthrough authentication in *Chapter 3, Governance* we can access the location of the file directly, with no need for a mount point, as shown in *Figure 4.45*:

Figure 4.45: Creating a view from ADLS directly

Notice that the only change from the AWS version is the value of the path. Now we can create a table from the view, as we did in *Recipe 31*. We have not created a schema in the Databricks workspace yet, so we must create one. Once it is created in command cell number three, we can create the table, as shown in *Figure 4.46*:

Figure 4.46: *Creating a Delta table with SQL in Azure*

Again, the only difference from the AWS version is the location. Notice the use of **IF NOT EXISTS** in command cell three and **OR REPLACE** in cell number four. This is a good practice. It ensures that the command will work correctly if executed multiple times. Additionally, recall that using **OR REPLACE** is important as it preserves the history of the table. We can now move on to creating a Delta table using Python to interact with Spark's Python API.

Recipe 36: Creating an external table with Python on Azure

It is not unusual to use Python to construct tables using DataFrames. One advantage of Databricks is the ability to switch languages between cells in a notebook. This allows the developer to use the best approach for the problem. The first step is to create a DataFrame, from a CSV file in ADLS Gen2. We do this using the **spark.read.csv** command, as shown in *Figure 4.47*:

```
Cmd 1

1    fileName = 'raw/Animal_Husbandry_TABLE_14_2012-13.csv'
2    containerName = 'lake'
3    storageAccountName ='lakehousecookbooklake'
4    fullUrl = 'abfss://'+containerName+'@' + storageAccountName + '.dfs.core.windows.net/' + fileName
5    df = spark.read.csv(fullUrl,header=True,inferSchema=True)
6    df = (df.withColumnRenamed("s. no.","sno")
7            .withColumnRenamed("states/uts","statesuts")
8            .withColumnRenamed("2008-09", "2008_09")
9            .withColumnRenamed("2009-10", "2009_10")
10           .withColumnRenamed("2010-11", "2010_11")
11           .withColumnRenamed("2011-12", "2011_12")
12           .withColumnRenamed("2012-13", "2012_13")
13   )
14   display(df)
```

▸ (3) Spark Jobs

▸ ▦ df: pyspark.sql.dataframe.DataFrame = [sno: string, statesuts: string ... 5 more fields]

Table ∨   +

	sno	statesuts	2008_09	2009_10	2010_11	2011_12	2012_13
1	1	Andhra Pradesh	183446.36	193958.45	201277.09	212103.27	222973.83
2	2	Arunachal Pradesh	360.5	380.15	407.42	419	438.69
3	3	Assam	4658.93	4671.22	4707.31	4705	4709.58
4	4	Bihar	10740.43	11001.77	7446.08	7552	8371.86
5	5	Chhattisgarh	9737.92	10520.01	12454.34	12984.44	13704.06
6	6	Goa	148.61	148	149	149.45	457.87
7	7	Gujarat	12675.35	12761.98	13269.23	14269.19	14558.39

⬇ 36 rows | 0.77 seconds runtime

Figure 4.47: Reading a CSV into a DataFrame in Azure

This code is very similar to that used to read the same CSV in AWS. The main difference is the way the string is constructed in line four. Notice we use the same **withColumnRenamed** commands. Once the DataFrame is constructed, the next step is to write the DataFrame as a table, as shown in *Figure 4.48:*

Figure 4.48: Create a Delta table from a DataFrame in Azure

We have now created an external table in Azure using Python. We can now move to GCP.

Recipe 37: Accessing GCP buckets from Databricks

The first step in creating an external table is accessing a cloud storage service. In GCP, we store data in buckets. For simplicity, this example will use mount points and service principles. For more on using service principles in GCP, see **https://docs.gcp.databricks. com/administration-guide/users-groups/service-principals.html**. During cluster creation, ensure you use the Google Service Account field, located in the **Advanced options** section of the cluster properties page, as shown in *Figure 4.49:*

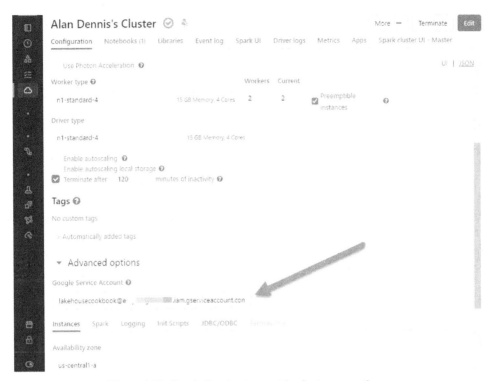

Figure 4.49: Google Service Account in cluster properties page

Once the cluster is up and running, you can create a mount point, as shown in *Figure 4.50*:

```
1   bucket_name = "lakehousecookbook"
2   mount_name = "lakehousecookbook"
3   myProjectId = "e-c           l3"
4   mountPoint = f"/mnt/{mount_name}"
5   if any(mount.mountPoint == mountPoint for mount in dbutils.fs.mounts()):
6       print(f"Already mounted {mount_name}")
7   else:
8       print(f"Mounting {mount_name}")
9       dbutils.fs.mount(
10      f"gs://{bucket_name}",
11      mountPoint,
12      extra_configs = {"fs.gs.project.id": myProjectId}
13      )
```

```
Mounting lakehousecookbook

Command took 11.21 seconds -- by alanatucumberlands@gmail.com at 6/18/2023, 4:19:06 PM on Alan Dennis's Cluster

Cmd 2
```

```
1   dbutils.fs.ls("/mnt/lakehousecookbook")
```

```
Out[20]: []

Command took 0.33 seconds -- by alanatucumberlands@gmail.com at 6/18/2023, 4:19:21 PM on Alan Dennis's Cluster
```

Figure 4.50: Creating a mount point to a bucket in GCP Databricks

This code is a bit more advanced because it checks to see if the mount point has already been mounted on line 5. If you use mount points, we recommend putting this code in a shared notebook wrapped inside a Python function. Also, we need to supply a project identifier, set in line 3 and used in line 12. Ideally, this information would be stored in a secret store. Now that we have mounted the bucket, the next step is to put some data in it and then create a table using SQL and then Python.

Recipe 38: Creating an external Delta table in SQL on GCP

We first need to get some data into our bucket to turn it into a table. For this example, we will use a data set ranking popular breeds of dogs found at **https://data.world/len/akc-popular-dog-breeds**. Since we are using mount points, the code is relatively simple. The first step after having uploaded the data is to create a **TEMPORARY VIEW** from the CSV file, as shown in *Figure 4.51:*

```
Cmd 1

1   CREATE OR REPLACE TEMPORARY VIEW AKC_Popular_Breeds USING CSV OPTIONS (
2     path "/mnt/lakehousecookbook/source/AKC_Popular_Breeds_2013-2016.csv",
3     inferschema "true",
4     header "true",
5     mode "FAILFAST"
6   )

▶ (2) Spark Jobs

OK

Command took 12.00 seconds -- by alanatucumberlands@gmail.com at 6/18/2023, 4:39:03 PM on Alar
```

Figure 4.51: Creating a temporary view from a CSV in GCP

As we have learned, **VIEWS** do not have storage information. It just has the schema when you use the **DESCRIBE EXTENDED** command as we do in *Figure 4.52:*

```
1   DESCRIBE EXTENDED AKC_Popular_Breeds
```

Table ∨   +

	col_name	data_type	comment
1	Breed	string	null
2	2016 Rank	int	null
3	2015 Rank	int	null
4	2014 Rank	int	null
5	2013 Rank	int	null

Figure 4.52: Describe extended on a temporary view in GCP

As we can see, four columns have spaces in their names. This means we will have to do the mapping exercise, as shown in *Figure 4.53*:

```
1    CREATE SCHEMA IF NOT EXISTS lakehousecookbook
```

OK

Command took 0.76 seconds -- by alanatucumberlands@gmail.com at 6/18/2023, 4:40:52 PM on Alan Dennis's Cluster

Cmd 5

```
1    CREATE OR REPLACE TABLE lakehousecookbook.Bronze_AKC_Popular_Breeds
2    LOCATION "/mnt/lakehousecookbook/bronze/DataWorld/lenFishman/AKC_Popular_Breeds"
3    COMMENT "Bronze version of AnimalHusbandry"
4    as SELECT Breed,
5      `2016 Rank` as 2016Rank,
6      `2015 Rank` as 2015Rank,
7      `2014 Rank` as 2014Rank,
8      `2013 Rank` as 2013Rank
9    FROM  AKC_Popular_Breeds
```

▸ (6) Spark Jobs

Query returned no results

Command took 35.55 seconds -- by alanatucumberlands@gmail.com at 6/18/2023, 4:47:08 PM on Alan Dennis's Cluster

Figure 4.53: *Creating a table from a view with column name mapping in GCP*

Notice that we created the **SCHEMA** if it does not exist in the first command cell. Lines 5 through 8 show removing the space from the name. We can finish the process by looking at the detailed properties of the table by using the **DESCRIBE EXTENDED** function, as shown in *Figure 4.54*:

```
1    DESCRIBE EXTENDED lakehousecookbook.Bronze_AKC_Popular_Breeds
```

Table ∨   +

col_name	data_type
1 Breed	string
2 2016Rank	int
3 2015Rank	int
4 2014Rank	int
5 2013Rank	int
6	
7 # Detailed Table Information	
8 Catalog	spark_catalog
9 Database	lakehousecookbook
10 Table	Bronze_AKC_Popular_Breeds
11 Type	EXTERNAL
12 Comment	Bronze version of AnimalHusbandry
13 Location	dbfs:/mnt/lakehousecookbook/bronze/DataWorld/lenFishman/AKC_Popular_Breeds
14 Provider	delta
15 Owner	root
16 Table Properties	[delta.minReaderVersion=1,delta.minWriterVersion=2]

Figure 4.54: *Details of the table created using SQL in GCP*

Notice that line 13 references the mount point. Also, notice that the type is external. We can now move to create an external table in GCP using Python.

Recipe 39: Creating an external Delta table in Python on GCP

As we have done in this chapter, the next step is to clean the column names (if needed) and then save the DataFrame to cloud storage and create the table. In this section, we see two ways of removing spaces from column names, and the first is shown in *Figure 4.55:*

Hand coded mapping

Cmd 2

```
1    fullUrl = '/mnt/lakehousecookbook/source/AKC_Popular_Breeds_2013-2016.csv'
2    df = spark.read.csv(fullUrl,header=True,inferSchema=True)
3    df = (df.withColumnRenamed("2016 Rank","2016_Rank")
4         .withColumnRenamed("2015 Rank","2015_Rank")
5         .withColumnRenamed("2014 Rank", "2014_Rank")
6         .withColumnRenamed("2013 Rank", "2013_Rank"))
7    display(df)
```

▸ (3) Spark Jobs

▸ 📊 df: pyspark.sql.dataframe.DataFrame = [Breed: string, 2016_Rank: integer ... 3 more fields]

Table ∨   +

	Breed	2016_Rank	2015_Rank	2014_Rank	2013_Rank
1	Retrievers (Labrador)	1	1	1	1
2	German Shepherd Dogs	2	2	2	2
3	Retrievers (Golden)	3	3	3	3
4	Bulldogs	4	4	4	5
5	Beagles	5	5	5	4
6	French Bulldogs	6	6	9	11
7	Poodles	7	8	7	8

Figure 4.55: A hand-coded way of cleaning column names

This approach is like what we have done previously. It works and is easy to understand. However, as the number of columns grows, this approach becomes tedious. An alternative is to replace spaces in column names programmatically, as shown in *Figure 4.56:*

Code mapping

Cmd 4

```
1    from pyspark.sql import functions as FUNC
2    fullUrl = '/mnt/lakehousecookbook/source/AKC_Popular_Breeds_2013-2016.csv'
3    df = spark.read.csv(fullUrl,header=True,inferSchema=True)
4    df = df.select([FUNC.col(col).alias(col.replace(' ', '_')) for col in df.columns])
5    display(df)
```

▸ (3) Spark Jobs

▸ 📊 df: pyspark.sql.dataframe.DataFrame = [Breed: string, 2016_Rank: integer ... 3 more fields]

Table ∨   +

	Breed	2016_Rank	2015_Rank	2014_Rank	2013_Rank
1	Retrievers (Labrador)	1	1	1	1
2	German Shepherd Dogs	2	2	2	2
3	Retrievers (Golden)	3	3	3	3
4	Bulldogs	4	4	4	5
5	Beagles	5	5	5	4
6	French Bulldogs	6	6	9	11
7	Poodles	7	8	7	8

⬇ 189 rows | 2.74 seconds runtime   Refreshed now

Figure 4.56: Programmatic replacement of spaces in column names

The advantage of the approach presented in *Figure 4.55* is that you can apply multiple tests, filtering all invalid characters. Additionally, this is less error-prone than manually creating the statements to replace the spaces in column names. The results are the same, the approach to use is often a personal choice. Next, we need to create the table, as shown in *Figure 4.57*:

Code mapping

Cmd 4

```
1   from pyspark.sql import functions as FUNC
2   fullUrl = '/mnt/lakehousecookbook/source/AKC_Popular_Breeds_2013-2016.csv'
3   df = spark.read.csv(fullUrl,header=True,inferSchema=True)
4   df = df.select([FUNC.col(col).alias(col.replace(' ', '_')) for col in df.columns])
5   display(df)
```

▸ (3) Spark Jobs

▸ ▦ df: pyspark.sql.dataframe.DataFrame = [Breed: string, 2016_Rank: integer ... 3 more fields]

Table ⌄ +

	Breed	2016_Rank	2015_Rank	2014_Rank	2013_Rank
1	Retrievers (Labrador)	1	1	1	1
2	German Shepherd Dogs	2	2	2	2
3	Retrievers (Golden)	3	3	3	3
4	Bulldogs	4	4	4	5
5	Beagles	5	5	5	4
6	French Bulldogs	6	6	9	11
7	Poodles	7	8	7	8

↓ 189 rows | 2.74 seconds runtime   Refreshed now

Figure 4.57: *Create an unmanaged table using Python in GCP*

The last step is to examine the details of the created table using **DESCRIBE EXTENDED**, as shown in *Figure 4.58*:

Cmd 7

```
1   %sql DESCRIBE EXTENDED lakehousecookbook.BronzeAKCPopularBreedsPy
```

▸ ▦ _sqldf: pyspark.sql.dataframe.DataFrame = [col_name: string, data_type: string ... 1 more field]

Table ⌄ +

	col_name	data_type
1	Breed	string
2	2016_Rank	int
3	2015_Rank	int
4	2014_Rank	int
5	2013_Rank	int
6		
7	# Detailed Table Information	
8	Catalog	spark_catalog
9	Database	lakehousecookbook
10	Table	BronzeAKCPopularBreedsPy
11	Type	EXTERNAL
12	Location	dbfs:/mnt/lakehousecookbook/bronze/DataWorld/lenfishman/AKCPopularBreedsPy
13	Provider	delta
14	Owner	root
15	Table Properties	[delta.minReaderVersion=1,delta.minWriterVersion=2]

Figure 4.58: *Table details for the table created in Python in GCP*

We can also take a brief look at the contents of the table using a **SELECT** statement, as shown in *Figure 4.59*:

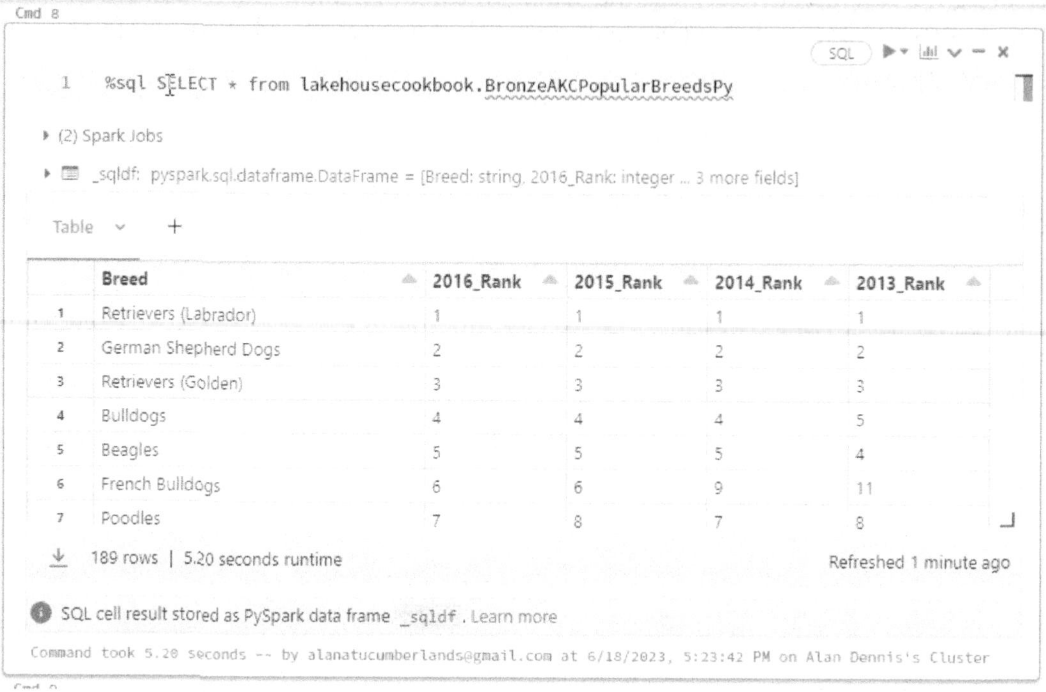

Figure 4.59: Contents of a table created with Python in GCP

We have created tables using Python and SQL in the three Databricks cloud providers. We have used several ways of doing the same thing and discussed the benefits of each. Hopefully, you see that the variations between cloud providers mostly center on access to external data sources.

Conclusion

In this chapter, we discussed Delta Lakes in detail. We examined the types of Delta tables and created each kind in the three Databricks cloud offerings. We discussed how to read a language reference and used that information to create tables. A key takeaway for this chapter is that access to the storage cloud system is the challenge, rather than the ability to create external tables. It is also important to use secret scopes to protect sensitive information.

The next chapter will start with data profiling and analysis using various approaches. We will then shift to the various data modeling approaches used in Lakehouse construction.

CHAPTER 5
Data Profiling and Modeling in the Lakehouse

Introduction

Understanding your data is essential. We start this chapter by examining many ways to examine and understand your data. Then we shift to creating models using that data. Modeling data appropriately is essential for successful Lakehouse adoption. The most popular data modeling approaches are explored, with hands-on examples. The benefits and challenges of each approach are covered, along with recommendations for adoption.

Structure

In this chapter, we will cover the following topics:

- Data profiling
- Data modeling

Objectives

By the end of this chapter, you will understand common ways to profile data using the Databricks Lakehouse Platform. You will be familiar with native profiling tools, commonly used third-party tools and data modeling approaches. You will also learn how to apply those common modeling approaches to Databricks Lakehouse.

Data profiling

Understanding your data is essential. The first thing most data scientists, engineers, architects, or analysts do when encountering a new data set is examine the contents to get a sense of the data. There are many ways to profile data. We will start with the capabilities natively available in Databricks, then we will examine commonly used third-party tools.

When working in a professional setting, data sets are supplied by the organization. Someone gives you the information necessary to access the systems where the data resides. We will go through a similar exercise, using Azure Data Factory to ingest data to our Lakehouse, then we will do some data profiling using several approaches.

Recipe 40: Using Azure Data Factory to ingest raw

Azure Data Factory (**ADF**) version 2 is a commonly used data ingestion mechanism in the Azure ecosystem. While it can do some transformations, it is most powerful as a data pump. For our purposes, we will use ADF's metadata-driven ingestion.

After launching ADF Studio, click on **Ingest** to indicate that you wish to create an ingestion, as shown in the following figure:

Figure 5.1: Selecting ADFs Ingest

You will be presented with a screen like that in *Figure 5.2*. You will then select a **Metadata-driven copy task** marked with the callout labeled 1. This will allow you to ingest many items using the metadata available in the source system. ADF relies on linked services to access system data. We happen to have a linked service already configured, with an uninspiring name **linkedService1** (marked with callout 2). You can think of linked services as a pointer to a system. It is where connection information is stored. In this case, my linked service is using a self-hosted integration runtime that allows ADF to access an instance of SQL Server on my home desktop.

You will need to select a **Control table data store** (as marked callouts 3 and 4). In our case, we will use a schema called **dbo** and a table name **MainControlTable_WorldWideImporters**. In a production environment, we typically do not use **dbo**, but for a demo, it is acceptable. The control table keeps track of the names of the items of interest and, if you are ingesting incremental data, the last watermark. We will talk more about watermarks, but for now, think of it as a way to keep your place. This allows ADF to ingest only the records that have changed or are new after that point in time. Since this is a demo, we only want to run the ingestion once or on demand (callout 5). You can now click the **Next** button, marked with callout 6. Refer to the following *Figure 5.2*:

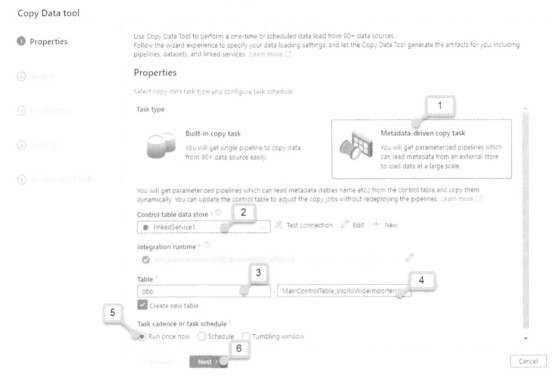

Figure 5.2: Copy Data tool setting properties

Now, you are asked to pick the source. In this case, we are using a **SQL server** (callout 1) that is using a self-hosted integration runtime (callout 3), as shown in *Figure 5.3*. The connection name is **SqlServer1** (callout 2). This connection has the name of the database server, login information, and the name of the database to connect to. Assuming the connection is successful, you will see a list of tables. In our case, we wish to ingest all tables. We do this by clicking the box next to **Select all** (callout 4). If the selection is successful, you will see the selected count change from zero. We are now ready to click the **Next** button (callout 5) and proceed to the configuration step. Refer to the following *Figure 5.3*:

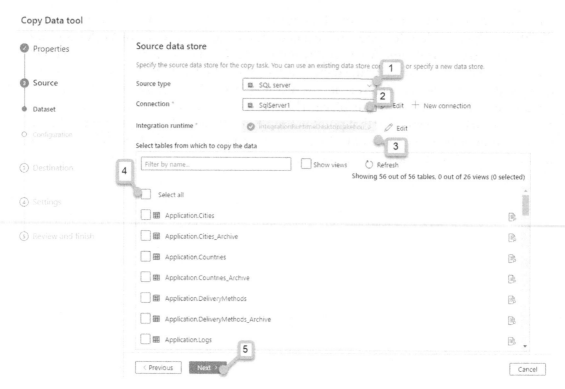

Figure 5.3: Copy Data tool selecting the source

We are now ready to determine how the data is to be ingested. You will be presented with two choices. One is to perform a full load of all the tables. The other is to configure how you wish to load each table.

Selecting choosing to configure each table takes more time but allows you to load the data that has changed incrementally. This is an essential part of a Lakehouse. Ideally, everything will be loaded incrementally in a Lakehouse. The reality is that some things cannot be loaded using a delta or differential loading mechanism with an associated watermark table and column.

The term watermark describes the maximum value for a particular table that has been ingested or refined. The idea is that initially, you will load data from the beginning of time, which in the data world, is the first of January 1900. When you complete processing the item, you will note the maximum value you have seen in a column that indicates the modification or creation date and store it in a special table. The next time you ingest that data item, you will consult the table where you stored that maximum value, and it will become the minimum value for the current ingestion or refinement. The process repeats with you saving the maximum value each time to a watermark table.

One of the tables in the Wide World Importers (available from GitHub at **https://github.com/microsoft/sql-server-samples/tree/master/samples/databases/wide-world-**

importers) dataset is **Application.Logs**. It contains a column named **EventTime**, which is an ideal watermark candidate. By selecting the **Delta load** option, as shown in *Figure 5.4*, you can specify the column name and the initial value.

You might notice that not all columns show up in the watermark column field because to use a column as a watermark, it must be in orderable. Date and time columns are the most common watermarks, but occasionally integer and other numeric columns are used as watermark columns (refer to *Figure 5.4*):

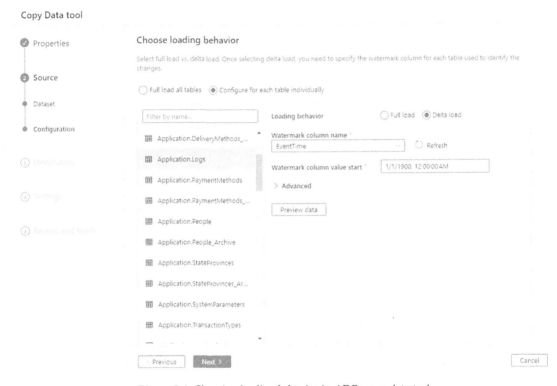

Figure 5.4: Choosing loading behavior in ADFs copy data tool

After you have selected each table's loading behavior, you will click the **Next** button at the bottom of the form. If you have correctly configured the table loading behavior, you will move to select the destination. As with selecting the source, you start by selecting the type of system. In our case, we will use **Azure Data Lake Storage Gen2**.

Next, you will either create or select a connection. Again, this is a linked system that allows access to a system of a particular type. Once you have the connection established, the next step is to specify the destination path and file name suffix, as shown in *Figure 5.5*. The folder path structure should be oriented around the system that the data is coming from. Also, notice that we are using a raw location. The suffix we are using is Avro because we will use Avro as the format for our files.

Avro is a good choice when using ADF because it preserves the data types using a schema and does not have the requirement of Java, which using an Apache Parquet file does. Ideally, when exporting files, preserve the schema. It might be easier to export CSV files, but that may require data type mapping during ingestion.

Clicking **Next** will bring you to the configuration screen as shown in *Figure 5.5*:

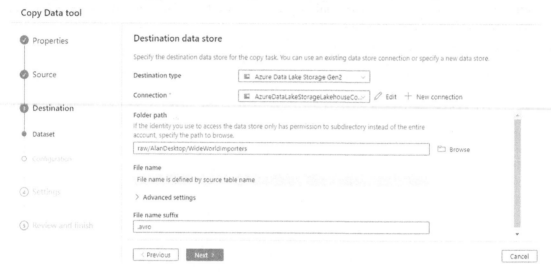

Figure 5.5: Selecting destination path

The configuration screen allows you to specify the file format along with compression type and level. Notice that if you select **Parquet**, you will get a warning regarding the required **Java Runtime Environment (JRE)** that is required on the machine running the integration runtime, as shown in *Figure 5.6:*

File format settings

File format

| Parquet ⌄ |

Compression type

| snappy ⌄ |

⚠ In addition to an Integration Runtime, JRE 8 (Java Runtime Environment) is also required on the Integration Runtime machine. Please download the appropriate version at Java downloads

Figure 5.6: JRE warning

Selecting **Avro** removes the warning and allows you to specify the compression type and level, as shown in *Figure 5.7*. Compression is an important thing when dealing with large datasets. Setting a medium compression level allows for an acceptable level of space savings without undue processing time during compression and decompression:

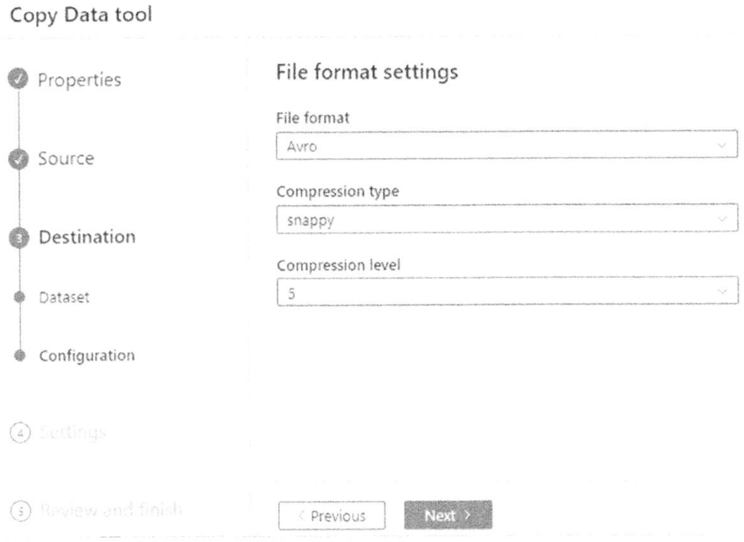

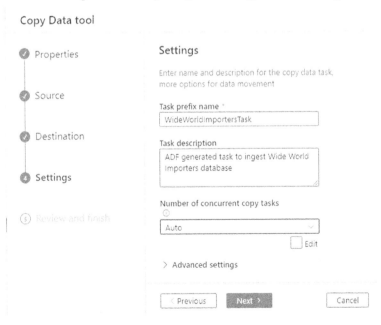

Figure 5.7: *Selecting Avro file format*

Once you have selected the file format, the next step is to set the task prefix which will be used on the automatically created ADF pipelines. It is best to give the tasks a name that associates them with the operation they are performing, as seen in *Figure 5.8.*

Figure 5.8: *Set the task prefix*

There are many advanced settings available. These allow you to control the degrees of concurrency if you want data consistency validation (which includes using a checksum to ensure valid transfers), logging, and other settings. You can adjust these depending on the situation. Some of the changes will have cost implications, so verify your choices. Often, the default settings are sufficient.

Once you complete adjusting the settings, you will be presented with a page to review the information that you supplied, as shown in *Figure 5.9*. This is a common pattern in Azure. Often, you enter information in a wizard-like experience and then the information you supplied on a conformation page are shown. This allows you to double-check your inputs before completing the activity:

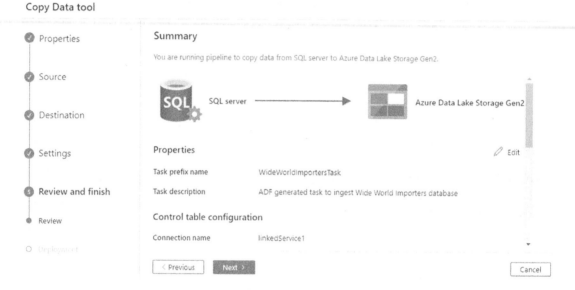

Figure 5.9: *Review supplied information*

Once you click **Next** on the review screen, you will be informed that the deployment is completed. You will also see an SQL script. Copy that script and execute it on the SQL Database associated with the linked server from *Figure 5.2*. This script will create the control table, which is used during ingestion and to track watermarks, as shown in *Figure 5.10*:

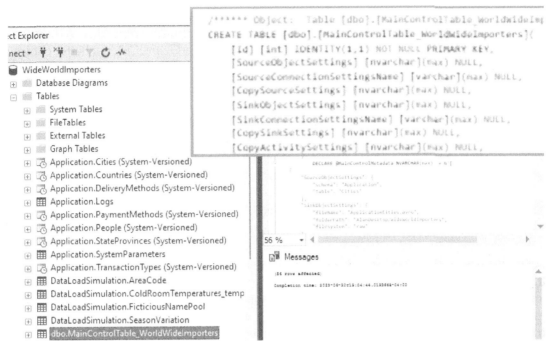

Figure 5.10: *Created control tables*

We can now run the pipelines and populate the lake with the data from the database. The wizard creates three pipelines. The name of the pipelines is based on the prefix you supplied in *Figure 5.8*. You will want to manually trigger (and possibly schedule for repeated execution) the pipeline that ends with **_TopLevel**, as shown in *Figure 5.11*:

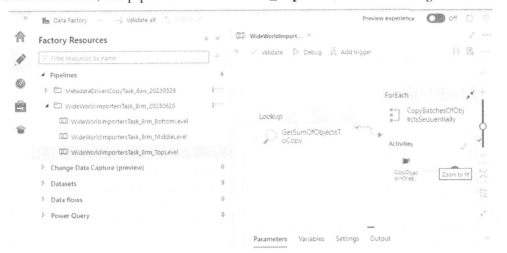

Figure 5.11: *ADF pipelines*

To start the pipelines, you can either click **Debug** or **Add trigger**. Debug starts an interactive debugging environment, which is useful when authoring pipelines. In this case, clicking **Add trigger**, and selecting **Trigger now**, as shown in *Figure 5.12*, is a better choice. The **Add trigger** menu is also where you would schedule the pipeline. Please refer to *Figure 5.12* below:

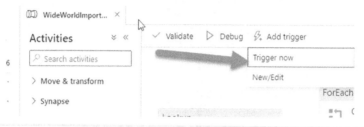

Figure 5.12: *Trigger the pipeline*

Switching over to the monitor view of ADF lets us see the results of our pipeline executions. If you use the `WideWorldImporters` data set, you will see several errors related to an unsupported data type conversion (`SqlGeography`); you can safely ignore those for this exercise. If you were doing this in a production environment, you would find a way to transform the `SqlGeography` data type to a Databricks supported data type.

You can use Microsoft Azure Storage Explorer to examine, interact with, and remove files stored in containers. For example, we can examine the raw layer that we just populated with files, as shown in *Figure 5.13*:

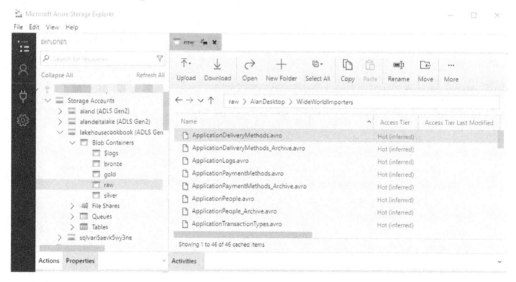

Figure 5.13: *Azure storage explorer viewing raw files*

You can download Microsoft Azure Storage Explorer from
https://azure.microsoft.com/en-us/products/storage/storage-explorer

Once you download it, you will need to log in to associate it with your Azure subscription. We now have data in our data lake and can switch back to Databricks to load it into Delta tables and then do some data profiling.

Recipe 41: Reorganize files

We have files in our raw zone, but they are a little hard to deal with. Generally, files are organized into directories, with multiple related files in the directory. To convert our list of files to a list of folders with files in each folder, we can use Python and **dbutils**. We start by setting up some variables containing important values. Creating a Python function is a way to organize your code. In this case, we create a function that takes a path and creates a folder name by removing the **.avro** extension. Then the function moves the file specified by the path into the newly created folder. We apply this function to all the files in the path we are working with, resulting in a directory containing directories, as shown in *Figure 5.14:*

```
Cmd 1

1   path = "abfss://lake@lakehousecookbooklake.dfs.core.windows.net/raw/AlanDesktop/WideWorldImporters/"
2   fileList = dbutils.fs.ls(path)

Command took 0.18 seconds -- by alan.dennis@gmail.com at 6/21/2023, 7:09:48 PM on Power User Cluster
```

```
Cmd 2

1   # Moves a file to a folder with the same name as the file, minus .avro
2   def CreateFolderAndMoveFile(path):
3       print("path= " + path)
4       folderName= path.replace(".avro","")
5       dbutils.fs.mkdirs(folderName)
6       print("Made Folder, calling move")
7       dbutils.fs.mv(path,folderName)
8       print("Moved to ",folderName)

Command took 0.06 seconds -- by alan.dennis@gmail.com at 6/21/2023, 7:03:43 PM on Power User Cluster
```

```
Cmd 3

Move the files into a folder per file

Cmd 4

1   for row in fileList:
2       path = row.path
3       name = row.name
4       try:
5           CreateFolderAndMoveFile(path)
6       except Exception as ex:
7           print("Exception: ",ex)

Cmd 5
```

Figure 5.14: *Function to move files into directories*

This gives us a directory containing a folder per file we previously ingested. This simplifies ingestion. Ideally, your ingestion tool or framework should organize raw files into a folder per file. If that does not happen, you may need to do what is shown in *Figure 5.14*.

You can, however, see the contents of our folder in *Figure 5.15*:

```
fileList = dbutils.fs.ls(path)
display(fileList)
```

▸ (2) Spark Jobs

Table ∨ +

	path	name	size	modificationTime
1	abfss://lake@lakehousecookbooklake.dfs.core.windows.net/raw/AlanDesktop/WideWorldImporters/ApplicationDeliveryMethods/	ApplicationDeliveryMethods/	0	1687386928000
2	abfss://lake@lakehousecookbooklake.dfs.core.windows.net/raw/AlanDesktop/WideWorldImporters/ApplicationDeliveryMethods_Archive/	ApplicationDeliveryMethods_Archive/	0	1687386928000
3	abfss://lake@lakehousecookbooklake.dfs.core.windows.net/raw/AlanDesktop/WideWorldImporters/ApplicationLogs/	ApplicationLogs/	0	1687386929000

***Figure 5.15**: Contents of our directory after reorganizing the files*

Now that we have our files organized correctly, we can move on to creating a table for the files so that we can proceed with data profiling.

Recipe 42: Creating tables from a directory programmatically

We could create a table for each file by hand. That would be tedious, given that we have over 40 files. Instead, we can create the bronze tables programmatically. The process is like that we used for moving the files, but instead of moving them, we will load them into a DataFrame, and then save that DataFrame as a Delta table into the bronze zone. We create a Python function and then call it within a loop, as shown in *Figure 5.16:*

Cmd 6

```
# Given a Directory containing a Directory per Avro File, Create Unmanaged Bronze Delta tables
def CreateDeltaTable(path,name):
    print("path= " + path)
    name =name.replace("/","")
    print("name=" + name)
    print(dbutils.fs.ls(path))
    tableName = "lakehousecookbook.Bronze" + name
    print("Table Name :" + tableName)
    bronzePath = path.replace("/raw/","/bronze/")
    print("bronzePath :"+ bronzePath)
    df = spark.read.format("avro").load(path)
    df.write.mode("overwrite").option("path",bronzePath).saveAsTable(tableName)
```

Command took 0.04 seconds -- by alan.dennis@gmail.com at 6/21/2023, 7:05:23 PM on Power User Cluster

Cmd 7

```
for row in fileList:
    path = row.path
    name = row.name
    CreateDeltaTable(path,name)
```

▸ (60) Spark Jobs

```
path= abfss://lake@lakehousecookbooklake.dfs.core.windows.net/raw/AlanDesktop/WideWorldImporters/Appl
name=ApplicationDeliveryMethods
[FileInfo(path='abfss://lake@lakehousecookbooklake.dfs.core.windows.net/raw/AlanDesktop/WideWorldImpo
eliveryMethods.avro', size=1175, modificationTime=1687386928000)]
Table Name :lakehousecookbook.BronzeApplicationDeliveryMethods
bronzePath :abfss://lake@lakehousecookbooklake.dfs.core.windows.net/bronze/AlanDesktop/WideWorldImpor
```

***Figure 5.16**: Creating tables programmatically*

While this is convenient, it is simplistic. We would need to handle more types of refinement in a production environment. This simplistic approach shows that we can use code to simplify many of our data engineering activities. More importantly, we now have tables to profile.

Recipe 43: Data profiling using Databricks native functionality

Databricks has continued to extend the capabilities of its offerings. This includes data profiling. Often when doing profiling, we start by listing the schemas and then the tables in the schemas. The USE command allows you to select a schema as the active schema. Once you have selected a schema, you do not need to include it when doing things like a selection of all records in the table, as shown in *Figure 5.17*:

Figure 5.17: *Selecting a schema as the active schema*

While this is not the first time, we have seen the results of a **SELECT** statement, look at the **plus sign** marked with the arrow. Clicking the **plus sign** brings up the context menu, as shown in *Figure 5.18*:

Figure 5.18: *Display grid's context menu*

We are instead in the **Data Profile** option. This will cause a **Data Profile** tab to be added to our output. This provides an analysis of the data within the table, including graphs, as shown in *Figure 5.19*:

Sort by
Feature order ▾ ☐ Reverse order   Feature search (regex enabled)

Features: ☑ int(7) ☑ string(6) ☑ unknown(3)

Numeric Features (7)

Chart to show
Standard ▾

	count	missing	mean	std dev	zeros	min	median	max	custom	☐log ☐expand
OrderID										
	1,701	0%	157k	491.18	0%	156k	157k	158k	data type: int	
CustomerID										
	1,701	0%	657.32	389.29	0%	1	664	1,338	data type: int	
SalespersonPersonID										
	1,701	0%	10.53	5.71	0%	2	13	20	data type: int	
PickedByPersonID										
	1,419	16.58%	9.32	5.52	0%	2	7	19	data type: int	
ContactPersonID										
	1,701	0%	711.65	393.57	0%	47	719	1,398	data type: int	

Figure 5.19: Data Profile tab

This is a powerful and easy-to-use feature. To understand this output, we will start with a single row, as shown in *Figure 5.20:*

	count	missing	mean	std dev	zeros	min	median	max	custom	☐log ☐expand
OrderID										
	1,701	0%	157k	491.18	0%	156k	157k	158k	data type: int	

Figure 5.20: Single row from the data profile

From left to right, we have the column name in bold, in this case, **OrderID**. We can see the row count is **1,701**. The next column is the percentage of missing records, and in this case, it is zero. Often, when doing data engineering, we need to handle missing values. There are several ways to deal with them, such as removing the record or performing imputation. Next is the mean and standard deviation of the records. Since this column is a system-generated identifier, these values are not useful. The percentage of records with zero we can see in the next column; in this case, it is also zero. Zeros can be as troubling as missing values. It can be difficult to determine if the zero indicates a data issue or if it is the correct value for the situation. Next, we see the minimum, median, and maximum values. Again, since this is a system-generated column, these values are useless. We use these to determine the shape of the data. To determine if there is skew. The histogram on the right of the row gives us that visualization. We can see there is an even distribution. That is a sign that the identifier is evenly distributed.

The native data profiling capabilities of Databricks are useful and powerful. It is convenient to access, making it a desirable choice. Next, we will look at other ways to profile data in Databricks.

Recipe 44: Listing row counts for all

One way of data profiling is to examine the entire collection of the data assets. In that case, it is often useful to know information about each table in a database, such as the number of rows. Be aware that this may take a while to run if you have large tables. However, it is not something that needs to be done often.

The approach to this problem uses a useful approach for other database interactions. To make this feature more accessible, we package it into a Python function (line 1). We start by getting a DataFrame of the schemas in the workspace, as shown in the following code, in line 2. In preparation for storing the results, we create an empty list on line 3. Next, we iterate across the rows in the DataFrame (line 4), and for each row, create a DataFrame (line 5) containing the tables in that schema. Given the schema/database and table name, we can retrieve the counts. To clarify how that SQL statement is constructed, we use variables to store the database (line 7) and table (line 8). We combine them to create the **SELECT** statement (line 9) that will return a column named **COUNT** containing the row count. Next, we execute the SQL statement (line 10) and extract the count, knowing it will be in the first record in a column named **COUNT** (line 11). We can now add the three items as a list to our list (13) to later convert it to a DataFrame (lines 14 and 15). Refer to the following code:

```
def GetTableCountsDataFrame():
    schemasDf = spark.sql('SHOW SCHEMAS')
    results = []
    for schema in schemasDf.collect():
        tablesDf = spark.sql('show tables from ' + schema['databaseName'])
        for table in tablesDf.collect():
            database = table['database']
            tableName = table['tableName']
            countSql = 'SELECT COUNT(*) as COUNT FROM `' + data-
base + "`.`" + tableName + '`'
            dfCounts = spark.sql(countSql)
            count = dfCounts.collect()[0]['COUNT']
            print(database, tableName,count)
            results.append((database, tableName,count))
```

```
columns = ['database', 'tableName', 'rowCount']
df = spark.createDataFrame(results, columns)
return df
```

To use our newly created function, we simply execute the cell and then invoke the method, as shown in *Figure 5.21:*

Figure 5.21: Calling the all-table row count function and descending sort the results

Notice that we sorted the results by the rowCount column in descending order (line 2) to see the table with the largest row count first. We have now identified the tables with the most records, and we will use them in the next section, where we summarize using DBUtils.

Recipe 45: Using DBUtils summarize

As we have discussed before, **dbutils** is a collection of helpful operations. One of those is in **dbutils.data**. Summarize takes a DataFrame as a parameter and returns a summary. Some values returned are approximations, such as the number of distinct values for a categorical column. Note that at the time of this writing, this function is in public preview and is available in Databricks Runtime 9.0 and higher. To learn more about the summarize method, we can use the help command, as shown in *Figure 5.22:*

Figure 5.22: dbutils data help

Notice the data area summary level of help, as shown in the first command. This tells you about the area, with a summary of available methods. Including the method's name in the help command's invocation returns a detailed description of the method's parameters and results. To use the summarize command, we need a DataFrame. We can construct one using the **spark.sql** command, as shown in *Figure 5.23*. The output should look familiar as it is the same as that returned during data profiling, discussed earlier in this chapter. The report display count, missing values, mean, standard deviation, zeros, minimum, median, and maximum values, along with a histogram. This method is useful if you want to display the information about a DataFrame while processing so that you can review it if there are issues later. Refer to the following *Figure 5.23*:

Figure 5.23: Creating a DataFrame and calling dbutils.data.summarize

We will now revisit some more basic statistical information about datasets by looking at the DataFrame's describe and summary functionality.

Recipe 46: Using a DataFrames describe and summary methods

As part of a DataFrame, we have methods for computing statistics, like the output of **dbutils.data.summarize** method. These methods lack graphs but can be useful while examining data. We start by examining the structure of a table, as shown in *Figure 5.24*:

Cmd 1

```sql
%sql
DESCRIBE TABLE lakehousecookbook.bronzesalesorderlines
```

▸ ▣ _sqldf: pyspark.sql.dataframe.DataFrame = [col_name: string, data_type: strin

Table ∨   +

	col_name	data_type	comment
1	OrderLineID	int	null
2	OrderID	int	null
3	StockItemID	int	null
4	Description	string	null
5	PackageTypeID	int	null
6	Quantity	int	null
7	UnitPrice	double	null

↓   12 rows | 1.01 seconds runtime

Figure 5.24: *Description of the table*

This gives us a general sense of the use of the table. In this case, we are looking at items that go into an order at a detail level. The next step is to load the table into a DataFrame and compare the schema information of the table (shown in *Figure 5.24*) to schema of the DataFrame's, as shown in *Figure 5.25*. Notice that the results are the same, except for **printSchema()**, returning the information in a tree structure instead of a table. Also, notice that the data types displayed are relative to the language. In SQL, an integer is an int, while the output in Python is an integer. Please refer to the following figure:

```
1    df.printSchema()
```

```
root
 |-- OrderLineID: integer (nullable = true)
 |-- OrderID: integer (nullable = true)
 |-- StockItemID: integer (nullable = true)
 |-- Description: string (nullable = true)
 |-- PackageTypeID: integer (nullable = true)
 |-- Quantity: integer (nullable = true)
 |-- UnitPrice: double (nullable = true)
 |-- TaxRate: double (nullable = true)
 |-- PickedQuantity: integer (nullable = true)
 |-- PickingCompletedWhen: string (nullable = true)
 |-- LastEditedBy: integer (nullable = true)
 |-- LastEditedWhen: string (nullable = true)
```

Figure 5.25: *Load DataFrame and print schema*

Now that we have compared the schemas, we can use the **describe** method. When invoked without parameters, the method returns the count, mean, standard deviation, minimum and maximum for all the columns, as shown in *Figure 5.26*:

```
1    display(df.describe())
```

▸ (2) Spark Jobs

Table ∨   +

	summary	OrderLineID	OrderID	StockItemID	Description
1	count	5238	5238	5238	5238
2	mean	495220.5	157341.83123329515	109.55975563192058	null
3	stddev	1512.2246856866211	473.95596462993745	62.69492771764987	null
4	min	492602	156458	1	"The Gu" red shi
5	max	497839	158158	219	Void fill 400 L ba

Figure 5.26: *Invoking describe on a DataFrame*

In *Figure 5.26*, we can see there are **5,238** records. Also, notice that an attempt was made to calculate descriptive statistics on the **Description** column, which is a string. While the output for identifier columns is not very useful, scrolling to the right, we can see that the mean, minimum, maximum, and standard deviation of the **Quantity** column is useful, as shown in *Figure 5.27*:

```
1   display(df.describe("Quantity","UnitPrice","TaxRate","PickedQuantity"))
```

▸ (2) Spark Jobs

Table ∨ +

	summary	Quantity	UnitPrice	TaxRate	PickedQuantity
1	count	5238	5238	5238	5238
2	mean	39.76078655975563	48.26134402443706	15.0	38.83886979763268
3	stddev	54.702157184883106	154.91543308493647	0.0	54.114299937499375
4	min	1	0.66	15.0	0
5	max	360	1899.0	15.0	360

Figure 5.27: Describe the output of the Quantity, UnitPrice, TaxRate, and PickedQuantity columns

The **summary** is another function available on a DataFrame that returns the same values as the **describe** method but includes approximate quartile information, as shown in *Figure 5.28*:

```
1   display(df.summary())
```

▸ (2) Spark Jobs

Table ∨ +

	summary	OrderLineID	OrderID	StockItemID	Description
1	count	5238	5238	5238	5238
2	mean	495220.5	157341.83123329515	109.55975563192058	null
3	stddev	1512.2246856866211	473.95596462993745	62.69492771764987	null
4	min	492602	156458	1	"The Gu" red shi
5	25%	493910	156950	55	null
6	50%	495219	157338	109	null
7	75%	496529	157748	164	null

Figure 5.28: Summary method output

To limit the columns that we want to see the results of, as we did with **describe**, we utilize the **select** method of the DataFrame, as shown in *Figure 5.29*:

```
1   display(df.select("Quantity","UnitPrice","TaxRate","PickedQuantity").summary())
```

▸ (2) Spark Jobs

Table ∨ +

	summary	Quantity	UnitPrice	TaxRate	PickedQuantity
1	count	5238	5238	5238	5238
2	mean	39.76078655975563	48.26134402443706	15.0	38.83886979763268
3	stddev	54.702157184883106	154.91543308493647	0.0	54.114299937499375
4	min	1	0.66	15.0	0
5	25%	5	13.0	15.0	5
6	50%	10	18.0	15.0	10
7	75%	60	32.0	15.0	60
8	max	360	1899.0	15.0	360

Figure 5.29: Limited columns using the summary method

Using the summary method allows us to see the distribution of items across the quartiles. This can provide a simpler view of a histogram and may be important when doing certain statistical methods. Now that we have looked at data using built-in **descriptive methods**, we will explore the use of Pandas profiling for Spark.

Recipe 47: Descriptive data analysis with Pandas profiling

Pandas profiling is a popular way of examining data. In the past, we could only use it on relatively small data sets, as it was not natively integrated with Spark. Now, thanks to a relatively new release, we can run what was previously called Pandas reports on large data. With this broader support, Pandas reports is now called **ydata-profiling**. The process of using the library starts by ensuring it is installed, as shown in *Figure 5.30*:

```
Cmd 1

For more information, see https://www.databricks.com/blog/2023/04/03/pandas-profiling-now-supports-apache-spark.html

Cmd 2

  1   %pip install ydata-profiling==4.0.0

Note: you may need to restart the kernel using dbutils.library.restartPython() to use updated packages.
Collecting ydata-profiling==4.0.0
  Using cached ydata_profiling-4.0.0-py2.py3-none-any.whl (344 kB)
Requirement already satisfied: pandas!=1.4.0,<1.6,>1.1 in /databricks/python3/lib/python3.10/site-packages (from yc
Requirement already satisfied: visions[type_image_path]==0.7.5 in /databricks/python3/lib/python3.10/site-packages
Requirement already satisfied: pydantic<1.11,>=1.8.1 in /databricks/python3/lib/python3.10/site-packages (from ydat
Requirement already satisfied: htmlmin==0.1.12 in /databricks/python3/lib/python3.10/site-packages (from ydata-prof
```

Figure 5.30: Install ydata-profiling using pip

Next, we select the data to process. For this example, we will use the Databricks hosted NYC Yellow Taxi Data. This is a popular data set and can be found by searching for "**TLC Trip Record Data**" in most search engines. The search result should have **https://www.nyc.gov/site/tlc/about/tlc-trip-record-data.page** as the top result location, as that is the source of this data set. This data set can be loaded using the code, as shown in *Figure 5.31*:

```
  1   # Load an example CSV and save it as a Delta table.
  2   raw_path = 'dbfs:/databricks-datasets/nyctaxi/tripdata/yellow/yellow_tripdata_2019-01.csv.gz'
  3   bronze = (
  4       spark.read.format('csv')
  5       .option('inferSchema', True)
  6       .option('header', True)
  7       .load(raw_path))
  8   bronze.write.format('delta').mode('overwrite').saveAsTable('yellowtaxi_trips')

  ▶ (12) Spark Jobs

  ▶ ▦ bronze: pyspark.sql.dataframe.DataFrame = [VendorID: integer, tpep_pickup_datetime: timestamp ... 16 more fields]

Command took 1.75 minutes -- by olan.dennis@gmail.com at 6/24/2023, 1:48:22 PM on Power User Cluster
```

Figure 5.31: Load the yellow taxi trip data

We can see in *Figure 5.31* that we are creating a table named **yellowtaxi_trips** based on the file within the Databricks datasets. Once the table has been created, we can create a DataFrame that references using the **spark.table** command, as shown in *Figure 5.32*:

```
1   df = spark.table('yellowtaxi_trips').cache()
2   display(df)
```

▸ (1) Spark Jobs

▸ ▦ df: pyspark.sql.dataframe.DataFrame = [VendorID: integer, tpep_pickup_datetime: timestamp ... 16 more fields]

Table ⌄ +

	VendorID	tpep_pickup_datetime	tpep_dropoff_datetime	passenger_count	trip_distance	RatecodeID	store_and_fwd_flag	PULocationID	DOLocat
1	1	2019-01-01T00:46:40.000+0000	2019-01-01T00:53:20.000+0000	1	1.5	1	N	151	239
2	1	2019-01-01T00:59:47.000+0000	2019-01-01T01:18:59.000+0000	1	2.6	1	N	239	246
3	2	2018-12-21T13:48:30.000+0000	2018-12-21T13:52:40.000+0000	3	0	1	N	236	236
4	2	2018-11-28T15:52:25.000+0000	2018-11-28T15:55:45.000+0000	5	0	1	N	193	193
5	2	2018-11-28T15:56:57.000+0000	2018-11-28T15:58:33.000+0000	5	0	2	N	193	193
6	2	2018-11-28T16:25:49.000+0000	2018-11-28T16:28:26.000+0000	5	0	1	N	193	193
7	2	2018-11-28T16:29:37.000+0000	2018-11-28T16:33:43.000+0000	5	0	2	N	193	193

Figure 5.32: *Loading a table into a DataFrame*

Now that we have a DataFrame, we can perform some simple descriptive analytics by using the summary command from the earlier section, as shown in *Figure 5.33*:

```
1   display(df.summary())
```

▸ (2) Spark Jobs

Table ⌄ +

	summary	VendorID	passenger_count	trip_distance	RatecodeID	store_and_fwd_flag	PULocationID	DOLocationID	paym
1	count	7667792	7667792	7667792	7667792	7667792	7667792	7667792	76677
2	mean	1.6367752281230372	1.5870782410373156	2.8010838491707664	1.0583713016732847	null	165.5009177348577	163.75290553004047	1.2917
3	stddev	0.5398204323494812	1.22443061523395	3.7375294029872803	0.6780886992671954	null	66.39179993938781	70.36445185660163	0.4733
4	min	1	0	0.0	1	N	1	1	1
5	25%	1	1	0.9	1	null	132	113	1
6	50%	2	1	1.53	1	null	162	162	1
7	75%	2	2	2.8	1	null	234	234	2
8	max	4	9	831.8	99	Y	265	265	4

Figure 5.33: *Summary of the DataFrame from the yellowtaxi_trips table*

From the summary, we can see that the maximum passenger count was 9 and that the mean was a little over one and a half. Our next step is to create a **ydata_profiling** report, as shown in *Figure 5.34*:

```
1   from ydata_profiling import ProfileReport
2   report = ProfileReport(df,
3                   title='NYC yellow taxi trip',
4                   infer_dtypes=False,
5                   interactions=None,
6                   missing_diagrams=None,
7                   correlations={"auto": {"calculate": False},
8                                 "pearson": {"calculate": True},
9                                 "spearman": {"calculate": True}})
```

▸ (1) Spark Jobs

Command took 28.39 seconds -- by alan.dennis@gmail.com at 6/24/2023, 1:48:59 PM on Power User Cluster

Figure 5.34: *Creating the ydata_profiling report*

As with many things in Spark, the time to define the report is quick (less than 30 seconds in this example). However, the time to produce the report can be considerable and is related to the size of the data set. In our example, we are dealing with over one and a half million records. Depending on the size of your cluster, this may take some time. The method `report.to_html` is used to produce displayed HTML, as shown in *Figure 5.35*:

```
1    report_html = report.to_html()
2    displayHTML(report_html)
```

Figure 5.35: *Producing the ydata_profiling HTML report*

In our case, it took a little over eight and a half minutes. The report contains **Overview**, **Variables**, **Correlations**, and **Sample sections**. The Overview section lists the characteristics of the dataset, as shown in *Figure 5.36*:

Overview

Overview	Alerts **21**	Reproduction			
Dataset statistics			Variable types		
Number of variables		18	Numeric		15
Number of observations		7667792	Date Time		2
Missing cells		0	Categorical		1
Missing cells (%)		0.0%			
Duplicate rows		0			
Duplicate rows (%)		0.0%			

Figure 5.36: *ydata_profiling Overview section of the report*

If you are not familiar with **ydata-profiling** or Pandas reports, consult the project's documentation at **https://ydata-profiling.ydata.ai/docs/master/index.html**. It is a powerful way of examining your data. As a final example, we can look at tip_amount, and see that many trips do not result in a tip, as shown in *Figure 5.37*. We can also see outliers, such as a maximum of **$787.25**:

tip_amount
Real number (3)

HIGH CORRELATION   ZEROS

Distinct	3362	Minimum	-63.5
Distinct (%)	< 0.1%	Maximum	787.25
Missing	0	Zeros	2410295
Missing (%)	0.0%	Zeros (%)	31.4%
Infinite	0	Negative	105
Infinite (%)	0.0%	Negative (%)	< 0.1%
Mean	1.827367	Memory size	0.0 B

More details

Statistics   Histogram   Common values   Extreme values

Quantile statistics		Descriptive statistics	
Minimum	-63.5	Standard deviation	2.5012129
5-th percentile	-63.5	Coefficient of variation (CV)	1.3687523
Q1	0	Kurtosis	1910.9131
median	1.32	Mean	1.827367
Q3	2.16	Median Absolute Deviation (MAD)	1.32
95-th percentile	787.25	Skewness	13.265064
Maximum	787.25	Sum	14011870
Range	850.75	Variance	6.2560658
Interquartile range (IQR)	2.16	Monotonicity	Not monotonic

Figure 5.37: Detailed information about tip_amount

Now that we have discussed ways to learn about our data, we will move on to ways to model it.

Data modeling

In *Chapter 3, Connecting to Storage,* we discussed general data lake design. Recall the basic idea was to keep data elements organized by source system through the silver zone. The idea was that it should be easy to determine the source system each silver item comes from. Once we start modeling our data, that approach becomes challenging, mainly because the true value of data becomes clear when multiple systems are combing. Instead, in the silver and gold layers, we will often organize our data based on modeling paradigms, as well as for consumption-enabling denormalization. In the following sections, we will discuss common modeling approaches and present how they should be organized in a Lakehouse architecture.

Common modeling approaches

There are many ways to model data. In this section, we present the most commonly occurring modeling approaches. We will also briefly describe how those modeling approaches can be utilized in a Lakehouse.

Entity-relationship data modelling

Given its historical importance, discussing data modeling without mentioning entity-relationship modeling is difficult. As the name implies, this type of modeling is about identifying entities and the relationships between them. As an example, consider the simple **Entity-Relationship Diagram (ERD)** in *Figure 5.38:*

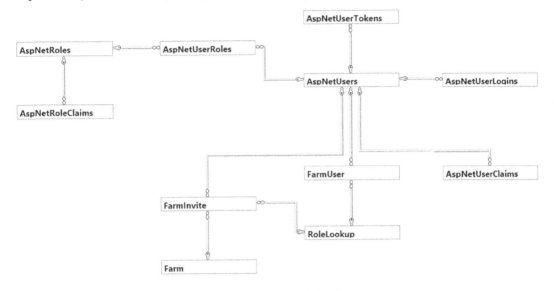

Figure 5.38: *Example ERD*

ERDs take multiple formats. Microsoft SQL Server Management Studio was used to generate this example. Most database management tools support the creation of ERD from database tables and tables from ERDs. One defining characteristic of ERD is that there can be a relationship between a table that, in turn, has a relationship with another entity.

We typically model this type of data in a Lakehouse by ingesting the data that is in an entity into a bronze Lakehouse table. Next, we apply business rules and remove duplication to produce silver tables. The foreign key relationships persist, as the values that define the relationships are unmodified. However, without a higher-level construct like Unity Catalog or a commercial product, it is difficult to enforce referential integrity or other constraints. Instead, we are forced to write functions to validate.

Star schema

Star schemas have been around since the 1990s. The basic concept is to have a table that contains core information, we call that the fact table. Associated to that table are dimensional tables. An example of a dimension is time, such as month, quarter, year, and so on. It is organized around fact and dimensional tables. The relationships between these tables give rise to the name, as the model often looks like a star, as shown in *Figure 5.39:*

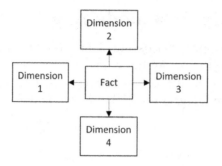

Figure 5.39: Typical star schema

Star schemas are a good way of representing data, but they sometimes encounter limitations. To overcome these limitations, star schemas were extended to create a snowflake schema.

Snowflake schema

While the star schema works for many situations, there are times when the dimensions need more flexibility. The snowflake extends the star schema by enabling the dimensions to have subdimensions, as shown in *Figure 5.40*:

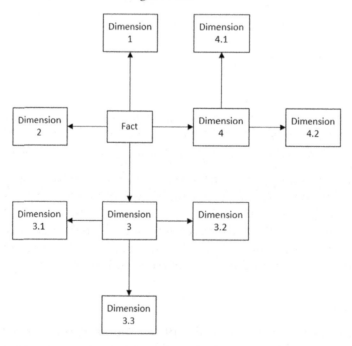

Figure 5.40: Example snowflake schema

From a Lakehouse perspective, the main difference between a star and snowflake schema is that performance can be problematic for the latter. Sometimes there needs to be clarity between a snowflake schema and the cloud company Snowflake, which is often seen as a competitor to Databricks. Snowflake schemas are useful in certain circumstances and often support business intelligence workloads. Another approach used to support business analytics workloads is to apply standardized data models.

Standardized data models

During the implementation of data projects, system integrators, architects, and business stakeholders often found similarities between various companies' business models. This phenomenon was more common across companies in the same industries. These data models had various names, including **Common Data Models (CDM)**, **Industry standard models (ISDM)**, and **Standard Data Models (SDM)**. This commonality has led to the creation of standards. These standards are sometimes governed by industry standards boards, such as OSCRE and its Industry Data Model, **https://www.oscre.org/Industry-Data-Model/Introducing-the-Data-Model**. Often software vendors create standardized models, such as Microsoft's Common Data Model, **https://learn.microsoft.com/en-us/common-data-model/**.

The goal of these models is to bring standardization across companies and reduce the time to value during the implementation phase of a data project. The idea is that a vendor can implement dashboards and reports that source data from a standardized model. This standardization enables the vendor to focus on the population of the models rather than creating a unique software deployment. Remember that this approach only works if an organization is willing to conform to the standard.

As with some of the previously discussed modeling approaches, it may be necessary to perform transformations to improve retrieval performance. In the next section, we discuss the types of retrieval optimization that might be needed.

Retrieval optimized models

Retrieval of information quickly is essential in a Lakehouse. Databricks has spent considerable efforts to improve the retrieval time of items stored in a Delta Lakehouse. These operations include some form of denormalization, in other words, taking values from a standardized storage approach and transforming them so they are faster to load. This is a classic trade-off of storage space for performance. When doing these forms of transformations, data lineage must be maintained somehow. Additionally, an effort should be made to make the transformations as fast as possible.

These transformations are beyond the typical maintenance and optimizations performed on Delta tables. Rather, it involves creating tables with consumption optimization as the primary goal. While this may be wasteful in terms of space, it may be faster to merge tables and produce a denormalized output as the source tables change than to perform that operation during a retrieval.

Regardless of the modeling approaches used, it is important to start with a design in hand. Otherwise, tables and associated external files may be created in inconsistent locations. This lack of governance will make ongoing support more challenging.

Design approach

In *Chapter 3, Connecting to Storage,* we discussed the importance of designing a data lake. That design approach is appropriate as we move into more various types of modeling, as shown in *Figure 5.41:*

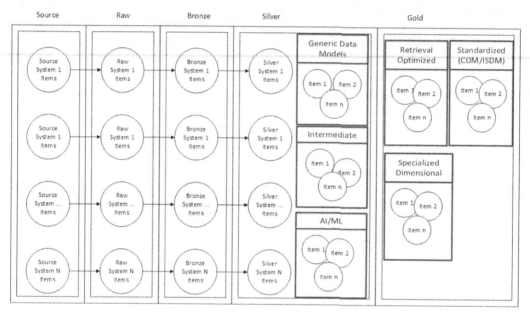

Figure 5.41: A design approach for a Lakehouse

As a refresher, items should be organized by the source system, any containers on that system, and the item by layer. Once things are in the silver layer, we know we can use those items for business purposes. However, we often need transformations to get the data ready to be used for business purposes in the gold layer. It is common to join a table with lookup tables and save the result as an intermediate table. The table is not meant to address a particular business question but is fit for use as it has had rules applied and is ensured to be free of duplications or other data quality issues. In this model, we would place those items in an intermediate container within the silver layer.

Likewise, data scientists, people doing Artificial Intelligence experiments, and users focusing on machine learning activities need to create tables that will likely not be used directly for a business purpose but may produce things (such as trained models) that are.

This approach should be considered a guiding principle, not a fixed rule set. The basic idea is to create containers for types of things that are related, such as standardized models.

Conclusion

In this chapter, we discussed how to explore data. We discussed types of data profiling and descriptive statistics mechanisms. We then discussed data modeling approaches and how they fit into a Lakehouse architecture.

In the next chapter, we shift to the building area of this book. We will discuss hands-on steps to ingest from source systems to bronze.

Join our book's Discord space

Join the book's Discord Workspace for Latest updates, Offers, Tech happenings around the world, New Release and Sessions with the Authors:

https://discord.bpbonline.com

CHAPTER 6

Extracting from Source and Loading to Bronze

Introduction

The population of a Lakehouse can be performed in several ways. We will explore various ways and discuss the tradeoffs associated with each approach. Native Databricks functionality is discussed, along with third-party solutions. Supporting stream processing is an important characteristic of a Lakehouse solution. Stream ingestion is discussed in depth, along with examples of various solutions.

Structure

The chapter covers the following topics:

- To raw or not to raw
- Loading files using self-managed watermarks
- Loading files using Auto Loader
- Loading files using Delta Live Tables
- Loading streaming data

Objectives

By the end of this chapter, you should understand the many ways that data can be ingested into a Lakehouse. You will have a good understanding of Delta Live Tables, Databricks Auto Loader, and Spark's Structured Streaming.

To raw or not to raw

When ingesting data, the first question to answer is where it goes. That may seem like a basic question, but the answer is more complex than you might think. The approach we typically use is that if the data comes from a source with access to a schema, we skip the raw layer and go directly to a Delta table in the Bronze zone, especially if that source is an enterprise-class system, such as the database for a **Customer Relationship Management (CRM)** system.

If the data is coming from a file-based system that lacks schema support, landing the raw layer is a good idea. This allows you to apply a schema during ingestion to the Bronze table. Additionally, it allows you to have a history of the files you received in case of a defect related to your raw-to-Bronze transformation.

As a Bronze layer holds the history of all changes, we typically want to avoid data duplication by having that same data in the raw zone. It comes down to balancing the risk of data corruption with the cost of added storage. It is possible to bypass the raw zone, but that comes at a higher risk. Regardless of the destination, we recommend using Databricks' **Change Data Feed (CDF)** for all Delta tables. In the next section, we will discuss CDF in depth.

Using change data feed

CDF allows row-level tracking of changes in a Lakehouse. This enables functionality like **Change Data Capture (CDC)** available in many relational database systems. We will go over CDF discussing its importance to the Lakehouse architecture.

Overview of change data feed

It is common to need to know the changes within a table. For example, relational systems often implement CDC to help track changes and minimize effort in synchronizing systems. Similarly, Delta tables have CDF. CDF allows row-level tracking.

CDF is critical to Lakehouse architecture in that it is the enabling technology of incremental processing. With CDF, we can identify the subset of records to process from layer to layer. This reduces processing time and, in turn, costs.

Recipe 48: Creating a table with change data feed on

CDF is associated with a Delta table and is stored in **TBLPROPERTIES**. To enable CDF for a table, you need to set the **TBLPROPERTIES delta.enableChangeDataFeed** to **true**, as shown in *Figure 6.1*:

```
Cmd 3

1   CREATE TABLE IF NOT EXISTS LakehouseCookbook.Watermarks  (
2     schemaName string,
3     tableName string,
4     watermarkType string,
5     timestampWatermark TIMESTAMP,
6     integerWatermark INT,
7     bigIntWatermark BIGINT,
8     stringWatermark string
9   ) TBLPROPERTIES (delta.enableChangeDataFeed = true)

▶ (4) Spark Jobs

OK

Command took 9.85 seconds -- by alan.dennis@gmail.com at 7/1/2023, 3:11:59 PM on Power User Cluster

Cmd 4

1   DESCRIBE HISTORY lakehousecookbook.Watermarks

▶ (1) Spark Jobs

Table ∨   +
```

	version	timestamp	userId	userName	operation	operationParameters
1	0	2023-07-01T19:12:02.000+0000	2270508095937838	alan.dennis@gmail.com	CREATE TABLE	▶ {"isManaged": "true", "descrip

Figure 6.1: Creating Table using SQL with CDF enabled

The main addition is the **TBLPROPERTIES** section on line 8 of command 3. This instruction tells Databricks to set the **delta.enableChangeFeed** table property to **true**. We can also examine the history of a given table. In this example, the only operation performed on this table was its creation. Since we have added the **IF NOT EXISTS** clause, running command 3 repeatedly will not add additional records to the table history, as no changes will occur.

In general, if you are working with tables that are fully loaded each time, use the **OR REPLACE** clause. If you are working with incrementally loaded tables, ensure you use the **IF NOT EXISTS** clause, as we have most recently done here. As you can see in command 4, replacing a table retains the table's history, something desirable in a Lakehouse architecture. Next, we will discuss a similar approach using Python.

Recipe 49: Using Python to enable CDF

One of the benefits of Databricks is its broad support for programming languages. In this book, we focus mostly on Python and SQL. Keep in mind that Databricks also supports R and Scala natively. Python is used here because it is a popular language in data engineering, data science, and machine learning. Often, the easiest way to use Python is to create an SQL string and use the **spark.sql** interface, as shown in *Figure 6.2*:

```
Cmd 3

    1    def TurnCDFOn(schema,tableName):
    2        spark.sql("ALTER TABLE " + schema + "." + tableName + "  SET TBLPROPERTIES (delta.enableChangeDataFeed = true)")
    3        print("TurnCDFOn: Turned CDF on for ",schema,tableName)

 Command took 0.06 seconds -- by alan.dennis@gmail.com at 6/30/2023, 6:48:56 PM on Power User Cluster

Cmd 4

    1    TurnCDFOn("default","yellowtaxi_trips")

 ▸ (4) Spark Jobs

 TurnCDFOn: Turned CDF on for  default yellowtaxi_trips
 Command took 1.97 seconds -- by alan.dennis@gmail.com at 6/30/2023, 6:48:57 PM on Power User Cluster
```

Figure 6.2: *Using Python to turn on CDF*

In this example, we use the **SQL ALTER TABLE** command to turn on CDF for the yellow taxi trips table. One challenge with blindly applying an **ALTER TABLE** command is that you are impacting the table's history, as each update is recorded, as you can see in *Figure 6.3*:

```
Cmd 5

    1    %sql DESCRIBE HISTORY  default.yellowtaxi_trips

 ▸ (2) Spark Jobs

 ▸ ▥ _sqldf: pyspark.sql.dataframe.DataFrame = [version: long, timestamp: timestamp ... 13 more fields]

 Table  ∨    +
```

	version	timestamp	userId	userName	operation
1	4	2023-06-30T22:48:58.000+0000	2270508095937838	alan.dennis@gmail.com	SET TBLPROPERTIES
2	3	2023-06-30T22:17:50.000+0000	2270508095937838	alan.dennis@gmail.com	SET TBLPROPERTIES
3	2	2023-06-25T22:55:07.000+0000	2270508095937838	alan.dennis@gmail.com	SET TBLPROPERTIES
4	1	2023-06-24T17:50:06.000+0000	2270508095937838	alan.dennis@gmail.com	CREATE OR REPLACE TABLE
5	0	2023-06-24T16:34:29.000+0000	2270508095937838	alan.dennis@gmail.com	CREATE OR REPLACE TABLE

Figure 6.3: *History of a table with CDF repeatedly being turned on*

If we look closer at the results of the DESCRIBE HISTORY command, we can see the operational Parameters, as shown in *Figure 6.4*:

userName	operation	operationParameters
alan.dennis@gmail.com	SET TBLPROPERTIES	▸ {"properties": "{\"delta.enableChangeDataFeed\":\"true\"}"}
alan.dennis@gmail.com	SET TBLPROPERTIES	▸ {"properties": "{\"delta.enableChangeDataFeed\":\"true\"}"}
alan.dennis@gmail.com	SET TBLPROPERTIES	▸ {"properties": "{\"delta.enableChangeDataFeed\":\"true\"}"}
alan.dennis@gmail.com	CREATE OR REPLACE TABLE AS SELECT	▸ {"isManaged": "true", "description": null, "partitionBy": "[]", "properties": "{}"}
alan.dennis@gmail.com	CREATE OR REPLACE TABLE AS SELECT	▸ {"isManaged": "true", "description": null, "partitionBy": "[]", "properties": "{}"}

Figure 6.4: *Table history's operational parameters*

You can see in the operationalParameters column that the **delta.enableChangeDataFeed** property was being repeatedly set to true. To avoid this, it is better to see if CDF is on before enabling it. There are several ways to do this, but a simple approach is shown in *Figure 6.5:*

```
Cmd 2

1    def IsCDFOn(schema,tableName):
2        tblPropertiesDf = spark.sql("SHOW TBLPROPERTIES " + schema + "." + tableName)
3        tblProperties = tblPropertiesDf.where(tblPropertiesDf.key == "delta.enableChangeDataFeed").collect()
4        numMatching = len(tblProperties)
5        if (numMatching ==0):
6            print("IsCDFOn: No CDF table properties found ",schema,tableName)
7            return False
8        else:
9            if numMatching == 1:
10                isOn = tblProperties[0][1]
11                if isOn != "true":
12                    return False
13                else:
14                    return True
15        print("IsCDFOn: CDF - This should not happen. Should be 1. ",numMatching)
16

Command took 0.05 seconds -- by alan.dennis@gmail.com at 6/30/2023, 7:02:48 PM on Power User Cluster

Cmd 3

1    print(IsCDFOn("default","yellowtaxi_trips"))

▸ (1) Spark Jobs

True
```

Figure 6.5: *Checking if CDF is enabled*

The approach used in *Figure 6.5* is to retrieve a DataFrame that contains the specified table's TBLPROPERTIES. Next, a where operation is applied to the DataFrame to select only the rows that have the key matching CDF being enabled on line 3. If there are no rows, then CDF is not on. If there are rows, then there should be a single row with a Boolean value indicating if CDF is on. We test for that on line 10, where we get the first row and select the second column. Ideally, we should ask for the cell based on the key's property, but this approach is sufficient for most situations. We can see by the results of command 3 that CDF is on for the yellow taxi trips table.

Recipe 50: Ensure CDF is enabled for all tables

We now have the building blocks to ensure that CDF is turned on for all Delta tables. This approach iterates across all tables in all schemas and invokes a method that first checks if CDF is on and, if not, turns it on, as shown. As CDF is critical to the Lakehouse architecture, ensuring it is turned on will reduce the number of issues met. The source code for this approach is available from the publisher's companion site, but can be viewed in *Figure 6.6*:

Cmd 7

```
1   def EnsureCDFIsOn(schema,tableName):
2       isOn = IsCDFOn(schema,tableName)
3       if isOn:
4           print(schema,tableName,"EnsureCDFIsOn: CDF already on")
5           return
6       TurnCDFOn(schema,tableName)
7       print(schema,tableName,"Turned CDF on")
```

Command took 0.06 seconds -- by alan.dennis@gmail.com at 6/30/2023, 7:20:08 PM on Power User Cluster

Cmd 8

```
1   def TurnCDFOnForAllTables():
2       schemasDf = spark.sql('SHOW SCHEMAS')
3       results =[]
4       for schema in schemasDf.collect():
5           tablesDf = spark.sql('show tables from ' + schema['databaseName'])
6           for table in tablesDf.collect():
7               EnsureCDFIsOn(table['database'],table['tableName'])
```

Command took 0.13 seconds -- by alan.dennis@gmail.com at 6/30/2023, 7:20:09 PM on Power User Cluster

Cmd 9

```
1   TurnCDFOnForAllTables()
```

▶ (53) Spark Jobs

```
default bronzeapplicationdeliverymethods EnsureCDFIsOn: CDF already on
default yellowtaxi_trips EnsureCDFIsOn: CDF already on
lakehousecookbook bronze_basetable EnsureCDFIsOn: CDF already on
lakehousecookbook bronze_lookuptable1 EnsureCDFIsOn: CDF already on
lakehousecookbook bronzeanimalhusbandry EnsureCDFIsOn: CDF already on
lakehousecookbook bronzeanimalhusbandrypy EnsureCDFIsOn: CDF already on
lakehousecookbook bronzeapplicationdeliverymethods EnsureCDFIsOn: CDF already on
lakehousecookbook bronzeapplicationdeliverymethods archive EnsureCDFIsOn: CDF already on
```

Figure 6.6: Ensure CDF is on for all tables

The first function checks if CDF is turned on for the supplied schema and table parameters, and if it is, it prints a message and exits (lines 2 through 5). Since we know CDF is not on, we can turn it on (line 6). To apply this to all tables, we get the schemas (line 2 of command 8) and then ask for all tables in each schema (line 5 of command 8). Then we iterate across the tables invoking EnsureCDFIsOn on each schema/database and table pair.

CDF is an important part of the Lakehouse architecture. It is a tool provided by Databricks that is not part of the Apache Spark distribution. We will revisit CDF extensively in

Chapter 7, Transforming to Create Silver and in *Chapter 8, Transforming to Create Gold for Business Purposes*. Before we can perform those transformation, we need to have loaded into Bronze tables. In the next section, we will discuss loading files using self-managed watermarks.

Loading files using self-managed watermarks

There are many ways to load (also called ingest) data from data sources to a Lakehouse. Some require more work than others. One way to do this, is to manage the watermark information with your own code. Other approaches take care of this for you, but it is important to understand the processes involved. There are several types of ingestion, but incremental ingestion is the preferred mechanism with the Lakehouse architecture. In the next section, we discuss this approach of moving data from source systems to the Lakehouse.

Incremental ingestion example

There are several situations where incremental ingestion is required. Often, Lakehouses consume data from enterprise systems, such as customer relationship management systems. In this situation, the data we see changing has both a column that can be used to order the data (referred to in this book as a watermark) and a unique identifier that can be used to find existing instances of a changing record.

An example of this pattern is an employee database that includes name, address, and phone number. To determine which employee is which, we use a **unique** identifier or key, likely called an **employee id**. Typically, there are also at least two timestamp records on the employee's record tracking record creation and revision, as shown in *Table 6.1*:

EmPId	FirstName	LastName	Address1	CreatedOn	ModifiedOn
1	Leonardo	da Vinci	123 First St.	12/31/2024	12/31/2024
2	Napoleon	Bonaparte	234 Second St.	12/31/2024	12/31/2024
3	Charles	Darwin	345 Third St.	12/31/2024	12/31/2024
4	Albert	Einstein	456 Fourth St.	12/31/2024	12/31/2024
5	Thomas	Jefferson	678 Fifth St.	12/31/2024	12/31/2024

Table 6.1: Simplified employee table

Due to space limitations, we use a grossly simplified employee table. During the initial ingestion of the employee table, we would load all records, keeping track of the maximum modification column value. We would save that value in a table, like that which we created in *Table 6.1*. To review, that table includes fields for schema, table name, and type of watermark. For this example, the watermark type would be date and we would use the timestamp column. As all these records have the same modified date, we would start that date in the watermark table.

If an employee moves to a new residence, we update that employee's record with their new address, also changing the revision timestamp. When we ingest records from the employee database, we would only get those records which have changed, in other words, the records which have a modified date greater than our previously stored date watermark.

In our example, **Albert** decided to move to a different location. We update the address in the employee database table along with the modified date. Often modification timestamps are system managed. We can see the updated employee database in *Table 6.2*:

EmPId	FirstName	LastName	Address1	CreatedOn	ModifiedOn
1	Leonardo	da Vinci	123 First St.	12/31/2024	12/31/2024
2	Napoleon	Bonaparte	234 Second St.	12/31/2024	12/31/2024
3	Charles	Darwin	345 Third St.	12/31/2024	12/31/2024
4	Albert	Einstein	160 Spear St	12/31/2024	5/1/2025
5	Thomas	Jefferson	678 Fifth St.	12/31/2024	12/31/2024

Table 6.2: Employee table after modifications

When extracting data from this table into our Lakehouse, only records with modification dates greater than 12/31/2024 will be extracted. This will result in a dataset similar to that in *Table 6.3*:

EmPId	FirstName	LastName	Address1	CreatedOn	ModifiedOn
4	Albert	Einstein	160 Spear St	12/31/2024	5/1/2025

Table 6.3: Extract from employee table

Only the updated record would be inserted into the Bronze table. This is important to understand. The Bronze table will contain all changes made to the source table, as shown in *Table 6.4*:

EmPId	FirstName	LastName	Address1	CreatedOn	ModifiedOn
1	Leonardo	da Vinci	123 First St.	12/31/2024	12/31/2024
2	Napoleon	Bonaparte	234 Second St.	12/31/2024	12/31/2024
3	Charles	Darwin	345 Third St.	12/31/2024	12/31/2024
4	Albert	Einstein	160 Spear St	12/31/2024	12/31/2024
5	Thomas	Jefferson	678 Fifth St.	12/31/2024	12/31/2024
4	Albert	Einstein	160 Spear St	12/31/2024	5/1/2025

Table 6.4: Bronze table after ingesting modifications

Many struggle to understand that we only append to the Bronze table. The primary reason for this design decision is to preserve the history of changes. When constructing the silver table, which we discuss in *Chapter 7, Transforming to Create Silver*, you will see we take the most recent version of the table, and merge that version into the silver table based on the key, in this case **EMPID**.

Also, we often receive data from **Internet of Things (IoT)** device. When dealing with device data, we typically see data that has a date or timestamp that is increasing. In the next section, we will read data from an Azure Event Hub using Event Hub Capture to create our files.

Recipes 51: Using incremental load of files

IoT devices are commonly encountered when constructing a Lakehouse. One way that IoT devices send messages is through queue-based technologies, such as Azure Event Hub. Event Hubs are a **Platform as a Service (PaaS)** offering from Azure. They can be treated much the same as any Apache Kafka system, with reduced operational effort.

The data we use in this example comes from a simple Jupyter Python Notebook running on Windows. The notebook sleeps for a configurable number of minutes, then executes a speed test using the Python speedtest-cli package. For more about the speed test library, see **https://www.speedtest.net/apps/cli**. Once the speed test completes, the program sends the results to an Event Hub using **azure-eventhub**. The payload is a JSON string, as shown in *Figure 6.7:*

```
In [*]:   1  import time
          2  print("ready to start work")
          4  linesToWrite = []
          4  while (True):
          5      try:
          6          now = GetTimestamp()
          7          d, u, p,ip = test()
          8          print(d,u,p,ip)
          9      except  Exception as ex:
         10          print("exception",ex)
         11          d = -1
         12          u = -1
         13          p = -1
         14      ip = socket.gethostbyname(socket.gethostname())
         15      eventData = json.dumps( {"utc":now,"ip":ip,"download":d,"upload":u,"ping":p})
         16      SendToEventHub(eventData)
         17      print("sent to event hub")
         18      if sleepMinutes>0:
         19          print('sleeping',sleepMinutes)
         20          time.sleep(sleepMinutes * 10) # time.sleep takes seconds as parameter

execution queued 10:49:08 2023-07-08

ready to start work
GetTimestamp 1688827748 time.struct_time(tm_year=2023, tm_mon=7, tm_mday=8, tm_hour=14, tm_min=49, tm_sec=8, tm_wday=5, tm_yday
=189, tm_isdst=0)
{'ip': '98.97.19.239'}
98.97.19.239
17897527.560420774 9300811.476445962 48.418 98.97.19.239
enter SendToEventHub {"utc": 1688827748, "ip": "98.97.19.239", "download": 17897527.560420774, "upload": 9300811.476445962, "pi
ng": 48.418}
Sent data
sent to event hub
sleeping 10
```

Figure 6.7: Example run of speed test sending to Event Hub

Now that we know what the payload should look like, the next step is to get the files containing that information. For simplicity, and because it is cloud-agnostic we use mount points for this example. Once you have configured Event Hub Capture to write to a location in your source data lake, mount that location with a name similar to **SourceData**, as shown in *Figure 6.8*:

```
Cmd 3

   1   %run ./Utilities

Command took 0.78 seconds -- by alan.dennis@gmail.com at 7/1/2023, 11:41:01 AM on Power User Cluster

This file is part of Databricks Lakehouse Cookbook, by Alan L. Dennis (c) 2023 - Published by BPB Publications

All source code in this Repository is Licensened under https://www.apache.org/licenses/LICENSE-2.0.txt

Cmd 4

   1   accountKey = dbutils.secrets.get(scope = "LakehouseCookbook", key = "lakehouseSourceAccountKey")
   2   mountPoint = "/mnt/sourceData"
   3   if  IsMounted(mountPoint):
   4       print(mountPoint, "already mounted")
   5   else:
   6       print(mountPoint," no mounted, this will take a little bit")
   7       dbutils.fs.mount(
   8       source = "wasbs://source@lakehousecookbook.blob.core.windows.net",
   9       mount_point = mountPoint,
  10       extra_configs = {"fs.azure.account.key.lakehousecookbook.blob.core.windows.net":accountKey})
  11

/mnt/sourceData already mounted
```

Figure 6.8: *Mounting source data location*

Note that in command 3 we use the **%run magic** command. This includes the notebook named Utilities into the context of the current notebook. To learn more about this and related approaches of notebook orchestration see **https://docs.databricks.com/notebooks/notebook-workflows.html**. While using **%run** is a good solution to our problem (including the contents of one notebook into multiple) it does have many limitations. If you need to supply parameters (called widgets in Databricks) or are concerned with the output or result of the notebook, you should use the dbutils.notebook.run method instead. We will discuss dbutils.notebook.run in detail in *Chapter 15, Tips, Tricks, Troubleshooting, and Best Practices*.

Within the Utilities notebook, you will see a collection of function definition, including the one used in *Figure 6.8*. This is a useful approach to simplify your development. The goal should be to provide an easy-to-understand set of functions, ideally that include documentation. Over time, you might find it beneficial to construct a Python class containing those functions. Be cautious, however, that the construct might become overly complex and fail to provide the required simplicity.

Creating a common set of functions and making them accessible to all notebooks can bring standardization and increase efficiency. In this example, the function tests if the mount path has previously been mounted using iteration across the known mounts, as shown in *Figure 6.9*:

```
Utilities    Python ∨                                          ▶ Run all    ● Power User (

File   Edit   View   Run   Help    Last edit was 2 hours ago    Provide feedback


        Cmd 8


        1     def TurnCDFOnForAllTables():
        2         schemasDf = spark.sql('SHOW SCHEMAS')
        3         results =[]
        4         for schema in schemasDf.collect():
        5             tablesDf = spark.sql('show tables from ' + schema['databaseName'])
        6             for table in tablesDf.collect():
        7                 EnsureCDFIsOn(table['database'],table['tableName'])


     Cmd 9


        1     def IsMounted(mountName):
        2         if any(mount.mountPoint == mountName for mount in dbutils.fs.mounts()):
        3             return True
        4         else:
        5             return False
```

Figure 6.9: Utility function definition to see if a path has been mounted

We now have a mount point that lets us access our source files. To use this mount point, we need to retrieve the files found within the mount and ingest those not previously ingested into a Bronze table. To get the list of files in a folder, we can use a function that recursively traverses the directory structure using dbutils.fs.ls. Note that **dbutils.fs.ls** returns a list of FileInfo **objects**. Each object has isFile and isDir methods, useful to determine if the item is a directory that might contain files or a file.

Event Hub Capture typically writes files in a directory structure based on the Event Hub namespace, the event hub's name, partition identifier, and then a time slices directory structure based on year, month, day, hour, and so on. To learn more about Event Hub Capture, visit **https://learn.microsoft.com/en-us/azure/event-hubs/event-hubs-capture-enable-through-portal**.

The code we will use may seem slightly confusing as it is recursive. The process starts by invoking the function and supplying a path and an optional list of FileInfo objects. We check whether the supplied list is None, Python's null equivalent. If so, we set a flag to indicate that when we exist the method, we should convert the file info list to a directory. Next, we look for the contents of the current directory using the **dbutils.fs.ls** method. We work through that list, checking whether the item is a file or directory. If it is a file, we add the FileInfo to the list. If it is a directory, we call the same function (recursing), supplying the path of the FileInfo object along with the current list of FileInfo objects. The process repeats until we hit the terminating condition; in this case, we encounter a folder containing only files or no subdirectories, as shown in *Figure 6.10*:

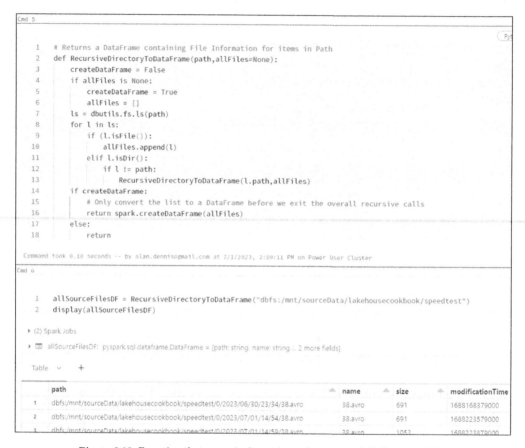

```
Cmd 5

                                                                                          Pys
    1   # Returns a DataFrame containing File Information for items in Path
    2   def RecursiveDirectoryToDataFrame(path,allFiles=None):
    3       createDataFrame = False
    4       if allFiles is None:
    5           createDataFrame = True
    6           allFiles = []
    7       ls = dbutils.fs.ls(path)
    8       for l in ls:
    9           if (l.isFile()):
   10               allFiles.append(l)
   11           elif l.isDir():
   12               if l != path:
   13                   RecursiveDirectoryToDataFrame(l.path,allFiles)
   14       if createDataFrame:
   15           # Only convert the list to a DataFrame before we exit the overall recursive calls
   16           return spark.createDataFrame(allFiles)
   17       else:
   18           return

Command took 0.10 seconds -- by alan.dennis@gmail.com at 7/1/2023, 2:09:11 PM on Power User Cluster
```

```
Cmd 6

    1   allSourceFilesDF = RecursiveDirectoryToDataFrame("dbfs:/mnt/sourceData/lakehousecookbook/speedtest")
    2   display(allSourceFilesDF)

  ▶ (2) Spark Jobs

  ▶ ▦ allSourceFilesDF: pyspark.sql.dataframe.DataFrame = [path: string, name: string ... 2 more fields]

    Table  ∨     +
```

	path	name	size	modificationTime
1	dbfs:/mnt/sourceData/lakehousecookbook/speedtest/0/2023/06/30/23/34/38.avro	38.avro	691	1688168379000
2	dbfs:/mnt/sourceData/lakehousecookbook/speedtest/0/2023/07/01/14/54/38.avro	38.avro	691	1688223579000
3	dbfs:/mnt/sourceData/lakehousecookbook/speedtest/0/2023/07/01/14/59/38.avro	38.avro	1053	1688223879000

Figure 6.10: *Function that recursively retrieves the names of all files in a folder*

We can see the results of invoking the method in command 6. Notice that the files are AVRO format and nested in folders based on the time of the arrival of the message to the Event Hub. Now that we have a DataFrame containing all the files within the mount point, next, we need a method to get and update a record in our watermark Delta table.

Dealing with watermarks can be confusing. Having helper functions simplifies that process. We created the table we will use in Recipe 46. The table has columns to store the schema and table names of the table whose watermarks we store and a column to differentiate the type of watermark being used. It is not usual to encounter unexpected watermark types. The only determining characteristic of a watermark is that it can be sorted. For the example we will use the BIGINT datatype associated with the modificationTime.

We must handle the case that we have not previously ingested the table. In this situation, we want a minimum value so that we will load all existing records. For our example we will use zero as our minimum value and create the existing watermark DataFrame if there is not a record in the Delta table matching the schema and table names, as shown in *Figure 6.11*:

```
1    from pyspark.sql import functions as F
2    def GetWatermark(schemaName, tableName):
3        watermarkTable = "lakehousecookbook.watermarks"
4        df = spark.read.table(watermarkTable)
5        df = df.where((F.col("schemaName") == schemaName) & (F.col("tableName") == tableName))
6        df.cache()
7        count = df.count()
8        print(count)
9        if count == 1:
10            return df
11        elif count == 0:
12            updateWatermarkTableSchema = "schemaName string,tableName string,watermarkType string,timestampWatermark timestamp,
                 integerWatermark integer,bigintWatermark BIGINT,stringWatermark string"
13            updatesList = [{
14                "schemaName": schemaName, "tableName": tableName,
15                "watermarkType": "bigint", "timestampWatermark": None,
16                "integerWatermark": None, "bigintWatermark": 0,
17                "stringWatermark": None,
18            }]
19            dfUpdates = spark.createDataFrame(updatesList, updateWatermarkTableSchema)
20            dfUpdates.show()
21            return dfUpdates
22        else:
23            return None
```

Command took 0.06 seconds -- by alan.dennis@gmail.com at 7/1/2023, 1:24:55 PM on Power User Cluster

Cmd 9

```
1    startingWatermarkDF = GetWatermark("LakehouseCookbook","speedtest")
```

▶ [3] Spark Jobs

▶ ▦ startingWatermarkDF: pyspark.sql.dataframe.DataFrame = [schemaName: string, tableName: string ... 5 more fields]

0

```
+-----------------+---------+-------------+------------------+----------------+---------------+---------------+
|       schemaName|tableName|watermarkType|timestampWatermark|integerWatermark|bigintWatermark|stringWatermark|
+-----------------+---------+-------------+------------------+----------------+---------------+---------------+
| LakehouseCookbook|speedtest|       bigint|              null|            null|              0|           null|
+-----------------+---------+-------------+------------------+----------------+---------------+---------------+
```

Figure 6.11: *Get watermark function with example output*

This may seem overwhelming at first, however, understanding it will also help you comprehend other common Lakehouse activities. We start by importing functions from the pyspark.sql library. We need functions to use the col notation as seen on line 5. On line 3 we set the name of our watermark table. If this method was part of a class, the watermark table name would be an important property. Next, we read the watermark table with a **where** clause based on the supplied parameters (line 5). On line 6, we tell Databricks to cache the DataFrame after it has transformed with an operation such as **count**. Without using a cache Databricks may be forced to perform the operations defined on a DataFrame repeatedly. For more information on cache, see **https://kb.databricks.com/scala/best-practice-cache-count-take**. If we have a single record matching our query, we return the DataFrame. If the number of records returned is zero, we create a placeholder DataFrame (line 19) using spark.createDataFrame after having created a list of objects (lines 13 to 18) and the watermark table's schema (define on line 12 and used on line 19). You can see in command 9 that we have created a DataFrame with one record with watermarkType set to bigint.

We now have a means to get watermark values; the next step is to be able to update. For this, we want to perform an operation often called an upsert. The word is formed by combining update and insert. It means we want to update a record if it exists; if not, we want to insert it. A function of Delta tables is a **merge**. We can use the **merge** command to combine a DataFrame with an existing Delta table, as shown in *Figure 6.12*:

```
Cmd 10

  1   from delta import *
  2
  3   def UpsertWatermark(dfUpdates):
  4       watermarkTable = 'lakehousecookbook.watermarks'
  5       print("watermarkTable",watermarkTable)
  6       print(watermarkTable)
  7       watermark = DeltaTable.forName(spark,tableOrViewName=watermarkTable)
  8       watermark.alias('watermark').merge(
  9           dfUpdates.alias('updates'),'watermark.schemaName = updates.schemaName AND watermark.tableName = updates.tableName'
 10           ).whenMatchedUpdateAll() .whenNotMatchedInsertAll() .execute()

Command took 0.07 seconds -- by alan.dennis@gmail.com at 7/1/2023, 3:49:28 PM on Power User Cluster

Cmd 11

  1   UpsertWatermark(startingWatermarkDF)

  ▸ (9) Spark Jobs

watermarkTable lakehousecookbook.watermarks
lakehousecookbook.watermarks
```

Figure 6.12: *Update the watermark record*

Line 1 in command 10 imports everything from the Delta library. We do this because line 7 requires it. That line, 7, is how we retrieve get the Delta table so we can interact with it, using the table's name, rather than the location of its files. You can use the fromFiles method to retrieve a reference to a Delta table based on the location where files are serialized. Lines 8 through 19 are where the upsert occurs. On line 8 we create an alias for the watermark table and start the **merge** command. Next, we indicate that the dfUpates DataFrame should have an alias, named update. The **next** clause is the condition to use to determine when a match is found. The **final** clauses on line 10 tell Databricks what to do when there is a match and when there is not. In the case of a match, we want to update all fields. In the case there is not a match, we want to insert all the records from the dfUpdates DataFrame.

This is a simplistic version of what we will do when merging into silver tables in *Chapter 7, Transforming to Create Silver*. The main difference is that in our example here, there is always a single record in the update DataFrame. When merging to silver, we will need to remove duplicates from the update DataFrame, taking the most recent version. We can now check to see if there is a record in our watermark table, as shown in *Figure 6.13*:

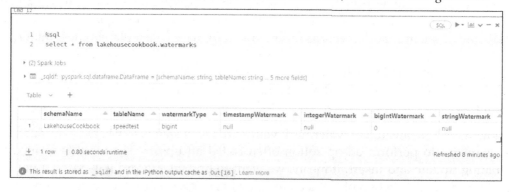

Figure 6.13: *Viewing contents of watermark table*

Since we created the table with CDF turned on, we can also review the table history of the watermarks table, as shown in *Figure 6.14*:

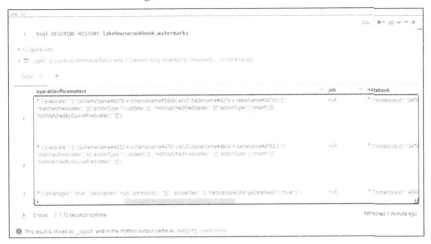

Figure 6.14: Watermark table history

Notice that revision 1 was when we created the table. This sort of information can be useful in detecting stale data or unsanctioned operations. Back to the task at hand, we have the means to retrieve files, filter them using a watermark that is persisted in a Delta table, and update that table. We are close to our solution, but first, we need two helper methods. When we retrieve a watermark, we will get a DataFrame with a single row. We need to extract the value from the row so we can use it to filter the files. To do that, we need a method that can return the correct value, as shown in *Figure 6.15*:

```
def GetWatermarkValue(startingWatermarkDF):
    watermarkRow = startingWatermarkDF.collect()[0]
    # Get the watermark value based on watermarkType on the row
    watermarkType = watermarkRow.watermarkType
    print(watermarkType)
    if watermarkType == "bigint":
        watermarkValue = watermarkRow.bigIntWatermark
    elif watermarkType == "timestamp":
        watermarkValue = watermarkRow.timestampWatermark
    elif watermarkType == "integer":
        watermarkValue = watermarkRow.integerWatermark
    elif watermarkType == "string":
        watermarkValue = watermarkRow.stringWatermark
    else:
        print("Unknown watermark type", watermarkType)
        watermarkValue = None
    return watermarkValue
```

Figure 6.15: Helper method to convert watermark DataFrame to value

The **next** method we need takes a value and updates the watermark DataFrame so that we can send it to the method that merges it with the table. The main challenge with this method is that we must use the **lit** method to say our values are **literals**, as shown in *Figure 6.16*:

Cmd 15

```
1   # Update the Supplied WatermarkRow with the value, based on watermarkType on the row
2   from pyspark.sql.functions import lit
3   def UpdateWatermarkValue(watermarkDf,maxValue):
4       print(maxValue)
5       #watermarkTable = "lakehousecookbook.watermarks"
6       watermarkRow = startingWatermarkDF.collect()[0]
7       watermarkDf.createOrReplaceTempView("tempWatermarkRow")
8       watermarkType = watermarkRow.watermarkType
9       if watermarkType == "bigint":
10          watermarkDf = watermarkDf.withColumn("bigIntWatermark",lit(maxValue))
11      elif watermarkType == "timestamp":
12          watermarkDf = watermarkDf.withColumn("timestampWatermark",lit(maxValue))
13      elif watermarkType == "integer":
14          watermarkDf = watermarkDf.withColumn("integerWatermark",lit(maxValue))
15      elif watermarkType == "string":
16          watermarkDf = watermarkDf.withColumn("stringWatermark",lit(maxValue))
17      return watermarkDf
```

Figure 6.16: Updating the watermark DataFrame with the maximum value

We are almost there. To recap, we can retrieve and update the watermark that lets us retrieve the list of files that have changed since the last time we ingested the data. However, so far, we have not read those files. Instead, we have just gotten the list of files that have arrived or changed since the last time we checked. Now we need to read those files and construct the DataFrame that will be used to create and update the Bronze Delta table, as shown in *Figure 6.17*:

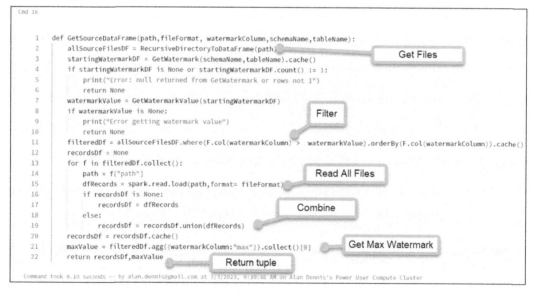

Figure 6.17: Retrieve source file records

As this has gotten more complex, we have added annotations to add clarity. We start by using the function that recursively captures the files in a path, which we created in *Figure 6.10*. Next, we filter the files so that our filtered DataFrame only has files we have not previously processed. Then we read each one of the filtered file paths into a DataFrame. We use the DataFrame's union operator to combine existing records with new ones. We also initialize that accumulator to None and check for that case. When it is None, this is the first DataFrame being used so that we know we can accept it as the base DataFrame with which the next DataFrame will be combined. Since we need both the DataFrame with the results and the maximum watermark value, we return a tuple. A tuple is an ordered immutable collection. To learn more about tuples, see **https://www.w3schools. com/python/python_tuples.asp**. We test this method to ensure it is working correctly, as shown in *Figure 6.18*:

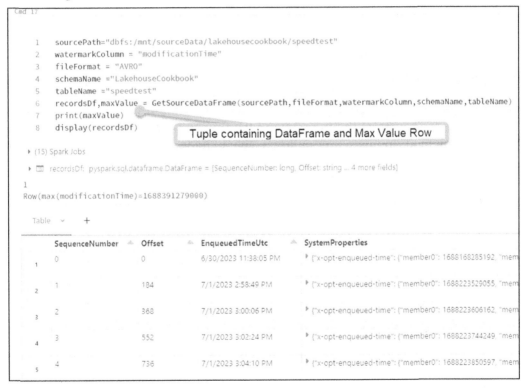

Figure 6.18: Testing retrieval of source file records

We are finally to the place we can pull all of this together in a unified operation. We have all the pieces built so we can finally incrementally ingest a set of files from a mount point that is receiving new files over time, as seen in *Figure 6.19*:

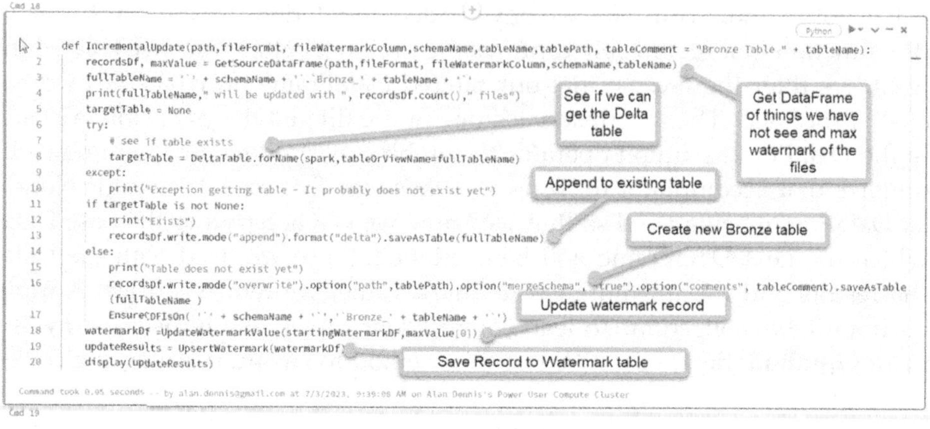

Figure 6.19: *Method to ingest files incrementally*

There is a lot going on in this method, so we will walk through it line by line. In the first line, we define the method, asking for the parameters necessary for processing. In line 2, we get a DataFrame that contains all records from the files in the supplied path that are newer than the supplied watermark, along with the maximum watermark value for the files. In line 3, we construct the full name of the Bronze Delta table. Line 4 prints out a **diagnostic** method. In line 5, we set targetTable to **None**. We do this because there will be an exception if the table does not exist, in line 8. We use a **try** and **except** clause to handle that occurrence. This is not a best practice, but we encountered issues with incorrect values returned by DeltaTable.isDeltaTable. If the table exists, we append the incremental DataFrame to it, in line 13. If not, we create the table in line 16. In line 17, we call our helper method EnsureCDFIsOn. Line 18 updates the watermark record with the max value returned in line 2. In line 19 we update the watermark table with the record from line 18. We do this at the end of the function to ensure that we only save the watermark if the process completes successfully. Now we need to try it, as shown in *Figure 6.20*:

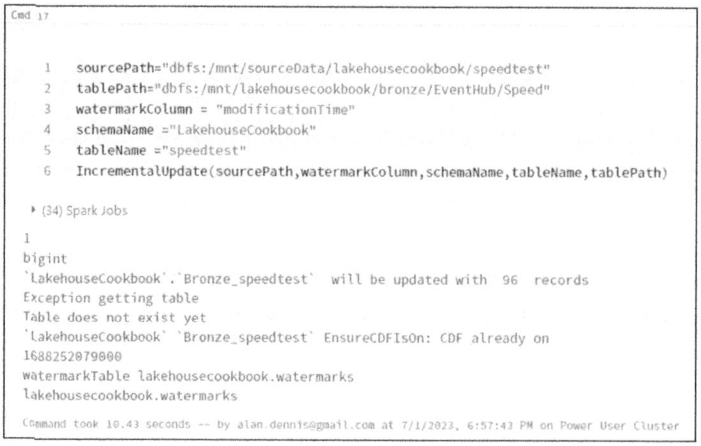

Figure 6.20: *Executing the incremental update*

You can see that we updated the table with 96 records. The exception error message can be ignored, as that is indicating that the Bronze Delta table did not exist. So far, we have not incrementally ingested files, as we have loaded everything that was in the folder. However, if we wait a few minutes and run the commands again we can see that only one file was ingested, as shown in *Figure 6.21*:

```
Cmd 17

    1   sourcePath="dbfs:/mnt/sourceData/lakehousecookbook/speedtest"
    2   tablePath="dbfs:/mnt/lakehousecookbook/bronze/EventHub/Speed"
    3   watermarkColumn = "modificationTime"
    4   schemaName ="LakehouseCookbook"
    5   tableName ="speedtest"
    6   IncrementalUpdate(sourcePath,watermarkColumn,schemaName,tableName,tablePath)


  ▶ (28) Spark Jobs

1
bigint
`LakehouseCookbook`.`Bronze_speedtest`  will be updated with  1  records
Exists
1688252379000
watermarkTable lakehousecookbook.watermarks
lakehousecookbook.watermarks

Command took 8.54 seconds -- by alan.dennis@gmail.com at 7/1/2023, 6:59:41 PM on Power User Cluster
```

Figure 6.21: One new file being ingested

We have successfully incrementally ingested to a Bronze table. Let us look at the table and its contents.

Recipes 52: Convert Event Hub data to JSON

Ideally, we should see JSON like what it looked like when it was created, as shown in *Figure 6.7*. As you can see in *Figure 6.22*, it is different:

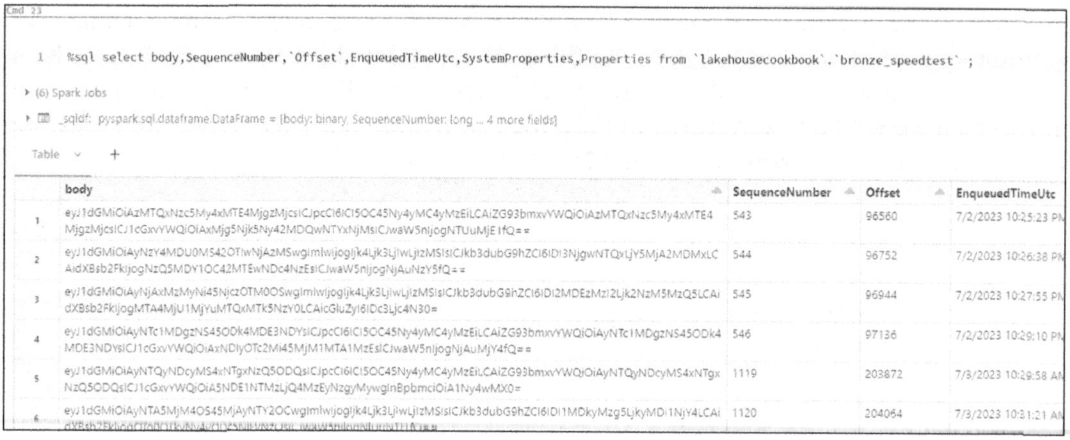

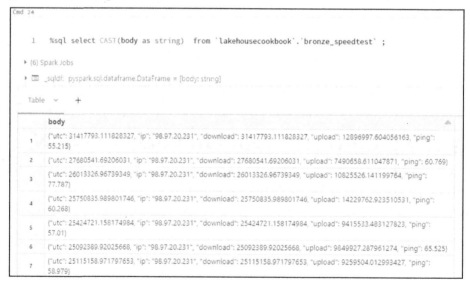

Figure 6.22: SQL view of the incrementally loaded table

This is because sending data in event streams often involves serializing it, adding tracking information, and other values necessary to ensure at least once delivery. In the case of Azure Event Hubs, the payload sent to the hub is converted to a binary array using Base64 encoding. If you search the Internet for ways to decode the body of the message, you may see overly complex solutions. The simplest way to decode the message body is to cast it as a string, as shown in *Figure 6.23*:

Figure 6.23: Decoding a Base64 body to string

Notice that the output is closer to that in *Figure 6.7*. However, it is still a string, not an object. In the Databricks Lakehouse we can interact with objects, like that in programming languages, like Python. To make the conversion seems straight forward, read the string as a JSON object and save it. The method typically used for this purpose is from_json.

This method is similar to json.loads in that both take a string and return an object. The difference is that from_json requires a schema. If you have the schema, it is not an issue. However, typically we do not have one. Luckily there is a way to get it programmatically, as shown in *Figure 6.24:*

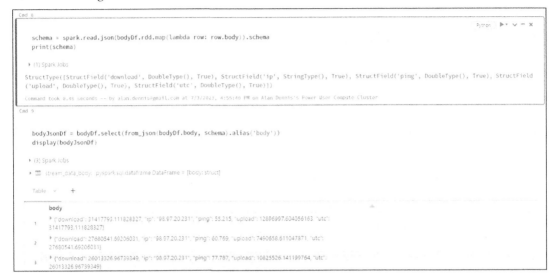

Figure 6.24: Determining a schema and using it in from_json

This relatively small amount of code can save a considerable amount of time. In command 8 we use **spark.read.json** to load the body field of our DataFrame and then expose the schema. Writing these schemas by hand is tedious and error-prone. We take that schema and use it in command 9 to use the **from_json** command and create a DataFrame with a single column called **body**. Notice the small triangle by each row. That indicates that the field is an object. You can expand that row and see the sub elements of that object, as shown in *Figure 6.25:*

```
      body
  ▼ object
        download: 31417793.111828327
        ip: "98.97.20.231"
  1     ping: 55.215
        upload: 12896997.604056163
        utc: 31417793.111828327
```

Figure 6.25: Sub elements of an object

This is interesting, however not as interesting as applying math operation on using dot notation, as shown in *Figure 6.26:*

```
Cmd 9

    tablePath="dbfs:/mnt/lakehousecookbook/bronze/EventHub/SpeedJson"
    tableComment = "Json version of speed table"
    bodyJsonDf.write.mode("overwrite").option("path",tablePath).option("overwriteSchema", "true").option("comments", tableComment).saveAsTable
    ("`lakehousecookbook`.`bronze_speedtest_json`")

  ▸ (6) Spark Jobs

  Command took 12.59 seconds -- by alan.dennis@gmail.com at 7/3/2023, 5:17:08 PM on Alan Dennis's Power User Compute Cluster

Cmd 10

    %sql select avg(body.download)/1024/1024 avgMbs from `lakehousecookbook`.`bronze_speedtest_json`

  ▸ (5) Spark Jobs

  ▸ ▦ _sqldf: pyspark.sql.dataframe.DataFrame = [avgMbs: double]

    Table  ∨    +

        avgMbs                 ▲
  1   16.1418665079944
```

Figure 6.26: Accessing nested values using dot notation

In command 9 we create a table to save the value as objects. In command 10 we compute the average download value in bits per second, and then convert it to megabytes per second. One option is to explode the fields within a nested structure to columns. That is appropriate in situations where the values are highly used and computationally expensive to access. If you are unsure if the values will be used, often you leave them in the object structure. Ideally, this transformation would be done as part of incremental ingestion. If not, then it would be performed as incremental refinement. To perform that operation, we would need to utilize a watermark table, to ensure we process values once. We have finally made sense of the incrementally loaded data. We will now shift our focus to full loading of data.

Recipes 53: Full load of files

We are revisiting fully loading tables. We talked about it in *Chapter 4, Data Profiling and Modeling in the Lakehouse*. We return to the topic with a few modifications. The code we used earlier was a bit simplistic. We will build on that learning and utilize a method to do our loading. We will start by revisiting converting Base64 encoded payloads to usable objects. Much of the code will look familiar, but it is presented in a combined function, as seen in *Figure 6.27*:

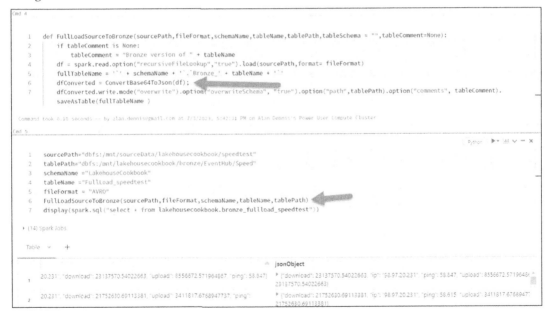

Figure 6.27: *Function to convert Base64 encoded text to a JSON object*

You can see that all the code in the function was used in Recipe 51. However, we now have an easy to call method that converts our encoded data to a usable object, as shown in *Figure 6.28*:

Figure 6.28: *Full load of a table calling ConvertBase64ToJson*

The important commands are highlighted in commands 4 and 5. In command 5, line 6 invokes the function to perform a full load of the files from source and create a table. In command 4 we see the call to convert the encoded body field to an object. This approach adds columns to the DataFrame. Likely, you will want to remove the columns that were added by Event Hub.

At this point we have loaded files both incrementally and fully. However, it was a consider amount of effort. For those using the helpers we constructed, it will be simpler. Databricks has created a tool to treat data storage as a stream. We will discuss Databricks Autoload in detail in the next section. You will see it has considerable advantages over doing incremental ingestion yourself.

Loading files using Auto Loader

Databricks Auto Loader is a proprietary solution for loading files from cloud storage systems, such as AWS S3, ADLS Gen2, GCS, and other cloud-based storage systems. It allows us to treat a file system as a stream and process it like any other. This approach simplifies ingestion and reduces the amount of required code in Recipe 50 dramatically. In the next few sections, we will explore Auto Loader and apply it to several situations.

Auto Loader overview

Auto Loader is a useful tool. It allows reading files in JSON, CSV, PARQUET, AVRO, ORC, TEXT, and BINARY format. We access those files using Spark Structured Streaming. Internally, Auto Loader keeps track of the ingestion process using RocksDB in a checkpoint location specified in the Auto Loader pipeline. This is like our watermarks table in Recipe 50. This checkpointing mechanism ensures once, and only once, ingestion of data. The real power of Auto Loader is that it makes the work we did in Recipe 50 look simple, as we will see in the next section.

Recipe 54: Incremental ingestion of files Avro using Auto Loader in Python

Databricks Auto Loader is a significant element of the Lakehouse platform. It is often taken for granted, in part because it works well. Auto Loader lets you treat a directory, and arriving files, as a stream. This means you can read from it and get only those records which are new since the last time you checked. This is accomplished by using checkpoints to record your progress. The overall result is that the amount of code required to incrementally ingest a file-based system is significantly reduced, as you can see in *Figure 6.29:*

```
Cmd 7
 1   def CreateTableFromFile(cloudFilesformat,sourcePath,filePath,schema,tableName,schemaHints= None,readOptions=None):
 2       if not tableName.startswith("bronze_"):
 3           tableName = "bronze_" + tableName
 4       schemaLocation = filePath.replace("/bronze/","/schemas_bronze/")
 5       checkpointLocation =filePath.replace("/bronze/","/checkpoints_bronze/")
 6       dbutils.fs.mkdirs(schemaLocation)
 7       dbutils.fs.mkdirs(checkpointLocation)
 8       # Setup the Input Stream
 9       dataStreamReader = spark.readStream.format("cloudFiles").option("mergeSchema", "true").option("cloudFiles.inferColumnTypes", "true")
10       dataStreamReader = dataStreamReader.option("cloudFiles.format", cloudFilesformat).option("cloudFiles.schemaLocation",schemaLocation)
11       if schemaHints is not None:
12           dataStreamReader = dataStreamReader.option("cloudFiles.schemaHints", schemaHints)
13       else:
14           dataStreamReader = dataStreamReader.option("delta.columnMapping.mode", "name")
15       if readOptions is not None:
16           dataStreamReader = dataStreamReader.options(**readOptions)
17       df = dataStreamReader.load(sourcePath)
18       # Read the stream and create the DataFrame
19       result = (df.writeStream.trigger(once=True).format("delta").outputMode("append").option("checkpointLocation", checkpointLocation)
20                 .option("mergeSchema", "true").option("path", filePath).toTable(schema + "."+ tableName))
21       result.awaitTermination()
22       EnsureCDFIsOn(schema,tableName)
23       return result
```

Figure 6.29: Function using autoloader to incrementally retrieve files from a mount point

The most important lines are highlighted with arrows. The first part of the function (lines 1 to 7) is used to construct the path to the checkpoint and schema directories. As we did with Recipe 51, Auto Loader determines the schema of input (when possible) and stores it if a location is specified. Also, as mentioned previously, checkpoints are essential for incremental processing. We must tell Auto Loader where to write its checkpoint files, by specifying a checkpoint location. Lines 9 through 17 configure the reading data stream reader. You can tell that we are using Auto Loader by seeing that the **cloudFiles** format is being used, as shown on line 9. Once we have the data reader configure, we configure the data writer (lines 19 and 20). One part of Auto Loader that can be daunting is that you are writing a streaming application. It is a simple one, but you are very much creating a stream to serialize to a table. Because of that, we must wait for the streaming job to terminate, using the awaitTermination statement on line 21. Notice on line 19, we use the statement **trigger** with the parameter once being **True**. This tells Spark to run this until the data is exhausted or until some other terminating condition is met. Invoking the function is a little different, in that you will see progress as the method executes, as shown in *Figure 6.29:*

```
Cmd 8
 1   sourcePath = "/mnt/sourceData/lakehousecookbook/speedtest"
 2   bronzePath = "/mnt/lakehousecookbook/bronze/AlanDesktop/EventHubSource/SpeedTestAutoLoader/"
 3   result = CreateTableFromFile("avro",sourcePath,bronzePath,"lakehousecookbook","SpeedTestAutoLoader")
 4   display(spark.sql("SELECT * FROM lakehousecookbook.bronze_speedtestautoloader order by EnqueuedTimeUtc desc"))

Cancel   • Listing the input directory to include existing files to streaming source.
```

Figure 6.30: CreateTableFromFile running

Once the command completes, the results are like other methods we have discussed in this book, as shown in *Figure 6.31:*

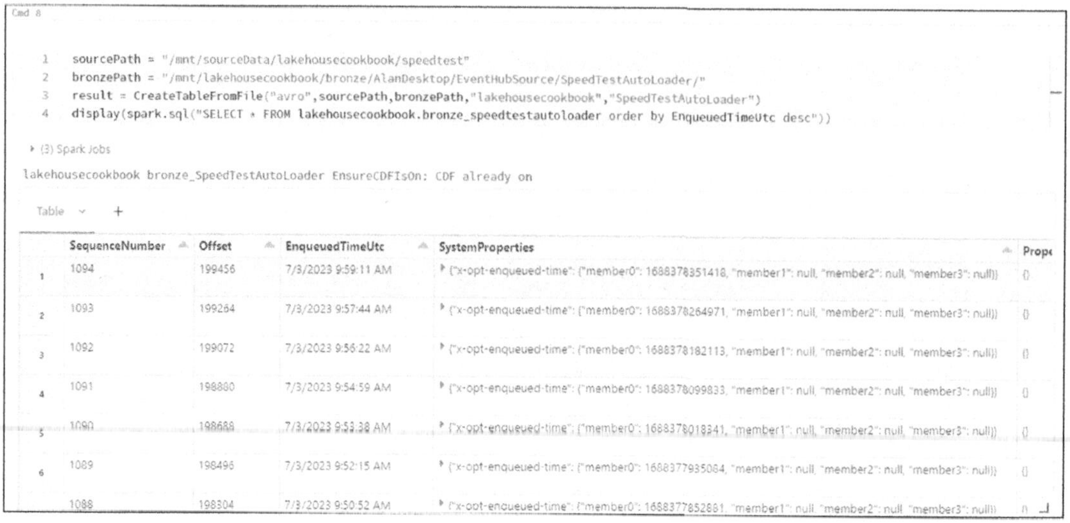

Figure 6.31: Results of reading folder incrementally with Auto Loader

We have successfully read a collection of AVRO files incrementally and populated a Bronze table. In the next section, we will repeat the process using CSV files.

Recipe 55: Incremental ingestion of CSV files using Auto Loader in Python

Earlier in this chapter we discussed incremental ingestion using the example of famous employees. We will revisit that example from an incremental ingestion perspective. For convenience, our data is housed in an Excel spreadsheet, as shown in *Figure 6.32:*

	A	B	C	D	E	F	G	H	I	J	K	L
1	EmployeeId	FirstName	LastName	Address1	Address2	City	State	PostalCode	CreatedOn	ModifiedOn	CreatedBy	ModifiedBy
2	1	Leonardo	da Vinci	123 First St.		Seattle	WA	98101	12/31/2024	12/31/2024	Admin	Admin
3	2	Napoleon	Bonaparte	234 Second St.		Seattle	WA	98101	12/31/2024	12/31/2024	Admin	Admin
4	3	Charles	Darwin	345 Third St.		Seattle	WA	98102	12/31/2024	12/31/2024	Admin	Admin
5	4	Albert	Einstein	456 Fourth St.		Seattle	WA	98103	12/31/2024	12/31/2024	Admin	Admin
6	5	Thomas	Jefferson	678 Fifth St.		Seattle	WA	98104	12/31/2024	12/31/2024	Admin	Admin

Figure 6.32: Excel spreadsheet of employee data

We are using Excel because it is easy to go from spreadsheet to CSV. While we would like to tell you that you will never encounter data housed in Excel in a commercial environment, that is sadly untrue. In Excel, generating a CSV file from a spreadsheet is as easy as selecting File, and Save a Copy and change the file format to CSV. In our example, we place the CSV in a storage account using the storage browser. As shown in *Figure 6.33:*

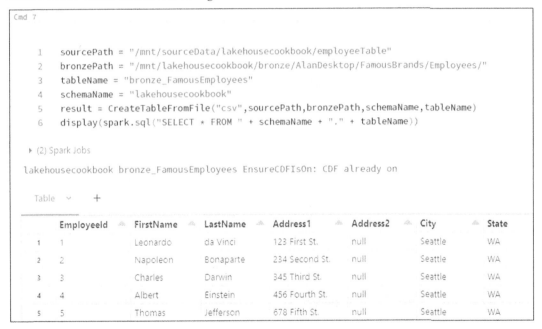

Figure 6.33: *Storage browser listing of employee files*

Notice the **Upload** function at the top and middle of the form. This makes it simple to upload data, and the **Add Directory** function allows you to create the directory structure. As you can see, we have already placed a file in the folder. Now, we need to convert it to a Bronze Delta table, as shown in *Figure 6.34*:

```
Cmd 7

1    sourcePath = "/mnt/sourceData/lakehousecookbook/employeeTable"
2    bronzePath = "/mnt/lakehousecookbook/bronze/AlanDesktop/FamousBrands/Employees/"
3    tableName = "bronze_FamousEmployees"
4    schemaName = "lakehousecookbook"
5    result = CreateTableFromFile("csv",sourcePath,bronzePath,schemaName,tableName)
6    display(spark.sql("SELECT * FROM " + schemaName + "." + tableName))

▶ (2) Spark Jobs

lakehousecookbook bronze_FamousEmployees EnsureCDFIsOn: CDF already on

Table  ∨    +
```

	EmployeeId	FirstName	LastName	Address1	Address2	City	State
1	1	Leonardo	da Vinci	123 First St.	null	Seattle	WA
2	2	Napoleon	Bonaparte	234 Second St.	null	Seattle	WA
3	3	Charles	Darwin	345 Third St.	null	Seattle	WA
4	4	Albert	Einstein	456 Fourth St.	null	Seattle	WA
5	5	Thomas	Jefferson	678 Fifth St.	null	Seattle	WA

Figure 6.34: *Using helper method to create Bronze table from CSV*

You can see that we are using the same method as that in Recipe 52. The function **CreateTableFromFile** is useful enough to move it to our Utilities notebook. It will need some extension over time, but it is useful as it is. We can see that all the records made it into our table. Auto Loader does schema inference, as we can see in *Figure 6.35*:

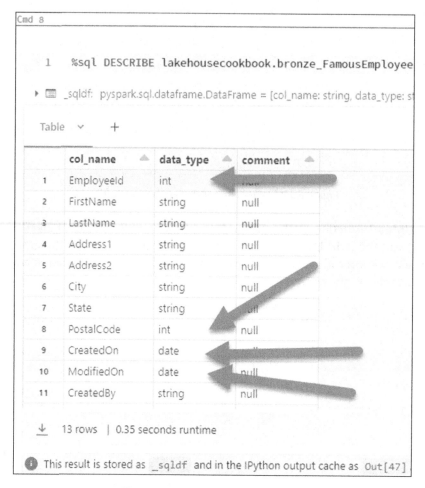

Figure 6.35: Employee table structure

Notice the columns that are not strings. This is important because CSV does not include schema information. Instead, Auto Loader examined the data and saw that id, for example, had only numeric values. Schema inference is not always successful, but it is a time saver.

Returning to our example that **Albert** moved, and we updated his address, as shown in *Figure 6.36:*

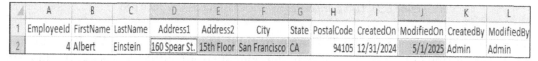

Figure 6.36: Updated address record

After creating and uploading the CSV to the storage account, we are ready to re-run our ingestion notebook, as shown in *Figure 6.37:*

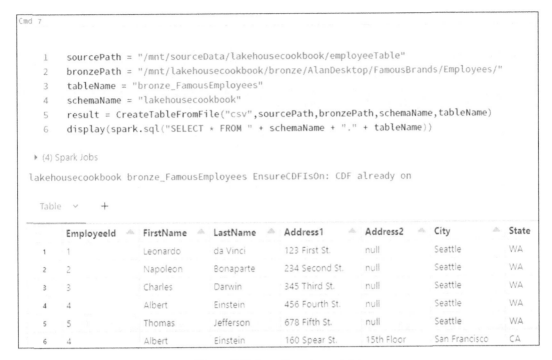

Figure 6.37: Ingesting changed data

Recall that in Bronze tables, we do have data duplication. We could handle this de-duplication process ourselves, by using constructs such as windows and ranking, but the performance would decrease as the table size grows. The solution is to utilize Delta's **Change Data Feed** (CDF) mechanism. We will discuss CDF and the process to remove duplications in depth in *Chapter 7, Transforming to Create Silver*. In the next section, we will explore Databrick's **Delta Live Tables** (DLT) and describe how to create pipelines to simplify ingestion.

Loading files using Delta Live Tables

Delta Live Tables (DLT) is a declarative method of constructing data pipelines. It simplifies data engineering and operations by providing a graphical representation of the execution of pipelines. We will provide an overview of DLT, and then use it to perform various types of ingestion.

Delta Live Tables overview

DLT is a powerful mechanism to ingest and refine data. We will revisit it multiple times in coming chapters. It supplies a simpler alternative than writing custom code or developing your own framework. There is an added cost to use DLT, but the value it returns makes it an attractive solution.

There are two ways you can construct DLT pipelines, using SQL or a Python API. Understand that when you write notebooks that will become DLT pipelines, the code you are writing is used to construct the pipelines but is not executed directly (especially in the case of SQL). In the coming sections we will utilize both approaches, so you can determine which is best for you. Often, people are stronger in SQL and prefer that approach. Others may prefer the power of the Python API approach.

Recipe 56: Using the DLT SQL API to ingest JSON

We start creating a DLT pipeline by creating a Databricks notebook. In that notebook, we use a variation of the CREATE TABLE command we have previously used, as shown in *Figure 6.38*:

```
Cmd 2

 1   CREATE STREAMING LIVE TABLE Bronze_Employee_DLT
 2   COMMENT "Famous Brands Employee Table"
 3   TBLPROPERTIES ("quality" = "bronze")
 4   AS
 5   SELECT * FROM cloud_files("dbfs:/mnt/sourceData/lakehousecookbook/employeeJson/","json",
 6       map('multiline', 'true',
 7       'recursiveFileLookup','true',
 8       'schemaEvolutionMode','rescue',
 9       'autoMerge','true',
10       'cloudFiles.inferColumnTypes', 'true'));
```

Figure 6.38: Create DLT Table

Remember that the purpose of the SQL in *Figure 6.38* is to tell DLT what you want to occur. The code itself is not executed. Rather it lets DLT know what you would like to occur. The syntax is very similar to traditional SQL **CREATE Table**. Note the addition of the words STREAMING LIVE to the table creation statement. This indicates that this table is a Delta Live Table. Also, notice the TBLPROPERTIES keyword, where we set the quality to Bronze. This is for information and is not used programmatically. Also notice the **MAP** starting on line 6. Many of these values are not required, as they may be the default. The purpose is to show how we control the options in DLT. For our data, we do need the multiline setting, as our JSON spans multiple lines. Also notice that we set the schemaEvolutionMode to rescue. This causes an additional column to be added to the Bronze table that would contain any columns that are not in the schema. The idea is to allow you to recover from schema changes without missing data.

Given the amount of work that was required for us to manage our own incrementally updating table in Recipe 49, you can see how much less effort was required to configure incremental ingestion files using DLT. To use the notebook, we need to create a pipeline. We do this in the **Workflows** section, and under the **Delta Live Tables** tab, as shown in *Figure 6.39*:

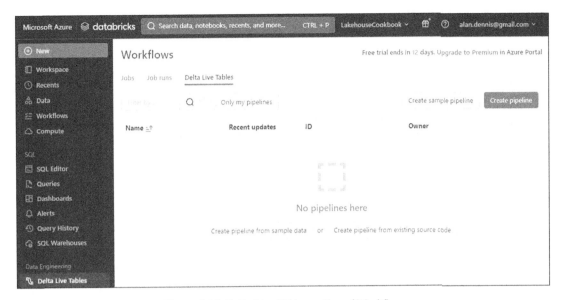

Figure 6.39: Delta Live Tables section of Workflows

You can also navigate to the page by clicking on **Delta Live Tables** in the left navigation, if you have the new UI enabled. As of this writing, near the bottom of the page is a control that enables a unified UI, as shown in *Figure 6.40:*

Figure 6.40: Controlling the UI

We create a pipeline by clicking the **Create pipeline** button in the upper right corner of the page. After clicking the button, we see a page that allows us to enter the **pipeline's name**, select the **product edition**, and select the **notebooks** we wish to use as the source code for the pipeline, as seen in *Figure 6.41:*

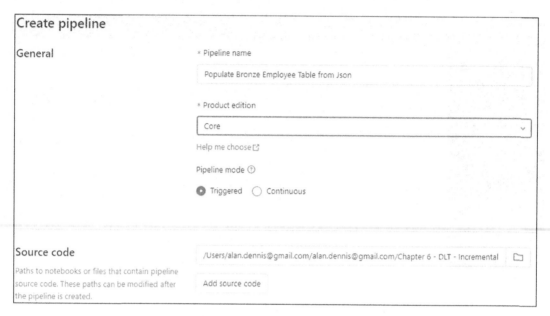

Figure 6.41: Configure the pipeline

There are several important elements on this page. The first is the product edition. Databricks has three editions of DLT. The main difference is the support for certain functions. The advanced product has all features enabled. Moving down to pro you lose support for expectation rules and policies, and data quality observability. We will discuss expectations in depth in *Chapter 7, Transforming to Create Silver*. For now, understand they are how we express the conditions that must be met for data to be inserted into a table. Moving from pro to core removes **Change Data Capture (CDC)** and **Slowly Changing Dimension (SCD)** features. Depending on your cloud provider, the pricing varies significantly from core to advanced, with advanced being almost twice as expensive. You can learn more about the product editions at **https://www.databricks.com/product/pricing/delta-live**. For our purposes, core is sufficient.

The next important thing to notice is the pipeline mode. This selection controls the execution model of your pipeline. The choices are triggered and continuous. For most applications, triggered is sufficient. You would only select continuous if you were required to meet a **Service Level Agreement (SLA)**, such as tables must update within one minute. There is a considerable difference in cost between the two execution patterns.

Now that we have the pipeline's general information captured, we can move to source code and destination information, as shown in *Figure 6.42*:

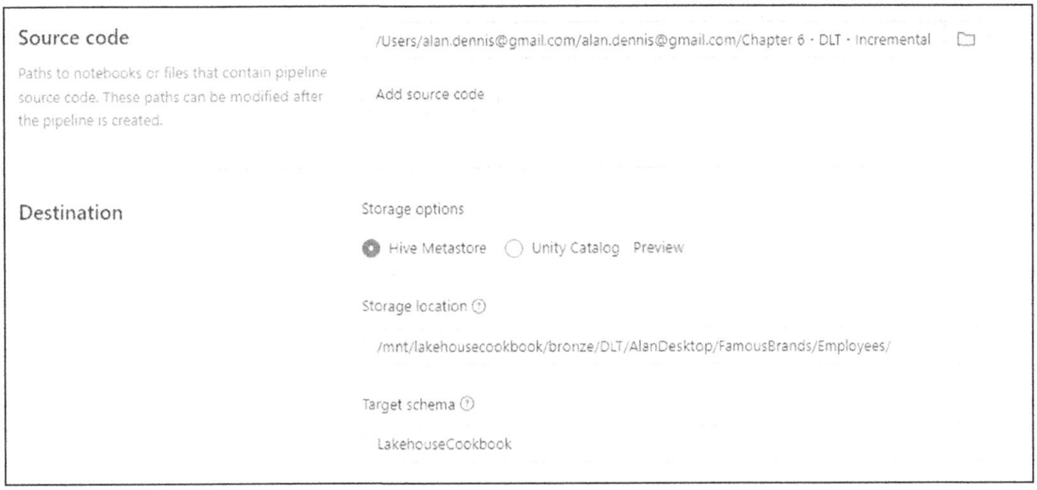

Figure 6.42: *Source code and destination information*

The **Source Code** section is where you reference the notebooks you wish to have evaluated to construct the pipeline. You can browse to them by clicking the folder icon, or you can paste the path the notebook in directly. To find the path to a notebook, you can click the **three dots** on the end of the notebook's name in the Workspace explorer and then select to **Copy** and then **Path**, as shown in *Figure 6.43*:

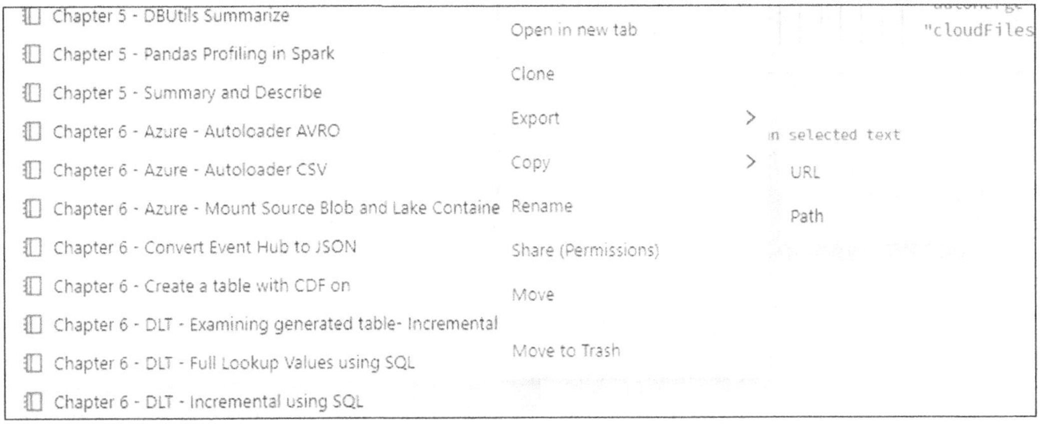

Figure 6.43: *Getting a notebook path*

Once you have supplied the paths of any notebooks you wish to include in the pipeline, you select the **storage** option. The choices are **Hive Metastore** and **Unity Catalog**. As of this writing, targeting Unity Catalog was in preview. For our case, we will select the Hive Metastore. You also have the choice of managing the storage location for the created files. In our case, we place it in a folder like that used in previous recipes. You also have the option of specifying the schema the table will be placed in. In our case we selected

LakehouseCookbook as our schema. We can now move on to configuring the **Compute** section of the pipeline, as shown in *Figure 6.44:*

Figure 6.44: Pipeline Compute section

You have the option to select a **Cluster policy** and **Cluster mode**. Cluster mode controls how the cluster handles load. The choices are a fixed size, which we selected. This means that regardless of the load on the cluster, it will stay at the size specified. As a review of how Spark works, each cluster has a driver node and one or more work nodes. When we set the **Cluster mode** to fixed size and specify one worker node, it means that there will be one driver node and one worker node. Ideally, you size the cluster using fixed size, as doing so will avoid cluster resizing, which can take considerable time. If you want the cluster to be able to change size, you have two choices to choose from **Enhanced and Legacy Autoscaling**. The advantage of autoscaling is that it can lower your cost if the workloads you are performing a change in load over the execution lifetime. Advanced auto-scaling improves on legacy auto-scaling by finding underutilized nodes. To learn more about autoscaling, visit **https://docs.databricks.com/delta-live-tables/auto-scaling. html**.

You also have the choice to **enable Photon**. Photon is at least two times faster than Scala-based Spark, and up to eight times faster for certain workloads. It also comes at a higher price. Typically, the faster execution time results in a lower overall cost. To learn more about Photon visit **https://www.databricks.com/product/photon**. You can assign tags to clusters. Tags are often used to track costs. Tags are name-value pairs. The last two section are **Notifications and Advanced**, as shown in *Figure 6.45:*

Notifications Preview   Add notification

Advanced   Configuration
                                         Add configuration

                                         Channel ⓘ
                                         Current   ⌄

Figure 6.45: Notifications and Advanced section

Clicking **Add notification** causes a text box to display, along with a set of checkboxes. These boxes control the type of notification that is sent, as shown in *Figure 6.46:*

Figure 6.46: Notifications section

Send emails on success may lead to people ignoring emails. Instead, it is best to send emails when there is a failure and intervention is required. Often, distribution lists are utilized for this purpose, rather than an individual's email address.

Advanced is the last section when creating a pipeline. You can **add configuration** values, which are name value pairs. These values will be passed to the Spark cluster as configuration values. The **Channels** option lets you determine the runtime to utilize. Selecting **preview** causes a newer, and possibly less stable, runtime to be utilized. You can learn more about channels at **https://docs.databricks.com/release-notes/delta-live-tables**.

We can now click **create** and create our pipeline. Initially, you will see an empty canvas, with a message saying the graph will be generated when the pipeline starts. To start the pipeline, click the **start** button in the upper right-hand corner, as shown in *Figure 6.47:*

Figure 6.47: *Pipeline overview page*

Once you click Start, you will see messages describing progress of executing the pipeline. It takes a while to provision the resources. Once the resources are provisioned, the cluster is initialized. Then the pipeline will run and then the graph will be rendered on the screen. The graph is a dependency graph, showing the order of execution and you will also see **events** in the bottom panel, as shown in *Figure 6.48:*

Figure 6.48: *Pipeline status*

As execution progresses, additional status updates appear in the bottom of the screen. Eventually, if things go well, you will see several messages with the word COMPLETED in them. Also, you will see the status of the pipeline run turn to **completed** in the right side of the screen, as shown in *Figure 6.49*:

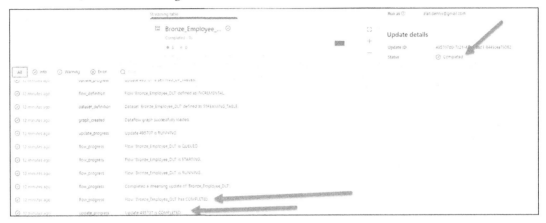

Figure 6.49: Successful creation of Bronze table using DLT

If we look at the newly created table, we will see the data is present, but the order of the columns has changed. This is a characteristic of JSON and should not impact processing. If a certain order is required, you can supply a schema in the notebook that contains the definition of the DLT. We can see that **Albert's address** has not changed, as shown in *Figure 6.50*:

	Address1	Address2	City	CreatedBy	CreatedOn	EmployeeId	FirstName	LastName	ModifiedBy	ModifiedOn	PostalCoc
1	123 First St.		Seattle	Admin	12/31/2024	1	Leonardo	da Vinci	Admin	12/31/2024	98101
2	234 Second St.		Seattle	Admin	12/31/2024	2	Napoleon	Bonaparte	Admin	12/31/2024	98101
3	345 Third St.		Seattle	Admin	12/31/2024	3	Charles	Darwin	Admin	12/31/2024	98102
4	456 Fourth St.		Seattle	Admin	12/31/2024	4	Albert	Einstein	Admin	12/31/2024	98103
5	678 Fifth St.		Seattle	Admin	12/31/2024	5	Thomas	Jefferson	Admin	12/31/2024	98104

Figure 6.50: View of generated DLT data

To prove out the incremental nature of file processing, we create a new folder and upload the file with a single record in it, reflecting the updated address for Albert. We can then re-execute the pipeline by clicking the Run button. Recall that this DLT is configured to run when triggered. We can schedule the pipeline by clicking the Schedule button next to the Run button, as shown in *Figure 6.51*:

Figure 6.51: *Schedule management of DLT*

Clicking Add a Schedule brings up a form where you can supply a name for the job, set the schedule, and control who is notified of job activity, as shown in *Figure 6.52*:

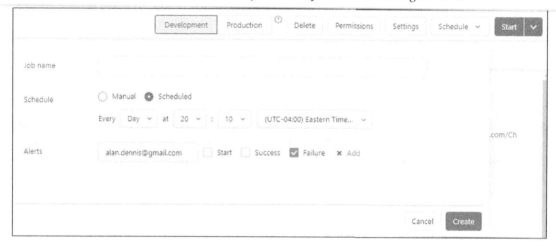

Figure 6.52: *Scheduling a job*

We will discuss scheduling in more detail in *Chapter 14, Operations.*

Back to our update testing, we can check to see that the table has been updated by re-running our **select** statement, as shown in *Figure 6.53*:

CreatedBy	CreatedOn	EmployeeId	FirstName	LastNam
Admin	12/31/2024	1	Leonardo	da Vinci
Admin	12/31/2024	2	Napoleon	Bonapart
Admin	12/31/2024	3	Charles	Darwin
Admin	12/31/2024	4	Albert	Einstein

Figure 6.53: *Listing contents of Bronze DLT to see updates*

We have now successfully created a notebook that describes the DLT operations we want to perform, created a pipeline using that notebook and tested it. In the **next** section we will repeat the process using the Python API approach.

Recipe 57: Incremental ingestion using DLT using Python API

Python is a popular language for data engineering. Databricks included support for it when they were designing DLT's APIs. To create a DLT pipeline, we start by defining the table in a Python cell, as shown in *Figure 6.54*:

```python
import dlt
@dlt.table( comment="Famous Brands Employee Table using Python DLT API",
    table_properties=("delta.enableChangeDataFeed": "true", "quality": "bronze")]hive_metastore.lakehousecookbook.employee_dlt_python)
def employee_dlt_python():
    return spark.readStream.format("cloudFiles").option("multiline", "true").option("cloudFiles.format", "json").load("dbfs:/mnt/sourceData/
    lakehousecookbook/employeeJson/")
```

Figure 6.54: *Defining a DLT pipeline using Python*

The first line imports the dlt library. We use it to create the definition of the table. We define our DLT table by creating a function that returns a DataFrame. The name of the function becomes the name of the table. We can add comments and table properties by passing them as parameters to @dlt.table. We use Auto Loader in this example to incrementally load the files. Registering this as a DLT pipeline is the same as in Recipe 54. We have successfully created a DLT pipeline using the Python API. Using Data Explorer, we can see that the data is what we expect and that the comment was added, as shown in *Figure 6.55*:

lakehousecookbook ›
🔲 lakehousecookbook.bronze_employee_dlt_python

△ Delta △ …. ⌄ 4.1KiB, 1 file ○ Hide comment

📄 Famous Brands Employee Table using Python DLT API

Columns | Sample Data | Details | Permissions | History

Address1	Address2	City	CreatedBy	CreatedOn	EmployeeId	FirstName	LastName	ModifiedBy	ModifiedOn	PostalCode	State	_rescued_data
160 Spear St.	15th Floor	San Francisco	Admin	12/31/2024	4	Albert	Einstein	Admin	5/1/2025	94105	CA	
123 First St.		Seattle	Admin	12/31/2024	1	Leonardo	da Vinci	Admin	12/31/2024	98101	WA	
234 Second St.		Seattle	Admin	12/31/2024	2	Napoleon	Bonaparte	Admin	12/31/2024	98101	WA	
345 Third St.		Seattle	Admin	12/31/2024	3	Charles	Darwin	Admin	12/31/2024	98102	WA	
456 Fourth St.		Seattle	Admin	12/31/2024	4	Albert	Einstein	Admin	12/31/2024	98103	WA	
678 Fifth St.		Seattle	Admin	12/31/2024	5	Thomas	Jefferson	Admin	12/31/2024	98104	WA	

Figure 6.55: *Data Explorer view of Python DLT API created table*

We have successfully created Delta tables using DLT's Python API. In the **next** section we will repeat the process, but instead of incremental ingestion we will fully load the files.

Recipe 58: Full ingestion using DLT using SQL API

Sometimes we need to load a file without using incremental ingestion. This is common with small files or files that infrequently change. For this example, we will use data related to fisheries and aquaculture infrastructure development from the Indian government website at **https://data.gov.in/catalog/fisheries-and-aquaculture-infrastructure-development-fund-fidf-scheme**.

To access the file, we can use a select statement that references a JSON file, as shown in *Figure 6.56*:

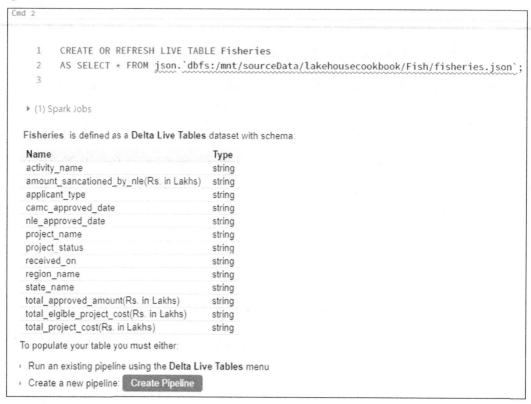

Figure 6.56: Create full load DLT using SQL

Notice the use of JSON and the backtick to specify the file to load. This is the preferred way to load small files in DLT. For more on this approach see **https://docs.databricks.com/delta-live-tables/load.html**.

After running the DLT pipeline we can see that we constructed a materialized view, as shown in *Figure 6.57*:

Figure 6.57: DLT materialized view

A materialized view saves data, resulting in better performance than views. To learn more about materialized views, views, and tables, see: **https://docs.databricks.com/delta-live-tables/transform.html**.

Recipe 59: Full ingestion using DLT using Python API

To load a small or static file using the DLT Python APIs, we use spark.read command, as shown in *Figure 6.58:*

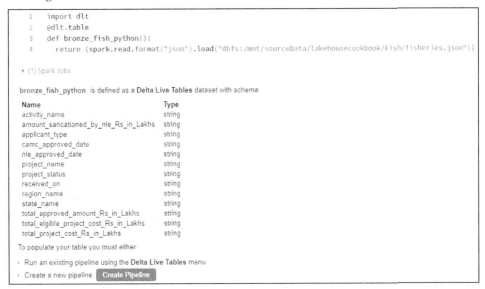

Figure 6.58: Create full load DLT using Python

The syntax is similar to that of the incremental load, but relies on spark.read instead of Auto Loader. This approach is appropriate if the files are small, such as lookups. We have now covered the common usage patterns of DLT. There are many other features in the offering, and we will return to them in *Chapter 7, Transforming to Create Silver* and in *Chapter 8, Transforming to Create Gold for Business Purposes*. In the next section, we will explore streaming ingestion using DLT and using Spark Structured Streaming.

Loading streaming data

Stream processing is an essential element of the Lakehouse architecture. A stream can be viewed as a continually growing table. The idea is that each time you look for records, there may be new ones since the last time you checked. You can process streams in a continuous fashion, or you can start a job, connect to the stream, retrieve records, and then end the process. Which pattern depends on cost constraints and the freshens of the data demands.

Before we start our discussion of using DLT to process streams, we need to cover parameterizing pipeline. This is similar in concept to the use of widgets in notebooks. In the next recipe, we will review how to use parameters and why it is important.

Recipe 60: Parameterizing pipelines

Most programming environments support some form of parameters. It allows you to develop generalized solutions and reuse them by varying the parameters. We can recall that in *Figure 6.45* we discussed the **Advanced** section of the DLT pipeline configuration page. One of the items in that page is the **Advanced** section. Within that section is a subsection called configuration which is used to set name-value pairs passed to the Spark cluster. DLT uses this mechanism to pass values to pipelines during their execution. We can see examples of these settings in *Figure 6.59:*

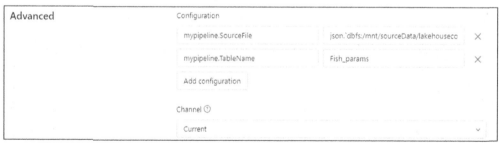

Figure 6.59: DLT configuration

Using these values differs between the SQL DLT API and the Python version. The SQL API uses a tag approach, as shown in *Figure 6.60:*

```
Cmd 2

  1    CREATE OR REFRESH LIVE TABLE ${mypipeline.TableName}
  2    AS SELECT * FROM ${mypipeline.SourceFile}
```

Figure 6.60: Retrieving a configuration parameter in DLT SQL

The tags are enclosed within ${}.Using this approach, you can create multiple pipelines using the same notebook but with different parameters. The Python approach relies on using the spark.conf.get function. The result of this function is assigned to a variable. That variable is then used to control the execution, as shown in *Figure 6:61:*

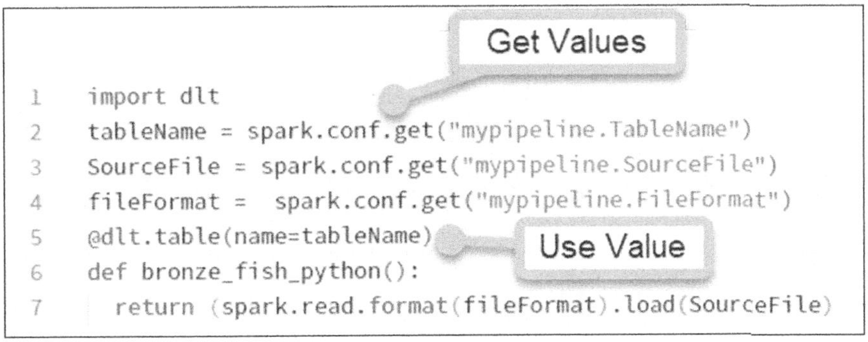

```
1   import dlt
2   tableName = spark.conf.get("mypipeline.TableName")
3   SourceFile = spark.conf.get("mypipeline.SourceFile")
4   fileFormat = spark.conf.get("mypipeline.FileFormat")
5   @dlt.table(name=tableName)
6   def bronze_fish_python():
7       return (spark.read.format(fileFormat).load(SourceFile)
```

Figure 6.61: Using configuration parameters using DLT's Python API

Now that we have a means to send parameters to a DLT pipeline, we can use this approach to configure our Event Hub Listener. In the next section, we will continue our discussion of DLT and use it to retrieve values from an Event Hub.

Recipe 61: Stream processing with DLT Python API

Event Hub is a common communication in the Azure environment. We will revisit streaming using Kafka in *Chapter 15, Tips, Tricks, Troubleshooting, and Best Practices.* For now, we will use an example from Microsoft and Databricks for inspiration. We have modified it, but you find the original version at:

https://learn.microsoft.com/en-us/azure/databricks/delta-live-tables/event-hubs

For this example, we revisit the speed test Event Hub we used earlier in the chapter. This time, we connect directly to the Event Hub rather than relying on Event Hub Capture. To connect to an Event Hub, we need some information. The easiest way to use that information is to use a connection string, sometimes referred to as connect string. To get a connection string for an Event Hub, you need to create or use a shared access policy, as shown in *Figure 6.62:*

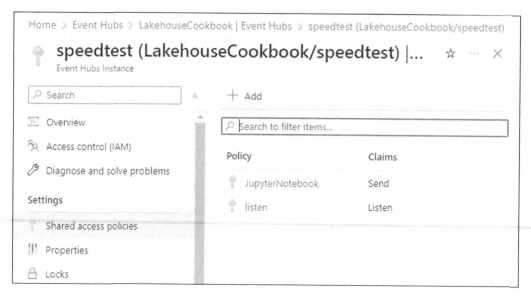

Figure 6.62: Event hub shared access policies

Shared access policies are used to control types of operations that are allowed, such as manage, send, or listen. In our case, we want to listen to the Event Hub so we will use the **Listen** policy, as show in *Figure 6.63*:

Figure 6.63: Event hub listen policy

We will use the primary connection string in this and the next example. As with all sensitive values, we store this in a secret store, in this case Azure Key Vault. Since we have a secret scope linked to it, that makes the connection string available in Databricks. We will break down the DLT source notebook into manageable section, discussing each. We start with retrieving the Event Hub configuration information, as shown in *Figure 6.64*:

```
1    import dlt
2    import pyspark.sql.types as T
3    from pyspark.sql.functions import *
4
5    # Event Hubs configuration
6    EH_NAMESPACE              = spark.conf.get("iot.ingestion.eh.namespace")
7    EH_NAME                   = spark.conf.get("iot.ingestion.eh.name")
8    EH_CONN_STRING            = spark.conf.get("iot.ingestion.eh.connectstringSecretName")
9    SECRET_SCOPE              = spark.conf.get("io.ingestion.eh.secretsScopeName")
10   EH_CONN_STR               = dbutils.secrets.get(scope= SECRET_SCOPE, key = EH_CONN_STRING)
11   # Kafka Consumer configuration
12
```

Non-sensitive configuration values

Name of the secret containing the event hub connection string

Figure 6.64: *DLT streaming example, retrieving values from key vault via secret scope*

In lines 6 to 8, we retrieve information needed to connect to the Event Hub that are not considered sensitive. These values often appear inline in code. The connection string contains sensitive information and is stored in the key vault. We retrieve it by getting the secret's name in line 10, and then we use **dbutils.secrets.get** to retrieve the actual value. Next, we create an object that contains the Kafka connection information, as shown in *Figure 6.65*:

```
13   KAFKA_OPTIONS = {
14     "kafka.bootstrap.servers"   : f"{EH_NAMESPACE}.servicebus.windows.net:9093",
15     "subscribe"                 : EH_NAME,
16     "kafka.sasl.mechanism"      : "PLAIN",
17     "kafka.security.protocol"   : "SASL_SSL",
18     "kafka.sasl.jaas.config"    : f"kafkashaded.org.apache.kafka.common.security.plain.PlainLoginModule required username=\"$ConnectionString\" password=\"{EH_CONN_STR}\";",
19     "kafka.request.timeout.ms"  : spark.conf.get("iot.ingestion.kafka.requestTimeout"),
20     "kafka.session.timeout.ms"  : spark.conf.get("iot.ingestion.kafka.sessionTimeout"),
21     "maxOffsetsPerTrigger"      : spark.conf.get("iot.ingestion.spark.maxOffsetsPerTrigger"),
22     "failOnDataLoss"            : spark.conf.get("iot.ingestion.spark.failOnDataLoss"),
23     "startingOffsets"           : spark.conf.get("iot.ingestion.spark.startingOffsets")
24   }
```

Connection string from line 10

Figure 6.65: *Set Kafka connection information*

The Spark specific configuration settings (such as **startingOffsets**) are described in detail at **https://spark.apache.org/docs/2.2.0/structured-streaming-kafka-integration. html**. They control how communication with the event hub is performed. Line 18 contains the connection string, supplied as a password.

Recall that we are sending a JSON object. It has five fields that are: utc (big integer), ip (string), upload, download, and ping (doubles), as shown in *Figure 6.66*:

```
{
    "utc": 1688827748,
    "ip": "98.97.19.239",
    "download": 17897527.560420774,
    "upload": 9300811.476445962,
    "ping": 48.418
}
```

Figure 6.66: *Example payload*

We want to convert the payload we receive back to that structure. To do that, we use a transformation that will be applied during ingestion, as shown in *Figure 6.67*:

```
25
26    # PAYLOAD SCHEMA - Updated for Speed Test                                    Schema of
27    payload_ddl = """utc long, ip STRING,download DOUBLE, upload DOUBLE, ping DOUBLE"""    our Event
28    payload_schema = T._parse_datatype_string(payload_ddl)                         Stream
29       ⌷
30    # Basic record parsing and adding ETL audit columns
31    def parse(df):                                                        Convert string to
32       return (df                                                         JSON objects
33         .withColumn("records", col("value").cast("string"))
34         .withColumn("parsed_records", from_json(col("records"), payload_schema))
35         .withColumn("UTC_timestamp", expr("cast(from_unixtime(parsed_records.utc) as timestamp)"))
36         .withColumn("eh_enqueued_timestamp", expr("timestamp"))
37         .withColumn("eh_enqueued_date", expr("to_date(timestamp)"))
38         .withColumn("etl_rec_uuid", expr("uuid()"))
39    )
40
```

Figure 6.67: Transformation method named parse

Note that lines 27 and 28 define a schema that matches that of *Figure 6.66*. Line 33 converts the value encoded to a string from Base64 encoding. Line 34 uses the schema we defined on 27 and 28 to convert the string body to a JSON object. Line 35 converts the utc property that was just created to a timestamp from a long. These transformations make the resulting table more usable and returns it to the object that was serialized and added to the Event Hub. Next, we pull it all together by creating our DLT table, as shown in *Figure 6.68*:

```
41    @dlt.create_table(
42       comment="Speedtest",  table_properties={"quality": "bronze","pipelines.reset.allowed": "false" },
43    )
44    def bronze_iot_speedtest():  return (
45       spark.readStream
46         .format("kafka")                    Use the options we defined earlier
47         .options(**KAFKA_OPTIONS)
48         .load()
49         .transform(parse)
50    )                                        Use the parse method to change the structure of table
```

Figure 6.68: Define the DLT that will be created

Line 41 begins the DLT definition that will be used when we create the DLT pipeline. Notice that we use the Kafka options we defined earlier on line 47. On line 49, we add a transform supplying the function that deserializes the message payload and converts the result to a JSON object using the supplied schema. The pipeline settings are like those we have used previously, supplying the required parameters, as shown in *Figure 6.69*:

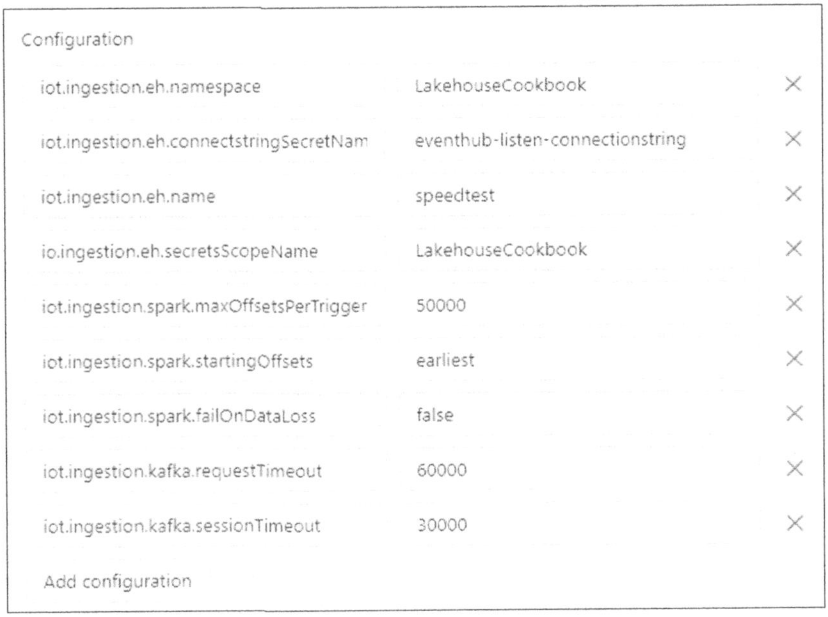

Figure 6.69: Properties of the DLT pipeline for event hub ingestion

These properties align with those which we are expecting in the source code we presented in *Figure 6.64*. The execution of the pipeline should not take more than a few seconds once the cluster is running. Selecting development mode in the top menu reduces restart time by keeping the cluster running.

Tip: Set a storage location, it makes it easier to remove the files if you drop the table.

We can examine the contents of the table using traditional SQL statement. The first thing we typically do when looking at a new dataset is to examine the schema. We can do that using the DESCRIBE command, as shown in *Figure 6.70:*

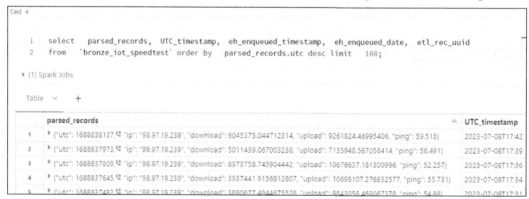

Cmd 3

```sql
I    DESCRIBE bronze_iot_speedtest
```

Table ∨   +

	col_name	data_type	comment
1	key	binary	null
2	value	binary	null
3	topic	string	null
4	partition	int	null
5	offset	bigint	null
6	timestamp	timestamp	null
7	timestampType	int	null
8	records	string	null
9	parsed_records	struct<utc:bigint,ip:string,download:double,upload:double,ping:double>	null
10	UTC_timestamp	timestamp	null
11	eh_enqueued_timestamp	timestamp	null
12	eh_enqueued_date	date	null
13	etl_rec_uuid	string	null

Notice the structure

Figure 6.70: *Describe the DLT pipeline created table*

Notice that row 9 contains the definition for the parse_records. Because we applied the parse transformation during ingestion we have a structure, rather than a string. We can use this functionality for simplified processing. Depending on the consumption model, we may leave the data nested. In part, accessing the values is simple, as shown in Figure 6.71:

Cmd 4

```sql
1    select    parsed_records,  UTC_timestamp,  eh_enqueued_timestamp,  eh_enqueued_date,  etl_rec_uuid
2    from    `bronze_iot_speedtest` order by    parsed_records.utc desc limit    100;
```

▶ (1) Spark Jobs

Table ∨   +

	parsed_records	UTC_timestamp
1	▶ {"utc": 1688838137, "ip": "98.97.19.239", "download": 6045375.044712314, "upload": 9261824.46995406, "ping": 59.515)	2023-07-08T17:42
2	▶ {"utc": 1688837973, "ip": "98.97.19.239", "download": 5011439.067003238, "upload": 7135948.567056414, "ping": 56.491)	2023-07-08T17:39
3	▶ {"utc": 1688837809, "ip": "98.97.19.239", "download": 6973758.745904442, "upload": 10676637.181300996, "ping": 52.257)	2023-07-08T17:36
4	▶ {"utc": 1688837645, "ip": "98.97.19.239", "download": 3937441.9156812807, "upload": 10698107.276832577, "ping": 55.731)	2023-07-08T17:34
5	▶ {"utc": 1688837482, "ip": "98.97.19.239", "download": 3880677.4944675528, "upload": 8843056.469067378, "ping": 54.88)	2023-07-08T17:31

Figure 6.71: *Using extract object values*

Notice that we are ordering by the utc value in the parsed_records column. This accessibility simplifies interaction with complex data. Also, if we wish to convert the values to columns, it is as easy as using a statement like parsed_records.*, as shown in *Figure 6.72*:

```
    1    select parsed_records.* from bronze_iot_speedtest
```

▸ (1) Spark Jobs

Table ⌄   +

	utc	ip	download	upload	ping
1	1688834152 ☎	98.97.19.239	9423401.082858438	6963407.276282442	63.407
2	1688834315 ☎	98.97.19.239	13869459.471134959	7094532.973217701	67.979

Figure 6.72: Expanding an object to columns

We can see that the values are present in the table and can be manipulated as needed. We have constructed a table using DLT pipelines from an Event Hub. In the next section, we will perform the same operation using Spark Structured Streaming.

Recipe 62: Using Spark structured streaming

In the previous section we covered connection string for Event Hubs. We will reuse that secret in the key vault in this example. To consume events using Spark Structured Streaming, we must be able to encrypt the connection string. To do this, we need to install a library on our cluster. We know the library's name (azure-eventhubs-spark_2.12), so we go to our cluster by navigating to the **Compute** section of the left navigation menu. Then we select the cluster we want to configure by clicking its name. On the cluster detail page, we click on **Libraries** in the top navigation, as shown in *Figure 6.73*:

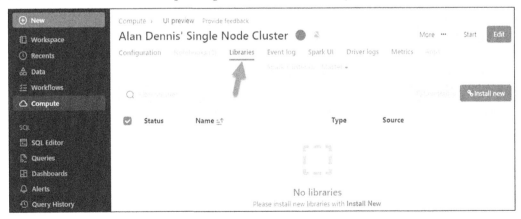

Figure 6.73: Libraries section of the cluster detail page

Clicking the Install new button (on the right side of the screen) bring ups the **Install** library page, as shown in *Figure 6.74*:

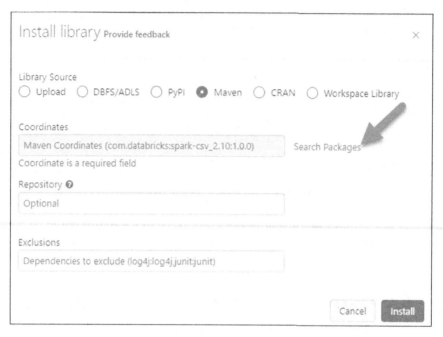

Figure 6.74: Install Library

Switch the **Library Source** to **Maven**. If you do not know the Mavin coordinates, click on the Search Packages text, to bring up the Search packages screen. You may be given the coordinates of a package to install, however, if you are not search for the package, as shown in *Figure 6.75*:

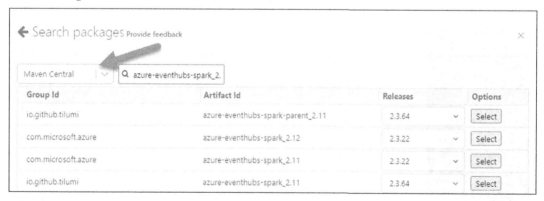

Figure 6.75: Searching for event hub utilities

The first thing you do when the screen opens is switching the combo box from **Spark Packages** to **Maven Central**. Next enter the name of the library you are looking for. You should see a list of matching results. In this case, we want to select the second one whose name ends with 2.12. Clicking the **Select** button returns you to the **Install** library page with the coordinates field populated, as shown in *Figure 6.76*:

Figure 6.76: *Populated coordinates field on install library page*

The last step in the library installation process is to click **install**. This function will install the library and return you to the cluster detail page. We can now return to the process of connecting to an Event Hub with Spark Structured Streaming.

Like the previous section, we need to construct an object containing configuration information. We keep the settings to a minimum, as shown in *Figure 6.77*:

Figure 6.77: *Spark Structured Streaming configuration*

We get the same connection string we used with the DLT streaming example. However, as mentioned before, we need to encrypt it, as it travels across the Internet. One additional property is required, a consumer group. Consumer groups are a way that multiple processes can consume one Event stream. In the case of Azure Event Hub, you go to the Event Hub Namespace, navigate to the **Event Hub**, and select **Consumer Groups** from the left navigation, as shown in *Figure 6.78*:

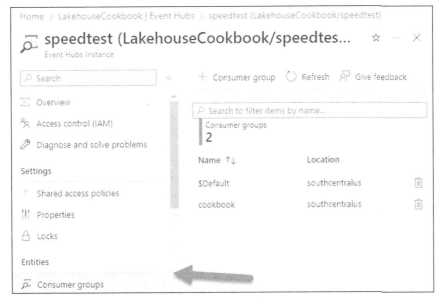

Figure 6.78: *Creating a Consumer Group in Azure Event Hub*

The **$Default** consumer group is automatically created when an Event Hub is created. The DLT streaming example used the default. Our example uses a newly created consumer group called **cookbook**. That is the value that is set on line 4 in *Figure 6.77*.

We are now ready to pull together the code that will pull values from Event Hub and save them to a Delta table, as shown in *Figure 6.79*:

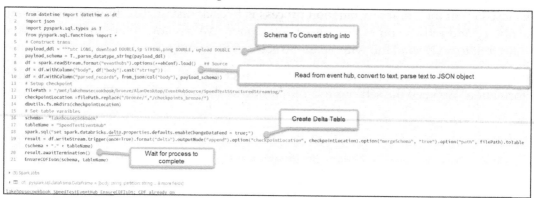

Figure 6.79: *Retrieve values from Event Hub and save to Delta Table*

There is a fair amount in this code, so we will go through it. We start by doing required imports (lines 1 to 4). We then define the schema we wish to use to convert the JSON string to an object (lines 6 and 7), as we did in the previous section. Next, we create a DataFrame using spark.read with format eventhubs (line 8), and convert the body column to a string from the Base64 content (line 9). We then apply the from_json statement to convert the JSON string to an object (line 10) using the schema from lines 6 and 7. Since consuming from an Event Hub in a streaming fashion requires a checkpoint, we setup a checkpoint location based on the file path where we will write the Delta files of our unmanaged table (lines 12 to 14). A key instruction is on line 18, it ensures that all tables created will have **Change Data Feed** (CDF) turned on. So far, all we have done is tell Spark what we want to happen. No data has been ingested to this point. We want to tell Spark where to write the data and how it should be triggered (line 19). Since stream processing is asynchronous, we must pause until the process completes (line 20). At this point, we have created a Delta table using Spark Structured Streaming.

Doing a little data profiling is always a good idea to ensure our job did what we think it did. We start by doing a **SELECT** ordering the fields with the ones we care the most about first and ordering the records by the time the Jupyter Notebook created the records, as shown in *Figure 6.80*:

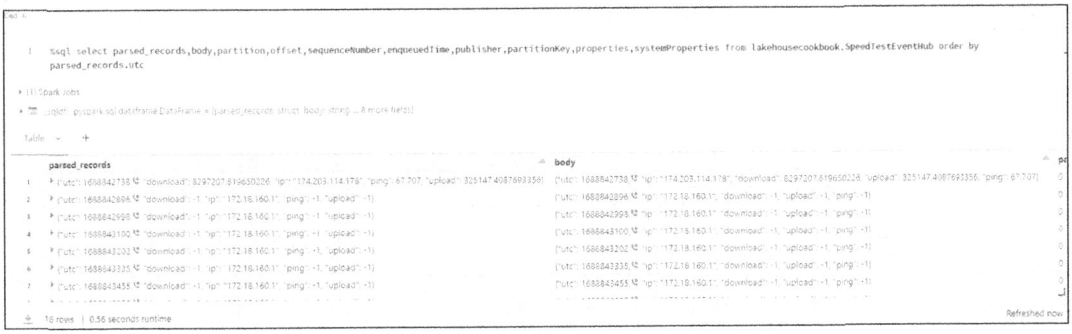

```
1   %sql select parsed_records,body,partition,offset,sequenceNumber,enqueuedTime,publisher,partitionKey,properties,systemProperties from lakehousecookbook.SpeedTestEventHub order by
    parsed_records.utc
```

▸ (1) Spark Jobs

▸ _sqldf: pyspark.sql.dataframe.DataFrame = [parsed_records: struct, body: string ... 8 more fields]

	parsed_records	body	pa
1	▸ {"utc": 1688842738, "download": 8297207.619650226, "ip": "174.203.114.178", "ping": 67.707, "upload": 325147.4087693356}	{"utc": 1688842738, "ip": "174.203.114.178", "download": 8297207.619650226, "upload": 325147.4087693356, "ping": 67.707}	0
2	▸ {"utc": 1688842896, "download": -1, "ip": "172.18.160.1", "ping": -1, "upload": -1}	{"utc": 1688842896, "ip": "172.18.160.1", "download": -1, "upload": -1, "ping": -1}	0
3	▸ {"utc": 1688842998, "download": -1, "ip": "172.18.160.1", "ping": -1, "upload": -1}	{"utc": 1688842998, "ip": "172.18.160.1", "download": -1, "upload": -1, "ping": -1}	0
4	▸ {"utc": 1688843100, "download": -1, "ip": "172.18.160.1", "ping": -1, "upload": -1}	{"utc": 1688843100, "ip": "172.18.160.1", "download": -1, "upload": -1, "ping": -1}	0
5	▸ {"utc": 1688843202, "download": -1, "ip": "172.18.160.1", "ping": -1, "upload": -1}	{"utc": 1688843202, "ip": "172.18.160.1", "download": -1, "upload": -1, "ping": -1}	0
6	▸ {"utc": 1688843335, "download": -1, "ip": "172.18.160.1", "ping": -1, "upload": -1}	{"utc": 1688843335, "ip": "172.18.160.1", "download": -1, "upload": -1, "ping": -1}	0
7	▸ {"utc": 1688843455, "download": -1, "ip": "172.18.160.1", "ping": -1, "upload": -1}	{"utc": 1688843455, "ip": "172.18.160.1", "download": -1, "upload": -1, "ping": -1}	0

16 rows | 0.56 seconds runtime   Refreshed now

***Figure 6.80**: Examining the contents of the Spark Structured Streaming populated table*

We can see that the body is a string, while the parsed_records is converted to a JSON object, as is shown by the black triangle. Additionally, we are ordering the results by parsed_records.utc. For completeness, we will examine the structure of the table using the DESCRIBE statement, as shown in *Figure 6.81:*

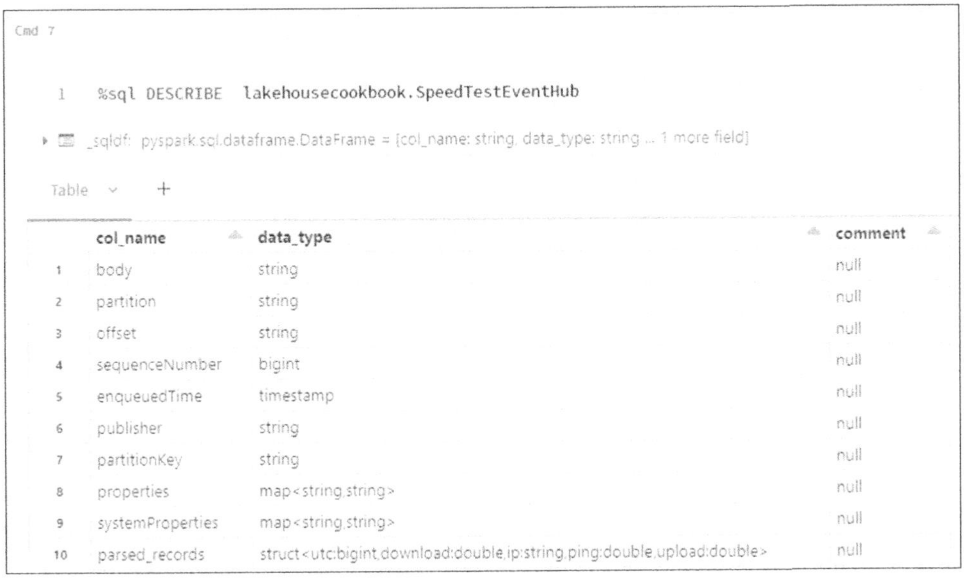

Cmd 7

```
1   %sql DESCRIBE  lakehousecookbook.SpeedTestEventHub
```

▸ _sqldf: pyspark.sql.dataframe.DataFrame = [col_name: string, data_type: string ... 1 more field]

	col_name	data_type	comment
1	body	string	null
2	partition	string	null
3	offset	string	null
4	sequenceNumber	bigint	null
5	enqueuedTime	timestamp	null
6	publisher	string	null
7	partitionKey	string	null
8	properties	map<string,string>	null
9	systemProperties	map<string,string>	null
10	parsed_records	struct<utc:bigint,download:double,ip:string,ping:double,upload:double>	null

***Figure 6.81**: Structure of the table created by Spark Structured Streaming*

We can see that the column parsed_records is an object. As mentioned in the previous section, we can decide later if those values should be converted to columns. Additionally, we would typically remove all other columns, except for enqueuedTime and sequenceNumber, as they relate to the delivery of the messages. Once the records are in the Bronze layer they are of little value. We have successfully ingested data from Event Hub and used it to create a Bronze Delta table.

Conclusion

In this chapter, we covered the common elements of ingestion into the Bronze layer. There are others which we will revisit in *Chapter 15, Tips, Tricks, Troubleshooting, and Best Practices*. We discussed if data should be landed in a raw zone or go into Bronze. We examined Change Data Feed, which we will use extensively in *Chapter 7, Transforming to Create Silver*. We discussed the conceptual underpinnings of incremental ingestion and the importance of watermarks. We discussed an approach to loading data incrementally using watermarks and its complexity. We then moved on to using Auto Loader and saw that it significantly reduced the effort involved. Next, we used Delta Live Tables to ingest data from several sources, including Event Hubs. Lastly, we used Spark Structured Streaming to retrieve values from an Event Hub and write them to a Bronze Table.

In the next chapter, we will pick up those Bronze items we just ingested and refine them to business usable quality. This includes applying data quality rules and removing duplicates. Once data is in the silver zone, a business user knows it is safe. At that point, a business can derive value from its Lakehouse data.

Join our book's Discord space

Join the book's Discord Workspace for Latest updates, Offers, Tech happenings around the world, New Release and Sessions with the Authors:

https://discord.bpbonline.com

CHAPTER 7

Transforming to Create Silver

Introduction

Once data has been ingested into the bronze zone, the next step is to refine it and populate the silver zone. Recall that silver tables do not have duplicates and are fit for business use. This means that business rules have been applied to ensure the data conforms to the business expectations of the nature of the data. We will also cover the types of refinement commonly performed and how they are implemented using Delta Live Tables, Spark SQL, and PySpark.

Structure

The chapter covers the following topics:

- Bronze to silver incremental and full refinement
- Bronze to silver enrichment and table-splitting refinement
- Data quality rules and expectations
- Silver to silver refinement, including denormalization, JSON exploding, and projection reshaping

Objectives

By the end of the chapter, you will understand the mechanisms used to convert data to a usable level of quality and structure. You will also understand the common types of transformations and how they are implemented in the common Databricks Lakehouse environment.

Bronze to silver

In the last chapter, we populated bronze tables in various ways. We will continue the flow of data by transforming that data into silver tables. Recall that silver tables do not have duplications based on the table's key. This requires the use of a **merge** operation. Additionally, we will apply data quality rules expressed as expectations in DLT, **WHERE** clauses in Spark SQL, and **filter** or **where** operations in PySpark. We will start by examining incremental refinement, then shift to full. Then we will explore common operations that occur during bronze to silver operations.

Incremental refinement

In *Chapter 6, Extracting from Source and Loading to Bronze*, we incrementally loaded data into tables in various ways. We will continue that process by incrementally processing and loading data into silver tables from bronze. Recall that we introduced our famous employee dataset in *Chapter 6, Extracting from Source and Loading to Bronze*, to discuss incremental ingestion. We ingested the data from a JSON file using a mount point to a bronze table in Recipes 54 and 55. We will use that dataset in this section as it is simple and small. We start by using DLT to create our silver table.

Recipe 63: Incremental refinement using Delta Live Tables

Reflecting changes in transactional systems is an important part of a lakehouse. As we discussed in the previous chapter, if we are tracking employee information and an employee moves, changes their name, or is terminated, we must have a means of recognizing that information and updating silver tables appropriately.

To make things clearer, we recreate the table from Recipe 54, changing the name of the table. Combining the two commands into a single notebook making it easier to see the interactions. Additionally, DLT does not allow two pipelines to access the same Delta table. The code is relatively simple, as you can see in *Figure 7.1*:

Cmd 2

```
1   CREATE STREAMING LIVE TABLE Bronze_Employee_DLT_7 COMMENT "Famous Brands Employee Table"
2   TBLPROPERTIES ("delta.enableChangeDataFeed"="true", "quality" = "bronze")
3   AS SELECT * FROM cloud_files("dbfs:/mnt/sourceData/lakehousecookbook/employeeJson/","json",
4       map('multiline', 'true', 'recursiveFileLookup','true', 'schemaEvolutionMode','rescue',
5       'autoMerge','true', 'cloudFiles.inferColumnTypes', 'true'));
```

Cmd 3

```
1   CREATE OR REFRESH STREAMING LIVE TABLE Silver_Employee_DLT_7 COMMENT "Famous Brands Employee Table"
2   TBLPROPERTIES ("quality" = "silver","delta.enableChangeDataFeed"="true");
3
4   APPLY CHANGES INTO LIVE.Silver_Employee_DLT_7 FROM STREAM(LIVE.Bronze_Employee_DLT_7)
5   KEYS (EmployeeId) SEQUENCE BY ModifiedOn;
```

Figure 7.1: *Creating an incremental table*

To do incremental updates, we need to use the DLT **APPLY CHANGES INTO** method as this method is used to implement **Change Data Capture** (**CDC**). Note that as of this writing, the CDC functionality was in public preview. This means that the syntax used here might differ from the final release of CDC functionality. To use CDC, you must select the PRO produce edition. The **CDC** function is documented in the DLT SQL reference manual that can be found here: **https://docs.databricks.com/delta-live-tables/sql-ref.html#cdc**.

Notice that the bronze table we create in command 2 is referenced as a stream in command 3. Also, notice the inclusion of the **LIVE** prefix to the table names. We can see how many records were copied into each in *Figure 7.2:*

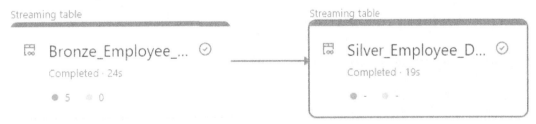

Figure 7.2: *Run of the DLT incremental ingest and update*

Notice the two dots at the bottom of each box. The first number is the records written, and the second is the records dropped. There is a UI bug where the **Silver** table is not showing any records written. A quick check of the table contents shows that the data was correctly inserted into the **Silver** table. We can now signal an update by dropping a file into the data lake and re-running the pipeline, as shown in *Figure 7.3:*

Figure 7.3: Run with changed data

Again, the **Silver** table shows no records processed. However, when we check the database, the values are correct, as shown in *Figure 7.4*:

```
Cmd 5
1   select * from bronze_employee_dlt_7;
▶ (5) Spark Jobs
Table  ∨   +
```

	Address1	Address2	City	CreatedBy	CreatedOn	EmployeeId	FirstName	LastName	ModifiedBy	ModifiedOn	PostalCode	State
1	123 First St.		Seattle	Admin	12/31/2024	1	Leonardo	da Vinci	Admin	12/31/2024	98101	WA
2	234 Second St.		Seattle	Admin	12/31/2024	2	Napoleon	Bonaparte	Admin	12/31/2024	98101	WA
3	345 Third St.		Seattle	Admin	12/31/2024	3	Charles	Darwin	Admin	12/31/2024	98102	WA
4	456 Fourth St.		Seattle	Admin	12/31/2024	4	Albert	Einstein	Admin	12/31/2024	98103	WA
5	678 Fifth St.		Seattle	Admin	12/31/2024	5	Thomas	Jefferson	Admin	12/31/2024	98104	WA
6	160 Spear St.	15th Floor	San Francisco	Admin	12/31/2024	4	Albert	Einstein	Admin	5/1/2025	94105	CA

```
↓  6 rows  |  2.32 seconds runtime                                    Refreshed 1 minute ago
Command took 2.32 seconds -- by alan.dennis@gmail.com at 7/18/2021, 6:50:33 PM on Alan Dennis's Cluster
Cmd 6
1   select * from silver_employee_dlt_7
▶ (3) Spark Jobs
Table  ∨   +
```

	Address1	Address2	City	CreatedBy	CreatedOn	EmployeeId	FirstName	LastName	ModifiedBy	ModifiedOn	PostalCode	State
1	123 First St.		Seattle	Admin	12/31/2024	1	Leonardo	da Vinci	Admin	12/31/2024	98101	WA
2	234 Second St.		Seattle	Admin	12/31/2024	2	Napoleon	Bonaparte	Admin	12/31/2024	98101	WA
3	345 Third St.		Seattle	Admin	12/31/2024	3	Charles	Darwin	Admin	12/31/2024	98102	WA
4	678 Fifth St.		Seattle	Admin	12/31/2024	5	Thomas	Jefferson	Admin	12/31/2024	98104	WA
5	160 Spear St.	15th Floor	San Francisco	Admin	12/31/2024	4	Albert	Einstein	Admin	5/1/2025	94105	CA

```
↓  5 rows  |  1.83 seconds runtime                                    Refreshed 1 minute ago
```

Figure 7.4: Bronze and silver tables

You might notice that command 6 results in 5 rows, as compared to the 6 rows in the bronze table in command 5. We can also observe that line 5 in command 6 has the updated address for **Albert**. We have successfully used CDC to **upsert** records in silver.

Next, we will perform the same operation using Python in Spark.

Recipe 64: Incremental refinement using PySpark

In *Recipe 48*, we created a self-managed process to ingest data using a watermark table in Delta incrementally. We will revisit that approach for refinement. Recall that we created a

Delta table to store watermark values. This allows us to process only the items that have changed since we last processed them. We also need to know the maximum value of the records we have processed, as it will become the starting point for our next refinement cycle.

As an example, consider a table with four records. Initially, the **Watermark** for that table should be the lowest value for the data type associated with the **Watermark** column, as shown in *Figure 7.5*:

Figure 7.5: *Incremental processing data*

Once the first four records are processed, the watermark is updated to reflect the **Watermark** value of the last processed record. When new records arrive, that persisted **Watermark** value is the starting point for processing, as shown in *Figure 7.6*:

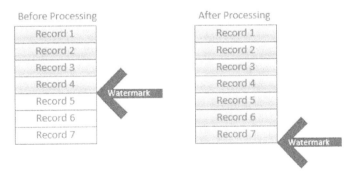

Figure 7.6: *Incremental processing with more data*

This serves several purposes. It reduces the amount of data being processed during each cycle. This, in turn, reduces the time needed for processing, along with reducing the cost to do that processing. Now, we will apply this concept to the speed test data we discussed in *Recipe 49, Using incremental load of files*.

For brevity's sake, we will skip imports and variable assignments and focus on the core elements of the example. Remember, the example notebooks are available in the GitHub repository. The first thing we need to do is get the current **Watermark**, as shown in *Figure 7.7*:

Cmd 7

```
1  # Get watermark for silver table
2  # This will be the max of the last values we ingested
3  silverWatermarkDf = GetWatermark(schemaName,silverTable,defaultWatermarkType='timestamp') # how far have we updated silver
4  silverDateTime = GetWatermarkValue(silverWatermarkDf)
5  print("silverDateTime",silverDateTime)
```

▸ (2) Spark Jobs

▸ 🔳 silverWatermarkDf: pyspark.sql.dataframe.DataFrame = [schemaName: string, tableName: string ... 5 more fields]

0

[{'schemaName': 'LakehouseCookbook', 'tableName': 'silver_speedtest', 'watermarkType': 'timestamp', 'timestampWatermark': datetime.date
rmark': 0, 'bigintWatermark': 0, 'stringWatermark': ''}]
past dfUpdates
silverDateTime 1900-01-01 00:00:00

Command took 2.82 seconds -- by alan.dennis@gmail.com at 7/14/2023, 7:17:01 PM on Alan Dennis's Cluster

Figure 7.7: *Getting the initial watermark*

This is like the before processing state in *Figure 7.5*. In this case, we are using a **timestamp** watermark. Since there is no record in the watermark table, the **GetWatermark** function returns a DataFrame with the minimum value for the **timestamp** datatypes. Now that we have the watermark, we can control which records are returned. Once we have selected the data that is greater than our watermark, we will need to find the maximum value of the watermark column, as shown in *Figure 7.8*:

Cmd 10

```
1   # Read the bronze table
2   df = spark.read.table(f"`{schemaName}`.`{bronzeTable}`")
3   # convert Base64 to text and object
4   payload_ddl = """"utc long, ip STRING,download DOUBLE, upload DOUBLE, ping DOUBLE"""
5   updatedDF = Base64ToStringAndJsonSqlDdl(df,'Body',payload_ddl) # turn base64 to text and parse it with the supplied SQL DDL
6   updatedDF =updatedDF.withColumn('utc',from_unixtime(updatedDF["Body_parsed.utc"])) # turn double to timestamp
7   silverProjection = ["utc","Body_parsed.ip","Body_parsed.download","Body_parsed.upload","Body_parsed.ping"] # turn object properties to columns
8   updatedDF = updatedDF.select(silverProjection).filter(col(watermarkColumn) > lit(silverDateTime)).distinct().cache() #Get new records
9   maxValueInBronze = updatedDF.agg({watermarkColumn: "max"}).collect()[0][0] # Find the max watermark value in the soon to be processed records
10  print(silverDateTime)
11  print(maxValueInBronze)
12  display(updatedDF)
```

▸ (10) Spark Jobs

▸ 🔳 df: pyspark.sql.dataframe.DataFrame = [SequenceNumber: long, Offset: string ... 4 more fields]
▸ 🔳 updatedDF: pyspark.sql.dataframe.DataFrame = [utc: string, ip: string ... 3 more fields]

1900-01-01 00:00:00
2023-07-15 12:52:38

Table ⌄ +

	utc	ip	download	upload	ping
1	2023-07-10 15:08:12	129.222.216.91	24519581.080767788	9796242.252609553	65.886
2	2023-07-14 01:37:06	129.222.216.91	18509840.85978379	4322135.518960425	61.764
3	2023-07-12 02:37:37	129.222.216.91	15581946.941108434	5530882.350320359	80.405
4	2023-07-12 16:01:02	129.222.216.91	25547633.243870668	11716697.366122972	50.411
5	2023-07-10 20:24:29	172.18.160.1	-1	-1	-1
6	2023-07-12 18:56:07	192.168.1.22	-1	-1	-1
7	2023-07-10 10:50:18	129.222.216.91	26118593.01858969	11764416.093551578	59.425

⤓ 2,811 rows | 9.09 seconds runtime

Command took 9.09 seconds -- by alan.dennis@gmail.com at 7/15/2023, 9:07:59 AM on Alan Dennis's Cluster

Figure 7.8: *Get new records based on watermark*

We start by reading the bronze table on line 2. We then parse it using the SQL schema definition on line 4. Ideally, this transformation would have been performed during the bronze table population. Since we did not do that in Recipe 49, we must do it now. We must also turn the **Unix time** (a big integer) into a timestamp and the unmodified column could have been used. However, it would have been harder to read than a date and time value.

Next, we change the shape of the data using a **select** statement. We are extracting the properties from the **Body_parsed** object and making the columns of the DataFrame. In line 8, we apply the projection and filter the records to be only those which are greater than the watermark. We apply the **distinct** method to ensure there are no duplicates. There should not be, however Event Hubs can sometimes send the same message multiple times. As this is telemetry, there would never be an instance where two records with the same values should exist. Since we are doing multiple things with this DataFrame, we use the **cache** operator. We find out the maximum value in the table by using the **aggregation** function in line 9.

Now that we have our DataFrame with the records we have not yet processed, we can move them into the silver table. Since this is telemetry, we only need to append records. However, since there are sometimes duplicates when dealing with streaming systems, we use the **merge** operation. This operation is what we would have to do if we were dealing with data from a transactional system. We need to determine if the silver table exists, and if not, we need to create it, as shown in *Figure 7.9:*

```
Cmd 12

1    if silverDateTime == maxValueInBronze or maxValueInBronze is None or silverDateTime is None:
2        print("Nothing to do")
3    else:
4        spark.sql("set spark.databricks.delta.properties.defaults.enableChangeDataFeed = true;") # Make CDF is on
5        if spark.catalog.tableExists(fullSilverTableName):
6            print(fullSilverTableName,"Exists")
7            silverTable = DeltaTable.forPath(spark,silverTablePath)
8            (silverTable.alias('source')
9             .merge(updatedDF.alias('target'), "source."+keyColumn +" = target." +keyColumn )
10            .whenMatchedUpdateAll()
11            .whenNotMatchedInsertAll()
12            .execute()
13            )
14        else:
15            print(fullSilverTableName, "Does Not Exist")
16            updatedDF.write.mode("append").option("path",silverTablePath).saveAsTable(fullSilverTableName)
17            print(fullSilverTableName, "Created")
18        UpsertWatermark(UpdateWatermarkValue(silverWatermarkDf,maxValueInBronze))

▶ (16) Spark Jobs

'LakehouseCookbook'.'silver_speedtest' Does Not Exist
'LakehouseCookbook'.'silver_speedtest' Created
watermarkTable lakehousecookbook.watermarks
lakehousecookbook.watermarks

Command took 51.98 seconds -- by alan.dennis@gmail.com at 7/15/2023, 9:11:33 AM on Alan Dennis's Cluster
```

Figure 7.9: *Create or append to the silver table and then save the new watermark*

We start by seeing if there is a change in the watermark and ensuring that neither the watermark nor the maximum value is null. If either is null, we could update the watermark table with a null value. Then on line 5, we use **spark.catalog.tableExists** to determine if the silver table has previously been created. If it does exist, we get the silver table and use the **merge** method to **upsert** the records.

We could have simply appended the records, but using **merge** ensures that if we get sent multiple records, we handle them appropriately. The **merge** statement takes a condition; in this case, we are comparing the key column in both source and destination. For the records that match, we update all the properties in the target table. For those that do not match, we insert all the columns in the source DataFrame into the target. In this example, we do not handle the deletion of records, as that does not occur with telemetry.

For the case where the table does not exist, we save the source DataFrame as a table, specifying a location. We use the **append** write mode, though it does not matter, given that we will only do this once. The last thing we do is save the maximum value as the new watermark value on line 18. Looking at the watermark table, we can see the new value, as shown in *Figure 7.10:*

Figure 7.10: *Updated watermark table*

You can see that the **silver_speedtest** table now has a record that is of **watermarkType** **timestamp**, and there is a value in the **timestampWatermark** column. Another form of validation is to examine the **silver_speedtest** table's contents, as shown in *Figure 7.11:*

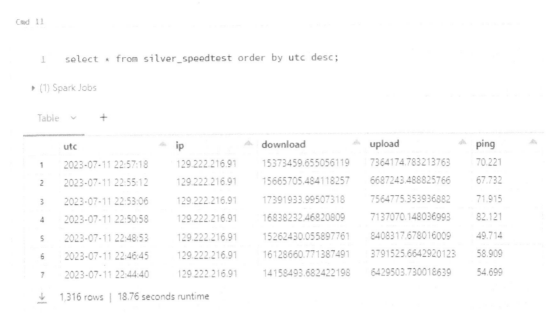

Figure 7.11: The silver speed test table's contents

The data in our silver table looks good. But one thing we did not do was filter out records that have values we do not want in a silver table.

For example, if an error occurs during the speed test, a -1 is sent in the **download**, **upload**, and **ping** columns. When dealing with data quality issues, the choices with missing values are to remove or filter the offending records, replace the value with null, or perform some form of imputation (such as replacing the values with averages from the dataset). We will discuss constraints and data quality rules later in this chapter.

To further test this example, we can execute a variant of the code from Recipe 49 to push new records into the bronze table. Once it completes, we can execute our code and see that we successfully merged our data, as shown in *Figure 7.12*:

Figure 7.12: History of the silver speed test table

We can see that the table was created in **version 1**, then merged into in **version 2**. We can consider this a successful creation and update of a silver table. Next, we will examine non-incremental or full refinement.

Full refinement

We try to avoid refining or processing an entire table. However, there are times it is unavoidable. When we do not have a way of finding a record, we must process the table in its entirety. This is because we cannot identify the target record and could produce duplicates. We will start with an example using Delta Live Tables.

Recipe 65: Full update refinement using Delta Live Tables

In Recipe 56 in *Chapter 6, Extracting from Source and Loading to Bronze*, we used a DLT SQL notebook to load Fisheries data. We will continue that example by refining the bronze materialized view that was created into a silver one. This is example is simplistic, so that we can focus on the concepts. Soon, we will discuss application of expectations and other operations that occur when converting a table from bronze to silver. For this example, we will add a timestamp column to the contents of the bronze table when constructing the silver table. As with creating other DLT pipelines, we start by creating a notebook. To make it clearer, we recreate the bronze table, with a bronze table name prefix, as shown in *Figure 7.13:*

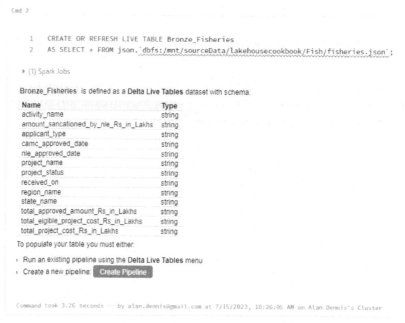

Figure 7.13: Bronze_Fisheries materialized view

This is identical to *Recipe 56*, except for the name of the table. Next, we need to create our silver DLT materialized view, as shown in *Figure 7.14*:

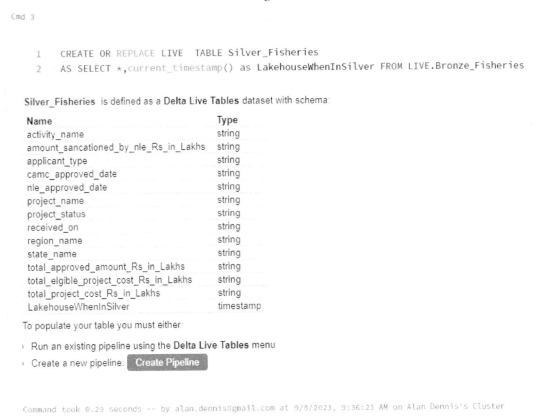

Figure 7.14: Silver_Fisheries materialized view

Notice the addition of the **LakehouseWhenInSilver** column to the SQL and the table preview. This is a common way to measure how quickly data flows through a lakehouse. Often, the time is captured when entering each zone. The output was trimmed to reduce space. We now have our notebook; the next step is to **Create Pipeline** and then run it, as shown in *Figure 7.15*:

Figure 7.15: Run of bronze and silver materialized view population

The final step is to examine the contents of the **Silver** table. Notice the addition of the **`LakehouseWhenInSilver`** column, as shown in *Figure 7.16:*

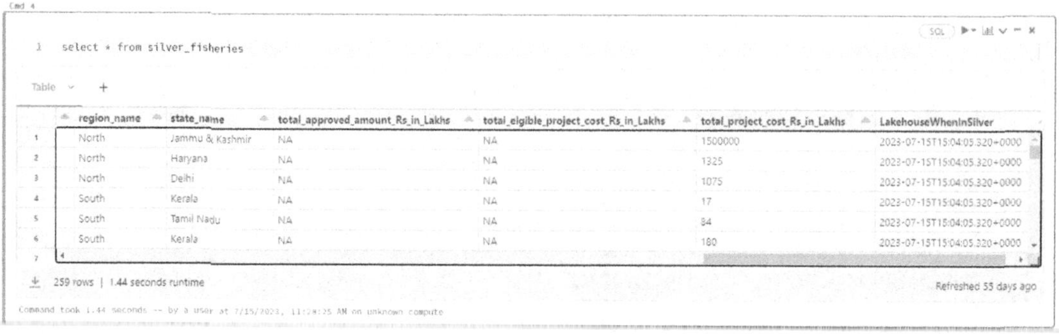

	region_name	state_name	total_approved_amount_Rs_in_Lakhs	total_elgible_project_cost_Rs_in_Lakhs	total_project_cost_Rs_in_Lakhs	LakehouseWhenInSilver
1	North	Jammu & Kashmir	NA	NA	1500000	2023-07-15T15:04:05.320+0000
2	North	Haryana	NA	NA	1325	2023-07-15T15:04:05.320+0000
3	North	Delhi	NA	NA	1075	2023-07-15T15:04:05.320+0000
4	South	Kerala	NA	NA	17	2023-07-15T15:04:05.320+0000
5	South	Tamil Nadu	NA	NA	84	2023-07-15T15:04:05.320+0000
6	South	Kerala	NA	NA	180	2023-07-15T15:04:05.320+0000
7						

***Figure 7.16**: Examining contents of silver fisheries data*

We have now constructed a DLT pipeline that fully loads and processes data. In the next section, we will perform the same operation using PySpark without using DLT.

Recipe 66: Full refinement using PySpark

In *Recipe 51*, we performed a full load of data from a location populated by Event Hub Capture. In this recipe, we will continue that process to convert and create a silver table. This workload most often occurs when performing a load of historical data. The typical consumption pattern for telemetry is to use a streaming ingestion pattern.

A variation of that approach is to use a streaming statement, but configure the processing to run until it consumes a predefined number of items or exhausts the queue, often called *trigger once.* This means you can capture events from the time you start retrieving them from the queue, but those which came before are not present. To compensate for that, we often load historical data into the same construct that the streaming data will and continue to update using the streaming approach.

We start the process by using the **`spark.read.table`** command and converting the big integer version of the timestamp into a readable timestamp using the **`from_unixtime`** operation, as shown in *Figure 7.17:*

```
Cmd 9

1    spark.sql("set spark.databricks.delta.properties.defaults.enableChangeDataFeed = true;")
2    df = spark.read.table(fullSourceTable)
3    df =df.withColumn('utc',from_unixtime(df["jsonObject.utc"])) # turn double to timestamp
4    silverProjection = ["utc","jsonObject.ip","jsonObject.download","jsonObject.upload","jsonObject.ping"] # turn object properties to columns
5    distinctDf = df.select(silverProjection).distinct() #Get new records
6    distinctDf = distinctDf.withColumn("LakehouseWhenInSilver", current_timestamp()).cache()
7    display(distinctDf)
```

▶ (5) Spark Jobs

▶ ▦ df: pyspark.sql.dataframe.DataFrame = [SequenceNumber: long, Offset: string ... 7 more fields]

▶ ▦ distinctDf: pyspark.sql.dataframe.DataFrame = [utc: string, ip: string ... 4 more fields]

Table ∨ +

	utc	ip	download	upload	ping	LakehouseWhenInSilver
1	2023-07-15 11:46:27	129.222.216.91	11923383.138649324	11786402.405754816	62.678	2023-07-15T19:12:37.707+0000
2	2023-07-15 11:56:56	129.222.216.91	10380415.73024663	11305591.845528843	38.405	2023-07-15T19:12:37.707+0000
3	2023-07-15 14:14:36	129.222.216.91	9657860.15654844	9146987.704572085	75.987	2023-07-15T19:12:37.707+0000
4	2023-07-15 15:13:09	129.222.216.91	7521926.929640849	13546060.636270512	48.681	2023-07-15T19:12:37.707+0000
5	2023-07-15 14:42:31	129.222.216.91	8969669.015221583	7061139.941774502	79.571	2023-07-15T19:12:37.707+0000
6	2023-07-15 15:21:36	129.222.216.91	8249685.474344337	10438567.809472296	62.269	2023-07-15T19:12:37.707+0000
7	2023-07-15 13:28:22	129.222.216.91	7517051.408147744	12051711.614594148	64.151	2023-07-15T19:12:37.707+0000

Figure 7.17: Loading full-load table

In line 1, we set the Delta defaults to always enable **Change Data Feed** (**CDF**). This may not always be advisable, but if you want to have insights into changes in a table, it is important. It also allows the option of streaming those changes to downstream tables. Not a great idea for a full load, but more useful to demonstrate the changes occurring and that replacing a table preserves history. The important tip is that if you want to have CDF available, this method will ensure it is active. Next, we let Spark know what table we want to read and that we want to change the **utc** column into a timestamp. Additionally, we expose the nested properties as columns, as we have done earlier in this chapter. We also apply the **distinct** operation and include the current timestamp to track arrival in the silver zone. Since we display the DataFrame, we enable caching. All that remains is to save the table, as shown in *Figure 7.18*:

```
1    distinctDf.write.mode("overwrite").option("mergeSchema", "true").option("path",silverTablePath).saveAsTable(fullSilverTable)
```

▶ (5) Spark Jobs

Command took 27.25 seconds -- by alan.dennis@gmail.com at 7/15/2023, 3:08:15 PM on Alan Dennis's Cluster

```
Cmd 11

1    %sql SELECT COUNT(*) FROM lakehousecookbook.silver_fullload_speedtest
```

▶ (3) Spark Jobs

▶ ▦ _sqldf: pyspark.sql.dataframe.DataFrame = [count(1): long]

Table ∨ +

	count(1)
1	143

Figure 7.18: Save DataFrame as table

We can see that the table was successfully created and is populated. We have successfully created a full refinement using PySpark. Next, we shift to discussing data quality rules, an important aspect of the lakehouse architecture.

Data quality rules

An important aspect of a lakehouse is trusting the data in the silver and gold zones. This means that they have had duplications removed, using operations such as **merge**, but also have had rules applied so that their contents are in line with the enterprise's expectations. A business owner should not examine a table and decide that the values are incorrect or have not been cleansed correctly. To ensure the data is correct, we will discuss several ways of ensuring data quality.

Recipe 67: Using expectations in DLT with SQL

DLT expresses business rules regarding data using a construct they named expectations. An expectation has a **Boolean** clause that is used to determine compliance. To keep things organized, they include a description, such as a name or unique identifier. This helps you track down which expectations were violated. Lastly, when a clause is violated, an action must occur. This type of action is configurable.

In such a scenario, three outcomes can occur. First, a **warning** records the failure to the metrics associated with the dataset but allows the records to populate the destination. Second, a **drop** action records the metric and does not allow the offending record into the target dataset. Lastly, a **fail** action terminates the entire operation associated with the dataset. This is reserved for severe failures and will require manual intervention to resolve. For more on expectations, visit:

https://docs.databricks.com/delta-live-tables/expectations.html.

For this example, we will revisit *Recipe 61*, which dealt with famous employees. We will extend it by requiring a few simple business rules before a record can enter or update a silver record, as shown in *Figure 7.19*:

```
Cmd 2

1  CREATE STREAMING LIVE TABLE Bronze_Employee_DLT_7_65
2  (
3      CONSTRAINT city_populated EXPECT (city is not null and length(city)> 2) ON VIOLATION DROP ROW,
4      CONSTRAINT state_populated EXPECT (state is not null and length(state)= 2) ON VIOLATION DROP ROW,
5      CONSTRAINT firstName_populated EXPECT (FirstName is not null and length(FirstName)> 0) ON VIOLATION DROP ROW,
6      CONSTRAINT positive_ping EXPECT (EmployeeId > 0) ON VIOLATION DROP ROW
7  )
8  COMMENT "Famous Brands Employee Table"
9  TBLPROPERTIES ("delta.enableChangeDataFeed"="true", "quality" = "bronze")
10 AS SELECT * FROM cloud_files("dbfs:/mnt/sourceData/lakehousecookbook/employeeJson/","json",
11     map('multiline', 'true', 'recursiveFileLookup','true', 'schemaEvolutionMode','rescue',
12     'autoMerge','true', 'cloudFiles.inferColumnTypes', 'true'));

Cmd 3

1  CREATE OR REFRESH STREAMING LIVE TABLE Silver_Employee_DLT_7_Filtered
2  COMMENT "Famous Brands Employee Table"
3  TBLPROPERTIES ("quality" = "silver","delta.enableChangeDataFeed"="true");
4
5  APPLY CHANGES INTO LIVE.Silver_Employee_DLT_7_Filtered FROM STREAM(LIVE.Bronze_Employee_DLT_7_65)
6  KEYS (EmployeeId) SEQUENCE BY ModifiedOn;
```

Figure 7.19: DLT with expectations

In this example, we require that the **City** property not be **null** and have a length greater than two characters. Additionally, we require the **State** property not to be **null** and be exactly two characters long. Next, we require the **FirstName** property not to be **null** and be one or more characters long. The last expectation is that the **EmployeeId** property is greater than zero. In all cases, if the condition is not met, the record the property belongs to will be dropped.

One interesting constraint is that tables with changes applied to them, as we do in this example, cannot have constraints on that table. This means the constraints must be applied to the bronze table or a table derived from the initial silver table (where duplications are removed). We take that approach in above *Figure 7.19*.

From a purist perspective, that is troubling. We must decide between dropping bronze records (not recommended) or creating a table in the silver zone that has not had constraints applied. An approach some have taken is to introduce more zones, such as a mapping zone. That has its challenges, as the intent of the medallion architecture is to be simple and intuitive. In this case, the less problematic approach is to apply the changes to a silver table with a name showing that the constraints have not been applied, as shown in *Figure 7.20*:

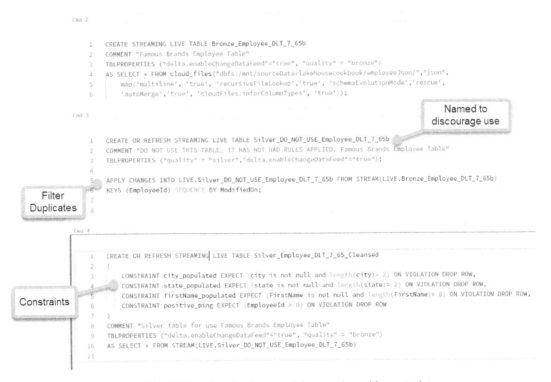

Figure 7.20: *DLT performing incremental processing with constraints*

This approach is not perfect, but at least the requirement that bronze should be a representation of the source data is preserved. Additionally, the intermediate table is named in a way to discourage its use. We often find these kinds of competing goals while building a lakehouse. The guiding principle should be clarity and that we are following the spirit of the design.

Recipe 68: Using expectations in DLT with PySpark

In this recipe, we will start by taking *Recipe 59* and extending it to use expectations. Recall that in *Recipe 59*, we connected to an Event Hub and retrieved speed test results. We did a certain amount of data transformation, primarily to return it to the original format. We reuse that code, changing the name of the table populated in this example. We then use that table as a source, applying rules to remove the records with -1 in the **update**, **download**, or **ping** fields, as shown in *Figure 7.21*:

```
44   def bronze_iot_speedtest_7():  return (
45       spark.readStream
46         .format("kafka")
47         .options(**KAFKA_OPTIONS)          New table name from Recipe 59
48         .load()
49         .transform(parse)
50   )
```

```
1    @dlt.table(
2      comment="Silver Speedtest",  table_properties={"quality": "silver","pipelines.reset.allowed": "false" },
3    )
4    @dlt.expect_or_drop("Download Not -1", "download > -1")
5    @dlt.expect_or_drop("Upload Not -1", "upload > -1")
6    @dlt.expect_or_drop("Ping Not -1", "ping > -1")
7    def silver_iot_speedtest_7():
8      return (                            Reference table created in this notebook
9        dlt.read("bronze_iot_speedtest_7").select("parsed_records.*","UTC_timestamp")
10     )
```

Figure 7.21: Refining data from event hub removing invalid records

After having created a pipeline referencing this notebook and executing it, we can tell that this notebook is working correctly by examining the produced data. We can now start by looking at the bronze table, as shown in *Figure 7.22*:

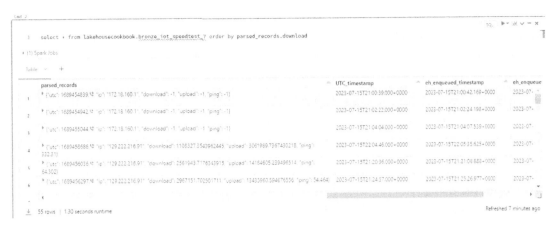

Figure 7.22: *bronze unfiltered event hub data*

Notice that in the JSON object, there are records with negative values. These records are created when a speed test is not successful. We can see they have been removed, along with the data restructured, in *Figure 7.23:*

Figure 7.23: *Silver refined item from event hub data*

We can see that three records were removed by looking at the row count in *Figures 7.22* and *Figure 7.23*. This is the same number of records as those having -1 for **speed**, **download**, and **ping**. We have seen that expectations can be used to filter records that do not confirm to the organization's policies. In the next section, we will explore what happens to silver tables once they arrive to prepare them for use in the gold layer.

Silver to silver

Once data has been used to populate silver tables, it can be used to answer business questions. However, it is often not in the ideal shape for that purpose. In this section, we discuss a set of operations that source data, from a silver table and populate a silver table. These silver-to-silver operations are often needed to prepare the data for use in the gold layer. We will explore the common types of required transformations and give examples of each.

Reshaping projection

Often data arrives in the silver layer with values that are valid but not needed by the business. We sometimes need to create additional tables that remove or change the way the attributes are within a table. We will start with how this is done in Python, then move to an example using DLT.

Recipe 69: Projection reshaping using Python

We have been doing some project reshaping previously, but we will discuss it in depth here. First, it is useful to know what a projection is. The name comes from the elements of a SQL **SELECT** statement which come between the word **SELECT** and the word **FROM**. In *Recipe 64*, we updated bronze data to silver. We will refine this further while adding a where operation to emulate a constraint with a drop action, as shown in *Figure 7.24*:

```
1    import datetime
2    from pyspark.sql.functions import *
3    df = spark.read.table(f"`{schema}`.`{sourceSilverTable}`")
4    df = df.withColumn("Date",to_date(df["utc"])).withColumn("Year",year(df["utc"])).withColumn("Month",month(df["utc"]))
5    df = df.withColumn("DayOfMonth",dayofmonth(df["utc"]))
6    df = df.withColumn("Hour",hour(df["utc"])).withColumn("Minute",minute(df["utc"]))
7    df = df.withColumn("DownMBS",df["download"]/1024/1024)
8    df = df.withColumn("UpMBS",df["upload"]/1024/1024)
9    df = df.withColumn("LakehouseWhenRefined",current_timestamp())
10   df = df.where(col('download')> 0).where(col('upload')> 0).where(col('ping')> 0)  # Remove items, similar to drop
11   df = df.cache() # so we can display this with out reprocessing
12   result = df.write.mode("overwrite").option("mergeSchema", "true").option("path",destSilverTableLocation).saveAsTable
     (fullDestSilverTable)
13   print(result)
14   display(df)
```

▸ (9) Spark Jobs

▸ ▦ df: pyspark.sql.dataframe.DataFrame = [utc: string, ip: string ... 13 more fields]

None

Table ∨ +

	Date	Year	Month	DayOfMonth	Hour	Minute	DownMBS	UpMBS	LakehouseWhenRefined
1	2023-07-15	2023	7	15	11	8	5.338220295138497	6.239585789847505	2023-07-16T16:30:01.8
2	2023-07-15	2023	7	15	11	23	7.210085431224569	11.020342584771162	2023-07-16T16:30:01.8
3	2023-07-15	2023	7	15	11	31	6.712758269065278	9.948322562092535	2023-07-16T16:30:01.8
4	2023-07-15	2023	7	15	13	5	9.435117143574399	8.045109664877907	2023-07-16T16:30:01.8
5	2023-07-15	2023	7	15	15	44	11.292894169811799	11.084484336115187	2023-07-16T16:30:01.8
6	2023-07-15	2023	7	15	13	34	6.233746260970782	10.35697998196772	2023-07-16T16:30:01.8

Figure 7.24: Refining a silver item while targeting a silver table

While we did not add any new data, the results are more useful. Additionally, by removing speed test failures, represented by -1, the results are easier to compute. In *Recipe 69*, we will return to this data and produce a table containing records that indicate when the speed test failed. By removing records that indicate a different condition, we can perform descriptive analytics on the remaining, as shown in *Figure 7.25*:

```
1    select min(DownMBS),max(DownMBS),avg(DownMBS),min(UpMBS),max(UpMBS),avg(UpMBS),avg(ping) from silver_fullload_speedtest_refined
```

▸ (2) Spark Jobs

Table ⌄   +

	min(DownMBS)	max(DownMBS)	avg(DownMBS)	min(UpMBS)	max(UpMBS)	avg(UpMBS)	avg(ping)
1	2.4474436642139925	13.784582166073415	8.026351367785189	1.0869930721546905	16.15809931155492	9.096740268655482	63.851485074626865

Figure 7.25: *Descriptive analysis of refined speed data*

We can see from the results that the average download speed in megabytes per second was around **8**. Had we not removed the records indicating the speed test had failed, the results would have been skewed lower. Next, we shift back to DLT and perform a similar refinement.

Recipe 70: Projection reshaping using Delta Live Tables

In *Recipe 66*, we explored applying expectations to control the quality of data. In this section, we will revisit that example from a projection reshaping perspective, as we did in Recipe 67. We extend the DLT refinement pipeline we created in *Recipe 66* to include a new table that produces the same projections as Recipe 67, as shown in *Figure 7.26*:

Cmd 3

```python
1    @dlt.table(
2      comment="Silver Speedtest",  table_properties={"quality": "silver","pipelines.reset.allowed": "false" },
3    )
4    @dlt.expect_or_drop("Download Not -1", "download > -1")
5    @dlt.expect_or_drop("Upload Not -1", "upload > -1")
6    @dlt.expect_or_drop("Ping Not -1", "ping > -1")
7    def silver_iot_speedtest_7_68():
8      return (
9        dlt.read("bronze_iot_speedtest_7_68").select("parsed_records.*","UTC_timestamp")
10     )
```

Cmd 4

```python
1    @dlt.table(
2      comment="Silver Speedtest",  table_properties={"quality": "silver","pipelines.reset.allowed": "false" },
3    )
4    @dlt.expect_or_drop("Download Not -1", "download > -1")
5    @dlt.expect_or_drop("Upload Not -1", "upload > -1")
6    @dlt.expect_or_drop("Ping Not -1", "ping > -1")
7    def silver_iot_speedtest_7_68_Refined():
8      df = dlt.read("silver_iot_speedtest_7_68")
9      df = df.withColumn("Date",to_date(df["UTC_timestamp"])).withColumn("Year",year(df["UTC_timestamp"])).withColumn("Month",month(df
         ["UTC_timestamp"]))
10     df = df.withColumn("DayOfMonth",dayofmonth(df["UTC_timestamp"]))
11     df = df.withColumn("Hour",hour(df["UTC_timestamp"])).withColumn("Minute",minute(df["UTC_timestamp"]))
12     df = df.withColumn("DownMBS",df["download"]/1024/1024)
13     df = df.withColumn("UpMBS",df["upload"]/1024/1024)
14     df = df.withColumn("LakehouseWhenRefined",current_timestamp())
15     return df
```

Figure 7.26: *Silver to silver reshaping using DLT*

We have created a more usable silver table. We did not create it to solve a certain problem but because we know that creating it will make subsequent operations easier. Often, when doing data engineering, we examine the produced results to ensure they are what we expected, as shown in *Figure 7.27:*

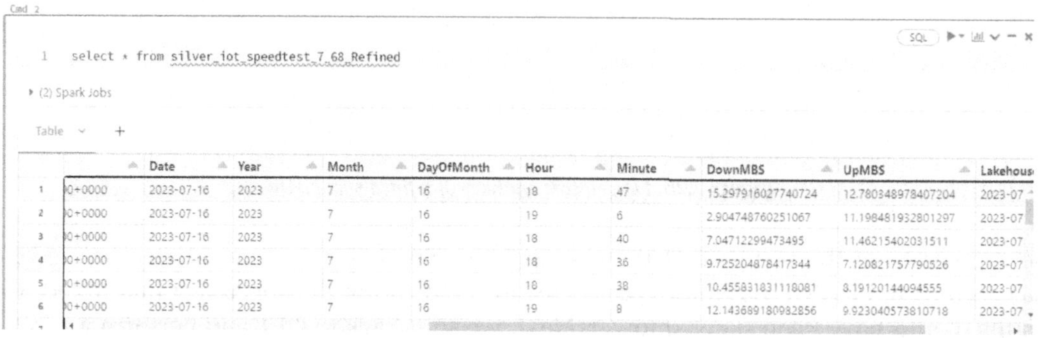

		Date	Year	Month	DayOfMonth	Hour	Minute	DownMBS	UpMBS	Lakehous
1	0+0000	2023-07-16	2023	7	16	18	47	15.297916027740724	12.780348978407204	2023-07
2	0+0000	2023-07-16	2023	7	16	19	6	2.904748760251067	11.198481932801297	2023-07
3	0+0000	2023-07-16	2023	7	16	18	40	7.04712299473495	11.46215402031511	2023-07
4	0+0000	2023-07-16	2023	7	16	18	36	9.725204878417344	7.120821757790526	2023-07
5	0+0000	2023-07-16	2023	7	16	18	38	10.455831831118081	8.19120144094555	2023-07
6	0+0000	2023-07-16	2023	7	16	19	8	12.143689180982856	9.923040573810718	2023-07

Figure 7.27: *Contents of a DLT reshaped table*

We will now examine a pattern when one silver table is used to produce multiple silver tables.

Splitting tables

Often, a table can be split into multiple tables. This is common in connected IoT devices. A common pattern is that a single table might have records that should be in different tables. We have that example in Recipe 67, where the table contains records where a speed test was successfully completed and records where the speed test failed. The failed speed tests might give us an indication of intermittent failures. Rather than just exclude those that resulted from a failed test, we should store them in a table for analysis.

Recipe 71: Splitting table into multiple in PySpark

It is not unusual for a table to contain records that logically belong to multiple sets. This is common when dealing with IoT devices. It also happens in legacy systems. Typically, the design pattern is not desirable, however as data engineers, we must address it. We will work through a simple example, based on the data we have been using. In *Recipe 67,* we removed records that contained a negative value in the **`download`, `upload`,** or **`ping`** columns. The Python code that produces the speed test data sends a -1 in those columns whenever there is an exception executing the speed test. This indicates a failure in the test. Rather than dropping those records, we should identify them as failure cases and store them for later analysis.

The main difference in the approach is that we will produce two DataFrames that will be saved as tables. One will contain records with passed tests and the full set of columns and the other will contain the failed test cases and the columns that do not reflect a speed test, such as **`download`, `upload`,** and **`ping`**, or derived from them, as shown in *Figure 7.28:*

```
1   import datetime
2   from pyspark.sql.functions import *
3   df = spark.read.table(f"`{schema}`.`{sourceSilverTable}`")
4   df = df.withColumn("Date",to_date(df["utc"])).withColumn("Year",year(df["utc"])).withColumn("Month",month(df["utc"]))
5   df = df.withColumn("DayOfMonth",dayofmonth(df["utc"]))
6   df = df.withColumn("Hour",hour(df["utc"])).withColumn("Minute",minute(df["utc"]))
7   df = df.withColumn("DownMBS",df["download"]/1024/1024)
8   df = df.withColumn("UpMBS",df["upload"]/1024/1024)
9   df = df.withColumn("LakehouseWhenRefined",current_timestamp()).cache()
```

(1) Spark Jobs

▤ df: pyspark.sql.dataframe.DataFrame = [utc: string, ip: string ... 13 more fields]

Command took 1.88 seconds -- by alan.dennis@gmail.com at 7/16/2023, 5:11:57 PM on Alan Dennis's Cluster

```
1   passedDf = df.where( (df.download > 0) & (df.upload > 0) & (df.ping > 0) )        # Remove failed items
2   passedDf = passedDf.cache() # so we can display this with out reprocessing
3   passedDf.write.mode("overwrite").option("mergeSchema", "true").option("path",destSilverTablePassedLocation).saveAsTable
    (destSilverTablePassed)
4
5   failedDf = df.where( (df.download <= 0) | (df.upload <= 0) | (df.ping <= 0) )     # Get Failed items
6   failedDf = failedDf.cache() # so we can display this with out reprocessing
7   failedDf = failedDf.select("utc","ip","Date","Year","Month","DayOfMonth","Hour","Minute","LakehouseWhenRefined","LakehouseWhenInSilver")
8   failedDf.write.mode("overwrite").option("mergeSchema", "true").option("path",destSilverTableFailedLocation).saveAsTable
    (destSilverTableFailed)
```

Figure 7.28: Creating two tables from one in the silver zone

The failed dataset contains a subset of the records and columns, as shown in *Figure 7.29*:

```
1   display(failedDf)
```

▸ (2) Spark Jobs

Table ∨ +

	utc	ip	Date	Year	Month	DayOfMonth	Hour	Minute	LakehouseWhenRefined
1	2023-07-15 15:03:13	172.18.160.1	2023-07-15	2023	7	15	15	3	2023-07-16T21:11:58.037+0000
2	2023-07-15 12:01:07	172.16.160.1	2023-07-15	2023	7	15	12	1	2023-07-16T21:11:58.037+0000
3	2023-07-15 15:04:55	172.18.160.1	2023-07-15	2023	7	15	15	4	2023-07-16T21:11:58.037+0000
4	2023-07-15 15:01:30	172.18.160.1	2023-07-15	2023	7	15	15	1	2023-07-16T21:11:58.037+0000

Figure 7.29: Failed speed test records

We have successfully split one silver into two using Python. In the next Recipe, we will use DLT to perform a similar operation.

Recipe 72: Splitting table into multiple in Delta Live Tables

Delta Live Tables simplifies data processing in part by detecting dependencies and ensuring the proper sequencing of operations. In Recipe 68, we used DLT to both apply expectations and drop records and to change the projection of our table to make it more usable. In this recipe, we will revisit that situation and save the different record types in different tables. As previously mentioned, the data contains records where a speed test was successfully completed and those where it failed. When a failure occurred, a -1 was used for the **download**, **upload**, and **ping** values. In this recipe we will separate those sets of records. We start by removing the constraints on the silver table populated from the bronze table, and from the reshaped table, as shown in *Figure 7.30*:

```
1    @dlt.table(
2      comment="Silver Speedtest",  table_properties={"quality": "silver","pipelines.reset.allowed": "false" },
3    )
4    def silver_iot_speedtest_7_70():                    No Expectations
5      return (
6        dlt.read("bronze_iot_speedtest_7_70").select("parsed_records.*","UTC_timestamp")
7    )
```

```
1    @dlt.table(
2      comment="Silver Speedtest",  table_properties={"quality": "silver","pipelines.reset.allowed": "false" },
3    )                                                   No Expectations
4    def silver_iot_speedtest_7_70_Passed():
5        df = dlt.read("silver_iot_speedtest_7_70")
6        df = df.withColumn("Date",to_date(df["UTC_timestamp"])).withColumn("Year",year(df["UTC_timestamp"])).withColumn("Month",month(df
         ["UTC_timestamp"]))
7        df = df.withColumn("DayOfMonth",dayofmonth(df["UTC_timestamp"]))
8        df = df.withColumn("Hour",hour(df["UTC_timestamp"])).withColumn("Minute",minute(df["UTC_timestamp"]))
9        df = df.withColumn("DownMBS",df["download"]/1024/1024)
10       df = df.withColumn("UpMBS",df["upload"]/1024/1024)
11       df = df.withColumn("LakehouseWhenRefined",current_timestamp())
12       df = df.where( (df["download"] > 0) & (df["upload"] > 0) & (df["ping"] > 0) )
13       return df
```

Figure 7.30: DLT with expectations removed and a where clause added

Since we removed the expectations, we must add a **where** clause to the table that expects valid **download, upload**, and **ping** values. Notice there are no expectations on either table. Next, we need to create a table to contain the records where the speed test failed. If it mirrors the past speed tests table, except that it does not include **download**, **upload**, or **ping** values or derived columns, as shown in *Figure 7.31*:

```
1    @dlt.table(
2      comment="Silver Speedtest",  table_properties={"quality": "silver","pipelines.reset.allowed": "false" },
3    )
4    def silver_iot_speedtest_7_70_Failed():
5        df = dlt.read("silver_iot_speedtest_7_70")
6        df = df.withColumn("Date",to_date(df["UTC_timestamp"])).withColumn("Year",year(df["UTC_timestamp"])).withColumn("Month",month(df
         ["UTC_timestamp"]))
7        df = df.withColumn("DayOfMonth",dayofmonth(df["UTC_timestamp"]))
8        df = df.withColumn("Hour",hour(df["UTC_timestamp"])).withColumn("Minute",minute(df["UTC_timestamp"]))
9        df = df.withColumn("LakehouseWhenRefined",current_timestamp())
10       df = df.where ( (df["download"] <= 0) | (df["upload"] <= 0) | (df["ping"] <= 0)  )
11       df = df.select("UTC_timestamp","ip","Date","Year","Month","DayOfMonth","Hour","Minute","LakehouseWhenRefined")
12       return df
```

Figure 7.31: DLT table for failed speed tests

When we create the DLT pipeline and run it, we can see the relationship between the tables, as shown in *Figure 7.32*:

Figure 7.32: *Dependencies between DLT tasks*

We can see from *Figure 7.32* that a **bronze** table is refined to a **silver** one, then that table is split into two tables. This matches our design and makes the successful and failed speed test data accessible. We have successfully split tables. In the next section, we will look at combining tables to enrich a dataset.

Enrichment

Often, relational data is broken down into various levels of normal form. While it can be deemed appropriate in relational systems, it can be problematic in a lakehouse. Moreover, device data is often combined with enterprise system data to supply a holistic view. In the next section, we will combine tables to create an output table that will be more useful but is not built for a specific problem.

Recipe 73: Creating lookup data from telemetry

When data is ingested, it is often from systems that purposefully segregate data into different tables. This is a form of data modeling referred to as normalization. The idea is to minimize the amount of storage space consumed by reducing data duplication. This is more desirable for transactional systems, however, when we are dealing with analytics workloads, it can be problematic.

When performing analytics, we sometimes need to combine multiple tables to provide richer data. While we could do that joining during query processing, it is often better to do it once and use the produced table rather than recomputing the results each time a query is performed. This process is referred to as denormalization and sometimes as materialized views. In this section, we will combine two tables together and save the result.

Before we can join tables together, we need to construct a lookup table. We have been processing speed test information, which includes an **Internet Protocol** (**IP**) address. Using a web API that returns geolocation based on IP, we can learn a considerable amount about an IP address. The API we use here is **http://ip-api.com**, which can be used to return JSON, as shown in *Figure 7.33*:

```
1  def GetISPInfo():
2      ipUrl = "http://ip-api.com/json"
3      response= json.loads(requests.get(ipUrl).content)
4      #print(response)
5      #print(response["query"])
6      return response
```
executed in 5ms, finished 17:29:31 2023-07-18

```
1  GetISPInfo()
```
executed in 147ms, finished 17:29:32 2023-07-18

```
{'status': 'success',
 'country': 'United States',
 'countryCode': 'US',
 'region': 'PA',
 'regionName': 'Pennsylvania',
 'city': 'Pittsburgh',
 'zip': '15212',
 'lat': 40.4339,
 'lon': -79.9996,
 'timezone': 'America/New_York',
 'isp': 'Verizon Business',
 'org': 'Verizon Business',
 'as': 'AS6167 Verizon Business',
 'query': '174.203.112.14'}
```

Figure 7.33: Geolocation information based on IP address

By running the script on a timing like the speed test script, we can capture speed and location information for IP addresses. This information is sent to a different Event Hub and captured to storage using Event Hub Capture. Next, we need to convert it to a bronze table, as shown in *Figure 7.33*:

Figure 7.34: Geolocation information in a bronze table

This is similar to the process we followed with speed data. Notice that there is considerable repetition of data. A more intelligent script could reduce duplication by only sending information when there is a change in IP address. We use the **query** property in the **ispinfo** field, as it is the public IP address of the requestor. For now, we use the data as it arrives and reduce it to the unique occurrences of IP address and organization (line 9 of *Figure 7.33*) and expose it as a table, as shown in *Figure 7.35*:

```
1    display(spark.sql(f"SELECT query,org FROM lakehousecookbook.silver_ipLookup "))
```

▸ (1) Spark Jobs

Table ⌄ +

	query	org
1	98.97.20.231	SpaceX Services, Inc
2	129.222.216.91	SpaceX Services, Inc
3	174.203.112.14	Verizon Business

Figure 7.35: Lookup table of IP address and Internet Service Provider (ISP) organizations

Now that we have a lookup table, we can combine it with our speed test data, which we do in the next section using DLT.

Recipe 74: Combining tables using DLT

Now that we have lookup data, we can use it with our past speed test data created in *Recipe 70*. For brevity, we will only focus on the new elements of this evolving example, as shown in *Figure 7.36*:

Figure 7.36: DLT table defined to use lookup data

Note that we read the table from *Recipe 70* using **dlt.read**, as it is a DLT, and **spark. read.table** for the lookup table. Lastly, we can look at the job run and see that only the DLT tables are displayed on the canvas, as they are the only ones being operated on, as shown in *Figure 7.37*:

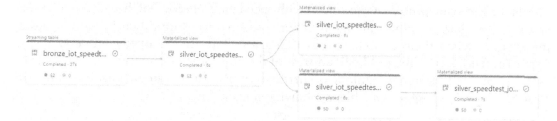

Figure 7.37: DLT pipeline run of the merge table process

We have now successfully joined tables to improve the data value within.

Conclusion

In this chapter, we have explored the various ways of creating and using silver tables. We have seen that DLT is a useful tool for creating pipelines that handle incremental, full load and processing patterns. Additionally, we have explored transformations where the source and destination tables are both silver tables.

In the next chapter, we will discuss using silver tables to create gold tables.

Join our book's Discord space

Join the book's Discord Workspace for Latest updates, Offers, Tech happenings around the world, New Release and Sessions with the Authors:

https://discord.bpbonline.com

CHAPTER 8

Transforming to Create Gold for Business Purposes

Introduction

Gold tables are created to address a particular business requirement. They are optimized for reading and are created using silver or other gold tables. There are common types of refinements associated with creating gold tables. Each of these types are explored. We review the types of aggregation used when converting from silver to gold and various modeling approaches. We provide a reusable way to create a time dimension and discuss creating dimensions from data. We close the chapter by reviewing optimization and maintenance often performed on gold tables to ensure they continue to meet consumption requirements.

Structure

The chapter covers the following topics:

- Silver to gold
- Gold to gold

Objectives

By the end of this chapter, you will be able to create gold tables using silver or gold tables. You should be familiar with the common approaches to creating gold tables. You will understand the ways to optimize tables for consumption.

Silver to gold

Until now, we have been refining data to make data easier to use or to ensure it is valid. We now shift to creating tables to answer a specific question. The tables in a gold layer are purpose-built. We are sure they are correct and know why they were created.

Aggregation

A common form of gold tables is to create aggregates. We want to reduce the number of records and perform some mathematical operation on them, such as an average or a sum. For example, you might want to know the sum of the sales for each region per year. That operation takes many records, groups them by location and time, and then adds up the groups. In the next section, we explore a hands-on example of creating gold aggregate tables.

Recipe 75: Aggregation in Delta Live Tables

We continue using speed test data as we discuss gold tables, partly because it is simple and allows us to focus on the core concepts. As a reminder, we previously combined **Internet Service Provider (ISP)** data with speed test data. We also converted the timestamp column to several date fields. Now we will use that data to answer the question, what is our average daily download speed by ISP?

In SQL, we would use the **GROUP BY** statement. Using the Python API to DLT, we do something similar but use the **groupBy** statement with an **agg** statement, as shown in *Figure 8.1:*

Cmd 7

```
1   @dlt.table(
2       comment="Silver Speedtest Joined",
3       table_properties={"quality": "silver", "pipelines.reset.allowed": "false"},
4   )
5   def silver_speedtest_joined_8_73():
6       df = dlt.read("silver_iot_speedtest_8_73_Passed")
7       schemaName = "LakehouseCookbook"
8       source_ispInfoLookupTableName = "silver_ipLookup"
9       lookupDf = spark.read.table(
10          f"`{schemaName}`.`{source_ispInfoLookupTableName}`"
11      ).select("query", "org")
12      joinedDf = df.join(lookupDf, df.ip == lookupDf.query, "left")
13      return joinedDf
```

Cmd 8

```
1   @dlt.table(
2       comment="Gold Speedtest Aggregation",
3       table_properties={"quality": "silver", "pipelines.reset.allowed": "false"},
4   )
5   def gold_speedtest_joined_8_73():
6       df = dlt.read("silver_speedtest_joined_8_73")
7
8       groupedDf = df.groupBy("org", "Date").agg(avg("downmbs").alias("avgDownMbs"))
9
10      return groupedDf
```

Figure 8.1: *Group records by date and calculate the average*

Notice the linkage with the previous table. This pattern of linking tables together is an important aspect of DLT. Also, notice that in line 8 of command 8 we use the **groupBy** command to group by organization and then date. Next, we average the download megabytes per second for that day. We can examine the results using SQL's **select** statement and then **order by date**, as shown in *Figure 8.2:*

Cmd 2

```
1   select * from gold_speedtest_joined_8_73 order by date desc
```

▶ (1) Spark Jobs

Table ∨   +

	org	Date	avgDownMbs
1	Verizon Business	2023-07-19	6.779595180294539
2	SpaceX Services, Inc	2023-07-19	18.993433542409424

Figure 8.2: *Results of aggregation*

We can also look at the data using Databricks' built-in visualizations, as shown in *Figure 8.3*:

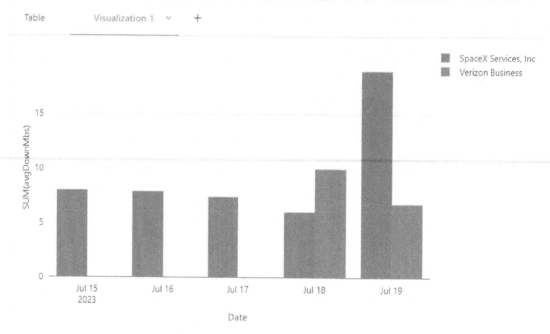

Figure 8.3: *Bar graph of download speeds*

We have now successfully created a table to answer a specific question and can move on to supporting many predefined answers by using dimensional modeling.

Dimensional tables using PySpark

In *Chapter 5, Data Profiling and Modeling in the Lakehouse*, we discussed dimensional modeling in the context of a star schema. We will revisit that discussion with an example. Time is a common dimension. We will start with a Recipe to create a dimension, then move on to using it.

Recipe 76: Creating a time dimension

Much of the data we analyze has a time element. Sometimes we want to know things like sales per quarter, which is knowable because we know when a transaction occurred to the exact second. In the case of a speed test, we do not care about a second, or even minute-level reporting as the data is typically not captured that frequently. Instead, we will construct a time dimension to the hour level, as shown in *Figure 8.4*:

```
1    Create or replace table LakehouseCookbook.Gold_DateDim as
2    SELECT
3      date_format(timestamp, "yyyyMMddHH") as id,
4      to_date(timestamp) AS date,
5      YEAR(timestamp) AS year,
6      QUARTER(timestamp) AS quarter,
7      MONTH(timestamp) AS month,
8      weekofyear(timestamp) AS weekofyear,
9      DAY(timestamp) AS day,
10     HOUR(timestamp) as hour,
11     WEEKDAY(timestamp) AS dayofweek,
12     date_format(timestamp, 'EEEE') as dayname,
13     date_format(timestamp, 'MMMM') as monthname,
14     CASE WHEN dayofweek(to_date(timestamp)) IN (1, 7) THEN 1 ELSE 0 END AS weekend,
15     CASE WHEN year(to_date(timestamp)) % 4 = 0 THEN 1 ELSE 0 END AS leapyear
16   FROM
17     (
18       SELECT explode( sequence(
19         TIMESTAMP '2023-06-01 00:00:00',
20         TIMESTAMP '2024-12-31 23:00:00',
21         INTERVAL 3600 SECOND) ) as timestamp
22     ) AS dates;
23   select * from LakehouseCookbook.Gold_DateDim
```

▸ (8) Spark Jobs

Table ⌄ +

id	date	year	quarter	month	weekofyear	day
1	2023060100	2023-06-01	2023	2	6	22	1
2	2023060101	2023-06-01	2023	2	6	22	1
3	2023060102	2023-06-01	2023	2	6	22	1

Figure 8.4: Creating a time dimension

Notice that the identifier for the dimension is **year**, **month**, **day**, and **hour** all with leading zeros. We populate the dimension table from June of 2023 to December of 2024. While our data is limited, this dimension could support reporting at a year or quarter level. In the next section, we revisit *Recipe 71*, where we created a lookup table from telemetry.

Recipe 77: Creating a dimension from telemetry

In *Recipe 71*, we created a table that contained ISP information from telemetry. We will extend that idea by creating a dimension from telemetry. As with all gold tables, dimensional modeling is about answering questions and solving problems. While the exact question may be vague, we know the area the dimensional model attempts to address. For example, in this case, we suspect there may be a difference in speed between different ISPs. With that general problem in mind, we set out to create a dimensional model using the **Time Dimension** we just created. Our dimensional model is simplistic, as shown in *Figure 8.5:*

Figure 8.5: Speed data dimensional model

We saw in *Recipe 74* that a dimension has different levels linked to a specific record. We will construct an approximation of that based on the telemetry we receive. The first step is to get the bronze data from *Recipe 71* into a format for constructing our **ISP dimension**, as shown in *Figure 8.6*:

```
1   ispinfoSilverPath = "/mnt/lakehousecookbook/Silver/AlanDesktop/EventHubSource/
    IspInfoForDim/"
2   ipLookupSilverPath = "/mnt/lakehousecookbook/Silver/AlanDesktop/EventHubSource/
    IspInfoIpLookup/"
3   ipLookupSilverTable = f"{schemaName}.silver_ipLookup"
4   ispinfoSilverTable = "silver_ispinfo_forDim"
5   ispinfoFullSilverTable = f"`{schemaName}`.`{ispinfoSilverTable}`"
6   ispinfoDf = spark.read.table(f"`{schemaName}`.`{ispInfoTableName}`")
7   ispinfoDf = ConvertBase64ToJson(ispinfoDf).cache()
8   forTable = ispinfoDf.select("jsonObject.*").distinct().cache()
9   forTable.write.mode("overwrite").option("mergeSchema", "true").option("path",
    ispinfoSilverPath).saveAsTable(ispinfoFullSilverTable)
10  display(forTable)
```

Figure 8.6: Preparing to create a dimension from telemetry

Notice that we have the ISP information in an object to create our **ISP dimension**. If you look at the data captured, it is ideal for a dimension. It contains hierarchical values, such as country, region, and city. As additional information is captured, the robustness of the dimension will increase. The next step is to get this data into a more accessible and distilled format, as shown in *Figure 8.7*:

```
1   ispDimDf = spark.read.table(ispinfoFullSilverTable)
2   ispDimDf = ispDimDf.select("ispInfo.*").distinct().where(col("query").isNotNull()).
    cache()
3   display(ispDimDf)
4   ispGoldDimPath = "/mnt/lakehousecookbook/Gold/AlanDesktop/EventHubSource/IspDim/"
5   ispGoldDimTable = f"`{schemaName}`.`Gold_IspDim`"
6   ispDimDf.write.mode("overwrite").option("mergeSchema", "true").option("path",
    ispGoldDimPath).saveAsTable(ispGoldDimTable)
```

▸ (12) Spark Jobs

Table ⌄   +

	as	city	country	countryCode	i:
1	AS14593 Space Exploration Technologies Corporation	New York	United States	US	S
2	AS14593 Space Exploration Technologies Corporation	New York	United States	US	S
3	AS6167 Verizon Business	Pittsburgh	United States	US	V
4	AS6167 Verizon Business	Pittsburgh	United States	US	V
5	AS14593 Space Exploration Technologies Corporation	New York	United States	US	S
6	AS6167 Verizon Business	Pittsburgh	United States	US	V

Figure 8.7: Creating a dimension from telemetry

We now have a link between each IP address (expressed as a query in our dimension) and information about that provider. The next step is to transform our speed telemetry into gold fact records.

Recipe 78: Creating a fact table from telemetry

We will revisit the approach we used in Recipe 52 to ingest data for this Recipe. Recall that in that Recipe, we used Auto Loader to read files from a mount point. Once we have loaded a DataFrame from the table created by **CreateTableFromFile**, we need to transform it for use and apply business rules. In this example, we will use business rules to exclude the record if **download**, **upload**, or **ping** are not greater than zero. We also convert the **unixtime** to a **timestamp** and convert **Bytes Per Second (BPS)** to **Megabytes Per Second (MBS)**. We then round all floating-point numbers to one decimal place to keep the output cleaner. Lastly, we save the newly constructed DataFrame to a table, as shown in *Figure 8.8*:

```
1   silverPath = "/mnt/lakehousecookbook/Silver/AlanDesktop/EventHubSource/SpeedTestForFact/"
2   schemaName= "Lakehousecookbook"
3   bronzeTable = "bronze_SpeedTest_ForFact"
4   silverTable = f"{schemaName}.silver_speedtest_forFact"
5   fullSilverTable = f"`{schemaName}`.`{silverTable}`"
6   bronzeDf = spark.read.table(f"`{schemaName}`.`{bronzeTable}`")
7   bronzeDf = ConvertBase64ToJson(bronzeDf)
8   silverDf = (bronzeDf.select("jsonObject.*")
9               .withColumn("timestamp", expr("cast(from_unixtime(utc) as timestamp)"))
10              .withColumn("DownMBS",round(col("download")/1024/1024,1))
11              .withColumn("UpMBS",round(col("upload")/1024/1024,1))
12              .withColumn("ping",round(col("ping"),1))
13              .where(col("download") >= 0)
14              .where(col("upload") >= 0)
15              .where(col("ping") >= 0)
16  ).cache()
17  display(silverDf)
18  silverDf.write.mode("overwrite").option("mergeSchema", "true").option("path",silverPath).saveAsTable(silverTable)
```

(9) Spark Jobs

▣ bronzeDf: pyspark.sql.dataframe.DataFrame = [SequenceNumber: long, Offset: string ... 7 more fields]

▣ silverDf: pyspark.sql.dataframe.DataFrame = [download: double, ip: string ... 6 more fields]

Table ∨ +

	download	ip	ping	upload	utc	timestamp	Dowr
1	8601171.580231367	129.222.216.91	66.3	11679382.825011991	1689589796	2023-07-17T10:29:56.000+0000	8.2
2	11683841.517972514	129.222.216.91	54.9	10827051.339742294	1689589923	2023-07-17T10:32:03.000+0000	11.1
3	7871846.892362514	129.222.216.91	68.1	10612308.764778273	1689590049	2023-07-17T10:34:09.000+0000	7.5

Figure 8.8: Creating a silver table

While we could have used an existing silver table for this exercise, we created a new one, partly so that this and related Recipes could be used independently. Now that we have a silver table, the last step is constructing a gold fact table, as shown in *Figure 8.9*:

```
1   goldPath = "/mnt/lakehousecookbook/Gold/AlanDesktop/EventHubSource/SpeedTest_Fact/"
2   schemaName = "Lakehousecookbook"
3   goldTable = f"{schemaName}.gold_speedtest_fact"
4   goldDf = silverDf.withColumn("dateId", date_format(col("timestamp"), "yyyyMMddHH"))
5   goldDf = goldDf.select("dateid", "ip", "downmbs", "upmbs", "ping", "timestamp").cache()
6   display(goldDf)
7   goldDf.write.mode("overwrite").option("mergeSchema", "true").option(
8       "path", goldPath
9   ).saveAsTable(goldTable)
```

▸ (9) Spark Jobs

▸ 🖥 goldDf: pyspark.sql.dataframe.DataFrame = [dateid: string, ip: string ... 4 more fields]

Table ∨   +

	dateid	ip	downmbs	upmbs	ping	timestamp
1	2023071710	129.222.216.91	8.2	11.1	66.3	2023-07-17T10:29:56.000+0000
2	2023071710	129.222.216.91	11.1	10.3	54.9	2023-07-17T10:32:03.000+0000
3	2023071710	129.222.216.91	7.5	10.1	68.1	2023-07-17T10:34:09.000+0000
4	2023071821	174.203.112.14	14.9	2.5	62.8	2023-07-18T21:59:37.000+0000

Figure 8.9: Constructing the speed fact table

Now that we have our dimensional model, we can execute a few queries to try it out. Our first query calculates the average download speed per month per ISP, as shown in *Figure 8.10*:

```
1   select
2     c.org,b.year,b.monthname,round(avg(downmbs),1) avgDownMbs,round(avg(upmbs),1) avgUpMbs,count(a.downmbs) readings
3   from
4     gold_speedtest_fact a
5     join gold_datedim b on a.dateid = b.id
6     join gold_ispdim c on a.ip = c.query
7   group by c.org,b.year,b.monthname
8   order by b.year,b.monthname
```

(4) Spark Jobs

Table ∨   +

	org	year	monthname	avgDownMbs	avgUpMbs	readings
1	Verizon Business	2023	July	7.4	2.9	295
2	SpaceX Services, Inc	2023	July	8.9	8.9	2398

Figure 8.10: Example usage of fact and dimensions

We can see that average download speeds are close, while there is a greater difference in upload speed. The value of a dimensional model is that supplies flexibility in calculating values along the established dimensions. In the earlier example, you can say that we rolled up the readings to a monthly level. While this Recipe is simplistic, it shows concepts associated with dimensional modeling in the lakehouse architecture.

Dimensional tables in Delta Live Tables

Now that we have explored creating a dimensional model using Auto Loader from Spark's Python interface, we will revisit the approach using Delta Live Tables.

Recipe 79: Dimensional models with Delta Live Table

As discussed in Recipe 74, we often organize data along temporal dimensions. We reuse the approach from Recipe 74 to create a time dimension table using DLT, as shown in *Figure 8.11*:

```
1   @dlt.table(
2       comment="Silver Speedtest",  table_properties={"quality": "gold","pipelines.reset.allowed": "false" },
3   )
4   def gold_dim_date_8_77():
5       return spark.sql("""
6   SELECT
7       date_format(timestamp, "yyyyMMddHH") as id,  to_date(timestamp) AS date,  YEAR(timestamp) AS year,
8       QUARTER(timestamp) AS quarter,  MONTH(timestamp) AS month,  weekofyear(timestamp) AS weekofyear,  DAY(timestamp) AS day,
9       HOUR(timestamp) as hour,  WEEKDAY(timestamp) AS dayofweek,
10      date_format(timestamp, 'EEEE') as dayname,  date_format(timestamp, 'MMMM') as monthname,
11      CASE WHEN dayofweek(to_date(timestamp)) IN (1, 7) THEN 1 ELSE 0 END AS weekend,
12      CASE WHEN year(to_date(timestamp)) % 4 = 0 THEN 1 ELSE 0 END AS leapyear
13  FROM  (
14      SELECT explode( sequence(TIMESTAMP '2023-06-01 00:00:00', TIMESTAMP '2024-12-31 23:00:00',INTERVAL 3600 SECOND) ) as timestamp
15  ) AS dates;""")
```

Figure 8.11: *Create a DLT date dimension*

Do you observe the three double quote strings on lines 5 and 15? This is a way of specifying a multiline string in Python. We can explore the table and ensure the results are as expected, as shown in *Figure 8.12*:

```
1   select * from gold_dim_date_8_77;
```

▸ (2) Spark Jobs

Table ⌄ +

	id	date	year	quarter	month	weekofyear	day	hour	dayofweek	dayname	montl
121	2023060600	2023-06-06	2023	2	6	23	6	0	1	Tuesday	June
122	2023060601	2023-06-06	2023	2	6	23	6	1	1	Tuesday	June
123	2023060602	2023-06-06	2023	2	6	23	6	2	1	Tuesday	June
124	2023060603	2023-06-06	2023	2	6	23	6	3	1	Tuesday	June
125	2023060604	2023-06-06	2023	2	6	23	6	4	1	Tuesday	June
126	2023060605	2023-06-06	2023	2	6	23	6	5	1	Tuesday	June

Figure 8.12: *Data exploration of the DLT-created date and time dimension*

Next, we need to construct the ISP dimension. We reuse the table from Recipe 75, as shown in *Figure 8.13*:

```
1   @dlt.table(
2       comment="Gold ISP Dim",  table_properties={"quality": "gold","pipelines.reset.allowed": "false" },
3   )
4   def gold_Dim_Isp_8_77():
5       df = spark.read.table("lakehousecookbook.gold_ispdim")
6       return df
```

Figure 8.13: *DLT ISP dimension*

Note the use of the existing gold table. Next, we need to focus on refining the speed test data. We start with creating the bronze table, as shown in *Figure 8.14*:

```
Cmd 9

1   payload_ddl = """utc long, ip STRING,download DOUBLE, upload DOUBLE, ping DOUBLE"""
2   payload_schema = T._parse_datatype_string(payload_ddl)
3
4   def parse(df):
5     return (df
6       .withColumn("records", col("Body").cast("string"))
7       .withColumn("parsed_records", from_json(col("records"), payload_schema))
8       .withColumn("timestamp", expr("cast(from_unixtime(parsed_records.utc) as timestamp)"))
9     )
10
```

```
Cmd 10

1   @dlt.table(
2     comment="bronze Speedtest",  table_properties={"quality": "bronze","pipelines.reset.allowed": "false" },
3   )
4   def bronze_SpeedTest_8_77():
5       df = spark.readStream.format("cloudFiles").option("cloudFiles.format","avro").load("/mnt/sourceData/lakehousecookbook/speedtest/")
6       return df.transform(parse).select("parsed_records.*","timestamp")
7
```

Figure 8.14: *Creating Bronze DLT for speed test data*

Notice that we use a **parse** method and invoke it using the DataFrame **transform** method. We then select the fields from the **parsed_records** along with the timestamp. Selecting the records provides a sanity check that the records are as we expect, as shown in *Figure 8.15*:

```
1   select * from bronze_SpeedTest_8_77
```

▶ (4) Spark Jobs

Table ∨   +

	utc	ip	download	upload	ping	timestamp
1	1689690666	98.97.20.231	2094976.7404184022	8226449.7647903	46.292	2023-07-18T14:31:06.000+0000
2	1689690793	98.97.20.231	2838208.229942732	9301261.634580104	53.924	2023-07-18T14:33:13.000+0000
3	1689645333	98.97.20.231	11141524.325672584	9883277.848353937	56.4	2023-07-18T01:55:33.000+0000

Figure 8.15: *Bronze records from DLT*

Next, we create the silver table that passed the condition that **download**, **upload**, and **ping** should be non-negative, as shown in *Figure 8.16*:

```
1   @dlt.table(
2     comment="Silver Speedtest",  table_properties={"quality": "silver","pipelines.reset.allowed": "false" },
3   )
4   def silver_iot_speedtest_8_77_Passed():
5       df = dlt.read("bronze_SpeedTest_8_77")
6       df = df.withColumn("Date",to_date(df["timestamp"])).withColumn("Year",year(df["timestamp"])).withColumn("Month",month(df["timestamp"]))
7       df = df.withColumn("DownMBS",df["download"]/1024/1024)
8       df = df.withColumn("UpMBS",df["upload"]/1024/1024)
9       df = df.where( (df["download"] > 0) & (df["upload"] > 0) & (df["ping"] > 0) )
10      return df
```

Figure 8.16: *DLT declaration of passed speed test table*

We highlight the **where** clause on line 9 to call out the silver requirement. Another sanity check of the table ensures the rules are applied as expected, as shown in *Figure 8.17*:

```
1    select * from silver_iot_speedtest_8_77_Passed order by download
```

▸ (1) Spark Jobs

Table ∨ +

	utc	ip	download	upload	ping	timestamp	
1	1689682719	98.97.20.231	81273.7528377321	95275.76851252174	4697.192	2023-07-18T12:18:39.000+0000	
2	1689437960	129.222.216.91	119971.47865551358	730290.1133063062	95.512	2023-07-15T16:19:20.000+0000	
3	1689802656	98.97.20.231	197017.9481304982	404381.4933351256	68.974	2023-07-19T21:37:36.000+0000	

Figure 8.17: *Silver speed test passed table ordered by download*

We are now at the place to create our gold table. Similar to what we did in *Recipe 76*, we expose the transformed data, along with the keys to the dimension tables, as shown in *Figure 8.18*:

```
1    @dlt.table(
2        comment="Gold Speedtest Fact",
3        table_properties={"quality": "gold", "pipelines.reset.allowed": "false"},
4    )
5    def gold_fact_speedtest_8_77():
6        df = dlt.read("silver_iot_speedtest_8_77_Passed")
7        df = df.withColumn("dateId", date_format(col("timestamp"), "yyyyMMddHH"))
8        df = df.select("dateid", "ip", "downmbs", "upmbs", "ping", "timestamp")
9        return df
```

Figure 8.18: *Gold DLT for speed test data*

Notice that the selected columns include the **dateid** column, which is used to join with the date dimension. We can double-check our work by listing a few of the records in the gold table, as shown in *Figure 8.19*:

```
1    select * from gold_fact_speedtest_8_77
```

▸ (2) Spark Jobs

Table ∨ +

	dateid	ip	downmbs	upmbs	ping	timestamp	
1	2023071511	129.222.216.91	2.4474436642139925	4.140687851900427	55.662	2023-07-15T11:10:49.000+0000	
2	2023071511	129.222.216.91	7.521755138145554	1.0869930721546905	83.343	2023-07-15T11:13:03.000+0000	
3	2023071511	129.222.216.91	8.918170176028458	7.387152804548598	74.529	2023-07-15T11:15:19.000+0000	
4	2023071511	129.222.216.91	8.136291394864628	4.9100705194564895	60.492	2023-07-15T11:17:25.000+0000	

Figure 8.19: *Gold speed test fact table*

We have constructed a dimensional model using DLT. Since gold tables are created in response to a specific business requirement, we cannot assume to cover the range of activities encountered during your day-to-day activities. We have presented several common patterns. They are by no means the only type of operations you will encounter. Next, we discuss another general variation of creating gold tables, populating Common Data Models.

Using Common Data Models with Delta Live Tables

There are many **Common Data Models (CDM)**. The idea of a CDM is that an industry has reoccurring patterns. This includes the types of data captured or the type of operations required. We will start our discussion with an overview of Microsoft's CDM.

Microsoft Common Data Model

The Microsoft CDM came out of the need to reduce the amount of duplicate work associated with data engineering activities across similar enterprise systems. Much of Microsoft's CDM is influenced by Dynamics 365. To learn more about Microsoft CDM, visit **https://learn.microsoft.com/en-us/common-data-model/**.

The model is organized into core entities and those specific to an industry or application type. Core entities include accounts, activities, addresses, appointments, organizations, and so on. CDM aims to reduce the amount of effort involved with system integration. A version of CDM has been released at **https://github.com/Microsoft/CDM**.

When dealing with CDM-related entities, there is a Spark connector that will simplify the interaction. The connector is available at **https://github.com/Azure/spark-cdm-connector**. The connector enables the use of the JSON files associated with each entity type. An example program walks you through the process of using a manifest file to connect to a location containing a CDM object. The main purpose of introduction this topic is to ensure you are prepared if you encounter such technology.

Gold to gold

A variation of creating gold lakehouse tables is when the tables used to produce them are themselves gold. Typically, we use silver tables to construct gold tables. However, there are cases when the source of gold table creation is one or more gold tables.

Table optimization for consumption

Once a gold layer is constructed, we often need to focus on improving read operation performance. As the gold layer is primarily concerned with serving data to consumers, it must perform well. We will briefly introduce ways to improve read performance.

We will revisit this topic in *Chapter 14, Operations*. We will then discuss the **optimize** command and then shift to the **vacuum** command.

To understand the importance of the **optimize** and **vacuum** commands, we must first discuss the nature of the Delta format. Delta is built leveraging the parquet file format, in part because of the effort that has been spent to optimize that format. Parquet files do not allow updates. Instead, a change to a parquet file requires rewriting the file. That is not an ideal solution for a Lakehouse.

To offset this limitation, Delta utilizes a set of JSON files containing a journal of operation on the table. For example, consider the fact table we created in *Recipe 77*. We constructed a gold table named **SpeedTest_Fact**. We stored that table externally, based on a mount point. We can view the contents of that folder using an explorer, as shown in *Figure 8.20*:

Name	Access Tier	Access Tier Last Modified	Last Modified	Blob Type
_delta_log			7/22/2023 12:44 PM	
part-00000-873cc5c9-ff76-48ef-b2c6-ffc0e09c0b31-c000.snappy.parquet	Hot (inferred)		7/22/2023 12:40 PM	Block Blob
part-00000-b946ac55-c478-472e-9f84-5f7083ad2937-c000.snappy.parquet	Hot (inferred)		7/22/2023 12:44 PM	Block Blob
part-00001-b29620b8-9405-4f3a-bf18-a82ca9187725-c000.snappy.parquet	Hot (inferred)		7/22/2023 12:44 PM	Block Blob
part-00001-bee92452-7438-414b-bdbc-4e87263c1de9-c000.snappy.parquet	Hot (inferred)		7/22/2023 12:40 PM	Block Blob
part-00002-8c9096c8-cd4a-4cfe-b8b6-60c57494548b-c000.snappy.parquet	Hot (inferred)		7/22/2023 12:44 PM	Block Blob
part-00002-c4899d13-5cc7-4208-a410-04bb72d2b0f7-c000.snappy.parquet	Hot (inferred)		7/22/2023 12:40 PM	Block Blob
part-00003-53d690b3-7fd2-48f0-9a56-07a48a089f52-c000.snappy.parquet	Hot (inferred)		7/22/2023 12:40 PM	Block Blob
part-00003-79b24686-6e98-43b8-a5ee-d5a28945c614-c000.snappy.parquet	Hot (inferred)		7/22/2023 12:44 PM	Block Blob

Figure 8.20: Folder contents of a Delta table

Notice that the selected row has the name **_delta_log**, while the other rows are parquet files. If we open the **_delta_log** folder, we see it is made up of some JSON and CRC files, as shown in *Figure 8.21*:

Name	Access Tier	Access Tier Last Modified	Last Modified	Blob Type	Content Type	Size	Status
__tmp_path_dir			7/22/2023 12:44 PM		Folder		Active
00000000000000000000.crc	Hot (inferred)		7/22/2023 12:40 PM	Block Blob	application/octet-stream	5.2 KB	Active
00000000000000000000.json	Hot (inferred)		7/22/2023 12:40 PM	Block Blob	application/octet-stream	4.3 KB	Active
00000000000000000001.crc	Hot (inferred)		7/22/2023 12:44 PM	Block Blob	application/octet-stream	5.2 KB	Active
00000000000000000001.json	Hot (inferred)		7/22/2023 12:44 PM	Block Blob	application/octet-stream	5.0 KB	Active

Figure 8.21: Contents of a _delta_log folder

These JSON files are the journal of the changes made to the tables. As the number of updates increases, the number of these files increases. As this occurs, elements of the parquet files are no longer being used, as they were deleted. We can think of this as being similar to fragmentation in traditional databases. Changes made to a Delta table over time leads to poor performance.

Optimize

To address this performance challenge, we use the **OPTIMIZE** command. There are several types of optimizations that can be performed. Compaction improves performance by combining smaller files into larger ones. Most big data systems suffer from the small file problem. Often systems cannot process many small files effectively. Rather, they perform better with fewer larger files. By rewriting the files, the **OPTIMIZE** command can greatly improve performance related to small files.

Another form of optimization is data skipping. By ordering data in certain columns (called **z-ordering**), data not needed for the current operation can be skipped over. Z-ordering is a form of near ordering, where records with values close to each other are physically stored closely.

Recipe 80: Manually optimize a table

In *Recipe 76*, we created a fact table from telemetry. As there were multiple executions of the notebooks, likely the table can benefit from optimization. We can run **OPTIMIZE** from multiple languages, such as SQL, as shown in *Figure 8.22:*

Figure 8.22: *Optimizing a Delta table*

The results of the command are a row that contains the folder impacted and the operational metrics. For example, we can see in this case that four files were removed and one added. **OPTIMIZE** is important enough that Databricks added auto-optimization. Even with such features, we still need to maintain our Delta tables, especially as they grow larger.

Vacuum

The **vacuum** command is another form of maintenance associated with optimizing Delta tables for reading. The **vacuum** command recursively removes files that are no longer needed. Optimize marks files as no longer being needed, so running the **OPTIMIZE** command and then running the **vacuum** command in your maintenance process is efficient. One-way files are no longer needed when the data they contain exceeds the retention interval associated with time travel. This marks the importance of correctly setting your desired retention period on a table, as vacuuming a table will make time travel before that period impossible.

You have the choice of performing a dry run of the **vacuum** command. This operation returns information about what will happen when the **vacuum** operation is performed. This will allow you to decide if the operation is advisable.

Recipe 81: Vacuum a Delta table

Returning to the fact table we created in *Recipe 76*, we can further optimize the table by running the **vacuum** command. Since the table is new, it is not expected that there will be any unused files in the folder. However, for completeness, we will execute **vacuum**, as shown in *Figure 8.23*:

Figure 8.23: *DRY RUN and vacuum of fact table*

Notice that when we ran the command with the **DRY RUN** clause, it returned no results. This is an indication that the operation was not likely to impact files. When we run it without the clause, it took roughly 20 seconds to complete but did not impact any records. We will return to these commands, along with other operations in *Chapter 14, Operations*. We have optimized gold tables for read operations.

Conclusion

In this chapter we learned how to construct gold tables. We discussed two ways of creating gold tables from silver. We also discussed the importance of understanding the business need before creating tables, as that is the definition of a gold table. We discussed two for purpose and a generic approach to creating tables (dimensional modeling and Common Data Models). In the next chapter, we will shift our focus to Machine Learning usage of the Lakehouse platform.

In the next chapter, we will review one of the common usages of the lakehouse architecture, machine learning, and data science. We will review Databricks' support for these workloads and provide examples.

Join our book's Discord space

Join the book's Discord Workspace for Latest updates, Offers, Tech happenings around the world, New Release and Sessions with the Authors:

https://discord.bpbonline.com

CHAPTER 9

Machine Learning and Data Science

Introduction

A common use of Lakehouse data is to support **Machine Learning (ML)** and **Data Science (DS)** activities. We start with a discussion of **AutoML**, an automated Machine Learning feature. Next, we will examine MLflow deeper and Databricks' Feature Store. We will then close the chapter by discussing ways to deploy models to production.

Structure

The chapter covers the following topics:

- Machine learning in Databricks
- Using AutoML
- Setting up and using MLflow
- Deploying models to production
- Using Databricks feature store

Objectives

By the end of this chapter, you should be able to use and understand basic ML concepts. You should be able to run AutoML to predict, classify, or perform regression. You will be able to understand MLflow's role in managing experiments and deploying models, including real-time scenarios. You will also have a basic understanding of Databricks' Feature Store.

Machine Learning in Databricks

Artificial Intelligence (AI), Data Science, and Machine learning are all disciplines focused on extracting business value from data. There is considerable discussion as to which discipline is a subset of the other, but the end goal is the same, to get value from data. For simplicity, we will use the term ML to describe these overlapping disciplines and approaches.

ML and most Big Data techniques often process all data rather than relying on sampling techniques. We do this because it typically yields better results and ensures we do not have a biased sample. The ways we solve these problems have been simplified with the advent of AutoML, which we will discuss next.

Using AutoML

Automated Machine Learning (AutoML) simplifies the process of creating ML models by creating and testing multiple models. The process typically starts by defining the type of ML problem being addressed, specifying the mechanism to rank output, and specifying the data to use. AutoML then creates, trains, and scores many models and presents the results ranked by the supplied mechanism. It is a compelling offering, as signified by the front-page placement on the Databricks landing page, as shown in *Figure 9.1*:

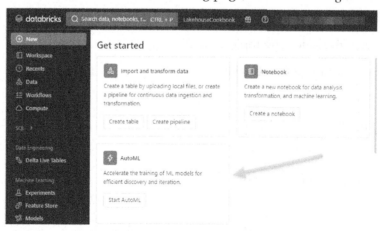

Figure 9.1: *AutoML in Databricks workspace*

Clicking **Start AutoML** brings up a new AutoML experiment. The first thing you will be asked to do is specify the cluster. The version of the ML runtime selected impacts the available features. As of this writing, the recommendation was to select an ML runtime of 12.2 LTS or higher to ensure the most extensive feature support. If you do not have any clusters running an ML runtime, you will be prompted to ask your administrator to create one.

Recipe 82: Creating an ML cluster

Creating a cluster is relatively straightforward; the main thing is to select an **ML Runtime**, as shown in *Figure 9.2*:

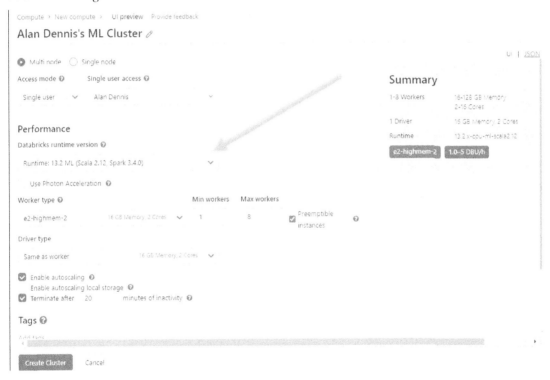

Figure 9.2: *Creating a cluster with an ML runtime*

Reading this form, we can tell this cluster will cost between 1 and 5 DBU per hour. A **Databricks Unit (DBU)** is a costing construct. It is a relative measure of cost. The exchange rate between DBUs and currency is handled contractually and is often affected by pre-commitment and other factors. The variable cost is a product of the cluster configured to auto scale. Autoscaling adjusts the cluster size based on worker utilization. When this cluster is at the maximum size of **8** workers, the cost will be 5 DBU per hour of execution.

There are other settings related to cluster creation. For example, this cluster is being created with pre-emptive instances for the workers. This is a similar concept to spot instances in

Azure. The idea is that when there is surplus capacity, you get a better rate in terms of DBUs. When the surplus capacity is exhausted, your worker may be terminated. Now that a cluster is created, we can shift back to AutoML.

On the **Configure AutoML experiment** page, select the ML cluster you wish to use, and specify the class of problem you are addressing. The choices are **classification**, **regression**, and **forecasting**. Next, you will need to supply the data. An easy way to add data is to use the Databricks data import feature.

Recipe 83: Importing data with the Databricks web page

On the Databricks landing page, notice the tile named **Import and transform data**, as shown previously in *Figure 9.1*. On that tile, notice the button labeled **Create table**. Clicking that starts the process of importing data, as shown in *Figure 9.3*:

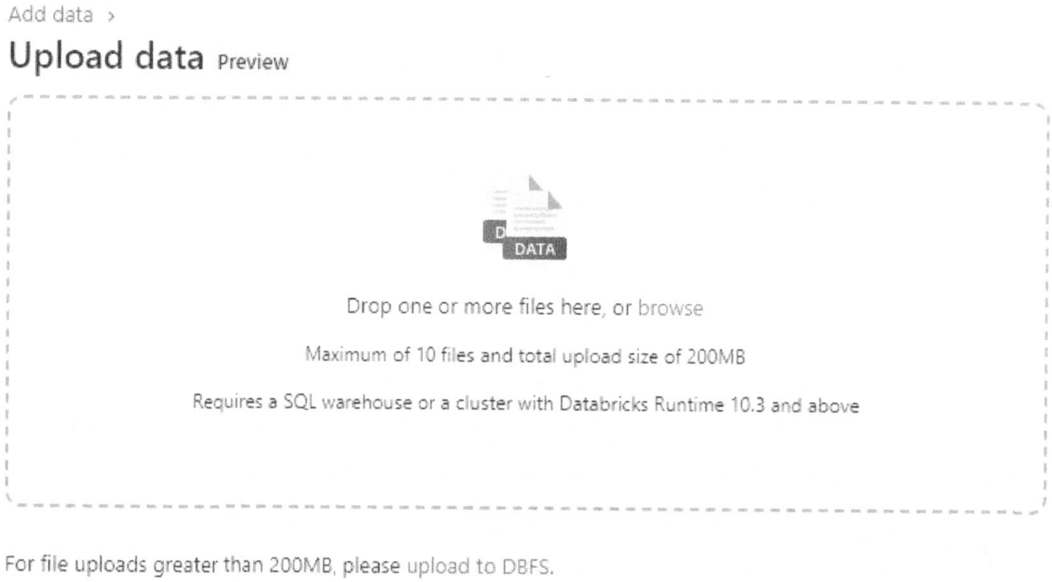

Add data >

Upload data Preview

Drop one or more files here, or browse

Maximum of 10 files and total upload size of 200MB

Requires a SQL warehouse or a cluster with Databricks Runtime 10.3 and above

For file uploads greater than 200MB, please upload to DBFS.

Figure 9.3: Import data screen

For this example, we will use a slightly modified version of the well-known and thoroughly studied dataset, **iris**, available at **https://archive.ics.uci.edu/dataset/53/iris**. The **iris** dataset is a commonly used dataset for learning about classification. It comes from studies in 1936 to determine the species of the iris flower based on measurements of its components. The dataset contains four features (each row's length and width of the petal and sepal) and the variety, as shown in *Figure 9.4*:

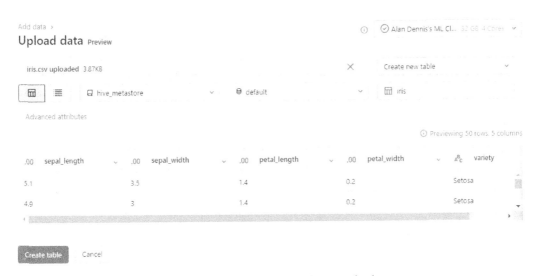

Figure 9.4: *Preview of data during upload*

Clicking the **Create table** button causes the table to be created. Note that feature names should not include periods, as it will cause the experiment to fail. It might take a little while to create.

Recipe 84: Creating and running an AutoML experiment

Once the table has been created, we can select it on the **Configure AutoML experiment** page, as shown in *Figure 9.5*:

Figure 9.5: *Configure AutoML experiment*

Once we have selected the dataset, we need to specify the target. The target will be the outcome of the classification. We can also see the **Schema** of the dataset on the right side of the page. Imputation is the process of handling missing values. In this case, we allow AutoML to handle them as it sees fit. The choices for impute are **auto**, **mean**, **median**, **most frequent**, and **constant**. Once we are satisfied with our settings, we can click on the **Start AutoML** button, located at the bottom of the page. The AutoML process can be time-consuming, in turn, leading it to be expensive. The process starts by analyzing the data and produces a data exploration notebook, as shown in *Figure 9.6*:

Variables

Select Columns ✔

sepal_length
Real number (ℝ)

Distinct	35	Minimum	4.3
Distinct (%)	23.3%	Maximum	7.9
Missing	0	Zeros	0
Missing (%)	0.0%	Zeros (%)	0.0%
Infinite	0	Negative	0
Infinite (%)	0.0%	Negative (%)	0.0%
Mean	5.8433333	Memory size	1.3 KiB

More details

Figure 9.6: Viewing the generated data exploration notebook

The report should look familiar, since it is generated using Pandas profile report we discussed in Recipe 45, in *Chapter 5, Data Profiling and Modeling in the Lakehouse*. As the experiment continues to run, we can monitor the process by clicking the **Refresh** button, as shown in *Figure 9.7*:

Figure 9.7: Results during the experiment run

Termination of the experiment is typically based on duration or reaching an acceptable metric, such as accuracy. In this case, the default value of a two-hour duration was used. We reached an **F1 score** (val_f1_score) of **0.969**, as shown in *Figure 9.8*:

Figure 9.8: F1 scores of the best models

The next step is to examine the generated model. Databricks AutoML allows you to see the notebook that was generated and then used to train and test the model. This is one of the distinguishing features of Databricks' approach to AutoML; since it is a **clear-box** approach, we can see and modify the generated code. Databricks is by no means the only company offering automatic ML. Still, their approach is compelling because you can extend the notebooks based on your skill and knowledge. When we click on a **model**, we land on a page that has a code for serving the model from a Databricks and Pandas DataFrame, as shown in *Figure 9.9*:

Figure 9.9: Model MLflow for using the model

You also have the option of registering the model. We will discuss serving the model in recipe 86, later in this chapter. If you scroll to the top of the page, you can see a link to the source notebook, as shown in *Figure 9.10*:

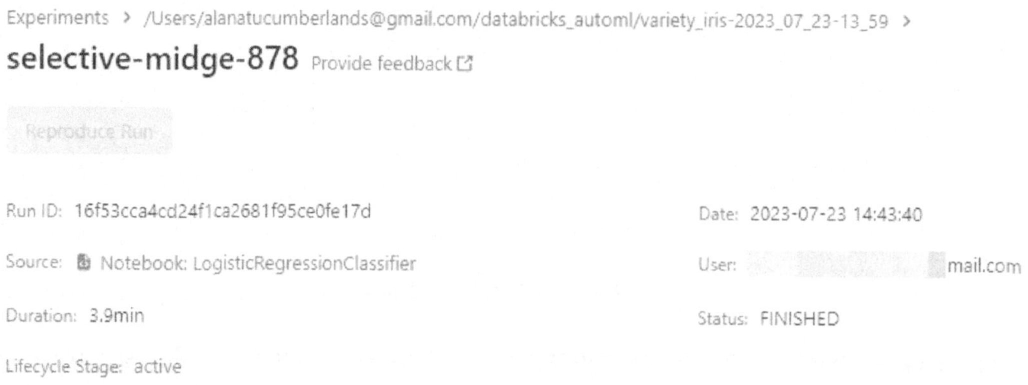

Experiments > /Users/alanatucumberlands@gmail.com/databricks_automl/variety_iris-2023_07_23-13_59 >

selective-midge-878 Provide feedback ⬈

Reproduce Run

Run ID: 16f53cca4cd24f1ca2681f95ce0fe17d   Date: 2023-07-23 14:43:40

Source: 📖 Notebook: LogisticRegressionClassifier   User: ▨▨▨▨▨▨▨ mail.com

Duration: 3.9min   Status: FINISHED

Lifecycle Stage: active

Figure 9.10: Link to source notebook

Clicking the link next to the **Source** label opens the MLflow page. If you are unfamiliar with ML, this is a good way to learn, as the notebooks follow best practices. This includes the use of the **Train – Validate - Test Split**. This is a common ML and DS practice to ensure high model quality by holding out a portion of the data for testing. In this case, the model uses a 60/20/20 ratio, as shown in *Figure 9.11*:

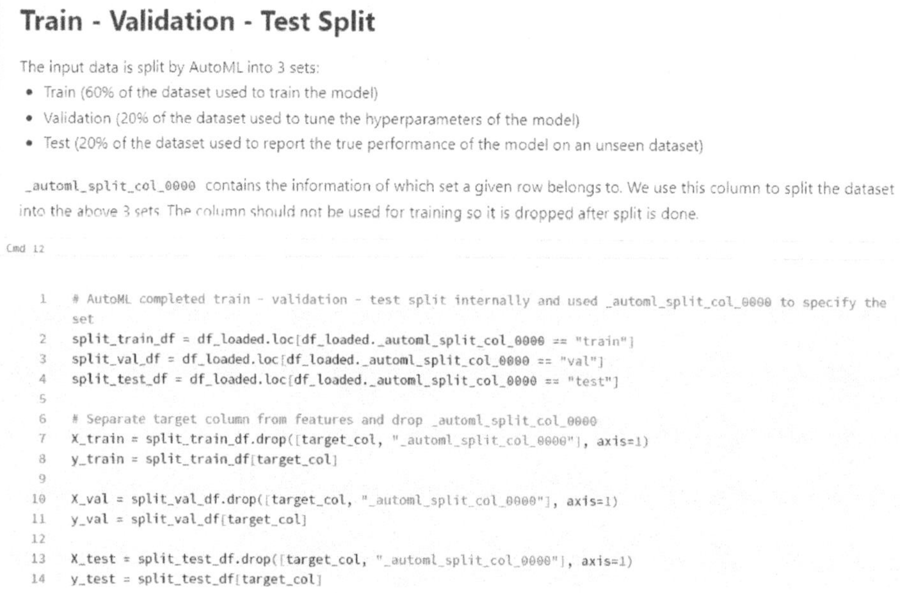

Train - Validation - Test Split

The input data is split by AutoML into 3 sets:

- Train (60% of the dataset used to train the model)
- Validation (20% of the dataset used to tune the hyperparameters of the model)
- Test (20% of the dataset used to report the true performance of the model on an unseen dataset)

_automl_split_col_0000 contains the information of which set a given row belongs to. We use this column to split the dataset into the above 3 sets. The column should not be used for training so it is dropped after split is done.

Cmd 12

```
1   # AutoML completed train - validation - test split internally and used _automl_split_col_0000 to specify the
    set
2   split_train_df = df_loaded.loc[df_loaded._automl_split_col_0000 == "train"]
3   split_val_df = df_loaded.loc[df_loaded._automl_split_col_0000 == "val"]
4   split_test_df = df_loaded.loc[df_loaded._automl_split_col_0000 == "test"]
5
6   # Separate target column from features and drop _automl_split_col_0000
7   X_train = split_train_df.drop([target_col, "_automl_split_col_0000"], axis=1)
8   y_train = split_train_df[target_col]
9
10  X_val = split_val_df.drop([target_col, "_automl_split_col_0000"], axis=1)
11  y_val = split_val_df[target_col]
12
13  X_test = split_test_df.drop([target_col, "_automl_split_col_0000"], axis=1)
14  y_test = split_test_df[target_col]
```

Figure 9.11: Train, validate, and test split

We have successfully used AutoML to solve a classification problem. Several of the other generated artifacts are useful as well. For example, the test **confusion matrix** is a good way to determine both the accuracy, but also the percentage of false positives and negatives, as shown in *Figure 9.12*:

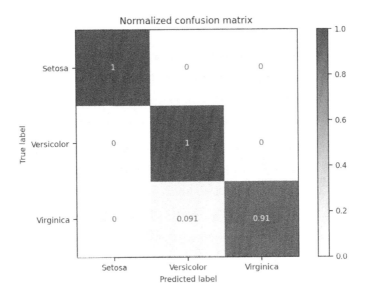

Figure 9.12: *Test confusion matrix*

We have seen the benefits of MLflow, without it being obvious. AutoML relies heavily on MLflow to perform the curation of the experiment results. In the next section, we explore MLflow.

Setting up and using MLflow

MLflow is an open-source project started and supported by Databricks. It manages the ML lifecycle by tracking experiments, packing ML code into reusable and reproducible packages, managing, and deploying models, and centrally storing and managing MLflow models. In this section, we will touch on only a few of the capabilities of MLflow. MLflow is part of the broader set of technologies associated with **Machine Learning Operations (MLOps)**. To learn more about MLflow, visit **https://mlflow.org**. We start our discussion of MLflow with how to set up an experiment.

Recipe 85: Setting up an MLflow experiment

With most softwares, we must first install it before we can use it however in the case of Mlflow, it is pre-installed with most Databricks runtimes. This means we can start using it without the installation or configuration. The process starts by importing the Mlflow libraries and turning on automatic logging for **sklearn**, as shown in *Figure 9.13*:

Cmd 3

Includes and sklearn Auto-logging

Cmd 4

```
1   import mlflow
2   import mlflow.sklearn
3   import matplotlib.pyplot as plt
4
5   from sklearn import datasets
6   from sklearn.decomposition import PCA
7   from sklearn.discriminant_analysis import LinearDiscriminantAnalysis
8   # Turn on MLflow's sklearn Autolog
9   mlflow.sklearn.autolog()
```

Command took 0.16 seconds -- by alanatucumberlands@gmail.com at 7/27/2023, 6:33:57 PM on Alan Dennis's ML Cluster

Figure 9.13: *Import MLflow libraries and enable auto logging*

The example we are using is taken from the scikit-learn website and deals with Linear **Discriminant Analysis (LDA)** and **Principal Component Analysis (PCA)** and can be found at:

https://scikit-learn.org/stable/auto_examples/decomposition/plot_pca_vs_lda. html#sphx-glr-auto-examples-decomposition-plot-pca-vs-lda-py.

The point of the exercise is not to discuss **pca** and **lda**, but rather to show how MLflow is integrated into the framework, as shown in *Figure 9.14*:

```
1    # Load Dataset
2    iris = datasets.load_iris()
3    # Set target, data, and target names
4    X = iris.data
5    y = iris.target
6    target_names = iris.target_names
7    pca = PCA(n_components=2)
8    X_r = pca.fit(X).transform(X)
9    lda = LinearDiscriminantAnalysis(n_components=2)
10   X_r2 = lda.fit(X, y).transform(X)
```

▼ (1) MLflow run

Logged 1 run to an experiment in MLflow. Learn more

```
2023/07/27 22:34:58 INFO mlflow.utils.autologging_utils: Created MLflow autologging run with ID 'aa09937a328b40af87fc0e3a0ec63573', w
hich will track hyperparameters, performance metrics, model artifacts, and lineage information for the current sklearn workflow
2023/07/27 22:34:59 WARNING mlflow.sklearn: Training metrics will not be recorded because training labels were not specified. To auto
matically record training metrics, provide training labels as inputs to the model training function.
2023/07/27 22:34:59 WARNING mlflow.sklearn: Failed to infer model signature: the trained model does not specify a 'predict' function,
which is required in order to infer the signature
2023/07/27 22:34:59 WARNING mlflow.sklearn: Model was missing function: predict. Not logging python_function flavor!
2023/07/27 22:35:06 WARNING mlflow.models.model: Model logged without a signature. Signatures will be required for upcoming model reg
istry features as they validate model inputs and denote the expected schema of model outputs. Please visit https://www.mlflow.org/doc
s/2.4.1/models.html#set-signature-on-logged-model for instructions on setting a model signature on your logged model.
2023/07/27 22:35:07 INFO mlflow.utils.autologging_utils: Created MLflow autologging run with ID '3b99b2cf2ddc4191864f81418157b284', w
hich will track hyperparameters, performance metrics, model artifacts, and lineage information for the current sklearn workflow
```

Command took 19.89 seconds -- by alanatucumberlands@gmail.com at 7/27/2023, 6:34:57 PM on Alan Dennis's ML Cluster

Figure 9.14: *Automatic logging results*

Notice that there are no explicit calls to log metrics or information. Rather, it is handled automatically. If you look on the right side of the screen, you see an icon that looks like a **beaker**. Clicking this opens the **Experiments** tab, as shown in *Figure 9.15*:

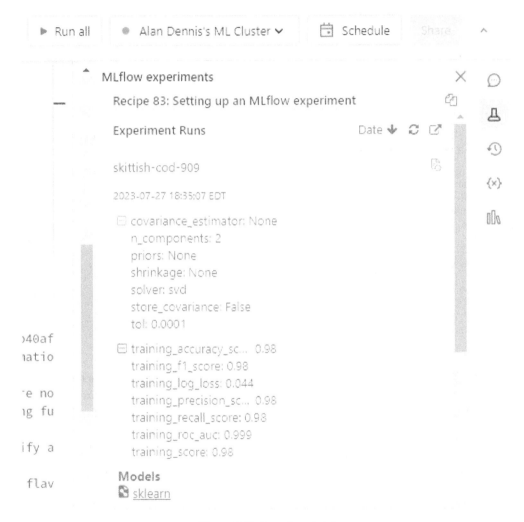

Figure 9.15: *Experiments tab*

We can see that the accuracy and other metrics were recorded automatically. This makes reproducing results easier and determining which parameters yielded the best results.

Recipe 86: Using MLflow for non-ML workflows

MLflow, as the name implies, was created to address machine learning problems. To use MLflow without an ML-configured runtime, you will need to install it, as shown in *Figure 9.16*:

```
1   %pip install mlflow
```

```
Python interpreter will be restarted.
Collecting mlflow
  Using cached mlflow-2.5.0-py3-none-any.whl (18.2 MB)
Collecting gunicorn<21
  Using cached gunicorn-20.1.0-py3-none-any.whl (79 kB)
Collecting docker<7,>=4.0.0
  Using cached docker-6.1.3-py3-none-any.whl (148 kB)
Requirement already satisfied: pytz<2024 in /databricks/python3/lib/python3.9/site-packages (from mlflow) (2021.3)
```

Figure 9.16: Installing MLflow in Python

Notice the use of **%pip** to invoke **pip**, the package installer for Python. If you are unfamiliar with pip, see **https://pip.pypa.io/**. Once we have installed MLflow, we can use it to record the start of a run, as shown in *Figure 9.17*:

```
1   import mlflow
2   mlflow.start_run()
3   mlflow.autolog()
4   tableName = "default.iris"
5   mlflow.log_param("tableName",tableName)
```

▼ (1) MLflow run

    Logged 1 run to an experiment in MLflow. Learn more

```
2023/07/29 18:07:21 INFO mlflow.tracking.fluent: Autologging successfully enabled for pyspark.
2023/07/29 18:07:21 INFO mlflow.tracking.fluent: Autologging successfully enabled for pyspark.ml.
```

Out[5]: 'default.iris'

Figure 9.17: Starting an experiment with MLflow enabled

You can see the **start_run** command on line 2, causing MLflow to create a new name and identifier. On line 5, we add a parameter, in this case, the table name we are operating on. Next, we run the **OPTIMIZE** command using **spark.sql**, as shown in *Figure 9.18*:

```
1    result = spark.sql(f"OPTIMIZE {tableName}").cache()
2    expandedResults = result.select("path", "metrics.*")
3    row = expandedResults.first()
4    names =expandedResults.schema.names
5    for name in names:
6        value = row[name]
7        if value is None:
8            continue
9        if name == "path":
10           mlflow.log_param(name,value)
11       else:
12           if isinstance(value,int) or isinstance(value,float):
13               mlflow.log_metric(name,value)
14   mlflow.end_run()
15   display(expandedResults)
```

▶ (6) Spark Jobs

▶ ▦ result: pyspark.sql.dataframe.DataFrame = [path: string, metrics: struct]

▶ ▦ expandedResults: pyspark.sql.dataframe.DataFrame = [path: string, numFilesAdded: long ... 20 more fi

Table ∨   +

path	numFilesAdded	numFilesRemoved	filesAdded
dbfs:/user/hive/warehouse/iris	0	0	▶ {"min": null,

Figure 9.18: Example operation using MLflow to store metrics

We start by constructing and executing the **sql** statement that **OPTIMIZE** the specified table on line 1. Next, we manipulate the resulting DataFrame to expand the top-level properties of a nested object on line 2. We know that the results of an **OPTIMIZE** statement is a single record, so we take the first row of the DataFrame. We then get the names of the columns using the DataFrame's **schema** property to iterate across them in line 5. We store the **path** of the table as a parameter and the integer and floating-point values as metrics in lines 10 and 13, respectively. We then end the MLflow run on line 14 and display the DataFrame on line 15. You can see that **filesAdded** is a nested object, which we ignore in this case.

You can click on an **Experiment** in the right MLflow **Experiments** tab and open the experiments detail, as shown in *Figure 9.19*:

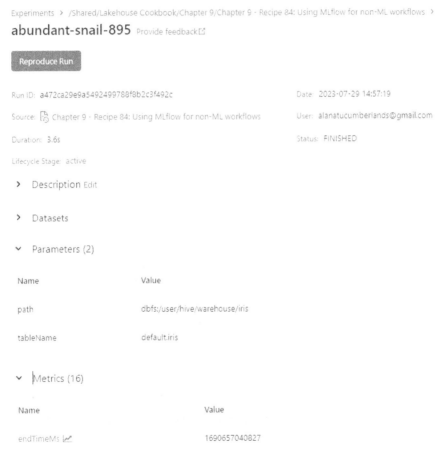

Figure 9.19: *Experiments detail page*

Notice the two parameters, **path** and **tableName**, along with the 16 metrics. This is not what MLflow was built for, but it can be useful for operations and optimization efforts. In the next section, we discuss deploying a model, such as that created in *Recipe 82*, to production.

Deploying models to production

Once a model is created, trained, and validated, the next step is to test and use it in a deployed environment. Typically, ML models are accessed via a web call using **Representational State Transfer** (**REST**). Databricks recommends deploying models using MLflow. Before deploying a model, we need to register the model with the model registry.

Recipe 87: Registering a model

In Recipe 84, we discussed MLflow. In *Figure 9.19*, we examined the experiment detail page. There is an **Artifacts** section lower on that same page, as shown in *Figure 9.20*:

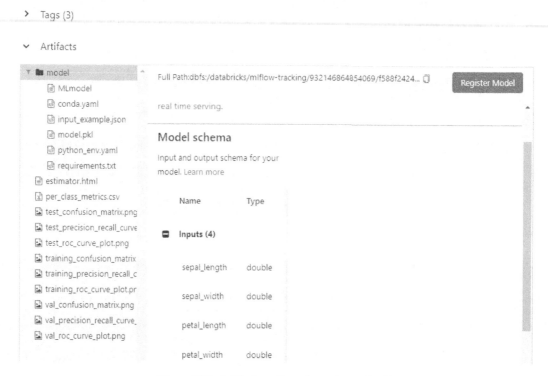

Figure 9.20: Artifacts section of experiment detail

This is where we can **Register Model**. In this case, we are examining the results from *Recipe 82*, where we used AutoML to create an **Iris** flower **classifier**. Clicking the **Register Model** button brings up the **Register Model** dialog, where we are asked to select or create a model. Selecting the combo box gives the option of creating a new model or selecting an existing one, as shown in *Figure 9.21:*

Register Model   ×

Model

+ Create New Model   ∨

Model Name

Iris classifier|

Cancel   **Register**

Figure 9.21: Register Model dialog

Once the **model** is registered, the button to **Create New Model** is replaced with the name of the model, as shown in *Figure 9.22*:

Figure 9.22: Experiment registered as a model

Now that we have registered the model, the next logical question is how one uses that registered model. Examining the Databricks workspace, notice the **Models** option under the **Machine Learning** section. Clicking it brings up the list of **Registered Models** in the workspace, as shown in *Figure 9.23*:

Figure 9.23: Registered models in a workspace

We have now registered a model. The next step will be to use that model for inference.

Recipe 88: Using a model for inference

One of the main reasons we use ML is to apply the models to respond to requests. Sometimes those requests are for classification, other times for regression. For example, a credit card company must decide if a transaction is fraudulent based on information such as location, amount, and so on. A model was developed to make that determination. Using that model is often referred to as using it for inference.

If we click on one of the models in our registered model list, it brings up a page with detailed information about that registration. The information includes the name of the model, a description if one was supplied, and the version history of the registration, as shown in *Figure 9.24*:

***Figure 9.24**: Registered model details*

Also, notice the button in the top right of the page with the title **Use model for inference**. Clicking that button brings up a form asking how you plan to serve the model. Your choices are **Real-time**, **Streaming (Delta Live Tables)**, and **Batch inference**. **Real-time** enables the model to be invoked by a REST API interface. **Streaming** inference is accomplished by integration with Delta Live Tables. **Batch** processing is done using more traditional processing approaches. In our case, we will use **Real-time**, as shown in *Figure 9.25*:

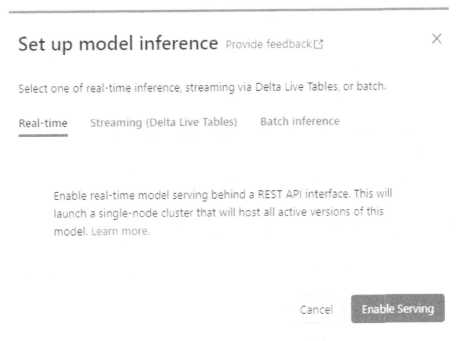

Figure 9.25: Specifying serving method

Note: Not all regions support real-time serving. Databricks will allow you to set it up, but it will not work.

The next step is to click the **Enable Serving** button at the bottom of the form. After serving is enabled, you are returned to a page associated with the REST API to serve the model, as shown in *Figure 9.26:*

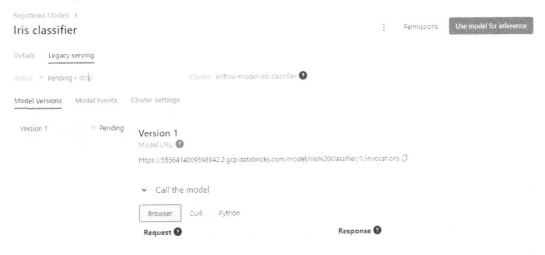

Figure 9.26: Model serving page

This page allows you to call the model using various testing mechanisms. The Browser method is simple to use and similar to that used in Swagger UI, **https://swagger.io/tools/swagger-ui**. Another alternative is to test using **Client for URL (cURL)**. cURL is a command line tool that enables interaction with websites. For more on cURL see **https://curl.se**. The last way to interact with the API is to use Python. An example Python program is supplied which uses the requests library to interact with the REST API. For more on requests, see **https://pypi.org/project/requests**. On the same form, you can examine the events associated with the model by clicking **Model Events**, as shown in *Figure 9.27*:

Status: ● Ready - Stop   Cluster: mlflow-model-Iris classifier ●

Model Versions   Model Events   Cluster Settings

Timestamp	Event Type	Version	Message
2023-07-29 17:38:43	VERSION_UPDATED	1	Model process ready
2023-07-29 17:35:43	VERSION_UPDATED	1	Launching model process
2023-07-29 17:35:40	ENDPOINT_UPDATED		Cluster became ready
2023-07-29 17:35:14	ENDPOINT_UPDATED		Initializing model environment
2023-07-29 17:29:04	ENDPOINT_UPDATED		Failed to get info for cluster 0729-212734-583vv6da. Retrying...
2023-07-29 17:27:34	ENDPOINT_UPDATED		Launched cluster 0729-212734-583vv6da

Figure 9.27: Model events

The same form also has a section for configuring the cluster serving the API. You can control the **Instance Type**, and associate tags, as shown in *Figure 9.28*:

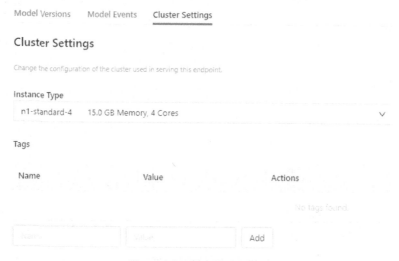

Figure 9.28: Cluster settings

Once the cluster is running, we can test out the model. We send the data using a JSON format. If you are uncertain of the structure of the data, you can click the **Show Example** button, as shown in *Figure 9.29*:

Figure 9.29: Example payload

We can tell that the expectation is to send the data as an array of arrays of four items. When you have your data ready, you click **Send Request**, as shown in *Figure 9.30*:

Figure 9.30: Sending data to the model

We have successfully queried the endpoint. We can see that the model predicted Setosa for both records supplied in the request. We have also briefly covered the common ML workloads. Next, we will discuss using the Databricks Feature Store.

Using Databricks feature store

Knowing information about the data being used in ML and DS workloads is critical. To discuss the feature store, we first need to discuss features and feature engineering. When data arrives at a Lakehouse, it is rarely in the format needed for ML experiments. The cleansing efforts required are similar to those required to reach the silver layer but go further. A feature is a property of an item. For example, petal length is a feature in the iris dataset. Feature engineering is the process of taking already high-quality data and transforming it to be used in a model. A feature store is a centralized storage location that stores a given feature and how those features were transformed.

For this section, we will be using an example notebook from Databricks, located at **https://docs.databricks.com/_extras/notebooks/source/machine-learning/feature-store-basic-example.html**.

This is a basic example of interacting with the feature store.

Recipe 89: Importing an HTML notebook

Databricks makes it easy to **Import Notebook** stored as DBC archives or on the web as HTML files. If you open the link above, you will see it is an HTML page, as shown in *Figure 9.31:*

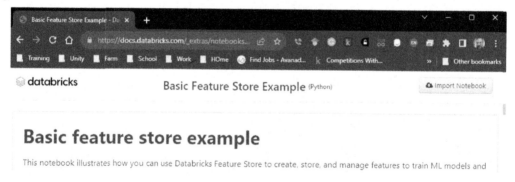

Figure 9.31: Example notebook page

Not only is this easy to read, but it can also be imported into the Databricks using the **Import** feature, as shown in *Figure 9.32:*

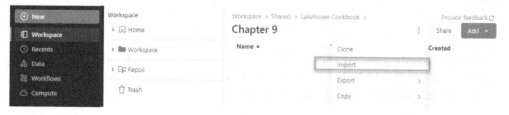

Figure 9.32: Import feature

Clicking on **Import** brings up the **Import form**. On this form, you can select to import a **File** or a **URL**, as shown in *Figure 9.33*:

Figure 9.33: *Importing a URL*

After clicking **Import,** the notebook is available for use. In the next section, we will walk through this example notebook.

Recipe 90: Basic interaction with Databricks Feature Store

Feature store requires a Databricks ML runtime, or you need to install it using **%pip**, as shown in *Figure 9.34*:

```
Cmd 2

1   %pip install databricks-feature-store

Note: you may need to restart the kernel using dbutils.library.restartPython() to use updated packages.
Collecting databricks-feature-store
  Downloading databricks_feature_store-0.14.0-py3-none-any.whl (201 kB)
                                    ─── 201.1/201.1 kB 3.6 MB/s eta 0:00:00
Collecting dbl-tempo<1,>=0.1.23
```

Figure 9.34: *Installing Feature Store library*

The process begins with the typical includes. Note the inclusion of the feature store library, as shown in *Figure 9.35*:

```
1    import pandas as pd
2
3    from pyspark.sql.functions import monotonically_increasing_id, expr, rand
4    import uuid
5
6    from databricks import feature_store
7    from databricks.feature_store import feature_table, FeatureLookup
8
9    import mlflow
10   import mlflow.sklearn
11
12   from sklearn.model_selection import train_test_split
13   from sklearn.ensemble import RandomForestRegressor
14   from sklearn.metrics import mean_squared_error, r2_score
```

Figure 9.35: *Library includes*

Next, data is read from an example dataset and manipulated to fix issues with column names, such as spaces in the names. An identifier is added using the monotonically increasing **id** function. Since feature tables are Delta tables with additional functionality, the code ensures a schema/database exists named **wine_id**. Interacting with the feature store requires a client. The client supports multiple methods, such as **create_table**, as shown in *Figure 9.36:*

```
1    fs = feature_store.FeatureStoreClient()
2    fs.create_table(
3        name=table_name,
4        primary_keys=["wine_id"],
5        df=features_df,
6        schema=features_df.schema,
7        description="wine features"
8    )
```

▶ (23) Spark Jobs

2023/08/25 11:20:47 INFO databricks.feature_store._compute_client._compute_client: Created feature tabl
e 'hive_metastore.default.wine_db_c8478c'.
/databricks/python/lib/python3.10/site-packages/databricks/feature_store/entities/_feature_store_objec
t.py:9: FutureWarning: ``databricks.feature_store.entities.feature_table.FeatureTable.keys`` is depreca
ted since v0.3.6. This method will be removed in a future release. Use ``FeatureTable.primary_keys`` in
stead.
  yield prop, self.__getattribute__(prop)

Out[5]: <FeatureTable: keys=['wine_id'], tags={}>

Command took 16.47 seconds -- by alan.dennis@gmail.com at 8/25/2023, 7:20:18 AM on Alan Dennis Personal Compute Cluster

Figure 9.36: *Creating a feature store client*

In this example, we are creating a table using a DataFrame, as shown on line 4. You have the option of creating an empty table and using the **write_table** method. We now have a feature store table. We cannot see that table in the **hive_metastore**, but we can see it in the feature store section, as shown in *Figure 9.37:*

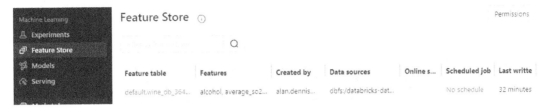

Figure 9.37: *Feature Store user interface*

The next step is to train a model using a feature store table. Since the target is not a feature, it cannot be stored in the feature store. However, it is required for training. The example mocks a wine feature that can only be observed during inference using a random number and associates it with the wine identifier and quality feature. Training is done using the holdout method, with a 20% test set. During training, we want model logging to go to the feature store, not MLflow. To accomplish this, we disable the auto-logging of models, as shown in *Figure 9.38*:

```
1   # Disable MLflow autologging and instead log the model using Feature Store
2   mlflow.sklearn.autolog(log_models=False)
3
4   def train_model(X_train, X_test, y_train, y_test, training_set, fs):
5       ## fit and log model
6       with mlflow.start_run() as run:
7
8           rf = RandomForestRegressor(max_depth=3, n_estimators=20, random_state=42)
9           rf.fit(X_train, y_train)
10          y_pred = rf.predict(X_test)
11
12          mlflow.log_metric("test_mse", mean_squared_error(y_test, y_pred))
13          mlflow.log_metric("test_r2_score", r2_score(y_test, y_pred))
14
15          fs.log_model(
16              model=rf,
17              artifact_path="wine_quality_prediction",
18              flavor=mlflow.sklearn,
19              training_set=training_set,
20              registered_model_name="wine_model",
21          )
22
23  train_model(X_train, X_test, y_train, y_test, training_set, fs)
```

▾ (1) MLflow run

Logged 1 run to an experiment in MLflow. Learn more

Figure 9.38: *Model training*

In line 2 we turn off automatic logging for models, and on lines 15 to 21 we log the model to the feature store. We can see the training results by looking at the MLflow experiments detail page, as we did during experiment 84. Now that we have a trained model, we can perform batch inference on a dataset, as shown in *Figure 9.39*:

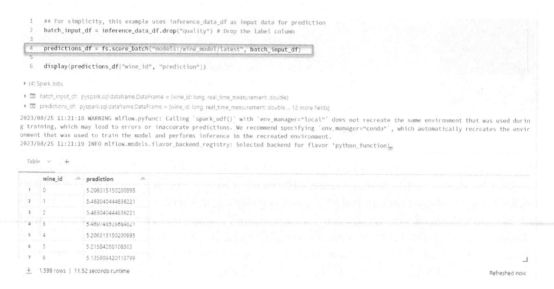

Figure 9.39: Batch inference

The example notebook demonstrates feature lineage by adding a new feature by averaging two existing features. Once the feature has been added, it can be used during training and inference. This shows the additional functionality available in feature store over traditional Delta tables.

Conclusion

We have briefly covered the ML capabilities in Databricks. We discussed the business motivation for using ML and how to use AutoML to generate and score multiple models quickly. We discussed how MLflow is a key technology for capturing and storing ML experiments. We used MLflow to deploy a model and perform inference. Lastly, we discussed feature stores in general and Databricks' feature store in more depth.

The next chapter discusses the SQL user persona and explores Databricks SQL Warehouses.

Join our book's Discord space

Join the book's Discord Workspace for Latest updates, Offers, Tech happenings around the world, New Release and Sessions with the Authors:

https://discord.bpbonline.com

CHAPTER 10
SQL Analysis

Introduction

The SQL Analysis persona is a common workload in a lakehouse. The process of creating SQL Analysis environments and related concepts is discussed. Writing queries is covered in depth, including queries often used in interviews. Using queries in dashboards or alerts is discussed. Lastly, cost and performance considerations and ways to monitor costs over time are presented.

Structure

The chapter covers the following topics:

- Databricks SQL
- Creating and managing a warehouse
- Using the SQL Editor
- Writing queries, including common interview queries
- Creating dashboards
- Setting alerts
- Cost and performance considerations

Objectives

By the end of this chapter, you should be able to create a Databricks SQL Warehouse, and create and run common queries using the SQL Editor. You should be able to use queries in dashboards and alerts. You should understand cost and performance and how to monitor each.

Databricks SQL

SQL is a pervasive programming language. It has existed since the 1970s and continues to experience an increase in usage and adapt to changing business needs. Data engineers, analysts, and many business users know SQL. Because of this extensive user base, Databricks has made SQL a supported language for data interaction.

One of the key concepts in SQL is that operations are performed on data sets. While performing iteration and changing a single record is possible, that is not a desirable pattern. Instead, operations should occur on sets of records. This fundamental concept applies to big data processing in general.

While there are many variations of SQL, there are groups of variations that are similar enough to be termed standard. Spark SQL can be configured to follow the ANSI standard, as discussed here: **https://spark.apache.org/docs/latest/sql-ref-ansi-compliance.html**.

Databricks runtimes have enabled the ANSI standard mode since 2021. Spark SQL will seem very familiar to users with a background in MySQL or similar products. If you come from a Microsoft SQL Server background, the main difference is the characters used to enclose schema and table names and how to limit the number of records returned by a query.

Databricks has been addressing the SQL-focused persona for some time. The product offerings have changed names several times. At one point, the features were called **SQL Analytics**. Later, the name changed to Databricks SQL. Regardless of the name, there are several key elements to the offering, such as simplified cluster management, robust query editing, dashboards, and alerts. We will discuss each in this chapter. We will include in the chapter common SQL queries, many of which are used during interviews.

Creating and managing a SQL Warehouse

Before we can run queries, we need an environment to execute them. For Databricks SQL, that is called a SQL Warehouse. A SQL Warehouse builds on the concepts of a cluster. In Spark, a cluster is made up of a driver node and one or more work nodes. A variation of that architecture called a single-node cluster combines the worker and driver nodes into a single node. Typically, that configuration is used for small workloads. The main concept is that worker nodes do the work. The driver node tells the worker nodes what tasks to perform. A SQL Warehouse builds on that, while hiding most of the complexity.

Creating a Spark cluster requires setting various values to control the shape, size, and nature of a cluster. An SQL Warehouse hides most of that complexity. A cluster is created using what is commonly called **T-Shirt Sizing**. The sizes range from the smallest (extra-extra-small) to the largest (extra-extra-extra-large). Since those are long names, we usually refer to them as 2X-small and 3X-Large, respectively. It is easy to change the size based on utilization and other factors. You still can control the scaling of a cluster, such as from 1 to 8. In the next section, we will walk through creating a SQL Warehouse.

Recipe 91: Creating a SQL Warehouse

SQL Warehouses are so important that Databricks provisions a **Starter Warehouse** for you. As the name implies, it is not large but is sufficient to do tasks such as importing data. You can see the list of your warehouses by selecting **SQL Warehouses** from the left navigation, as shown in *Figure 10.1:*

***Figure 10.1**: List of SQL Warehouses*

You can tell this warehouse is inactive by the square in the circle in the Status column. Also, the Size is clear, along with the type of warehouse. To create a warehouse, click the Create SQL warehouse button located in the top right of the screen. Doing so brings up a form used to supply information about the new warehouse, as shown in *Figure 10.2:*

Figure 10.2: Creating a new SQL Warehouse

Depending on the cloud provider, there are up to three types of SQL warehouses. The **Serverless** option leverages serverless technology, resulting in faster creation. Reduced waiting comes at the cost of a potentially higher DBU per hour. It is difficult to determine as the higher rate includes cloud instance costs. The **Pro** option performs better than **Classic** and provides additional functionality, but at a higher cost. For more information on the different types see **https://www.databricks.com/product/pricing/databricks-sql**. While the warehouse is being created, you are allowed to **Manage permissions**, as shown in *Figure 10.3*:

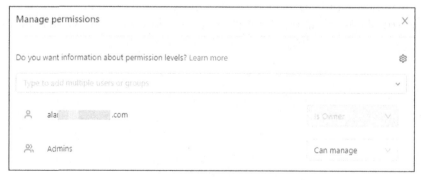

Figure 10.3: Manage permissions

The choices for users or groups are **Can manage** and **Can use**. Once you have configured the permissions, you can dismiss the screen and are returned to an overview of the Warehouse you just created, as shown in *Figure 10.4*:

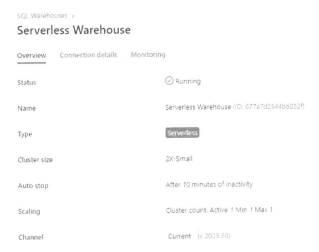

Figure 10.4: Serverless Warehouse overview

Now that you have a SQL Warehouse, you can run queries or connect to it from various sources. Switching to the **Connection details** section lets you see the information necessary to access the SQL Warehouse from various environments. The top of the form includes information such as **hostname**, **Port**, **Protocol**, and so on., as shown in *Figure 10.5:*

Figure 10.5: SQL Warehouse connection details

You can also retrieve information necessary to connect to common environments, as shown in *Figure 10.6*:

Figure 10.6: *Common tools access information*

Since **personal access tokens** are required to access a SQL Warehouse, the link to create one is included in this section of the form on the right side of the page. We can connect to this environment using Python or other listed tools and languages with this information.

Recipe 92: Connect to a SQL Warehouse from a Python Jupyter Notebook

Now that we have a Warehouse available, we can connect to it from a Python script, or Jupyter Notebook. To start, we need to capture the information required to connect, as shown in *Figure 10.7*:

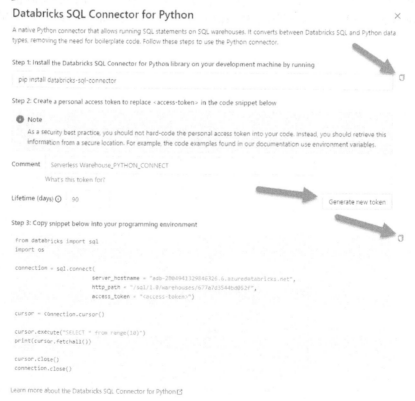

Figure 10.7: *Databricks SQL Connector for Python helping page*

The first step is to create a Jupyter Notebook or Python Script. Once that is created, copy the **pip install** command and run it. This installs the Databricks SQL Connector, which allows Python applications to connect to Databricks clusters and SQL Warehouses, as discussed at **https://pypi.org/project/databricks-sql-connector/**. Once the connector is installed, we must create a **personal access token**. Access tokens are an alternative to usernames and passwords. When you create an access token, you are asked to specify a lifetime for the token. The idea is that the token will expire at some point and need to be regenerated. Ensure you save the token after it is generated, as the value is not retrievable later. Next, copy the connection code into your script and update it with the recently generated access token, as shown in *Figure 10.8*:

```
1  from databricks import sql
2  import os
3  connection = sql.connect(server_hostname = "adb-2804941329846326.6.azuredatabricks.net",
4                           http_path = "/sql/1.0/warehouses/677a7d3544bd052f",
5                           access_token = accessToken)
6  cursor = connection.cursor()
7  cursor.execute("SHOW SCHEMAS")
8  print(cursor.fetchall())
9  cursor.close()
10 connection.close()
```
executed in 1.29s, finished 16:49:49 2023-08-03

```
[Row(databaseName='default'), Row(databaseName='lakehousecookbook')]
```

Figure 10.8: *Python connecting to SQL Warehouse*

Notice that the results of the execution are the two schemas in our workspace. We have successfully executed a Python Jupyter Notebook command after connecting to a SQL Warehouse. Note that if the SQL Warehouse had terminated, it would be restarted while the client waited. This section showed how to create and connect to a SQL Warehouse. In the next, we review the SQL Editor and start writing queries.

Using the SQL Editor

Now that we have a SQL Warehouse, we can start writing queries. To simplify this process, Databricks has created an SQL-focused editor, as shown in *Figure 10.9*:

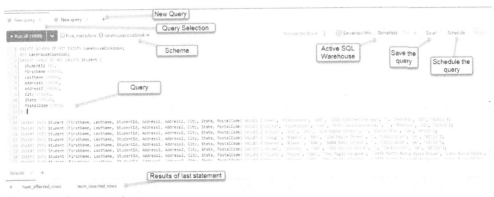

Figure 10.9: *SQL Editor overview*

The font is tiny, but the key thing to understand is where the important elements of the editor are located. We start by writing a query. Once it is close to the desired output, we can run it using the **Run all** button. We can switch between queries by selecting the name of the query. Clicking the **plus sign** creates a new tab and a blank query. Note that only the final statement's output is displayed when you run the query. At a glance, we can also tell what schema is active and the current SQL Warehouse. Clicking the **Save** button allows us to select a location to store the query and give it a meaningful name. Clicking the **Schedule** button allows for an easy selection of a refresh interval, such as once a day at a certain time, as shown in *Figure 10.10*:

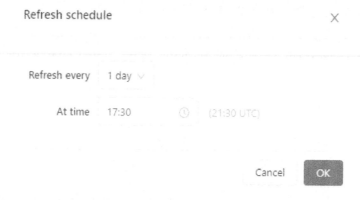

Figure 10.10: *Example refresh schedule*

Once the query has been saved, you can share it by selecting the **Share** button. For each identity or group, you choose to share a query with, you can control their access, as shown in *Figure 10.11*:

Figure 10.11: *Sharing a query example*

In addition to controlling if a user **Can View**, **Run**, **Edit**, or **Manage** a query, you can email the users with new access to a query. For convenience, you can also copy the link to the query into the clipboard by clicking **Copy link**.

In addition to easy-to-see items, clicking the **three dots** between **Provide feedback** and the SQL Warehouse information brings up a context menu. From that menu, you can **Clone** the selected query, **Edit query info**, and other helpful features, as shown in *Figure 10.12*:

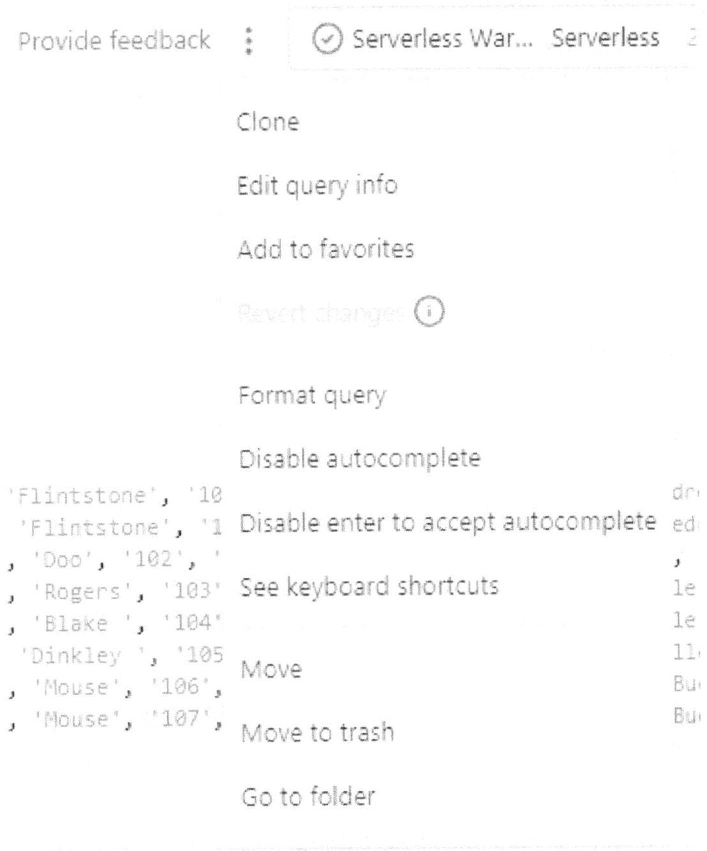

Provide feedback ⋮ ⊘ Serverless War... Serverless

Clone

Edit query info

Add to favorites

Revert change ⓘ

Format query

Disable autocomplete

```
'Flintstone', '10                             dr
 'Flintstone', '1  Disable enter to accept autocomplete  ed
, 'Doo', '102', '                             ,
, 'Rogers', '103'  See keyboard shortcuts      1e
, 'Blake ', '104'                             1e
 'Dinkley ', '105                             11
, 'Mouse', '106',  Move                       Bu
, 'Mouse', '107',                             Bu
```

Move to trash

Go to folder

Figure 10.12: SQL Editor menu

Autocomplete is a useful feature, but sometimes it can miss the user's intent. In those situations, you may wish to disable it. Also, **Format query** is useful for complex queries, but often the result is verbose. The **See keyboard shortcuts** option is helpful, as many shortcuts are poorly documented. We have now discussed the essential elements of the SQL Editor.

Writing queries

We discussed the SQL Editor in the previous section. While it is a useful and evolving tool, as of this writing, there are several limitations. There is no means to import and export a query. That limitation might not be an issue for typical workloads, but one of the goals of this book is to deliver usable code to the reader. As such, we will be delivering the queries as SQL Notebooks. The contents of which can be copied into a query if that is desired. Additionally, we can run the SQL notebooks using a SQL Warehouse, receiving the cost and latency benefits associated with that approach. Recall that a SQL Notebook is a notebook with the default language set to SQL. We can tell the language by looking to the right of the notebook's name, as shown in *Figure 10.13:*

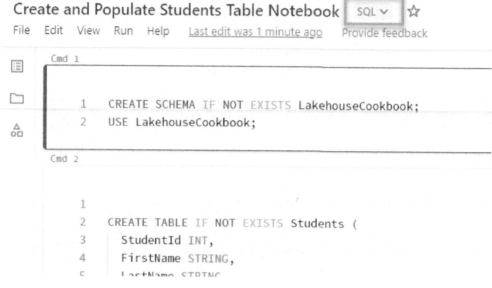

Figure 10.13: Example SQL Notebook

Notice the box around the **SQL** dropdown. This is where you can see the default language of the notebook. The star to the right is how you add a notebook to your favorites. In the next few sections, we will review some common queries, many of which appear in SQL-related interviews. We will discuss the concepts involved, as well as the actual query.

Common interview queries

Knowing how to operate is only part of the challenge. We must also be prepared for common questions when seeking a new job. We will cover some common questions and the theoretical foundations. The goal is to ensure you are prepared to understand why an organization might ask such questions. This is in no way a shortcut. You must understand the concepts to answer questions, as the specifics of these questions will vary. We will start with queries involving a single table, then examine those using multiple tables.

Recipe 93: Show the contents of a table

The most basic question is how you show what is inside a table. This is asking you to perform an unrestricted selection statement, as shown in *Figure 10.14:*

Figure 10.14: General select statement

Reading the query, **SELECT** is the keyword to indicate we wish to return rows. The asterisk indicates that we wish to return all columns. There will likely be follow up questions on when an asterisk should be used and when it should be avoided. The guidance here is that if you wish to retrieve all columns, even those added after the query is written, then the asterisk is appropriate. The conflicting concept is that we should not retrieve data unless we plan to interact with it or need to see it. The alternative is to list the columns, as shown in *Figure 10.15:*

Figure 10.15: Select statement listing columns

The list of columns is called a **projection**. When an asterisk is used, it is called a **wildcard** or **unrestricted projection**. Note that the order of returned rows is not guaranteed unless an **ORDER BY** clause is included. We will discuss ordering and filtering results in the next section.

Recipe 94: Select with filtered ordered limited result

Another common query involves filtering, ordering, and limiting the number of records returned. For example, you might be asked to return the students who live in Ohio ordered by last name, then first, and only display three records. To do this, we use the **WHERE**, **ORDER BY**, and **LIMIT** keywords, as shown in *Figure 10.16:*

```
1    SELECT * FROM LakehouseCookbook.students WHERE STATE = 'OH' ORDER BY LastName,FirstName LIMIT 3
```

Table ∨ +

	StudentId	FirstName	LastName	Address1	Address2	City	State	PostalCode
1	104	Daphne	Blake	9000 Easy Street		Coolsville	OH	45723
2	105	Velma	Dinkley	316 Circle Drive		Coolsville	OH	45723
3	102	Scooby	Doo	224 Maple Street		Coolsville	OH	45723

Figure 10.16: Limited, filtered, and ordered query

The **WHERE** clause filters records using a condition, in this case, equality. For a record to be included in the result set, it must pass the test of having a value of **OH** in the **State** column. Other conditions can be used, such as **LIKE** which is used for wildcard conditions. The **ORDER BY** clause controls the order in which records are returned. In this case, we are ordering by two levels, **LastName** and **FirstName**. Without an **ORDER BY** clause, there is no guarantee of the order that records will return. It could be in the order they are created or in random order. Limiting the number of records returned is performed using the **LIMIT** keyword. In this example, we return the first three records. This is similar to the **TOP** statement in some SQL variants but closer to the ANSI standard. We are performing a wildcard projection in this example; we could have listed the fields, as shown in *Figure 10.17*:

```
1    SELECT    StudentId, FirstName, LastName, Address1, Address2, City, State, PostalCode
2    FROM      lakehousecookbook.Students
3    WHERE     STATE = 'OH'
4    ORDER BY  LastName,  FirstName
5    LIMIT     3
```

Table ∨ +

	StudentId	FirstName	LastName	Address1	Address2	City	State	PostalCode
1	104	Daphne	Blake	9000 Easy Street		Coolsville	OH	45723
2	105	Velma	Dinkley	316 Circle Drive		Coolsville	OH	45723
3	102	Scooby	Doo	224 Maple Street		Coolsville	OH	45723

Figure 10.17: Explicit columns in a limited, filtered, and ordered query

Notice that we have formatted the query for easier viewing. The SQL language is case-insensitive and unaffected by white space, such as carriage returns or spaces. The goal of your scripts should be to make them as easy to read as possible. So far, we have been looking at the contents of a table without reducing it. In the next section, we will discuss aggregation.

Recipe 95: Aggregation of records

During SQL analytics we typically are looking at some form of data aggregation. For example, suppose you were asked to determine how many students live in the same

PostalCode. While you could count the records, this is only a viable option for small datasets. Instead, we leverage the **GROUP BY** construct, as shown in *Figure 10.18*:

```
1    SELECT COUNT(*) as COUNT, PostalCode
2    FROM LakehouseCookbook.students
3    GROUP BY PostalCode
```

Table ∨   +

	COUNT	PostalCode
1	2	32830
2	2	81411
3	4	45723

Figure 10.18: Grouping records by postal code

When performing a **GROUP BY**, there are restrictions on what can appear in the projection. The fields in the **GROUP BY** usually are in the projection. Other fields cannot be included in the projection. We typically use a mathematical operator in addition to the grouping projection, such as **COUNT**. If you attempt to include a field that is not in the aggregation, you will get an error message like that in *Figure 10.19*:

```
1    SELECT COUNT(*) as COUNT, PostalCode,STATE
2    FROM LakehouseCookbook.students
3    GROUP BY PostalCode
```

⊞ [MISSING_AGGREGATION] The non-aggregating expression "STATE" is based on columns which are not participating in the GROUP BY clause.
Add the columns or the expression to the GROUP BY, aggregate the expression, or use "any_valu e(STATE)" if you do not care which of the values within a group is returned.

Figure 10.19: Error projecting non-aggregated column

Adding State to the **GROUP BY** clause could cause unexpected results, as postal codes can span multiple states in the United States. In the next section, we explore adding filtering based on the results of a grouping.

Recipe 96: Using grouping to find duplicate records

A widespread problem with data is that sometimes there are duplicate records. There are many ways to find them, but we will explore a simple one and introduce the **HAVING** clause. In the previous section, we discussed the **GROUP BY** clause. We included the column we wished to aggregate as a field name in that example. We could also have supplied a **comma**-separated list of fields. Another choice is to use the keyword **ALL**, as shown in *Figure 10.20*:

```
1    SELECT COUNT(*) as COUNT,* FROM lakehousecookbook.students GROUP BY ALL
```

Table ∨   +

	COUNT	StudentId	FirstName	LastName	Address1	Address2
1	1	106	Mickey	Mouse	The Magic Kingdom	1675 North B
2	1	107	Minnie	Mouse	The Magic Kingdom	1675 North B
3	1	101	Wilma	Flintstone	1313 Cobblestone Way	
4	1	100	Fred	Flintstone	1313 Cobblestone Way	

Figure 10.20: Use of GROUP BY ALL

In this example, we count the instances of all columns after having grouped by all the fields and then descending order the result. This is one way to find duplicate rows, but a better approach is to use the **HAVING** clause, as shown in *Figure 10.21:*

```
1    SELECT *,COUNT(*) as COUNT FROM lakehousecookbook.students
2    GROUP BY ALL
3    HAVING COUNT >1 |
4    ORDER BY COUNT DESC
```

Query returned no results

Figure 10.21: Filtered results of GROUP BY ALL

The **HAVING** clause is similar to the **WHERE** clause in that it allows for conditional results filtering. The difference is that **HAVING** is applied after an aggregation operation. In this case, we restrict the results to groupings with more than one instance. That would return the duplicate records if any existed. In the next section, we continue our discussion of aggregation functions.

Recipe 97: Generating synthetic data

When testing operations, it is common to create synthetic or test data. Fortunately, Databricks has created **Databricks Labs Data Generator** (**dbldatagen**). You can read about dbldatagen at **https://databrickslabs.github.io/dbldatagen/public_docs/APIDOCS.html**. It allows for rapid creation of large amounts of data. In our case, we borrow the idea of a collection of cars for sales at dealerships. A car has a dealership identifier, color, price, and model. For our example, we create the schema and then populate it with data. We produce **10,000** records using 50 dealerships, eight models, and ten colors to keep time reasonable. Price is randomly assigned between **5,000** and **100,000**. Rather than writing this in code ourselves, we create a specification for the **DataGenerator** class to use, as shown in *Figure 10.22:*

```
1   spark.sql("CREATE OR REPLACE TABLE lakehousecookbook.carinventory (DealerID INT,Model STRING,Color STRING,Price DOUBLE)")
2   table_schema = spark.table("lakehousecookbook.carinventory").schema
3   models = ["Honda Accord","Toyota Corolla","Toyota Camry","Tesla Model Y",
4       "Toyota RAV4","Tesla Model 3","Ford 150","GMC Sierra",]
5   colors = ["White","Black","Gray","Silver","Green",
6       "Red","Blue","Beige","Orange","Brown",]
7   dataspec = dg.DataGenerator(
8       spark, rows=data_rows, partitions=partitions_requested
9   ).withSchema(table_schema)
10
11  dataspec = (
12      dataspec.withColumnSpec("DealerID", minValue=100, maxValue=150, random=True)
13      .withColumnSpec("Price", minValue=5000, maxValue=100000, random=True)
14      .withColumnSpec("Color", values=colors)
15      .withColumnSpec("Model", values=models)
16  )
17  df1 = dataspec.build()
18
19  df1.write.format("delta").mode("overwrite").saveAsTable(
20      "LakehouseCookbook.CarInventory"
21  )
```

▸ (11) Spark Jobs

▸ ▤ df1: pyspark.sql.dataframe.DataFrame = [DealerID: integer, Model: string ... 2 more fields]

Command took 5.22 seconds -- by alan.dennis@gmail.com at 3/5/2023, 4:06:57 PM on Alan Dennis's Cluster

Figure 10.22: DataGenerator usage to create vehicle data

We now have a table with 10,000 rows referencing dealerships with identifiers from **100 to 150**, based on line 12. We need to create a lookup table for use in subsequent recipes. Rather than writing 50 records, we grab a random 50 from a list of United States cities, removing unneeded columns and adding a sequential **Dealer** identifier, as shown in *Figure 10.23*:

```
1   %sql
2   -- Random selection from https://github.com/plotly/datasets/blob/master/us-cities-top-1k.csv
3   Use LakehouseCookbook;
4   CREATE TABLE Dealer
5   (
6       DealerId    INT,
7       City     STRING,
8       State    STRING,
9       CityPop INT
10  );
11
12  INSERT INTO Dealer (DealerId, City, State, CityPop) VALUES ('100', 'Doral', 'Florida', '50213');
13  INSERT INTO Dealer (DealerId, City, State, CityPop) VALUES ('101', 'Westminster', 'California', '91739');
14  INSERT INTO Dealer (DealerId, City, State, CityPop) VALUES ('102', 'Lubbock', 'Texas', '239538');
15  INSERT INTO Dealer (DealerId, City, State, CityPop) VALUES ('103', 'Overland Park', 'Kansas', '181260');
16  INSERT INTO Dealer (DealerId, City, State, CityPop) VALUES ('104', 'Jackson', 'Mississippi', '172638');
```

Figure 10.23: Creating a dealer table

We have successfully created and populated a lookup table and a detail table. We can test our generated data by joining the tables together, as shown in *Figure 10.24*:

```
1   %sql use lakehousecookbook;
2   select * from carinventory a join dealer b on a.DealerID = b.DealerId
```

▸ (3) Spark Jobs

▸ ▦ _sqldf: pyspark.sql.dataframe.DataFrame = [DealerID: integer, Model: string ... 6 more fields]

Table ∨   +

	DealerID	Model	Color	Price	DealerId	City	State	CityPop
1	147	Toyota RAV4	White	18426	147	Murrieta	California	107479
2	124	Tesla Model 3	Black	49334	124	East Providence	Rhode Island	47149
3	101	Ford 150	Gray	13188	101	Westminster	California	91739
4	135	GMC Sierra	Silver	10573	135	Philadelphia	Pennsylvania	1553165
5	125	Honda Accord	Green	54017	125	Urbandale	Iowa	41776
6	128	Toyota Corolla	Red	8254	128	Henderson	Nevada	270811
7	101	Toyota Camry	Blue	99819	101	Westminster	California	91739

⬇ 10,000 rows | 1.05 seconds runtime

Figure 10.24: *Joining lookup with a detail table*

Notice that the operation returns **10,000 rows**, an indication that there are no data issues. Now that we have created some data, we can move on to perform some more complex aggregations and joining of tables.

Recipe 98: Calculate rollups

Another form of aggregation is to perform a **ROLLUP** operation. We may want to perform an aggregation at a given level, then provide metrics at a higher level. For example, we want to know the makeup of our fleet by model and color. We can **GROUP BY Model** and then **Color**; however, if we include the keyword **WITH ROLLUP**, we can see how many of each color for each model and then how many of each model, as shown in *Figure 10.25*:

```
1   SELECT Model,Color,count(*) AS COUNT FROM lakehousecookbook.carinventory
2   GROUP BY Model,Color WITH ROLLUP
3   order by Model,Color
```

Table ∨   +

	Model	Color	COUNT
1	null	null	10000
2	Ford 150	null	1250
3	Ford 150	Blue	250
4	Ford 150	Gray	250
5	Ford 150	Green	250
6	Ford 150	Orange	250
7	Ford 150	White	250

⬇ 49 rows | 1.08 seconds runtime

Figure 10.25: *Group by with rollup*

Where **nulls** are present, we can see that it is a roll-up. For example, line 1 shows a total of **10,000** records. We can see on line 2 that **1,250** of those vehicles are **Ford 150**s. Then we can see the breakdown of Ford 150s per color. We are using synthetic data that did a round-robin assignment of color, causing our distribution to be overly uniform. If we extend our group to three levels to include the dealership, the breakdown becomes clearer, as shown in *Figure 10.26*:

```
1   SELECT DealerId, Model,Color,count(*) AS COUNT FROM lakehousecookbook.carinvento
2   GROUP BY DealerId, Model,Color WITH ROLLUP
3   order by DealerId, Model,Color
```

Table ⌄   +

	DealerId	Model	Color	COUNT
1	null	null	null	10000
2	100	null	null	111
3	100	Ford 150	null	16
4	100	Ford 150	Blue	3
5	100	Ford 150	Gray	2
6	100	Ford 150	Green	5
7	100	Ford 150	Orange	3
8	100	Ford 150	White	3
9	100	GMC Sierra	null	18
10	100	GMC Sierra	Beige	3

Figure 10.26: Three-level grouping with a rollup

We see a better distribution because the **DealerId** column was randomly assigned. Notice that dealer **100** has **111** vehicles, of which **16** are Ford 150s. Three of those are **blue**, and two are **gray**. This function supports analytics and is a common interview question. We now move on to queries that combine information from multiple tables.

Recipe 99: Types of joins

So far, we have focused on queries that interact with a single table. Now we move on to combining multiple tables. This operation is called a **join**. Joins take several forms. We will cover the most common forms in this recipe.

Inner

When most people think of a join in SQL, the **INNER JOIN** is what comes to mind. It matches records that exist in two tables and presents the combination, as shown in *Figure 10.27*:

```
1   SELECT * FROM lakehousecookbook.carinventory a INNER JOIN lakehousecookbook.dealer b on a.DealerID = b.DealerId
```

Table ∨ +

	DealerID	Model	Color	Price	DealerId	City	State	CityPop
1	147	Toyota RAV4	White	18426	147	Murrieta	California	107479
2	124	Tesla Model 3	Black	49334	124	East Providence	Rhode Island	47149
3	101	Ford 150	Gray	13188	101	Westminster	California	91739

⤓ 10,000 rows | 1.27 seconds runtime

Figure 10.27: INNER JOIN example

It is the default form of a join, so if you leave off the **INNER** clause, it behaves the same. Next, we have variations of outer joins. The idea of an outer join is that not all records match cleanly. One table may have references that do not exist in the other. That is where specifying the type of outer join becomes important. To demonstrate this behavior, we added two records to our dataset, one to each table.

Left and right outer joins

A left outer join tells you which table to include non-matching values from, as shown in *Figure 10.28*:

```
1   SELECT * FROM lakehousecookbook.carinventory a LEFT JOIN lakehousecookbook.dealer b on a.DealerID = b.DealerId order by a.dealerid desc
```

Table ∨ +

	DealerID	Model	Color	Price	DealerId	City	State	CityPop
1	200	No Dealer	Pink	1000000	null	null	null	null
2	150	Toyota Corolla	Red	55692	150	Southaven	Mississippi	50997
3	150	Honda Accord	Blue	43784	150	Southaven	Mississippi	50997

Figure 10.28: Left outer join

In this case, the left table is **carinventory**. Since no dealership has an identifier of **200** in the right table (dealer), we include null values for the columns normally populated by that table. Similarly, the **RIGHT OUTER JOIN** displays the tables when the match is on the other side, as shown in *Figure 10.29*:

```
1   SELECT * FROM lakehousecookbook.carinventory a
2   RIGHT OUTER JOIN lakehousecookbook.dealer b on a.DealerID = b.DealerId
3   order by a.dealerid
```

Table ∨ +

	DealerID	Model	Color	Price	DealerId	City
1	null	null	null	null	151	No Inventory
2	100	Tesla Model Y	Brown	73187	100	Doral
3	100	Honda Accord	White	40745	100	Doral

Figure 10.29: Right outer join

We have examined the left and right outer joins. A variation on the same theme is a full outer join, discussed in the next section.

Full outer join

Full outer joins handle the case of missing matching values by allowing **null**s on both the right and left sides, as shown in *Figure 10.30*:

```
1    SELECT * FROM lakehousecookbook.carinventory a
2    FULL OUTER JOIN lakehousecookbook.dealer b on a.DealerID = b.DealerId
3    where a.DealerID is null or city is null
```

Table ∨   +

	DealerID	Model	Color	Price	DealerId	City
1	200	No Dealer	Pink	1000000	null	null
2	null	null	null	null	151	No Inventory

Figure 10.30: *Full outer join*

In this case, the records were in the left and right outer join examples above. The choice of the type of join depends on the problem being addressed.

Cross join

A cross-join is sometimes called a **cartesian product**. Typically, it is only used to generate all combinations of items from two tables. The row count of a cross-join result is the same as the result produced by multiplying the row count of the involved tables. In our case, the dealer table contains 52 records, and our car inventory contains 10,001 (after having added records to not match for outer join testing). That means the row count of the cross will be the product of those two counts, as demonstrated in *Figure 10.31*:

```
1    SELECT count(*) FROM lakehousecookbook.carinventory a Cross JOIN lakehousecookbook.dealer b
```

Table ∨   +

	count(1)
1	520052

Figure 10.31: *Cross join*

We have covered common SQL queries. In the next section, we will explore how to create dashboards.

Creating dashboards

Dashboards are a way to review information interactively. There are many dashboarding technologies. In this section, we will briefly review Databricks' SQL Warehouse Dashboards. In *Chapter 12, Visualizations*, we will explore dashboards in greater depth. In the chapter, we will discuss, many ways of creating dashboards in Databricks exist. The following section explores creating a quick dashboard based on a single table.

Recipe 100: Creating a quick dashboard

There are many ways to create dashboards in Databricks. This section demonstrates creating a dashboard based on a single table. We start the process by navigating to the **Data Explorer**, as shown in *Figure 10.32*:

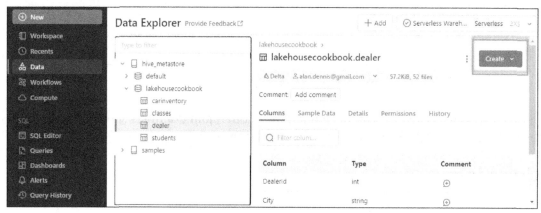

Figure 10.32: Data Explorer

Click the **Create** button, and select **Quick dashboard**, as shown in *Figure 10.33*:

Figure 10.33: Quick dashboard menu choice

Clicking the menu choice brings up the **Create quick dashboard** form. On this form, you select the **number**, **string**, **Boolean**, or **date** columns you want to include in your dashboard. As you select, a preview is generated, as shown in *Figure 10.34*:

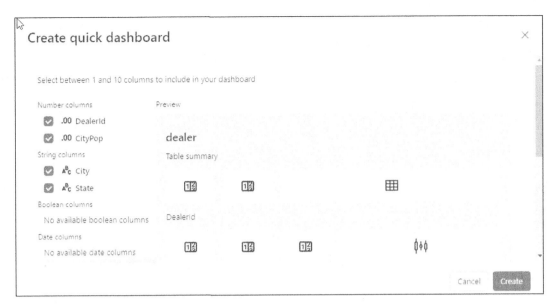

Figure 10.34: Create quick dashboard

If you do not have columns of a particular time, a message indicates that none are available for selection. Once you have selected the columns you are interested in, click the **Create** button. Once created, you are shown the dashboard in edit mode. In this mode, you can change the dashboard's name, colors, limit the number of records displayed, and add or remove sections from the dashboard. The generated report includes an overall analysis of the table, and then breaks down the details for each column, as shown in *Figure 10.35:*

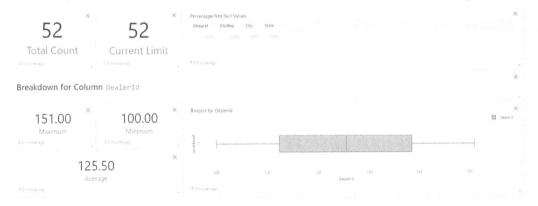

Figure 10.35: Editable version of the dashboard

In our case, the boxplot of **DealerId** is not useful, as it is based on both a generated identifier and based on synthetic data. We can remove the section by clicking the **X** in the upper right corner of the visualization. After clicking the **X**, you will see a prompt asking if you want to remove the selected widget. You can adjust the size of widgets by selecting the bottom right corner and dragging to the desired size. While it is useful to see the percentage of nulls, we do not need to control as wide. We can shrink it, and then move the breakdown of **DealerId** into the space created, as shown in *Figure 10.36*:

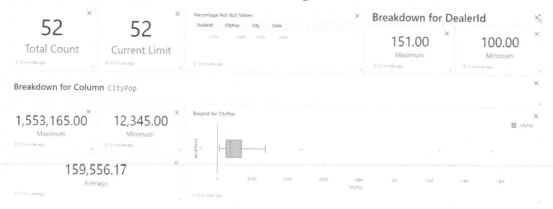

Figure 10.36: *Updated edit mode of the dashboard*

Working with a generated dashboard is a way to learn basic interaction skills. Notice that the scale of the **CityPop** is wide with the boxplot to the right. This is because the average is relatively small (about 160,000) while the max is over 1.5 million. This indicates that there are a few large cities in our table. Once satisfied with the dashboard, click on **Done Editing** (top right corner of the page). The display is not much different afterward, except the X's are removed along with controls to update or add controls. The use has the ability to schedule or refresh the dashboard as needed, as shown in *Figure 10.37*:

Figure 10.37: *Finished dashboard*

We have now successfully created a dashboard based on a specific table. In the next section, we discuss scheduling the refresh of a dashboard.

Recipe 101: Schedule dashboard refresh

In *Recipe 98*, we learned how to create a dashboard from a table. In this recipe, we discuss scheduling the refresh of a dashboard. The **Schedule** button is in the upper right-hand corner of the dashboard detail page, as shown in *Figure 10.38*:

Figure 10.38: Dashboard schedule button

Clicking **Schedule** brings up the scheduling page, as shown in *Figure 10.39*:

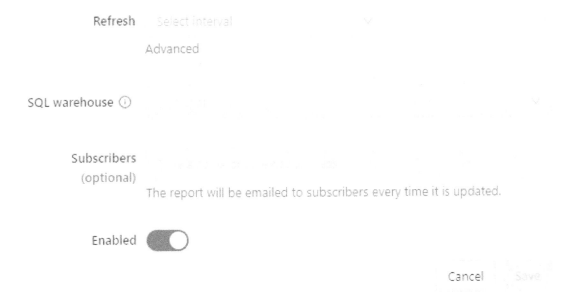

Figure 10.39: Schedule detail page

Selecting **Refresh** drops down a list of options, such as every minute, five minutes, ten minutes, and so on. Clicking **Advanced** brings up an adaptive display that allows you to control the details, such as shown in *Figure 10.40*:

Refresh every	1	∨	day	∨

At time	12:49	🕐	(16:49 UTC)

Back   Save

Figure 10.40: Detailed schedule

After selecting the **Refresh** interval, you can select the **SQL warehouse** for execution. You have the option of adding a list of subscribers. Those email addresses will receive an email when the dashboard is refreshed containing a thumbnail image and link to the report, as shown in *Figure 10.41*:

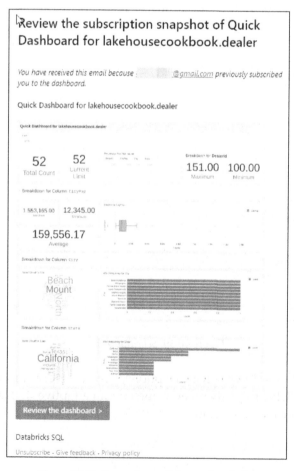

Figure 10.41: Example email from subscription

You can **Unsubscribe** or click the link and go to the interactive dashboard. This feature satisfies some executive requirements to receive emails with current metrics. We have successfully discussed scheduling a dashboard. In the next section, we will discuss setting alerts.

Setting alerts

Alerts are a way to be notified when a condition requires intervention. Typical business operations involve handling exception cases. Ideally, we never have alerts, but business owners or operations staff must be notified when a harmful condition exists. In Databricks SQL, alerts are a named link to a query written and saved in the query editor, with additional properties. This means that to create an alert, we must first create a query.

Recipe 102: Create a query for an alert

We discussed the query editor in detail earlier in this chapter. We need a query that returns values for testing to determine if we are alerting and should create an alert. For example, we should create an alert if we have cars with a **price** below a threshold, such as **$400**, as shown in *Figure 10.42*:

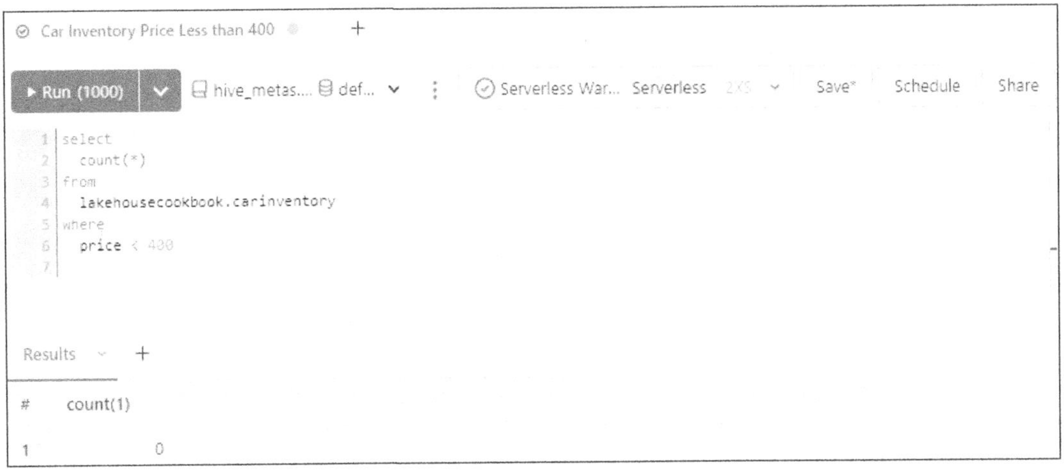

Figure 10.42: Query to detect cars with too low of a price

We can create an alert using it once we have created and saved the query. In the next section, we will create an alert using this query.

Recipe 103: Create an alert

When you click on the **Alert** section under SQL in the Databricks workspace, you see a list of alerts. If none exist, you see a prompt to create one, as shown in *Figure 10.43*:

Figure 10.43: *Empty Alert section*

There are multiple ways to create alerts, two of which are on this page. If you click on **Create alert**, you will be prompted for an **Alert name** and **Query**, as shown in *Figure 10.44*:

New alert

Alert name	Low car price
	Setup Instructions ❓

Query

    Search a query by name   🔍

    Car Inventory Price Less than 400

    Row Count for lakehousecookbook.dealer   QuickDashboard

    Summary for lakehousecookbook.dealer (1)   QuickDashboard

    Percentage Not Null for lakehousecookbook.dealer   QuickDashboard

    Distribution for column State   QuickDashboard

    Quick query for lakehousecookbook.dealer   QuickDashboard

    Summary for lakehousecookbook.dealer   QuickDashboard

    Distribution for column City   QuickDashboard

Figure 10.44: *Create alert page*

Selecting a query brings up the **Triggering condition, Notifications, Template, Refresh,** and **SQL warehouse** sections. We will discuss each section, starting with the **Trigger condition** section, as shown in *Figure 10.45*:

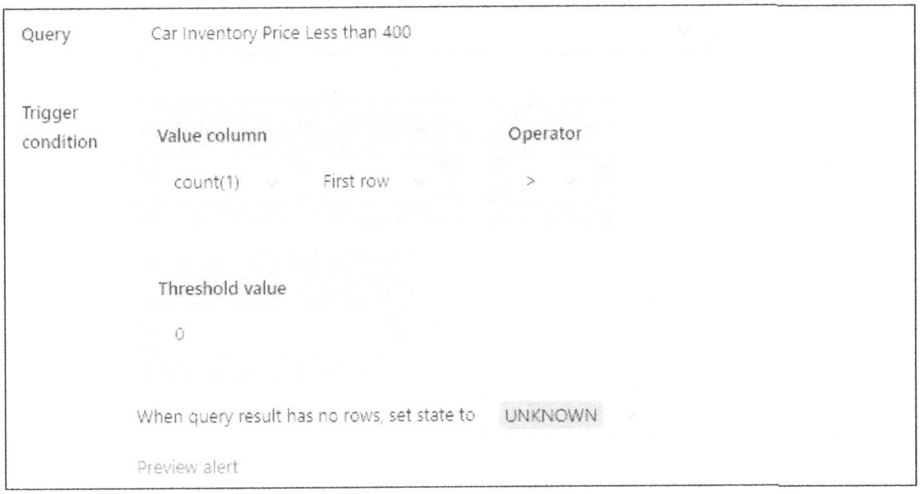

Figure 10.45: Triggering condition section

In this section, we determine how to respond to the values returned by the query. Our example is simple; we want to be alerted if cars are priced below **$400**, which means we need to be alerted if the count is greater than zero. We have the option of setting the start if there are no records returned. You have the option to **Preview alert**. This will run the query and see if an alert would occur. Clicking **Preview alert** returns the results of the query and the threshold, along with a resulting state, as shown in *Figure 10.46*:

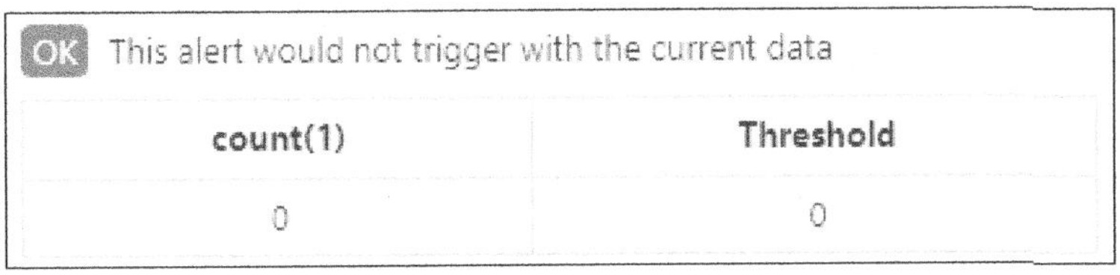

Figure 10.46: Results of alert preview

We can see that the query's result was zero, we would not raise an alert. Next, in the **Notifications** section, we decide what occurs **When alert is triggered**, as shown in *Figure 10.47*:

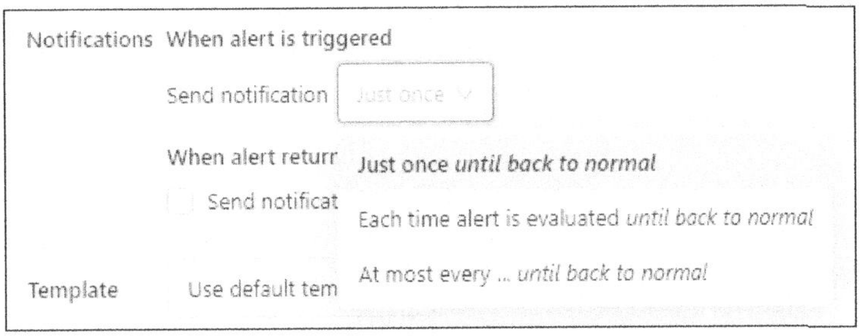

Figure 10.47: Notifications section of the alert page

There are several options when sending an alert while in a triggered state. One choice is to send the alert a single time. For many situations, that is sufficient. A more aggressive approach is sending an alert until the system returns to normal. This may result in many notifications, which may lead to recipients ignoring the alerts. The last choice is to send an alert at a configurable interval until the alert is resolved. For example, we may send a notification every hour until the system returns to a non-alerting status. The granularity goes from seconds to weeks, as shown in *Figure 10.48*:

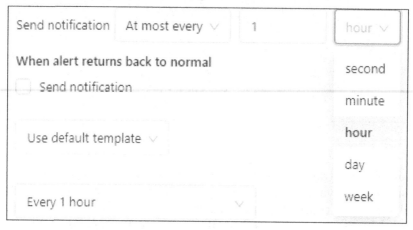

Figure 10.48: Repeating notification control

Once the condition is resolved, you can choose to receive a notification by selecting the checkbox under the **alert returns back to normal** section.

In the **Template** section, we can choose to **Use default template** or create a custom one. For details on templates, see **https://docs.databricks.com/en/sql/user/alerts**. The main concept is that a custom template uses a template language with tags of the form {{ALERT_NAME}}. If you have requirements that are not met by the default template, you have the option of creating your own.

The **Refresh** section controls when we run the query and evaluate the **Trigger condition**. When deciding the refresh frequency, you must consider both the cost of running the query and the **Service Level Agreement (SLA)** of notifications related to error states. If your SLA is hourly, you should run the query every 30 minutes to ensure you meet the SLA. Additionally, you can control when the refresh occurs based on the frequency interval. For example, if you specify that the refresh should occur daily, you can specify a time to run the refresh.

Once you have created the alert, you are taken to an alert detail page. On this page, you see the information we just entered, along with the configured **Destinations** and current state, as shown in *Figure 10.49*:

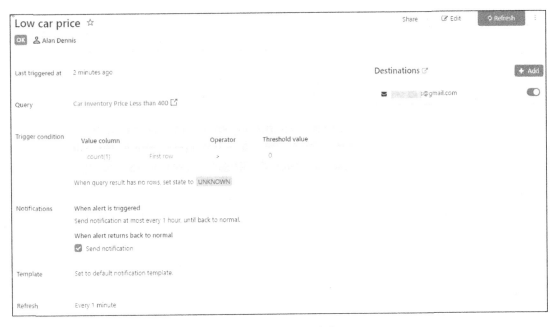

Figure 10.49: Created alert

Notice that we are in an OK state and after changing the query and saving it, we can cause a triggered state, as shown in Figure 10.50:

Figure 10.50: Triggered

The email that is sent uses the default template which contains sufficient information to review the alert and associated query, as shown in *Figure 10.51:*

Databricks SQL alert: Low car price
(TRIGGERED)

You're receiving this email because ███████@gmail.com defined an alert and added you as a recipient.

Low car price

Review the alert details.

Review the alert >

You can also view the query.

Databricks SQL

Unsubscribe - Give feedback - Privacy policy

Figure 10.51: Alert email

Clicking on **Review the alert** opens the alert detail page while clicking the **query** link takes you to the query used by the alert. We have created and managed alerts. In the next section we discuss cost and performance considerations.

Cost and performance considerations

SQL Warehouses are the most economical solution when running interactive SQL query workloads. Combining serverless computing with relatively small timeout windows minimizes the time the cluster is idle. When deciding on cluster size, starting small and increasing as needed is a good idea. One tool that will help with sizing is the **Monitoring** section of the Warehouse details. It displays the number of **Running queries**, **Queued queries**, **Active sessions**, the **Status** of the warehouse, and the number of **Clusters** being used. It also displays historical graphs of query count and the number of **Running clusters**, as shown in *Figure 10.52:*

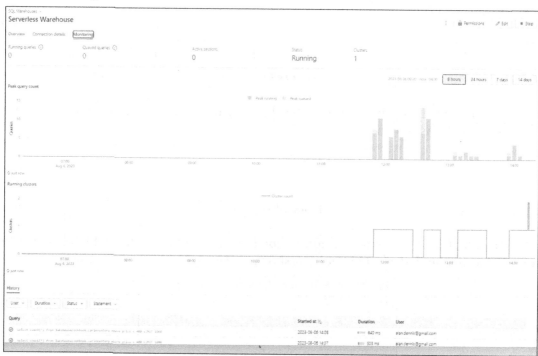

Figure 10.52: SQL Warehouse Monitor section

Of particular use is the **History** section at the bottom of the page. In this section, you can filter queries by **User**, **Duration**, **Status**, and the type of **Statement** used. This section lets you track down complaints and long-running queries. For example, find queries that take longer than ten seconds to run. To see that, we filter on **Duration**, as shown in *Figure 10.53:*

Figure 10.53: *Filtered queries based on duration*

With this kind of investigation, we can be proactive in tracking down undersized environments, or poorly performing queries.

Cost management is a complex topic. It differs by platform. The general concept utilized is to attach **Tags** to items, such as **SQL Warehouses**. When creating, or editing, a **SQL Warehouse**, you can specify multiple tags. **Tags** are name/value pairs. Selecting **edit**, opens the edit screen. On the bottom of the screen is a collapsed **Advanced options** section, as shown in *Figure 10.54*:

Figure 10.54: *Advanced Options of SQL Warehouse*

You can see we have set several example **Tags**. Usage information is reported based on **Tags**. For more information on tag usage, see **https://docs.databricks.com/en/administration-guide/account-settings/usage-detail-tags.html**. You can also review the cloud-specific tag documentation.

Conclusion

In this Chapter, we discussed Databricks' SQL Warehouses in depth. We discussed creating and managing them and using SQL Editor to author queries. We showed using SQL notebooks with a SQL Warehouse for execution. We wrote some common interview queries, explaining the associated concepts. We created a simple dashboard for a single table, used queries to create and manage alerts and discussed cost and performance considerations.

In the next chapter, we will discuss mathematical graph database operations.

Join our book's Discord space

Join the book's Discord Workspace for Latest updates, Offers, Tech happenings around the world, New Release and Sessions with the Authors:

https://discord.bpbonline.com

CHAPTER 11
Graph Analysis

Introduction

Graph analysis is ideal for examining connected information. However, we must ensure we are using the correct tool for a problem. In this chapter we will discuss graph and connected network operations. We will discuss how to determine when to use graph and network analysis. We will also examine the common graph algorithms and discuss when each is appropriate. We will close the chapter by examining 3rd party tools that integrate with Databricks.

Structure

The chapter covers the following topics:

- What is a graph
- When to use graph operations
- GraphX
- GraphFrames
- Graph operations and algorithms
- Neo4J and Databricks

Objectives

By the end of this chapter, you should be able to describe the components and purpose of a mathematical graph. You should be able to discuss GraphX and GraphFrame. You will have a basic understanding of graph algorithms and be able to apply them to common graph problems.

What is a graph

In this chapter, when we say graph, we mean a mathematical graph made up of **nodes** and **edges**. It is a way to represent information that is connected. In a simple form, we can have two nodes with an edge between them, as shown in *Figure 11.1:*

Figure 11.1: *Simple graph*

In this example, we have **Node 1** and **Node 2** connected by **Edge 1**. Notice that the edge is directed, meaning it goes from **Node 1** to **Node 2**, but not the reverse. Some edges are undirected, which means that they do not indicate a direction, just a relationship. As it is with many things, there are multiple names for these constructs. Nodes may also be called **vertices** or **points** and edges may be called **links** or **lines**; hence we will try to use consistent nomenclature in this chapter.

Nodes and edges by themselves are of limited use. Where they become more valuable is when we can attach properties (also called **attributes**) to both. This allows us to associate a named item with the characteristics, as shown in *Figure 11.2:*

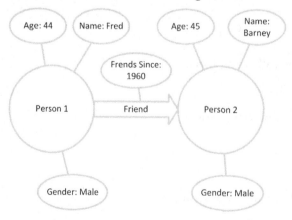

Figure 11.2: *Graph with properties*

By associating properties to nodes and edges, we can store complex data and perform operations on it. Notice that in this graph, **Fred** is a **Friend** of **Barney**, but **Barney** is not a **Friend** with **Fred**. We will discuss storing and processing this kind of data using Databricks. However, before we use graph algorithms, we will further discuss when to use them.

When to use graph operations

As with all tools, knowing the right time to use a graph algorithm is essential. There are two elements of the decision, the nature of the data and the type of analysis desired.

Graphs are intended to model networks of varying degrees of complexity. As we discussed, we can associate attributes to nodes and edges allowing for flexible and powerful modeling. However, even with this power and flexibility, applying graph processing to every situation does not make sense. Instead, the data associated with a problem should have relationships as an integral part of the data. While most relational problems could be modeled using graph technology, this only makes sense if graph technology offers an advantage to transaction processing.

This speaks to the second way of deciding when to use graphs, which is the type of analysis being performed. If the analytics involved is no more complex than traditional descriptive analysis, then using graph technologies does not make sense. However, if the situation being addressed benefits from the many graph algorithms, then using graph processing is appropriate. In the next section, we will discuss Spark's GraphX big data graph processing framework.

GraphX

GraphX is a low-level Spark-based graph processing framework. Before we can discuss it in great depth, we need to discuss Spark's internals in a little more than we have so far. Most likely, you will never use GraphX directly, however, if you do you will have a foundation to under how to proceed.

One of the key technologies that made Spark such a compelling and game-changing offering is the use of **Resilient Distributed Datasets (RDD)**. This technology served as the foundation for what became Spark. The idea of an RDD is that it keeps track of the operations to perform on a subset of the data being processed. If a worker becomes unavailable, only the portion of the work the worker was tasked with needs to be redone. This advancement also supported iterative workloads during big data processing, a shortcoming of traditional MapReduce and related approaches. For more on RDD programming, see **https://spark. apache.org/docs/latest/rdd-programming-guide.html**. However, keep in mind that the guidance from Spark and Databricks is to utilize DataFrames instead of the lower-level RDD elements.

RDD is relevant in that GraphX is an extension of RDD to support graph processing. It supports graph modeling using vertex/node and edge/link tables. The idea is that the nodes within the graph appear in the **Node Table**. A node has a unique identifier and any **Properties** associated with that node. The **Edge Table** contains a **Source** and **Destination** node name, along with any **Properties**, as shown in *Figure 11.3*:

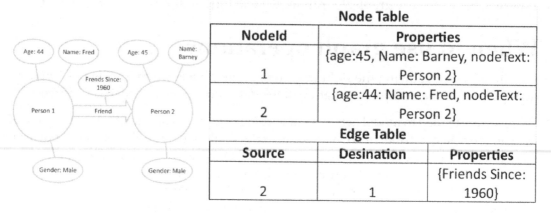

Node Table	
NodeId	**Properties**
1	{age:45, Name: Barney, nodeText: Person 2}
2	{age:44: Name: Fred, nodeText: Person 2}

Edge Table		
Source	**Desination**	**Properties**
2	1	{Friends Since: 1960}

Figure 11.3: *GraphX representation of a graph*

This representation is similar to that used in GraphFrames, which we discuss next. The key thing to take away from this discussion is that GraphX is an older technology used to process graphs in Spark. It is still relevant, as the graph operations performed in GraphFrames are supported by GraphX. Lastly, the general advice with RDD, and related technologies like GraphX, is to use them only if there is no alternative. In the next section, we explore GraphFrames in detail.

GraphFrames

GraphFrames is an Apache Spark library that uses DataFrame concepts to perform graph operations. It supports high-level APIs in Python, Scala, and Java. The key thing to understand about creating a GraphFrame is that you must first create two DataFrames. Just as GraphX represents a graph using two tables, a GraphFrame does the same thing. The difference is that those two tables are DataFrames. In the next section, we will create a very simple GraphFrame.

Recipe 104: Creating a GraphFrame

We will continue using our very simple graph of **Fred** and **Barney**. We start by creating a DataFrame for the nodes/vertices in the graph, as shown in *Figure 11.4*:

```
1    # Node/Vertex DataFrame
2    nodes = sqlContext.createDataFrame([
3      (1, "Fred", 44),
4      (2, "Barney", 45)
5    ], ["id", "name", "age"])
6    display(nodes)
```

▸ (2) Spark Jobs

▸ 🖽 nodes: pyspark.sql.dataframe.DataFrame = [id: long, name: string ... 1 more field]

Table   ∨   +

	id	name	age
1	1	Fred	44
2	2	Barney	45

Figure 11.4: *DataFrame containing nodes*

Next, we **createDataFrame** for the edges linking the nodes, as shown in *Figure 11.5*:

```
1    # Verticies/Edge DataFrame
2    edges = sqlContext.createDataFrame([
3      (2, 1, "friend",'1-1-1960')
4    ], ["src", "dst", "relationship","friendsSince"])
5    display(edges)
```

(2) Spark Jobs

🖽 edges: pyspark.sql.dataframe.DataFrame = [src: long, dst: long ... 2 more fields]

Table   ∨   +

	src	dst	relationship	friendsSince
1	2	1	friend	1-1-1960

Figure 11.5: *DataFrame containing the edges*

Once we have created the two DataFrames, we can create the **GraphFrame**, as shown in *Figure 11.6*:

```
1    from graphframes import *
2    # Create a GraphFrame
3    g = GraphFrame(nodes, edges)
4    display(g)
```

GraphFrame(v:[id: bigint, name: string ... 1 more field], e:[src: bigint, dst: bigint ... 2 more fields])

Command took 0.28 seconds -- by alan.dennis@gmail.com at 8/15/2023, 12:47:58 PM on Alan Dennis's Personal Compute Cluster

md S

```
1    display(g.vertices)
```

▸ (2) Spark Jobs

Table ⌄   +

	id	name	age
1	1	Fred	44
2	2	Barney	45

Figure 11.6: *Creating a simple GraphFrame*

The DataFrames for **nodes** and **edges** are available by accessing the vertices and edges properties of the **GraphFrame**. This graph is overly simple but does show the creation process. In the next section, we will learn how to create a graph quickly using a prepackaged example.

Recipe 105: Using example graphs

Learning graph processing techniques may be challenging for some. To simplify that process, the creators of **GraphFrames** include an example graph called friends. We can create an instance of it by passing the SQL connect as the constructor to the **Graphs** object and invoking the **friends()** method, as shown in *Figure 11.7*:

```
1    from graphframes.examples import Graphs
2    g = Graphs(sqlContext).friends()
3    display(g.vertices)
```

▸ (2) Spark Jobs

Table ⌄   +

	id	name	age
1	a	Alice	34
2	b	Bob	36
3	c	Charlie	30
4	d	David	29
5	e	Esther	32
6	f	Fanny	36

Figure 11.7: *Creating an instance of the friend graph*

Notice that we have six nodes in our graph. We can see the edges by displaying that DataFrame, as shown in *Figure 11.8*:

```
1    display(g.edges)
```

▸ (2) Spark Jobs

Table ∨   +

	src	dst	relationship
1	a	b	friend
2	b	c	follow
3	c	b	follow
4	f	c	follow
5	e	f	follow
6	e	d	friend
7	d	a	friend

Figure 11.8: Friends graph's edges

We can see the relationships between the friends. For example, we can see that **Alice** has a friend relationship with **Bob**, as shown in *Figure 11.9*:

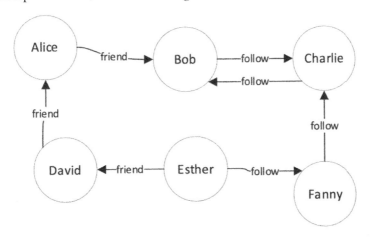

Figure 11.9: Drawing of relationships

We will use this example in the following examples. Next, we will discuss graph algorithms before exploring the more common graph algorithms available in GraphFrames.

Graph operations and algorithms

Graph theory is related to the study of networks, one made up of relationships between pairs of objects. The scope of graph theory is well beyond this Chapter; however, we will offer brief examples of common graph operations. The intent is to demonstrate the more common ways to analyze graphs without attempting to cover the topic exhaustively. In keeping with the structure of this book, we will present several recipes performing graph operations or analysis.

Recipe 106: Breadth-first search

We often need to determine if there is a way to travel from one node in a graph to another. If we can, we typically want to take the shortest route. One way to find that is to perform a breadth-first search. We begin the exercise by creating an instance of the friend's graph from Recipe 105. For our query, we want to see if there is a direct or indirect relationship between **Esther** to **Bob**. As we are dealing with a directed graph, the wording is important as there may be a relationship from **Esther** to **Bob** but not from **Bob** to **Esther**. We use the **bfs** method to find the matching routes, as shown in *Figure 11.10*:

```
1   paths = g.bfs("name = 'Esther'", "name = 'Bob'")
2   display(paths)
```

Figure 11.10: Results of breadth-first search

Because this is a very wide result, we manipulated the results to make it easier to see. The way to read this result is that there are two routes from **Esther** to **Bob**. One goes through **Fanny** to **Charlie** and then to **Bob**. A second route goes from **Esther** to **David** to **Alice** and then to **Bob**. We can tell that they are the same length. The key difference between the routes is that one comprises follow relationships while the other comprises friend relationships. There are other ways to find the shortest path; however, breadth-first search is a commonly used search strategy.

Recipe 107: PageRank

The **PageRank** algorithm is one of the more popular graph algorithms. It allows us to determine the most important elements in a graph. This is based on how important the pages (nodes) linked to a page are in a graph. It was created originally by Google and provided a revolutionary improvement in search by filtering out pages linked to many other pages to attempt to be more noticeable. It is common to see **PageRank** in most graph systems. We start as we did in the previous example by creating the friend graph. Next, we use the **pageRank** method to compute the results, as shown in *Figure 11.11*:

```
1    pageRankResults = g.pageRank(resetProbability=0.15, tol=0.01)
2    display(pageRankResults.vertices.orderBy('pageRank'))
```

▸ (4) Spark Jobs

Table ⌄   +

	id	name	age	pagerank
1	e	Esther	32	0.15262481250417587
2	f	Fanny	36	0.21749035781845O6
3	d	David	29	0.21749035781845O6
4	a	Alice	34	0.3374916166498589
5	c	Charlie	30	2.509883570845965
6	b	Bob	36	2.5650192843630992

Figure 11.11: PageRank results

In our graph, **Charlie** and **Bob** are the most important. Intuitively, you can see this by the number of edges connecting to them compared to the number of edges that start with them. Being able to determine the most important nodes in a graph quickly is a valuable capability and one that is frequently used.

Recipe 108: Shortest path

In Recipe 106, we performed a breadth-first search. An alternative search is to find the shortest paths for nodes of interest. We can accomplish this using the **shortestPaths** method, as shown in *Figure 11.12*:

```
1    results = g.shortestPaths(landmarks=["a","b","c","d","e","f"])
2    display(results)
```

▸ (7) Spark Jobs

▸ 🖾 results: pyspark.sql.dataframe.DataFrame = [id: string, name: string ... 2 more fields]

Table ∨   +

	id	name	age	distances
1	f	Fanny	36	▸ {"b": 2, "c": 1, "f": 0}
2	e	Esther	32	▸ {"e": 0, "f": 1, "a": 2, "b": 3, "c": 2, "d": 1}
3	d	David	29	▸ {"a": 1, "b": 2, "c": 3, "d": 0}
4	c	Charlie	30	▸ {"b": 1, "c": 0}
5	b	Bob	36	▸ {"b": 0, "c": 1}
6	a	Alice	34	▸ {"a": 0, "b": 1, "c": 2}

Figure 11.12: *Shortest paths in a graph*

When invoking the method, we supply a list of landmarks of interest. In this case, we ask for the shortest paths for all nodes in the graph. You can see that **Esther** has the most reachable nodes and the distance to each. In the next section, we will examine how components are connected.

Recipe 109: Connected components

Graphs may be made up of collections of connected components. The idea is that there may be subgraphs that are not connected. If the components are connected to each other (in either direction) then the graph is said to be connected. To test for and assign component membership in a graph, we can use the **connectedComponents** method, as shown in *Figure 11.13*:

```
1    sc.setCheckpointDir("/tmp/graphframes-example-connected-components")
2    result = g.connectedComponents()
3    display(result)
```

▸ (27) Spark Jobs

▸ 🖳 result: pyspark.sql.dataframe.DataFrame = [id: string, name: string ... 2 more fields]

Table ⌄   +

	id	name	age	component
1	f	Fanny	36	412316860416
2	e	Esther	32	412316860416
3	d	David	29	412316860416
4	c	Charlie	30	412316860416
5	b	Bob	36	412316860416
6	a	Alice	34	412316860416

Figure 11.13: *Testing for connected components*

Notice that all nodes are in the same graph because they share the same **component** identifier. If there were disconnected subgraphs, they would have differing **component** identifiers. In the next section, we continue investigating components by examining strongly **connectedComponents**.

Recipe 110: Strongly connected components

In graph theory, strongly connected components occur when the nodes in a directed graph are reachable from every other node. In our graph, this only occurs between **Charlie** and **Bob**, as shown in *Figure 11.14*:

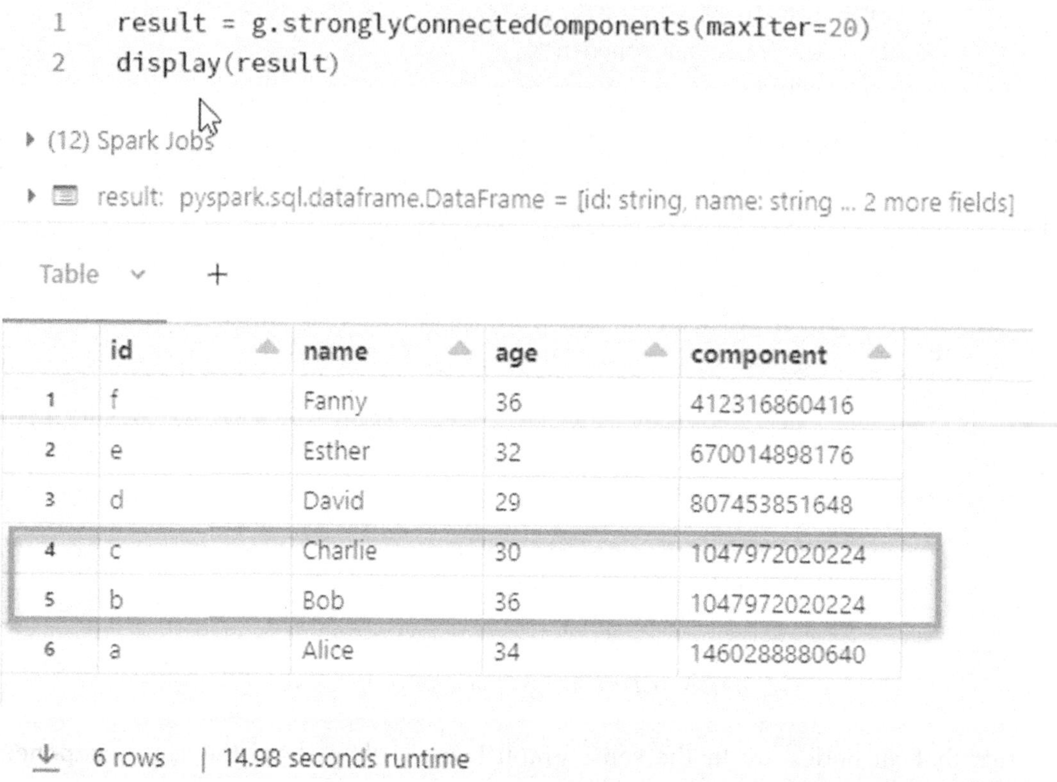

```
1    result = g.stronglyConnectedComponents(maxIter=20)
2    display(result)
```

▸ (12) Spark Jobs

▸ 🖽 result: pyspark.sql.dataframe.DataFrame = [id: string, name: string ... 2 more fields]

Table ⌄   +

	id	name	age	component
1	f	Fanny	36	412316860416
2	e	Esther	32	670014898176
3	d	David	29	807453851648
4	c	Charlie	30	1047972020224
5	b	Bob	36	1047972020224
6	a	Alice	34	1460288880640

⬇ 6 rows | 14.98 seconds runtime

Figure 11.14: Results of strongly connected components analysis

We can see this by examining the visual representation in *Figure 11.9*, where there are links from **Charlie** to **Bob** and **Bob** to **Charlie**. Next, we will examine the label propagation algorithm.

Recipe 111: Label Propagation Algorithm

In graph theory, there is the concept of a community. The idea is that some nodes are more related to each other than others. Using the **Label Propagation Algorithm (LPA)** is one way to detect nodes that have a relationship, as shown in *Figure 11.15*:

```
1    result = g.labelPropagation(maxIter=5)
2    display(result.orderBy("label"))
```

▸ (8) Spark Jobs

▸ 🖳 result: pyspark.sql.dataframe.DataFrame = [id: string, name: string ... 2 more fields]

Table ∨   +

	id	name	age	label
1	b	Bob	36	1047972020224
2	e	Esther	32	1382979469312
3	c	Charlie	30	1382979469312
4	a	Alice	34	1382979469312
5	f	Fanny	36	1460288880640
6	d	David	29	1460288880640

Figure 11.15: Results of LPA

We can apply these labels to our graph to visually see the labels, as shown in *Figure 11.16:*

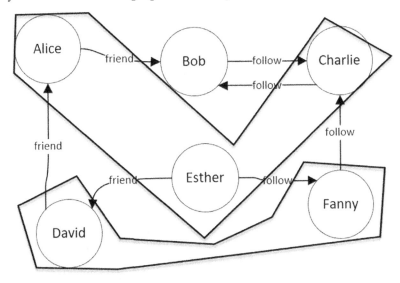

Figure 11.16: Labels applied to graph

LPA is a relatively simple algorithm where nodes send their community to their neighbors and then update based on the most frequently occurring community message they receive. It is iterative and may not converge. In the next section, we will examine looking at patterns in our graph using motifs.

Recipe 112: Motif finding

We often want to treat the nodes in a graph in a generic way. We look for patterns, such as a node that references a node that in turn references it. We can express this using an expression, as shown in *Figure 11.17*:

Figure 11.17: Motif to find circular reference in a graph

In this case, we ask for nodes that have an edge from them to another node and from that node back to the original node. We can see that **Charlie** and **Bob** match this **motif**. We may also want to know the connections of a certain length. If we want to know the nodes that connect from one to another and then to a third node, we can use the expression shown in *Figure 11.18*:

Figure 11.18: Motif with a length of three

We can see that **Esther** to **David** to **Alice** is one pattern matching our expression. This approach is often useful when learning about the shape of your graph.

We have covered many of the graph operations available on a GraphFrame. However, this is by no means an exhaustive treatment of the topic. Many more operations can be performed. To learn more about GraphFrames see the GraphFrame user guide at **https://graphframes.github.io/graphframes/docs/_site/user-guide.html**. In the next section, we will examine using Neo4J (a popular graph database system) with Databricks.

Neo4J and Databricks

Neo4J is a popular graph database system. It is available in several forms, including a managed cloud version.

Recipe 113: Using AuraDB

You can sign up for a free account by going to **https://neo4j.com/cloud/aura-free/**. You will either be prompted for your email address or your Google credentials. Once you have signed in, you can create a **New Instance** of the AuraDB, as shown in *Figure 11.19:*

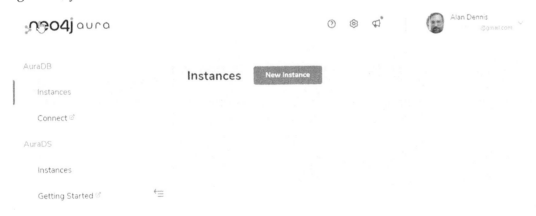

Figure 11.19: *AuraDB control page*

You will be prompted to select the instance type when you click the **New Instance** button. Your choices are **Free** or **Professional**. The free version is limited in memory size, number of nodes, and cloud provider, as shown in *Figure 11.20:*

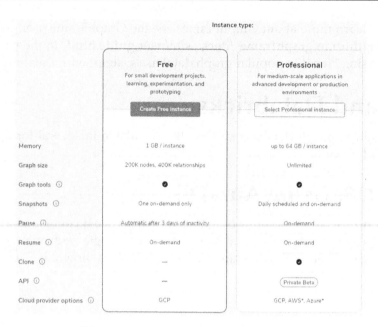

Figure 11.20: *AuraDB instance type selection*

For our purposes, the **Free instance** is sufficient. Selecting it creates the instance and opens a form with the credentials to access the new instance, as shown in *Figure 11.21*:

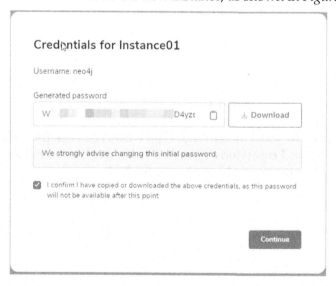

Figure 11.21: *AuraDB credentials*

It is advisable to **Download** the credentials and make a copy of them for future reference. After clicking **Continue**, you will be presented with your **New Instance**, as shown in *Figure 11.22*:

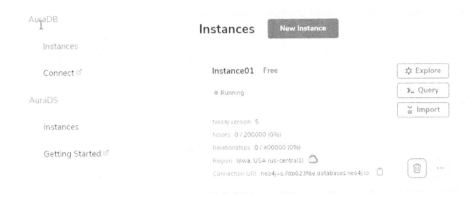

Figure 11.22: *New AuraDB instance*

Now that we have an instance, we can explore it by clicking the **Explore** button. This opens Neo4J's Bloom tool. As we have no data in our graph, the page is blank. Now that we have a graph database, we need to populate it. One way to do this is to leverage Excel to create the Cypher script to define a graph. For our example, we will use the concept of pre-requests in college classes. As most college students know, classes are often required before a student can take other classes. For our example, we will model a subset of a course catalog as a graph. The original Excel document used can be retrieved at **https://neo4j. com/blog/importing-data-into-neo4j-the-spreadsheet-way/**. While this is not a high-tech solution, it is sufficient for our needs.

As we have discussed earlier in this chapter, a graph is made up of nodes and edges. For this example, the nodes are classes, as shown in *Figure 11.23*:

Node	Type	Name	Label	CYPHER QUERIES for NODES
1	ITSS	ITSS 130	Application Software	create (n1:ITSS {id:1, name:'ITSS 130', fullname:'Application Software'})
2	ITSS	ITSS 131	Introduction to Object Oriented Programming	create (n2:ITSS {id:2, name:'ITSS 131', fullname:'Introduction to Object Oriented Programming'})
3	ITSS	ITSS 230	Fundamentals of Databases	create (n3:ITSS {id:3, name:'ITSS 230', fullname:'Fundamentals of Databases'})
4	ITSS	ITSS 232	Web Design	create (n4:ITSS {id:4, name:'ITSS 232', fullname:'Web Design'})
5	ITSS	ITSS 332	Database Administration	create (n5:ITSS {id:5, name:'ITSS 332', fullname:'Database Administration'})
6	ITSS	ITSS 333	Video Game Programming	create (n6:ITSS {id:6, name:'ITSS 333', fullname:'Video Game Programming'})
7	ITSS	ITSS 334	Web Programming	create (n7:ITSS {id:7, name:'ITSS 334', fullname:'Web Programming'})
8	ITSS	ITSS 337	Business Intelligence	create (n8:ITSS {id:8, name:'ITSS 337', fullname:'Business Intelligence'})
9	ITSS	ITSS 338	Programming of Mobile Devices	create (n9:ITSS {id:9, name:'ITSS 338', fullname:'Programming of Mobile Devices'})
10	ITSS	ITSS 435	Software Engineering	create (n10:ITSS {id:10, name:'ITSS 435', fullname:'Software Engineering'})

Figure 11.23: *Excel document of nodes and Cypher script*

Connecting the classes are relationships, such as pre-requisite, as shown in *Figure 11.24*:

=VLOOKUP(J18,B$3:D$33,3,FALSE)

Name	From	Relationship Type	To	Name	CYPHER QUERIES for RELATIONSHIPS
ITSS 131	2	PREREQ	6	ITSS 333	create (n2)-[:PREREQ]->(n6)
ITSS 131	2	PREREQ	7	ITSS 334	create (n2)-[:PREREQ]->(n7)
ITSS 230	3	PREREQ	7	ITSS 334	create (n3)-[:PREREQ]->(n7)
ITSS 232	4	PREREQ	7	ITSS 334	create (n4)-[:PREREQ]->(n7)
ITSS 230	3	PREREQ	8	ITSS 337	create (n3)-[:PREREQ]->(n8)
ITSS 131	2	PREREQ	9	ITSS 338	create (n2)-[:PREREQ]->(n9)
ITSS 131	2	PREREQ	10	ITSS 435	create (n2)-[:PREREQ]->(n10)
ITSS 230	3	PREREQ	10	ITSS 435	create (n3)-[:PREREQ]->(n10)
ITSS 130	1	PREREQ	11	ITSS 438	create (n1)-[:PREREQ]->(n11)

Figure 11.24: *Generated edge Cypher script*

We can take these Cypher scripts and past them into the Neo4J Browser to construct a graph as shown in *Figure 11.25:*

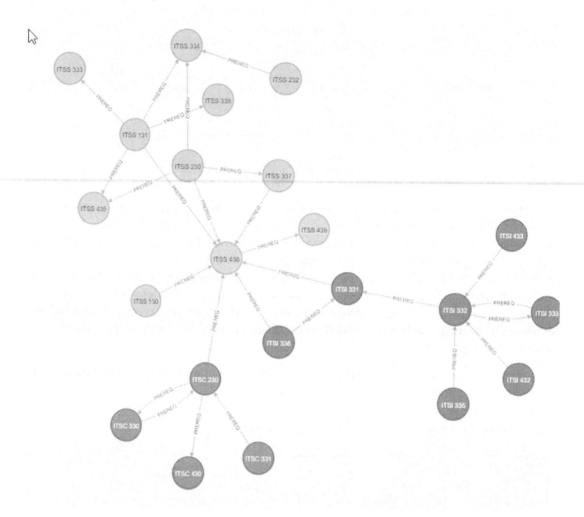

Figure 11.25: Neo4J graph of classes and relationships

Now that we have a graph, the next step is to connect to it from Databricks.

Recipe 114: Reading Neo4J's AuraDB from Databricks

In the previous section we created a free AuraDB account and populated it with a graph based loosely on a college course catalog. To read from AuraDB, the first step is to install the library that enables it, as shown in *Figure 11.26:*

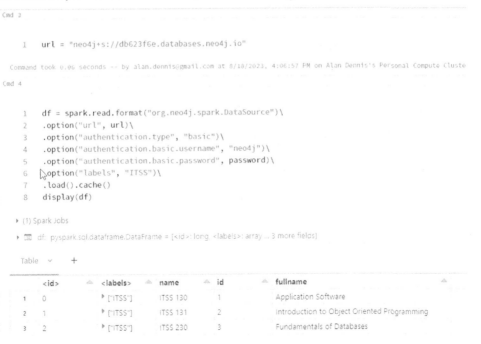

Figure 11.26: *Searching Maven for Neo4J spark connector*

To learn more about the library see **https://neo4j.com/docs/spark/current/overview/**. When installing the library, ensure that the version of the library matches the version of Scala in your Databricks runtime. Now that we have the library installed, the next step is to use it from a **spark.read** statement, as shown in *Figure 11.27*:

```
Cmd 3

1   url = "neo4j+s://db623f6e.databases.neo4j.io"

Command took 0.06 seconds -- by alan.dennis@gmail.com at 8/18/2023, 4:06:57 PM on Alan Dennis's Personal Compute Cluste

Cmd 4

1   df = spark.read.format("org.neo4j.spark.DataSource")\
2   .option("url", url)\
3   .option("authentication.type", "basic")\
4   .option("authentication.basic.username", "neo4j")\
5   .option("authentication.basic.password", password)\
6   .option("labels", "ITSS")\
7   .load().cache()
8   display(df)
```

▸ (1) Spark Jobs

▸ ▦ df: pyspark.sql.dataframe.DataFrame = [<id>: long, <labels>: array ... 3 more fields]

Table ∨   +

	<id>	<labels>	name	id	fullname
1	0	▸ ["ITSS"]	ITSS 130	1	Application Software
2	1	▸ ["ITSS"]	ITSS 131	2	Introduction to Object Oriented Programming
3	2	▸ ["ITSS"]	ITSS 230	3	Fundamentals of Databases

Figure 11.27: *Populating a DataFrame from Neo4J database*

This code should look familiar. The only real difference is the inclusion of the **FORMAT** clause, referencing the Neo4J data source, and the inclusion of the **labels** option on line six. To find the URL of your Neo4J **AuraDB**, navigate to the **Instances** screen and copy the **Connection URI**, as shown in *Figure 11.28*:

Figure 11.28: AuraDB connection URI

The AuraDB connection supports three retrieval methods, labels, relationships, and Cypher queries. In the earlier example, we retrieved based on labels. Retrieving by **relationship** returns **source** and **target** items, as shown in *Figure 11.29*:

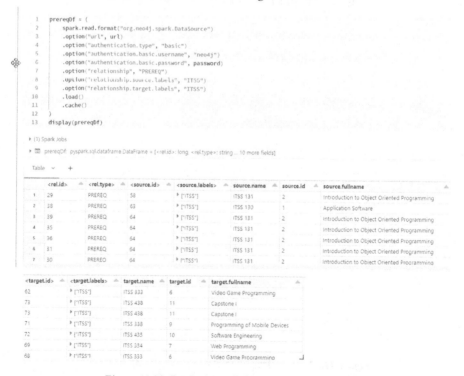

Figure 11.29: Retrieving relationships from AuraDB

There are other interaction patterns available to you when interacting with AuraDB from Databricks. We have covered two simple ways of retrieving data. You can also write from Databricks to AuraDB. You may choose to do this because **Neo4J** has superior graph visualization compared to Databricks. We have successfully interacted with **Neo4J**'s AuraDB using Databricks.

Conclusion

In this chapter, you were introduced to some of the graph functionality in Databricks. We discussed the nature of mathematical graphs and when it is appropriate to use graph operations. We briefly discussed GraphX and then moved to GraphFrames. We discussed several common graph algorithms and operations and we concluded the chapter by discussing accessing Neo4J's AuraDB from Databricks.

In the next chapter, we will discuss data visualization.

Join our book's Discord space

Join the book's Discord Workspace for Latest updates, Offers, Tech happenings around the world, New Release and Sessions with the Authors:

https://discord.bpbonline.com

CHAPTER 12
Visualizations

Introduction

Often visualization of data can be very powerful. The expression *a picture is worth a thousand words* is very true. In this chapter we will explore the common ways of presenting data visually, including a discussion of Power BI and the native Databricks visualization capabilities.

Structure

The chapter covers the following topics:

- Visualization best practices
- Databrick dashboards
- Visualization in Databricks notebooks
- Power BI

Objectives

By the end of this chapter, you should be able to discuss the benefits of using Databricks and Power BI dashboards. You should be able to articulate the benefits of each. You should be able to create simple visualizations and understand the basics of visualization design.

Visualization best practices

Before creating visualizations of data, we should review some best practices. While this might be a review for many, it is useful to remind ourselves of what makes a good data visualization. We will review best practices and provide guidance.

Visually appealing

This first point might be obvious to most. Still, as quantitative-oriented individuals often focus on finding the answer to a problem, it is important to make the presentation of that information visually appealing. This means that when creating a visualization, make it look good. We will attempt to define what good means in the following sections.

Keep it simple

In general, keep the visualization as simple as possible. If you have two ways of showing information, select the simpler approach. This allows your audience to focus on the information conveyed by the visualization rather than attempting to understand how it is presented. This does not mean that you should lower the fidelity of the visualization only to use a simpler visualization. Rather, if you can present your information using a line graph, do so. If you need something more complex, then ensure you explain it to the audience. This will be elaborated further in this chapter.

Explain unfamiliar graph types

In data analytics, there are a multitude of ways that information can be displayed. For example, within Databricks' Visualization Editor, there are over twenty visualization types (see **https://docs.databricks.com/en/visualizations/visualization-types.html**). Some types are familiar (line and bar graphs), while others (Sankey and Sunburst sequence) might be less so. If you use a less common visualization, tell the reader how to understand it. The goal is to inform the reader how to understand it so that they can reach their conclusions. Part of how we make sure they can understand it is by following conventions.

Follow conventions

Color choice and orientation must follow standard approaches. For example, we typically associate green with good or positive things and red with bad or negative things. Also, when discussing things like profit or income, we expect things to go from a low value at the bottom of the page to a high value at the top. While you could create a graph that rendered things differently, it likely confuses the reader.

Tell a story

While this may only sometimes be a possibility, it is important to help the data tell the story. For visualizations in Databricks notebooks, you can use Markdown (see **https://www.markdownguide.org/**) to add a narrative. It is more challenging with a dashboard, as the goal of a dashboard is to show information without distracting details. The idea is to capture the reader's attention and guide them through the analysis or synthesis of information.

Databricks dashboards

We explored Databricks dashboards briefly in *Chapter 10, SQL Analysis*. In this Chapter, we will go into greater depth. The goal of a dashboard is to present information in an easy-to-understand way. They use various visualizations like line graphs, bar charts, detail tables, or other controls. We will start by looking at some sample dashboards.

Recipe 115: Importing sample dashboards

Using a sample dashboard is a good way to learn. In Databricks, you can access the samples by navigating to the **Dashboards** section under the **SQL** area of the left navigation, as shown in *Figure 12.1:*

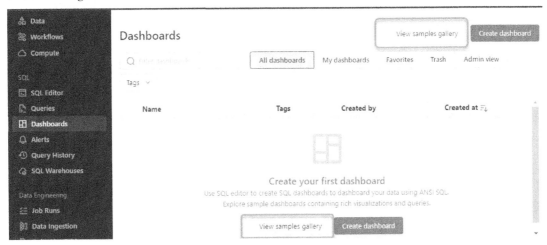

Figure 12.1: Dashboards landing page

As of this writing, the samples gallery has two samples. One is based on the **NYC Taxi Trip** data, while the other relates to **Retail Revenue & Supply Chain**. We will start by importing the **NYC Tax Trip Analysis** dashboard, as shown in *Figure 12.2:*

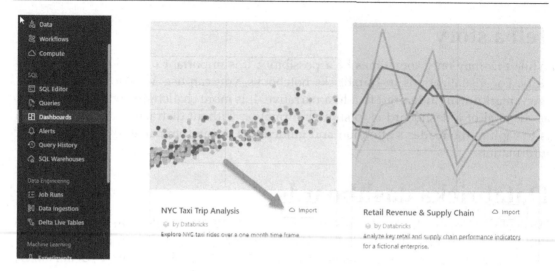

Figure 12.2: *Selecting NYC Tax Trip Analysis dashboard*

Clicking the **Import** button starts a SQL Warehouse, if one is not running. Once the SQL Warehouse has completed starting, the dashboard is displayed, as shown in *Figure 12.3*:

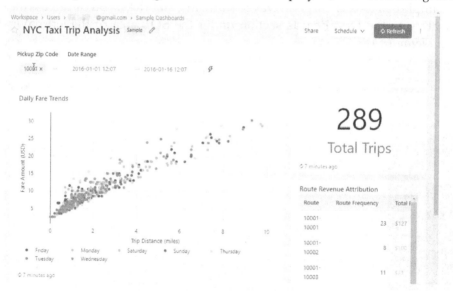

Figure 12.3: *Imported dashboard*

The first thing you likely notice is the scatter plot of **Trip Distance** on the X-axis and **Fare Amount** on the Y. Next, the **Total Trips** in the selected **Zip Code** and **Date Range** are prominently displayed. The **Route Revenue Attribution** table is below the total trips on the right side. This gives a sense of the frequency of certain routes and total fares. The last two visualizations on the dashboard are the **Pickup Hour** and **Dropoff Hour** distribution bar graphs, as shown in *Figure 12.4*:

Pickup Hour Distribution

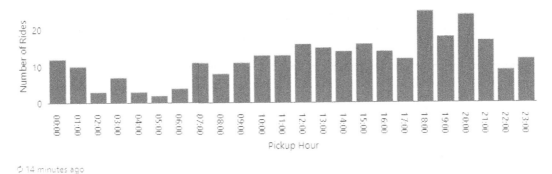

Dropoff Hour Distribution

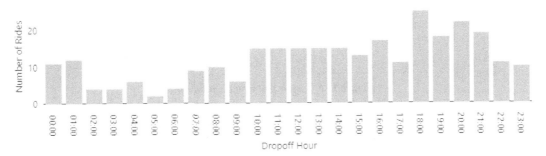

Figure 12.4: *Pickup and drop-off hour distribution bar graphs*

Selecting the **three dots** on the top right of the screen brings up a menu that includes an **Edit** option, as shown in *Figure 12.5*:

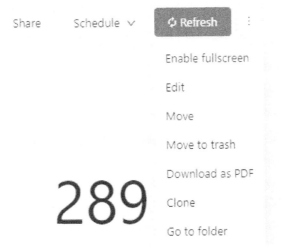

Figure 12.5: *Edit menu*

Selecting **Edit**, switches the dashboard into editable mode. This enables editing of each visualization by selecting the **three dots** in the upper right-hand of each control. Doing so on the **Scatter** plot, brings up the **Visualization** Editor, as shown in *Figure 12.6*:

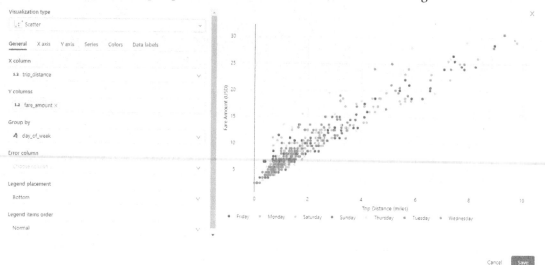

Figure 12.6: *Scatter plot visualization editor*

This **Edit** mode lets you pick the values on the **X column** and **Y columns**, use grouping, and control where the legend is placed and how it is ordered. You can also control the scale of each axis, along with the name. By clicking on the **Series** label, you could reorder the labels to follow the typical order of the days of the week.

You may decide that a line graph is a better representation of the rides per **Pickup Hour**. To change it, select **Edit** from and change the **Visualization type** from **Bar to Line**, as shown in *Figure 12.7*:

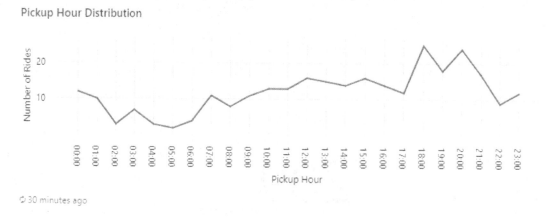

Figure 12.7: *Changed visualization type*

Once you are done editing the dashboard, select Done editing to return to presentation mode. Since one of the best practices is to ensure we are using the graphs correctly, we should switch to an area graph, as that more closely represents the nature of this data and looks better, as shown in *Figure 12.8*:

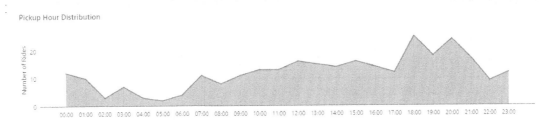

Figure 12.8: *Number of rides by pickup hour as an area graph*

We have explored the basic elements of dashboards. In the next section, we will manipulate sample data to prepare to create a new dashboard.

Recipe 116: Data preparation for a new dashboard

Often, reporting and creating dashboards involves a great deal of data manipulation. Ideally, the data will already reside in the silver or gold layers. However, often we must manipulate the data so it can be used. For this example, we will use a Databricks sample dataset. We can list those **datasets**, as shown in *Figure 12.9*:

```
display(dbutils.fs.ls('/databricks-datasets'))
```

▸ (2) Spark Jobs

Table ∨   +

	path	name	size	modificationTime
33	dbfs:/databricks-datasets/news20.binary/	news20.binary/	0	1692734924130
34	dbfs:/databricks-datasets/nyctaxi/	nyctaxi/	0	1692734924130
35	dbfs:/databricks-datasets/nyctaxi-with-zipcodes/	nyctaxi-with-zipcodes/	0	1692734924130
36	dbfs:/databricks-datasets/online_retail/	online_retail/	0	1692734924130
37	dbfs:/databricks-datasets/overlap-join/	overlap-join/	0	1692734924130
38	dbfs:/databricks-datasets/power-plant/	power-plant/	0	1692734924130
39	dbfs:/databricks-datasets/retail-org/	retail-org/	0	1692734924130

⤓ 55 rows | 0.92 seconds runtime

Figure 12.9: *Sample datasets*

For this example, we will use the **online_retail** dataset. We can read the dataset into a DataFrame, as shown in *Figure 12.10*:

```
df = spark.read.option("header", True).option("inferSchema",True).csv("dbfs:/databricks-datasets/online_retail/data-001/data.csv")
display(df)
```

▸ (3) Spark Jobs

▸ ▦ df: pyspark.sql.dataframe.DataFrame = [InvoiceNo: string, StockCode: string,... 6 more fields]

Table ∨ +

	InvoiceNo	StockCode	Description	Quantity	InvoiceDate	UnitPrice	CustomerID	Country
1	536365	85123A	WHITE HANGING HEART T-LIGHT HOLDER	6	12/1/10 8:26	2.55	17850	United Kingdom
2	536365	71053	WHITE METAL LANTERN	6	12/1/10 8:26	3.39	17850	United Kingdom
3	536365	84406B	CREAM CUPID HEARTS COAT HANGER	8	12/1/10 8:26	2.75	17850	United Kingdom
4	536365	84029G	KNITTED UNION FLAG HOT WATER BOTTLE	6	12/1/10 8:26	3.39	17850	United Kingdom
5	536365	84029E	RED WOOLLY HOTTIE WHITE HEART.	6	12/1/10 8:26	3.39	17850	United Kingdom
6	536365	22752	SET 7 BABUSHKA NESTING BOXES	2	12/1/10 8:26	7.65	17850	United Kingdom
7	536365	21730	GLASS STAR FROSTED T-LIGHT HOLDER	6	12/1/10 8:26	4.25	17850	United Kingdom

⬇ ∨ 10,000 rows | Truncated data | 2.29 seconds runtime   Refreshed 32 minutes ago

Figure 12.10: Reading sample dataset into DataFrame

Once we have loaded the **DataFrame**, we must make a few changes. For example, we calculate the total of each transaction by multiplying the **UnitPrice** by quantity, as shown in *Figure 12.11:*

```
from pyspark.sql.functions import from_unixtime,unix_timestamp,to_timestamp
from pyspark.sql.types import TimestampType
dfWithTotal = df.withColumn("Total",df.UnitPrice * df.Quantity)
dfFinished = dfWithTotal.withColumn("InvoiceDateTS",unix_timestamp(dfWithTotal.InvoiceDate, 'M/d/yy H:mm'))
dfFinished = dfFinished .withColumn("InvoiceDate",to_timestamp(from_unixtime(dfFinished.InvoiceDateTS)))
display(dfFinished )
```

▸ (1) Spark Jobs

▸ ▦ dfWithTotal: pyspark.sql.dataframe.DataFrame = [InvoiceNo: string, StockCode: string ... 7 more fields]

▸ ▦ dfFinished: pyspark.sql.dataframe.DataFrame = [InvoiceNo: string, StockCode: string ... 8 more fields]

Table ∨ +

		Quantity	InvoiceDate	UnitPrice	CustomerID	Country	Total	InvoiceDateTS
1	T-LIGHT HOLDER	6	2010-12-01T08:26:00.000+0000	2.55	17850	United Kingdom	15.299999999999999	1291191960
2		6	2010-12-01T08:26:00.000+0000	3.39	17850	United Kingdom	20.34	1291191960
3	OAT HANGER	8	2010-12-01T08:26:00.000+0000	2.75	17850	United Kingdom	22	1291191960
4	OT WATER BOTTLE	6	2010-12-01T08:26:00.000+0000	3.39	17850	United Kingdom	20.34	1291191960
5	HITE HEART.	6	2010-12-01T08:26:00.000+0000	3.39	17850	United Kingdom	20.34	1291191960
6	IG BOXES	2	2010-12-01T08:26:00.000+0000	7.65	17850	United Kingdom	15.3	1291191960
7	LIGHT HOLDER	6	2010-12-01T08:26:00.000+0000	4.25	17850	United Kingdom	25.5	1291191960

Figure 12.11: Data manipulation of DataFrame

We also convert the string representation of the **InvoiceDate** to a timestamp. This will allow us to do aggregation per unit of time, such as per hour. Next, we need to create a Delta table to hold our updated **DataFrame**, as shown in *Figure 12.12:*

```
table_name = "LakehouseCookbook.Silver_OnlineRetailSales"
dfFinished.write.mode("overwrite").option("overwriteSchema", "true").saveAsTable(table_name)
display(spark.sql("describe LakehouseCookbook.Silver_OnlineRetailSales"))
```

▶ (7) Spark Jobs

Table ⌄ +

	col_name	data_type	comment
1	InvoiceNo	string	null
2	StockCode	string	null
3	Description	string	null
4	Quantity	int	null
5	InvoiceDate	timestamp	null
6	UnitPrice	double	null
7	CustomerID	int	null

Figure 12.12: Create Delta table from DataFrame

We can reuse the date dimension that we discussed in *Recipe 74*. The only real change is exposing the **timestamp** and changing the start and end of the sequence, as shown in *Figure 12.13*:

Figure 12.13: Date dimension changes

The changes are highlighted in the above given *Figure 12.13*. By exposing the timestamp column, we can use it to join with aggregated data. We can use the Spark SQL Window grouping expression to aggregate the data. The **window** command can be used to create hopping windows, as shown in *Figure 12.14*:

Figure 12.14: *Creating an aggregated table and joining it with the date dimension*

This is a powerful way to process our data. To learn more about window operations, see **https://docs.databricks.com/en/sql/language-manual/functions/window.html**. We can now examine the total sales by hour and the **SmallestSale** and **LargestSale**. With this information in place, we are ready to create a dashboard.

Recipe 117: Creating a dashboard

To create a dashboard, we start by navigating to the **Dashboards** section of the left navigation and clicking **Create dashboard**. This will bring up a new dashboard prompt that asks for a **Dashboard name**, as shown in *Figure 12.15*:

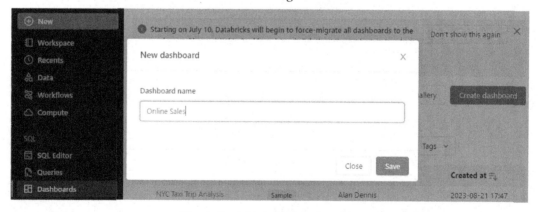

Figure 12.15: *New dashboard prompt*

Clicking **Save** brings you to a blank dashboard canvas, as shown in *Figure 12.16*:

Figure 12.16: *Newly created dashboard*

The next step is to select the SQL warehouse we wish to use. Once you have selected a warehouse, you need to construct the queries you wish to use, assuming they do not already exist. We will start by creating a **SQL Editor** query that joins the sales fact table to the date dimension, as shown in *Figure 12.17*:

Figure 12.17: *Joining sales fact with date dimension*

While this is sufficient, we will create queries that return each table in *Figure 12.17*. The next step is to add a visualization widget to our blank dashboard. Clicking the **Add** button displays the choices of things to add, as shown in *Figure 12.18*:

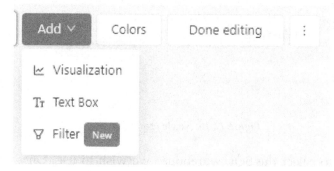

Figure 12.18: *Add to dashboard options*

Selecting **Visualization** brings up the **Add visualization widget** form. On this form you are asked to select a query that will be the base for the visualization, as shown in *Figure 12.19*:

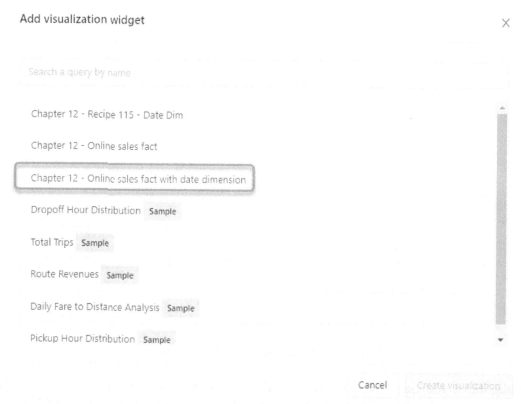

Figure 12.19: *Add visualization widget form*

In our case, we select the query that joins the sales fact table with the date dimension. Next, we are asked to **Select existing visualization** or **Create new visualization**, as shown in *Figure 12.20*:

Add visualization widget   ✕

Chapter 12 - Online sales fact with date dimension   ✕

◉ Create new visualization

◯ Select existing visualization

Results   ⌄

Title

Visualization - Chapter 12 - Online sales fact with date dimension   ⟋

Description

Sales combined with date dimension   ⟋

Cancel   **Create visualization**

Figure 12.20: Creating a new visualization

We can now select **Create visualization**, after having supplied a description and selected that we wish to create a new visualization. After clicking **Create visualization**, we briefly see a dialog explaining that the schema is being examined. We are now able to select the type of visualization and determine what elements go on which axis, as shown in *Figure 12.21:*

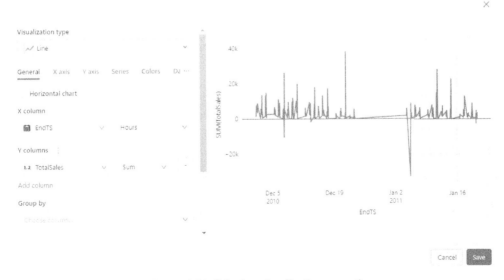

Figure 12.21: Selecting visualization properties

Since we have selected the **EndTS** column for the **X column**, we can select a date level. Also, we have selected **TotalSales** for the **Y column**, with the **Sum** operation being performed. Notice that there is a large spike and dip on the graph. If we change the date level to days, the spikes are less obvious, as shown in *Figure 12.22*:

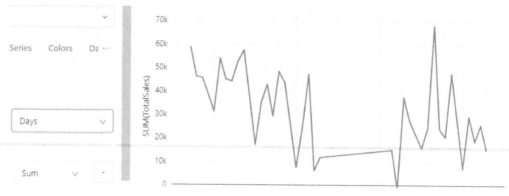

Figure 12.22: *Visualizing at a day level*

For those unfamiliar with the shopping patterns in the Western world, many transactions lead up to Christmas (December 25th), typically followed by many returns after January 1st. Moreover, there are fewer purchases during that period, as it is a holiday. For our purposes, we will select an hourly level. Note that we have not used the date dimension we joined with the sales information that was aggregated to an hourly level. Additionally, the visualization's ability to select different date levels questions whether the aggregation was necessary. However, it is a pattern often helpful for other reporting forms.

Now that we have created a visualization, we can see it on our **Dashboards**, as shown in *Figure 12.23*:

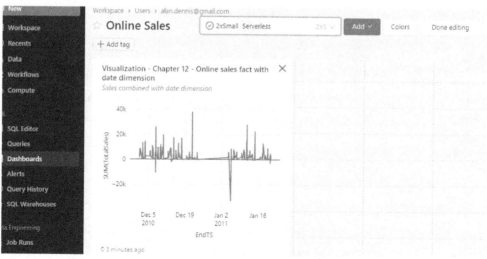

Figure 12.23: *Partially constructed dashboard*

At this point we can choose to change the size of the visualization by selecting the bottom right corner and dragging. Once you have selected an appropriate size, we can add a filter. A filter allows you to control the results of multiple visualizations. To learn more about filters, see **https://docs.databricks.com/en/sql/user/dashboards/index.html#filter-across-multiple-queries**. When adding a filter, you are asked to select what to **Filter on** per **Query** on the dashboard, as shown in *Figure 12.24*:

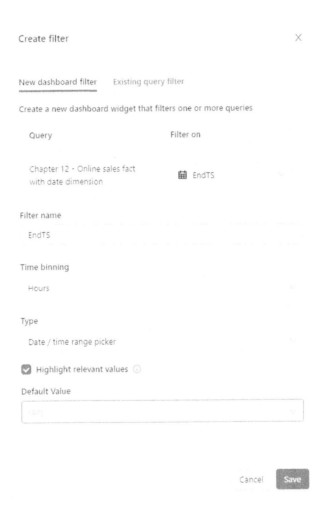

Figure 12.24: *Creating a filter*

In addition to the **Filter on** per **Query**, you can give the **Filter name**. You also select the time granularity by selecting **Time binning**. Then you select the **Type** of date and time selection you desire. Your choices are **Single select**, **Multi select**, **Date / time picker**, and **Date / time range picker**. In this case, we selected the **Date / time range picker**, as shown in *Figure 12.25*:

Type

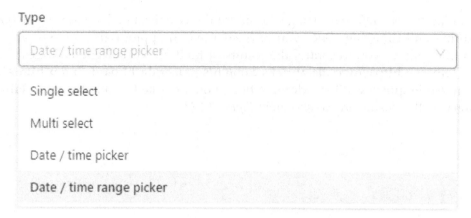

Figure 12.25: Date selection type

After all selections are complete, click **Save**. This will cause the selection mechanism to be placed on the dashboard. Once on the dashboard, we can experiment with the effects by entering a narrow range and clicking apply changes. It is often desirable to know the range of the data being displayed. To enable this, we create a simple query that returns the **min timestamp** and **max timestamp**, as shown in *Figure 12.26*:

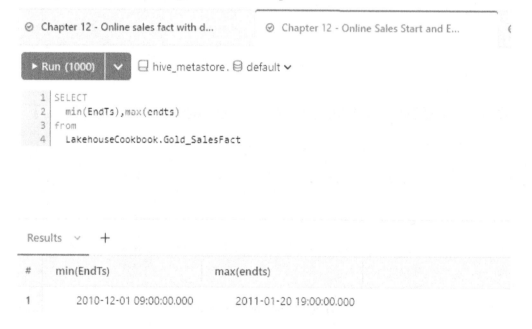

Figure 12.26: Query to return the range of the timestamps

We can use a different visualization type to display the two values returned, as shown in *Figure 12.27*:

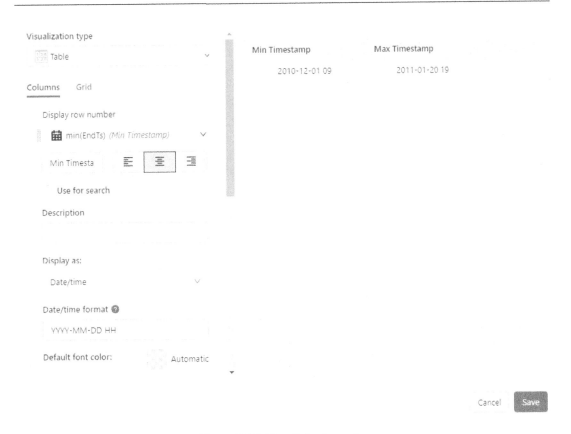

Figure 12.27: Visualizing two values

In this case, we select the **Visualization type Table**. When added, it renders as a grid with the two values side by side. Adding another visualization, such as a Counter displaying total sales, brings us close to a passable dashboard, as shown in *Figure 12.28:*

Figure 12.28: *Nearly complete dashboard*

A few more minor changes make a dramatic improvement in the resulting dashboard. For example, removing the word *Visualization* from the visualizations makes the results look more professional. Also, changing the filter's name to **End Timestamp** from **EndTS**, makes it more readable, as shown in *Figure 12.29*:

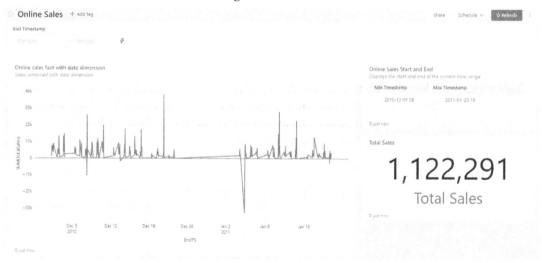

Figure 12.29: *Completed dashboard*

Often, the last few edits have the most impact on the appeal and success of a dashboard. We will now move to using visualizations in Databricks notebooks.

Visualizations in Databricks notebooks

In the previous section, we used several visualizations in a dashboard. In this section, we will present using visualizations in notebooks. Visualization can be used in several ways. They can provide an interactive and frequently updated report. Often, visualizations are combined with a narrative in Markdown to provide a compelling report-like experience. We will start by examining general visualization in notebooks.

Recipe 118: Using visualizations in notebooks

We will return to our online sales data, partly since it should be familiar to you. We aggregated the sales by the hour to combine them with a date dimension. We will start by creating Markdown cells, and adding text, as shown in *Figure 12.30*:

Figure 12.30: Markdown cell

Notice the **%md** magic string. This tells Databricks that this cell contains Markdown. Once rendered, the Markdown text becomes more appealing, as shown in *Figure 12.31*:

Figure 12.31: Rendered Markdown

As previously mentioned, Markdown is a simple textual representation language. For more on Markdown, see **https://www.markdownguide.org/**. Additionally, Databricks notebooks provide a generated table of contents using the Markdown headings information, as shown in *Figure 12.32*:

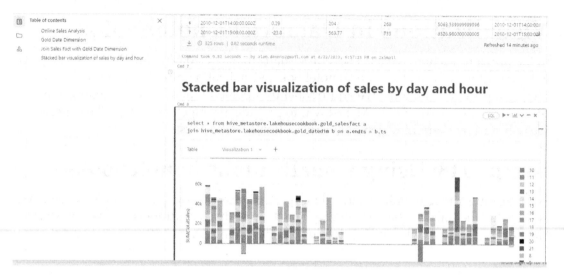

Figure 12.32: Generated table of contents

Additionally, the **Table of contents** provides for simplified navigation. Clicking the name in the **Table of contents** takes you to that section. *Figure 12.32* shows a visualization of the joined fact and dimension tables. To create a visualization, we click the **plus sign** next to the word **Table** in the results of a query, as shown in *Figure 12.33:*

Figure 12.33: Adding a visualization

Clicking **Visualization** brings up the **Visualization Editor**, which is similar to that used in dashboards. In our example, we created a bar graph with date as the **X column**. For the **Y column** we selected **TotalSales**. We then selected to **Group by hour** and enabled **Stacking**, as shown in *Figure 12.34:*

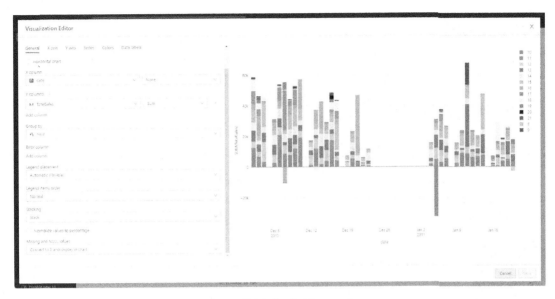

Figure 12.34: Stacked bar graphs

If you wish to change the name of the visualization after creating it, you can click on the **name** to change it, as shown in *Figure 12.35:*

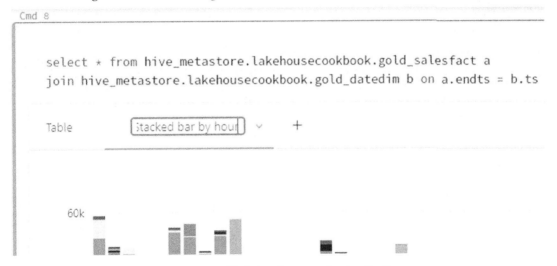

Figure 12.35: Updating the name of a visualization

While we have yet to exhaustively cover visualization, we have introduced the topic. Native visualization has become more powerful as Databricks continues to refine them. However, there are times we need a more powerful visualization tool. In the next section, we will discuss using Power BI to extend Databricks' visualization.

Power BI

Power BI is a popular visualization tool on the Windows Platform. It was created around July 2011 and has been updated regularly since. One compelling feature of Power BI is that it enables interactive business intelligence. In the next section, we will discuss connecting to Databricks from Power BI.

Recipe 119: Connecting Power BI to Databricks

There are several ways to connect Power BI to Databricks. We will show one of the simpler and more common approaches. It uses the **Partner Connect** area of Databricks, as shown in *Figure 12.36:*

Figure 12.36: Databricks Partner Connect

Partner Connect is organized by the type of tools offered. **Microsoft Power BI** is in the **BI and visualization** section. Notice that Power BI is not the only visualization tool available. Additionally, there are partners for **Data Ingestion**, Data preparation and transformation, Machine Learning, Data governance, Reverse ETL, Semantic layer, and **Other partners**.

Clicking on the **Microsoft Power BI** tile brings up the **Connect to partner** dialog. You are asked to select the **Compute** you wish to use and can then **Download connection file**, as shown in *Figure 12.37:*

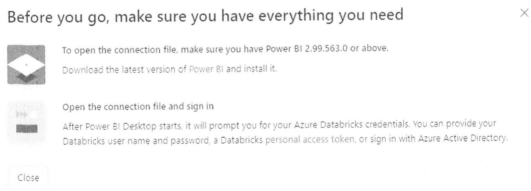

Figure 12.37: Power BI Connect to partner dialog

The compute resource is the mechanism that Power BI will use to connect to the Databricks endpoints. Clicking **Download connection file** will cause a file with the extension **pbids** to be downloaded. The screen will now be displaying tips to get you started using Power BI, as shown in *Figure 12.38:*

Before you go, make sure you have everything you need   ✕

To open the connection file, make sure you have Power BI 2.99.563.0 or above.

Download the latest version of Power BI and install it.

Open the connection file and sign in

After Power BI Desktop starts, it will prompt you for your Azure Databricks credentials. You can provide your Databricks user name and password, a Databricks personal access token, or sign in with Azure Active Directory.

Close

Figure 12.38: Post-download screen

Clicking on the file that was downloaded will cause Power BI to be opened. You will be prompted for an authentication mechanism. The choices for authentication are to use your Databricks username and password, a **Personal access token**, or to use **Azure Active Directory**. Although the choice is yours, the **Personal access tokens** are a simple way to authenticate. Recall that we create them by going to **User Settings**, by clicking on your email address in the upper right corner and selecting **User Settings**. This will bring you to the **User Settings** form where you can click **Generate new token**, as shown in *Figure 12.39*:

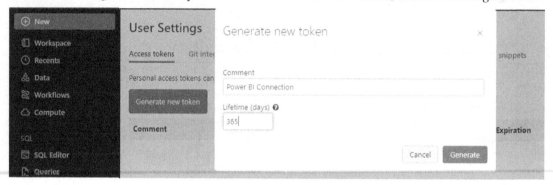

Figure 12.39: *Creating a user access token*

You will be prompted for the purpose of the token and ask to provide an expiration. Once you have provided the information, click **Generate**. This will bring up a form with the new token displayed. Make sure you save this value, as you cannot recreate it, as shown in *Figure 12.40*:

Figure 12.40: *New token*

Treat this token's value as you would a password, as it serves the same purpose. You can now go back to Power BI and enter the token into the field, as shown in *Figure 12.41*:

Figure 12.41: *Power BI Personal Access Token*

You can now click the **Connect** button. If all goes well, you will be presented with the **Navigator** screen, as shown in *Figure 12.42*:

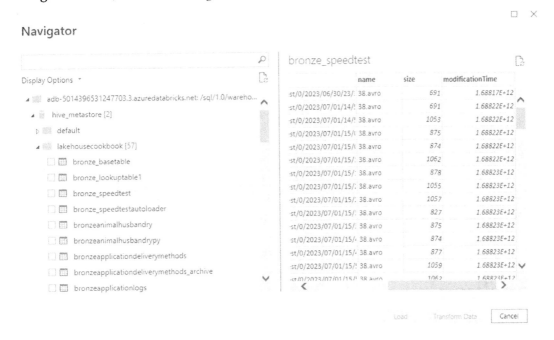

Figure 12.42: *Power BI Navigator screen*

This screen allows you to navigate the tables that exist in your Databricks workspace. Once you have identified the items of interest, check the box beside them and then click the **Load** button. This will bring the **Data** assets into Power BI, as shown in *Figure 12.43*:

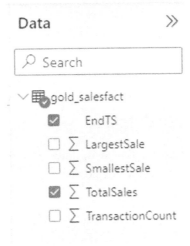

Figure 12.43: *Power BI Data tile*

Selecting a visualization renders the data, as shown in *Figure 12.44:*

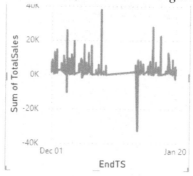

Figure 12.44: *Power BI visualization of Databricks data*

We have successfully displayed data in a Power BI visualization that originated in a Databricks workspace. This is a very brief introduction to visualization. However, we have shown the key elements required to expand your knowledge.

Conclusion

In this chapter, we discussed the best practices associated with visualization. We presented Databricks dashboards, first by examining a sample and then by preparing data and using it in a dashboard. We discussed native Databricks visualizations in notebooks, along with a discussion of the use of Markdown to enhance the quality of the notebooks. We concluded by connecting to Databricks from Power BI desktop.

The next chapter discusses data governance, which is essential for a successful Databricks Lakehouse.

Join our book's Discord space

Join the book's Discord Workspace for Latest updates, Offers, Tech happenings around the world, New Release and Sessions with the Authors:

https://discord.bpbonline.com

CHAPTER 13
Governance

Introduction

Without proper governance, data within a lakehouse will not be used or trusted. Organizations address these challenges by using data governance tools and concepts. In the Databricks Lakehouse architecture, Unity Catalog and Purview are two popular data governance tools. We will discuss the purpose of data governance and then walk through the process of provisioning and using each tool.

Structure

The chapter covers the following topics:

- Role of data governance
- Using Unity Catalog
- Installing and using Purview

Objectives

By the end of this chapter, you should be able to discuss the role of data governance in the Databricks Lakehouse architecture. You should be able to use Unity Catalog and Azure Purview. You should also be able to describe why organizations focus on data governance.

Role of data governance

Trusted data is essential for a data-driven organization. Data governance is a collection of activities performed to ensure that data is accurate, up to date, and correct, available to the right people, and unavailable to all others. This activity generally involves multiple systems, along with policies and procedures. In this chapter, we will go over commonly used data governance tools used in a Databricks Lakehouse.

Using Unity Catalog

Unity Catalog is a unified governance solution. It is used to manage data assets in the Databricks Lakehouse. Part of the value of Unity Catalog is that it enables centralized access control, lineage, and data discovery across multiple Databricks workspaces. Configuring Unity Catalog differs per cloud. To review the steps on AWS, see **https://docs.databricks. com/en/data-governance/unity-catalog/get-started.html**. The GCP instructions are similar and can be viewed at **https://docs.gcp.databricks.com/data-governance/unity-catalog/ get-started.html**. We will walk through the process of configuring Unity Catalog for Azure Databricks. To learn more about the process, see **https://learn.microsoft.com/en-us/azure/ databricks/data-governance/unity-catalog/get-started**.

Recipe 120: Configuring Unity Catalog in Azure

This process is complex, so we will highlight the major steps. The first thing we need to do is create a storage account for Unity Catalog to use to store tables.

Creating storage

Microsoft recommends selecting the premium performance level of Azure Data Lake Storage Gen2. Also, ensure you enable the hierarchical file system. Make sure you create the storage account in the same region as your Databricks instance. Because we discussed creating a storage account in *Chapter 3, Connecting to Storage*, we will discuss the second step which is, creating a managed identity to access the storage account.

Create a managed identity

We do this by locating the **Managed Identities** section of Azure. One way to do this is to enter `Managed Identities` in the search bar. Once you have located it, click the **Create** button, as shown in *Figure 13.1:*

Figure 13.1: Starting the creation process for a managed identity

Clicking **Create** brings up the **Create User Assigned Managed Identity** form. In this form, we will select the **Subscription**, **Resource group**, **Region**, and **Name**, as shown in *Figure 13.2*:

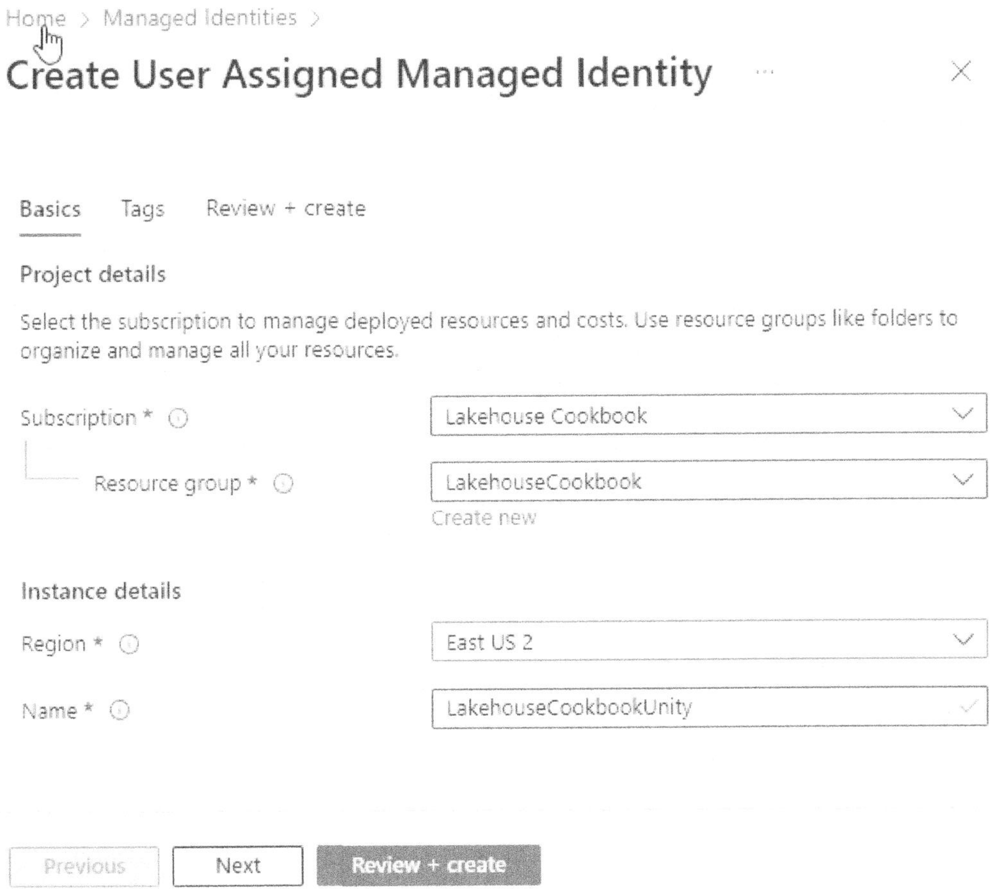

Home > Managed Identities >

Create User Assigned Managed Identity   ⋯   ✕

Basics   Tags   Review + create

Project details

Select the subscription to manage deployed resources and costs. Use resource groups like folders to organize and manage all your resources.

Subscription * ⓘ   [Lakehouse Cookbook   ∨]

⌐
└── Resource group * ⓘ   [LakehouseCookbook   ∨]
                          Create new

Instance details

Region * ⓘ   [East US 2   ∨]

Name * ⓘ   [LakehouseCookbookUnity   ∨]

[Previous]   [Next]   [**Review + create**]

Figure 13.2: Creating a managed identity

Next, you will be presented with a screen that includes legal verbiage about the term and conditions of using a managed identity, along with the information you just entered. Clicking **Create** will cause the identity to be created. Once created, you will be presented with a screen that allows navigation to the newly created resource.

Create Access Connector for Azure Databricks

Now that we have a managed identity and a storage account, we can move on to creating an Access Connector for Azure Databricks. To do this, search for **Access Connector for Azure Databricks** in the Azure search bar, as shown in *Figure 13.3*:

Figure 13.3: Searching for Access Connector for Azure Databricks

Next, click **Create** to start the creation process. This brings up the **create** page, as shown in *Figure 13.4*:

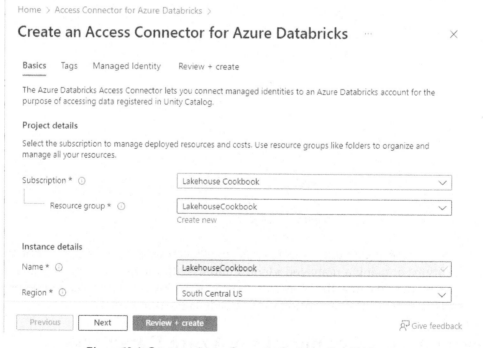

Figure 13.4: Create an Access Connector for Azure Databricks

Clicking the **Next** button brings up the **Tags** page. Enter the tag names and values if you want to use tags to track costs. Afterwards, click **Next** to move to the **Managed Identity** page. Ensure that the system-assigned managed identity is enabled. Clicking **Review +**

create displays the information you entered. If all is correct, click the **Create** button. After creating it, you will see a button to navigate to the newly created item.

Next, we will use the user-assigned managed identity created earlier in this section. We search for **Deploy a custom template** in the Azure search bar. After selecting the item, select **Build your own template in the editor**, as shown in *Figure 13.5*:

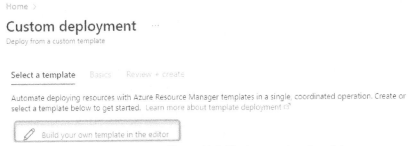

Figure 13.5: Deploy a custom template page

This will bring up the **Edit template** screen. Copy the JSON from the instructions page at **https://learn.microsoft.com/en-us/azure/databricks/data-governance/unity-catalog/azure-managed-identities# use-a-user-assigned-managed-identity** into the editor as shown in *Figure 13.6*:

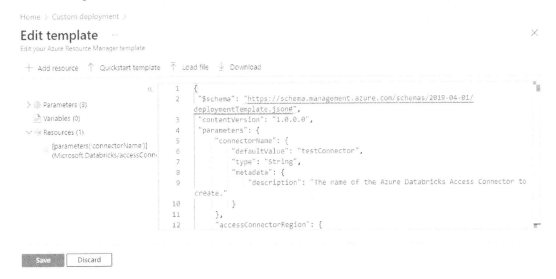

Figure 13.6: *Populated template editor*

Clicking **Save** takes you back to the custom deployment screen. On the **Basics** tab, populate the required values, as shown in *Figure 13.7*:

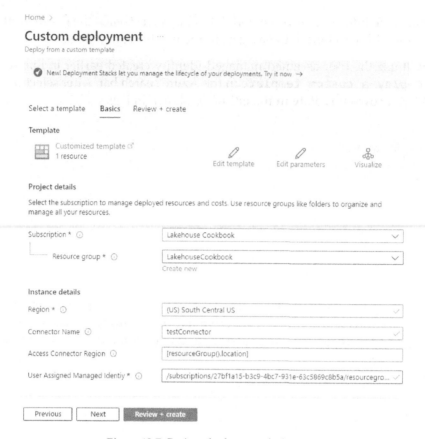

Figure 13.7: *Basics tab of custom deployment*

The first thing to populate is the subscription and resource group. Next, specify the region and name of the connector. You can leave the default value for Access Connector Region if the resource group region is the same as the connector's region. Lastly, supply the resource identifier for the user-assigned managed identity we previously created. The instructions are not clear on what identifier the form is expecting. If you navigate to the **Managed Identity Properties** section, you can copy the identifier, as shown in *Figure 13.8:*

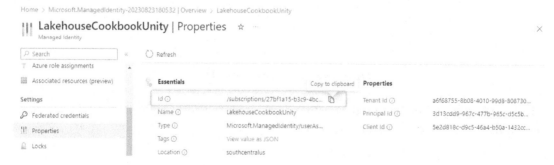

Figure 13.8: *Managed identities identifier*

Clicking **Review + create** displays the legal terms and conditions along with the values you just entered. After clicking **Create** and waiting for the creation process to complete, you can click on **Go to resource** to navigate to the recently created item. Make a note of the resource ID for the connector, as shown in *Figure 13.9*:

Figure 13.9: Newly created Access Connector for Azure Databricks

Grant managed identity access

Since we ensured that managed identity was on, we now need to grant it access to our storage account. To do this, we navigate to the storage account we created using the Azure portal. Select **Access Control (IAM)** from the left navigation, and then **Add**, as shown in *Figure 13.10*:

Figure 13.10: Selecting Add role in storage account

After clicking **Add role assignment**, search for `Storage Blob Data Contributor` and select it as shown in *Figure 13.11*:

Figure 13.11: Select role

After selecting the role, the red dot beside **Role** will disappear. Clicking **Next** brings up the **Member selection** screen. Select **Managed Identity** and then **+ Select Members**. You can choose to use the user-assigned managed identity or **Access Connector for Azure Databricks**. Alternatively, you can select both, as shown in *Figure 13.12:*

Figure 13.12: Selected members

Notice the red dot is no longer next to **Members**. Clicking **Review + assign** displays the information entered. After clicking **Review + assign** again you will see an indication the role is being added. We are now ready to use the managed identity to access Unity Catalog's root storage account.

Creating a metastore

Now that we have created a managed identity and configured the connector, we can create a metastore. Note that you must have an administrative account. Also, you may need to login to **https://accounts.azuredatabricks.net/** with your Azure AD credentials. You should see a screen similar to that in *Figure 13.13:*

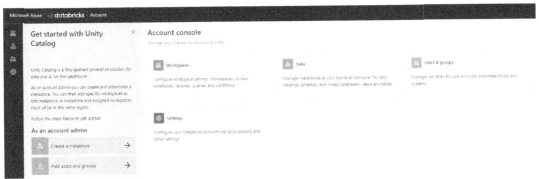

Figure 13.13: *Account console*

We are now prepared to create our metastore. Click **Create a metastore**. You will see a **Data** page listing your metastores, as shown in *Figure 13.14:*

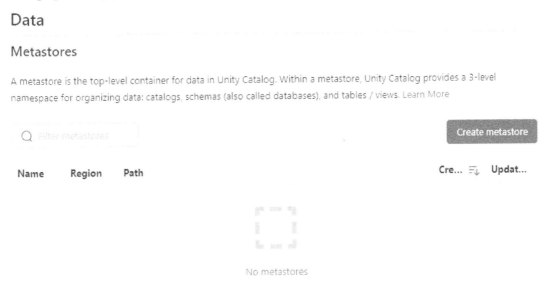

Figure 13.14: *Metastores list*

We are not to the place of creating the metastore. But first, we need to track down several pieces of information. We need to know the ADLS Gen2 path. This is string of the form **{containerName}@{storageaccount}.dfs.core.windows.net**. In our case we will use **unity@ lakehousecookbookunity.dfs.core.windows.net**. Next, we need to know the Access Connector ID which can be found by navigating to the connector's overview page, as shown in *Figure 13.15:*

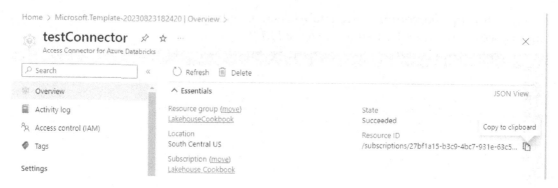

Figure 13.15: *Access Connector ID*

If you chose to create and use the user assigned managed identity, we can locate its identifier by navigating to the **identities** page and selecting **Properties**, as shown in *Figure 13.16:*

Figure 13.16: *Managed identity's resource ID*

Now that we have all these values, we can create the metastore, as shown in *Figure 13.17:*

Figure 13.17: *Populating the create metastore form*

Once the metastore is created, the next step is to assign Databricks Lakehouse workspaces to it. You will see a list of your workspaces in a grid. There is a checkbox in the first column that allows you to select them. Once selected, you can click **Assign**, as shown in *Figure 13.18*:

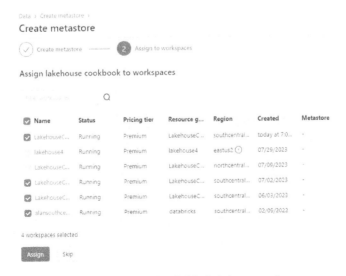

Figure 13.18: *Select Databricks Lakehouse workspaces*

Before enabling **Unity Catalog**, Databricks describes the consequences of the action, as shown in *Figure 13.19*:

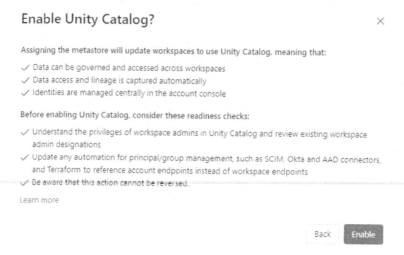

Figure 13.19: Unity Catalog consequences

After clicking **Enable**, you are given the option of opening navigating to a page containing example notebooks. We have successfully created a Unity Catalog. Now that we have created an instance of Unity Catalog, we should review its object mode.

Unity Catalog object model

Unity Catalog adds a layer above the traditional Hive metastore. Traditionally, Databricks workspaces had a Hive metastore that contained **Schemas**, and then **Tables**, as shown in *Figure 13.20:*

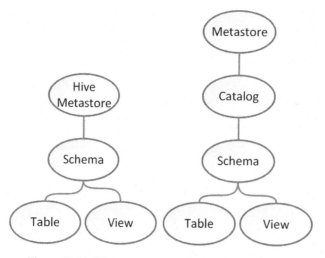

Figure 13.20: Hive metastore compared to Unity Catalog

This is a simplistic representation, hiding some of the other data elements in both Hive metastore and in Unity Catalog's metastore, catalog, and schemas. The main idea is to understand there is an additional organizational unit, the catalog. Note that after migration to Unity Catalog, you will see a catalog named **hive_metastore**. It is not the same as other catalogs in that it is not managed and does not have the same features as other catalogs. For more information on the elements of Unity Catalog, see **https://docs.databricks.com/ en/data-governance/unity-catalog/index.html**. Now that we have discussed the basics, we can create a new catalog.

Recipe 121: Creating a new catalog

Databricks extended Spark SQL to add support for the catalog construct. To see the catalogs, we can use the **SHOW CATALOGS** command, as shown in *Figure 13.21:*

Figure 13.21: Show catalogs

We can create a new catalog using the **CREATE CATALOG** command, as shown in *Figure 13.22:*

Figure 13.22: Creating a new catalog

Now that we have created the catalog, we can activate it using the **USE CATALOG** command, as shown in *Figure 13.23:*

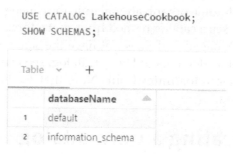

Figure 13.23: Selecting a catalog for use

Notice that the newly created catalog contains default schema/database, and a schema named **information_schema**. Information schemas are a mostly standardized way of describing the contents of a data store, such as a database. As tables or other data assets are created, the metadata about those items is updated in the information schema. To learn more about information schema, see **https://docs.databricks.com/en/sql/language-manual/sql-ref-information-schema.html**. Since we are focused on creating a Databricks Lakehouse we can create the layers as schemas, as shown in *Figure 13.24:*

Figure 13.24: Creating the medallion schemas

Recipe 122: Uploading data

One way to create tables is to use the Add data feature of Databricks. The process is the same as it was when we were using the Hive metastore, until the selection of the table name. Now, we must select a catalog, then a schema, and lastly specify the table name, as shown in *Figure 13.25:*

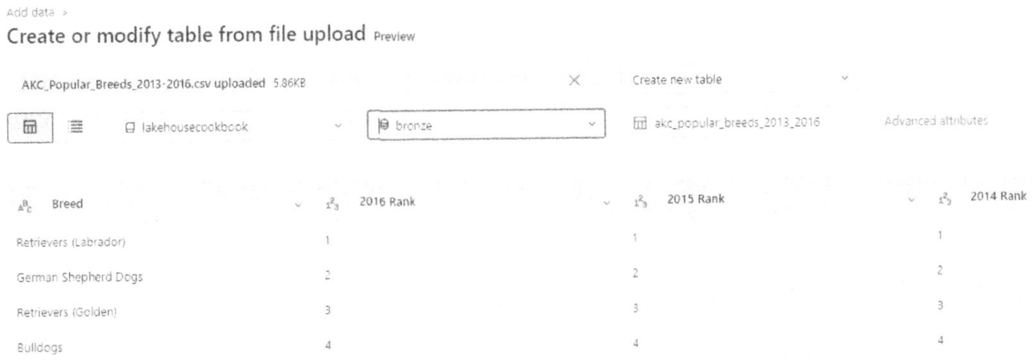

Add data >

Create or modify table from file upload Preview

AKC_Popular_Breeds_2013-2016.csv uploaded 5.86KB   ✕   Create new table ⌄

| ▦ ▤ | ⊟ lakehousecookbook ⌄ | ⚑ bronze ⌄ | ▦ akc_popular_breeds_2013_2016 | Advanced attributes |

ᴬᵇ_C Breed	⌄	¹²₃ 2016 Rank	⌄	¹²₃ 2015 Rank	⌄	¹²₃ 2014 Rank
Retrievers (Labrador)		1		1		1
German Shepherd Dogs		2		2		2
Retrievers (Golden)		3		3		3
Bulldogs		4		4		4

Figure 13.25: Adding data to a catalog

In this example, we are using the **lakehousecookbook** catalog and the **bronze** schema. At the bottom of the page is a **Create table** button. When clicked the table is created within the specified schema. In the next section we will revisit creating tables using SQL statements.

Recipe 123: Creating a table

Another way to create tables is to use SQL DDL statements. When using Unity Catalog, Databricks recommends using managed tables. External tables should be used when direct access to the data files is required. Generally, it is a best practice to allow Unity Catalog to manage access to the tables, and associated files. To create a table in a workspace with Unity Catalog enabled is the same as creating a managed table. We revisit the watermark table we created in *Chapter 6, Extracting from Source and Loading to Bronze*. There is little difference from that version, as shown in *Figure 13.26*:

```
USE CATALOG LakehouseCookbook;
CREATE SCHEMA IF NOT EXISTS PlatformHelpers;
USE SCHEMA PlatformHelpers;
```

OK

Command took 2.90 seconds -- by alan.dennis@gmail.com at 8/24/2023, 5:57:57 PM on 2xsmall -2

Cmd 2

```
CREATE TABLE IF NOT EXISTS Watermarks (
  schemaName string,
  tableName string,
  watermarkType string,
  timestampWatermark TIMESTAMP,
  integerWatermark INT,
  bigIntWatermark BIGINT,
  stringWatermark string
) TBLPROPERTIES (delta.enableChangeDataFeed = true)
```

Figure 13.26: Creating a watermark managed table

Note that we ensure that a schema named **PlatformHelpers** exists, and then activate it. Then we create the watermarks table. Note that when tables are created (such as when creating a table from a **SELECT** statement), relationships between then are automatically tracked for data lineage purposes. We have barely scratched the surface of Unity Catalog. To learn more about data lineage, see **https://docs.databricks.com/en/data-governance/unity-catalog/data-lineage.html**. In the next section we will discuss installing and configuring Azure Purview to integrate with Databricks.

Installing and using Purview

Azure Purview is a **Software as a Service (SaaS)** data governance offering. In this section we will walk through the process of creating a Purview account and configuring it to connect to Databricks.

Recipe 124: Installing Purview

To create a Purview account, search for **Purview** in the Azure search bar, as shown in *Figure 13.27:*

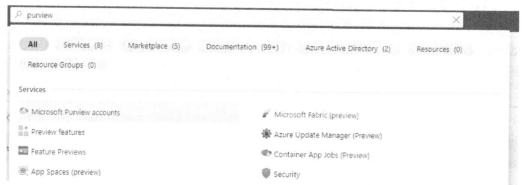

Figure 13.27: Searching for Purview

Selecting **Microsoft Purview accounts** brings you to a page that contains the list of your Purview accounts. If you do not have any, you will see a message indicating there are none to display and a link to create one, as shown in *Figure 13.28:*

No Microsoft Purview accounts to display

Maximize the business value of data with Microsoft Purview, a unified data governance solution.

Create Microsoft Purview account

Learn more ↗

Figure 13.28: No account message and create button

You can also create an account by clicking the + **Create** text in the menu. After clicking one of the mechanisms, you are taken to the create page, as shown in *Figure 13.29*:

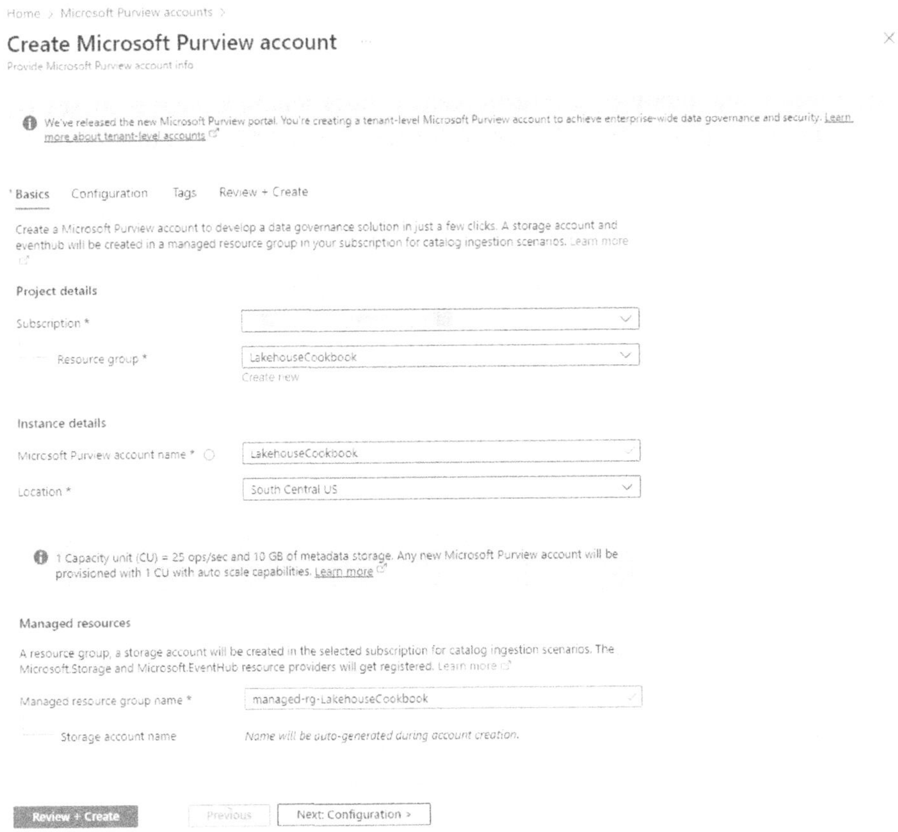

Figure 13.29: *Basics page of create Purview account*

On the configuration page you are offered the option to configure Event Hub Kafka topics. This is a way to integrate with Purview. When information is detected that is of interest, a message is added to a queue. A process listens for messages and processes them as appropriate. To learn more about using Event Hubs with Purview see **https://learn. microsoft.com/en-us/purview/configure-event-hubs-for-kafka**. For our purposes we will not configure Event Hubs. The tags page provides a place to add name/value pairs used for tracking during billing. The final page presents the entered information and offers a **Create** button. Clicking **Create** starts the provisioning. After the deployment succeeds, you will receive a link to the newly provisioned Purview account.

Recipe 125: Connecting Purview to Databricks

Now that we have a Purview account, the next step is to connect it to Databricks. As of this writing, metadata extraction, full scan, and lineage were supported by the Purview

Unity Catalog Databricks connector. To connect and scan a Databricks workspace using the Hive metastore, see **https://learn.microsoft.com/en-us/purview/register-scan-azure-databricks**. For this example, we will be connecting to the Databricks workspace we just migrated to Unity Catalog. To learn more about configuring the Unity Catalog connector see **https://learn.microsoft.com/en-us/purview/register-scan-azure-databricks-unity-catalog**. Purview is like many Azure resources in that there is a page related to a service and a way to launch a portal or editor on that page. The portal is undergoing a redesign that is related to the launch of Microsoft Fabric. Once you have navigated to the portal, find the **Data Map** pane, and select it. This will bring up a list of **Data sources**, as shown in *Figure 13.30:*

Figure 13.30: Purview data sources

Click **Register** to bring up the Register data source panel and then select **Azure Databricks (Preview)**, as shown in *Figure 13.31:*

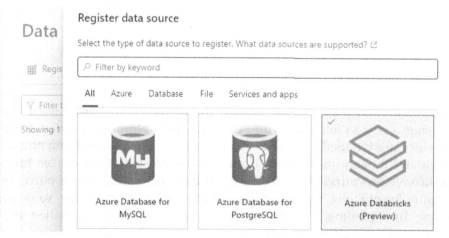

Figure 13.31: Register data source

Click **Continue**, located at the bottom of the page to bring up the **Register data source** panel. On this form you will supply a name for the source, be asked to select the Databricks workspace based on Azure subscription. Once you are happy with the information, click **Register**, as shown in *Figure 13.32:*

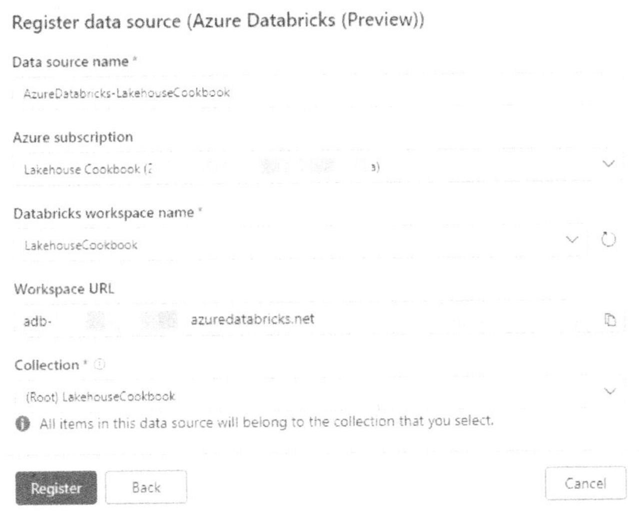

Register data source (Azure Databricks (Preview))

Data source name *

AzureDatabricks-LakehouseCookbook

Azure subscription

Lakehouse Cookbook (3)   ⌄

Databricks workspace name *

LakehouseCookbook   ⌄ ↻

Workspace URL

adb-   azuredatabricks.net   ▢

Collection * ⓘ

(Root) LakehouseCookbook   ⌄

ⓘ All items in this data source will belong to the collection that you select.

Register   Back   Cancel

Figure 13.32: Registering the Azure Databricks data source

Recipe 126: Scanning a Databricks workspace

Now that we have the workspace registered as a data source, we can scan it. To create a new scan, navigate to the newly created data source and click the **scan** icon, as shown in *Figure 13.33*:

Data sources

▦ Register   ↻ Refresh   **Map view**   Table view

▽ Filter by keyword

Showing 1 collection. 1 data source

LakehouseCookbook
The root collection.

▦   View details

⊖

AzureDatabricks-Lakeh...
Azure Databricks (Preview)

✎ ⟪ 🗑   View details

New scan

Figure 13.33: Create a new scan

This brings up the **Scan** form. Start by providing a scan name and selecting Unity Catalog as the extraction method. Credentials and HTTP path are a little harder to find, as shown in *Figure 13.34:*

Figure 13.34: *Scan details*

To create the credential, click chevron (V shape) on the right side and select **New**. This will bring up the **New credential** form. Make sure to select **Access Token** (the only choice available as of this writing). You will need to create a key vault connection before selecting the secret. Clicking the chevron and select **New** brings up the **New Key Vault** form. Again, you select an **Azure subscription** and then the **Key Vault** to use, as shown in *Figure 13.35:*

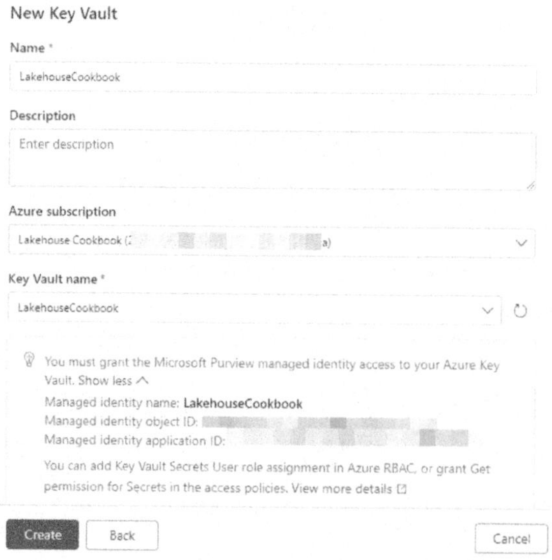

Figure 13.35: *Creating a new Key Vault connection*

You will need to create a Databricks personal access token and store it in the key vault before completing the next step. To create a personal access token, go to your Databricks workspace, select your email address in the upper right corner, and select **User Settings**. Then navigate to the **Developer** section and select **Manage** next to **Access tokens**. You will then see any access tokens you have previously created along with a **Generate new token** button. Clicking the button brings up a form asking what the token is for and how long it should last. Once you have created the token, save it as you will not be able to retrieve it in the future. Next, go into your Azure Key Vault and add a secret using the token's value along with a descriptive name. Once you have created the secret, you can create the key vault connection. This will close the form and return you to the **New credential** form. Enter the name of the secret, and then click **Create**, as shown in *Figure 13.36:*

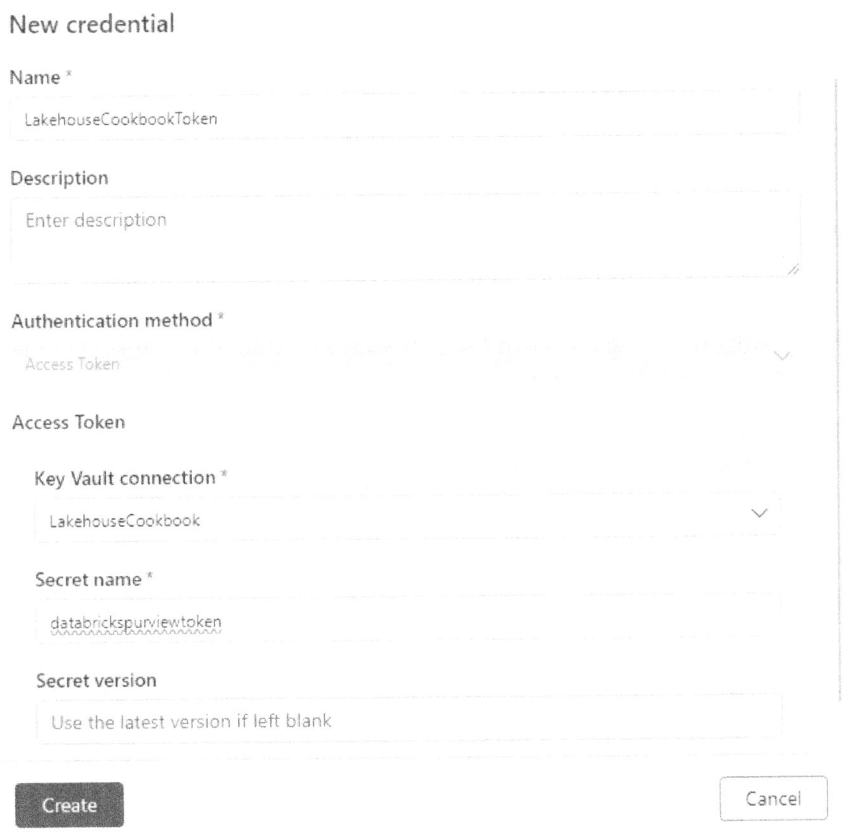

New credential

Name *

LakehouseCookbookToken

Description

Enter description

Authentication method *

Access Token

Access Token

Key Vault connection *

LakehouseCookbook

Secret name *

databrickspurviewtoken

Secret version

Use the latest version if left blank

Create   Cancel

Figure 13.36: New credential form

We are now back on the **Create Scan** form, with only one field left to populate, the **HTTP path**. This is the how Purview will connect to a Databricks SQL Warehouse. The connection information is on the ware's **Connection details** page, and named **HTTP path**, as shown in *Figure 13.37:*

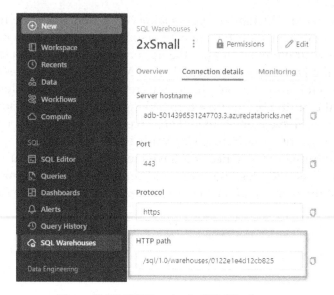

Figure 13.37: HTTP path of a SQL Warehouse

We now have all the information needed to finish creating the scan. You are now ready to test the connection. Ensure your SQL Warehouse is up and running. Also, make sure that the identity that is connecting to the Key Vault has **get secrets** permission. Note that clicking **More Info** will give a reason the connection failed. Once you have resolved any connectivity issues, click **Continue**.

You will then be asked to specify the scope of your scan, as shown in *Figure 13.38:*

Figure 13.38: Selecting the scope of the scan

Once you have selected the catalogs you want to scan, click **Continue**. This will bring you to a page where you can make the scan **Recurring** or **Once**. If you select **Recurring**, you will need to set the frequency and time. After selecting the frequency, you are presented with a page to review the information you added. Clicking **Save and run** will complete the editing process and start the scan. Clicking **View details** on the Databricks pane will bring a page where you can monitor the scan's progress, as shown in *Figure 13.39:*

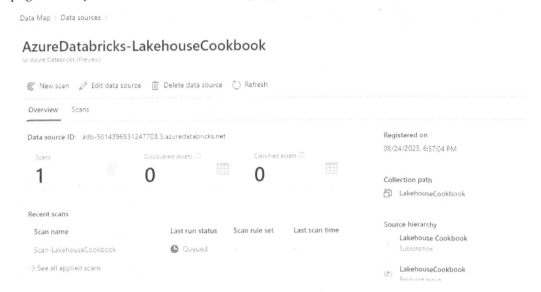

Figure 13.39: Data Source Detail information

Once the scan is finished, the status will change to **Completed**. Now that we have completed a scan, we can browse our assets.

Recipe 127: Browsing the Data Catalog

The landing page for Purview contains a panel for **Data Catalog**, as shown in *Figure 13.40:*

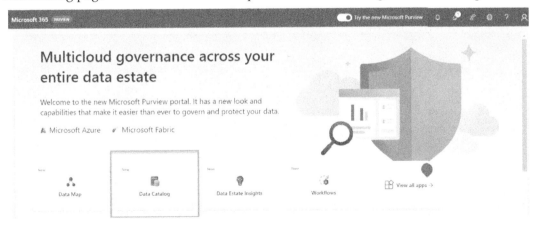

Figure 13.40: Purview landing page

Clicking it brings up the Purview **Data Catalog**. A **Data Catalog** is a way to organize and manage data assets for an organization. One thing that is useful is to browse the contents, as shown in *Figure 13.41:*

Figure 13.41: Browsing Purview Data Catalog by source type

The information from the Azure Databricks Unity Catalog is available in a centralized location. This makes finding and managing data assets simpler. The value of Purview increases with each new source that is added. It can provide insights into an organization's data ecosystem.

Conclusion

In this chapter we briefly discussed two Databricks Lakehouse data governance tools. We discussed the purpose of data governance within an organization. We then walked through the process to migrating to Databricks' Unity Catalog. Next, we revisited the process of creating tables, and adding data to them. We then discussed the process of provisioning and configuring Azure Purview to connect to Azure Databricks, created a scan and then examined the data assets that were discovered.

In the next chapter, we will discuss operations and the activities that are necessary to keep a lakehouse running smoothly.

CHAPTER 14
Operations

Introduction

Once the Lakehouse has been created, keeping it running is essential. Efforts must be made to ensure that the correct code is tested and used. System maintenance must be performed to keep the system running correctly, and cost must be attributed to the correct effort. These efforts will help ensure that data is kept fresh and valid. It will also help the system meet performance expectations. The steps needed to keep a Lakehouse running are discussed, along with ways to detect when a Lakehouse is in an error state.

Structure

The chapter covers the following topics:

- Source code management and orchestration
- Scheduled and ongoing maintenance
- Cost management

Objectives

By the end of this chapter, you should be able to discuss the importance of version control and orchestration within a Lakehouse. You should be able to discuss the common types of maintenance required for a Lakehouse. You should be able to discuss how to associate costs with things like jobs, clusters, and pools.

Source code management and orchestration

Most Databricks Lakehouses utilize code written in notebooks. Because this is essentially a software engineering effort, we should use learnings from that discipline. One pillar of effective software development is to utilize version control. This section will discuss how to connect a Databricks workspace to a repository and how to leverage that connection to ensure the correct code execution order.

Recipe 128: Use GitHub with Databricks

GitHub is a popular website that enables organizations to manage software. Your organization most likely has an established provider for managing software code. If you are developing code for your purpose, or you are part of a startup organization, you can sign up on GitHub or a similar Git-based offering. As of this writing, Databricks supports integration with GitHub/GitHub AE, Bitbucket cloud, GitLab, Azure DevOps, and AWS CodeCommit. In this recipe, we will be connecting to GitHub. To learn more about connecting to other providers, see **https://docs.databricks.com/en/repos/get-access-tokens-from-git-provider.html**.

Once you have logged into GitHub, you need to navigate to Settings, which is displayed after clicking your avatar in the upper-right-hand corner of the screen, as shown in *Figure 14.1:*

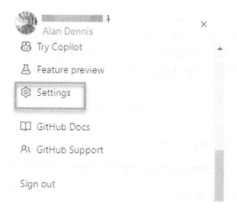

Figure 14.1: Settings section of GitHub account

Once you see the Settings screen, scroll down until you see < > **Developer Settings**. Clicking it will bring you to the **Developer Settings** area, where you will see Personal access token on the left side. After expanding the personal access tokens area, you will see Tokens (classic), as shown in *Figure 14.2:*

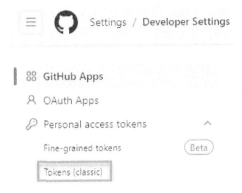

Figure 14.2: *Personal access tokens option*

Clicking will bring you to the list of tokens that you have created. You have the option of creating new tokens by selecting **Generate new token**, as shown in *Figure 14.3:*

Figure 14.3: *Personal access tokens management screen*

When you click it, you will likely see the choice between classic and fine-grained and repo-scoped tokens. Select the class option. You may be prompted to re-enter your credentials to confirm your identity. You will need to provide a note describing the purpose of the token and grant repo-level access, as shown in *Figure 14.4:*

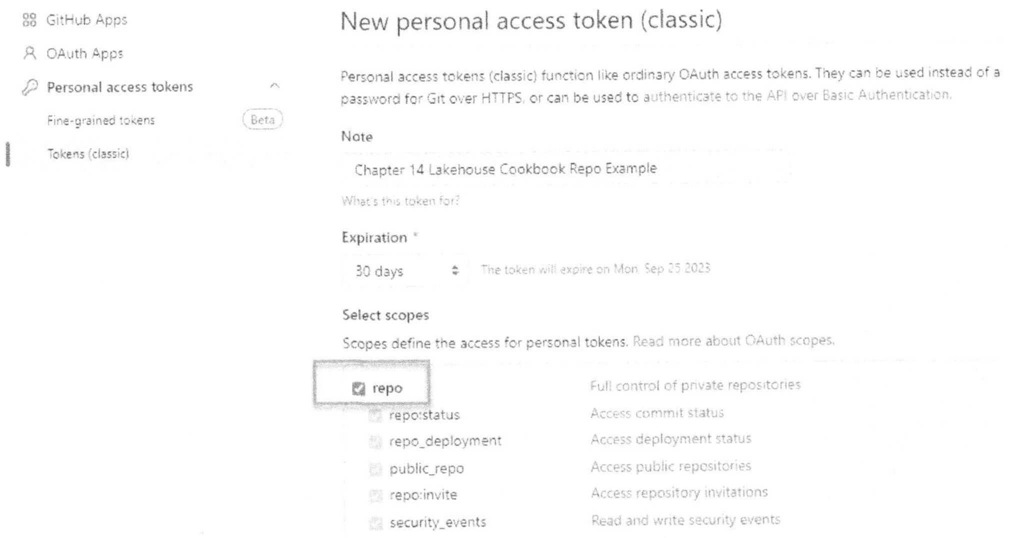

Figure 14.4: *Creating new classic personal access token*

Notice that you are asked to provide an expiration date for the token. You have the option of not using a date, that will likely provide a security issue later. Scrolling to the bottom of the form you will find a Generate token button. Clicking it creates the token and displays the value, as shown in *Figure 14.5:*

Figure 14.5: Generated token

Save the token value, as you will need to enter it in Databricks. Next, go to Databricks, and navigate to User Settings then **Linked accounts** as shown in *Figure 14.6:*

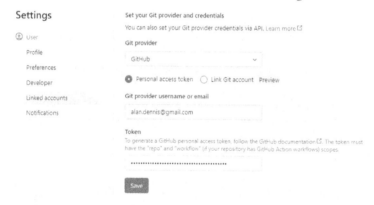

Figure 14.6: Enter token in Databricks

After clicking **Save**, you can navigate to the **Repos** section of the Workspace, as shown in *Figure 14.7:*

Figure 14.7: Databricks Repose area of Workspace

Clicking **Add Repo** enables you to add a repo using the repository URL, as shown in *Figure 14.8:*

Add Repo   ×

Location ⓘ
/Repos/ala

☑ Create repo by cloning a Git repository

Git repository URL ⓘ   Git provider

https://github.com/   /lakehousecookbook.   GitHub   ⌄

Repository name

lakehousecookbook

Advanced ⌄

                                                                     Cancel   **Create Repo**

Figure 14.8: Adding repo

Click **Create Repo** will cause the repo to be created, as shown in *Figure 14.9:*

Figure 14.9: Linked GitHub repo

Now that we have linked the repo, we can interact with it, including creating a new Folder and notebooks. The thing is to ensure you are doing your work in the Repos section of the workspace, not within your personal folder under Users, as shown in *Figure 14.10:*

Figure 14.10: Work in a repos folder

Once you want to commit to a branch, navigate to the repos Name and select **Git**…, as shown in *Figure 14.11*:

Figure 14.11: Opening the git menu

Once the Git page opens, you will be presented with the branch information along with the option to **Commit & Push** your changes, as shown in *Figure 14.12*:

Figure 14.12: Committing to a branch

In this case, we are working on the main branch, which is not good when the team size is greater than one. Ensure you connect with your team leads to understand your team and organization's branching strategy. After clicking Commit & Push, you can perform a Pull and create a pull request with the git provider. We have successfully linked a Databricks Workspace with a GitHub repo and added a folder and files to its contents.

Once this process is in place, the next step would be to set up **Continues Integration and Continuous Deployment (CI/CD)**. Databricks and git providers are continually improving this area. For larger teams, automated pipelines should be deployed to higher environments based on pull requests to associated branches. Because of the rate of change, we will likely revisit this topic with a blog post or article. In the next section, we will discuss how to control the order of execution of notebooks and other elements to ensure proper results.

Recipe 129: Create workflows to orchestrate processing

We have already used workflows, likely without being aware. When we created Delta Live Table pipelines, we were creating workflows. In Recipe 54, we created DLT pipelines in the **Workflows** section. Also, in *Chapter 6, Extracting from Source and Loading to Bronze*, in Recipe 49, we briefly discussed pipeline orchestration. This recipe will briefly discuss scheduling a notebook as a job and dependencies. For more information on workflows, see **https:// docs.databricks.com/en/workflows**. In Recipe 46, we created a table to store watermarks. We will build our workflow by invoking that notebook to ensure the watermark table exists. Navigating to the **Workflows** section brings up the list of existing jobs, as shown in *Figure 14.13:*

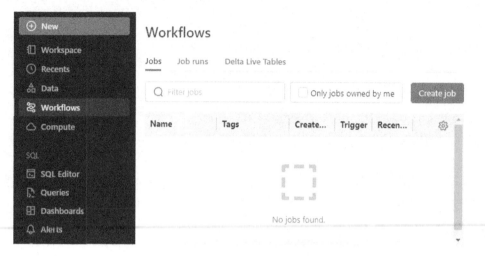

Figure 14.13: List of jobs in the Workflows section

Clicking **Create Job** opens the new job's canvas, prompting you to create the first task, as shown in *Figure 14.14*:

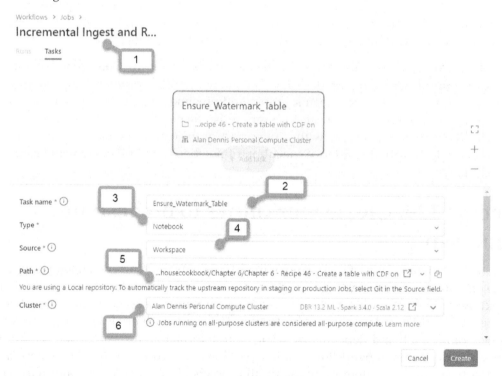

Figure 14.14: Creating a new job

There are a lot of fields on this form, so we will walk through them one at a time:

1. We will start by naming the overall job.

2. We will then assign a name to the current task we are specifying.

3. Next, we select the type of task. In this case, it is a notebook task.

4. The other types of tasks are **Python script**, **Python wheel**, **SQL**, **Delta Live Table pipeline**, **dbt**, **JAR**, and **Spark submit**. Note that new task types are being continually added. The next option is to specify the location of the contents of the job, in this case the notebook to execute. Our example specifies the current Databricks workspace

5. The other choice is a Git provider. This option allows for specifying a notebook housed in a Git provider, such as GitHub. We then specify where the item is located within the selected source, in this case the location of the notebook within the workspace.

6. Lastly, we specify where the job should run.

In this case, we are targeting an existing cluster. The alternative is to target a job cluster created to process the task. For performance reasons, if using multi-task jobs with job clusters, you should investigate using pools, as discussed in *Chapter 15, Tips, Tricks, Troubleshooting, and Best Practices.* Scrolling down shows additional options, as shown in *Figure 14.15:*

Figure 14.15: Additional job task options

Dependent libraries are things which are necessary for the task to process correctly. We used dependent libraries when creating DLT pipelines in Recipe 54 and others. Additionally, some tasks require runtime libraries, such as a specific library. This feature allows you to specify they must be loaded. Depending on the type of the task, you will likely see a dependent library selection tool that allows you to specify the source for the library (such as PyPI), and the library type.

Parameters are used to pass values to a task, such as passing a value to a notebook's widgets when using notebook tasks. Additionally, you can pass values about the current run of a job to it, as discussed in **https://docs.databricks.com/en/workflows/jobs/task-parameter-variables.html**.

The **Emails** option allows you to add an email address to be notified of various events, such as start, success, failure, or if the process is taking longer than allowed (discussed during the duration threshold section). You also have the option to mute skipped or canceled runs. You can also mute notifications until the final retry has been completed, as shown in *Figure 14.16:*

Figure 14.16: Email notification options

The **Retries** option controls the number of attempts Databricks will make when running the task. When you specify one retry, the task will be executed a maximum of two times. You also need to specify a wait period between retries. Lastly, you specify if the task should be retried on timeout, as shown in *Figure 14.17:*

Retry Policy   ✕

Jobs that fail are retried a number of times based on the following policy. You can specify a maximum number of attempts for a run and a minimal interval between attempts.

Retry at most   [1 time (2 total attempts) ⌄]   and wait   [15]   [mins ⌄]   between retries

☐ Retry on timeout

Cancel   [Confirm]

Figure 14.17: Task retry policy

As mentioned in the email notification section, we can also specify task duration thresholds. The first value to specify is a warning duration. This will control when the duration warning email is sent. The next setting is the timeout threshold, as shown in *Figure 14.18:*

Duration threshold   Warning ❸   Timeout ❸

[00h 30m 00s   ⊗]   [01h 00m 00s   ⊗]

Figure 14.18: Duration threshold settings

When the job takes longer than the timeout duration, Databricks will stop the job, and if a retry policy is configured, retry the task. Now that we have discussed and configured all the options, we can click on the Create button at the bottom of the form. This will take you to the **Tasks** section of the job, as shown in *Figure 14.19*:

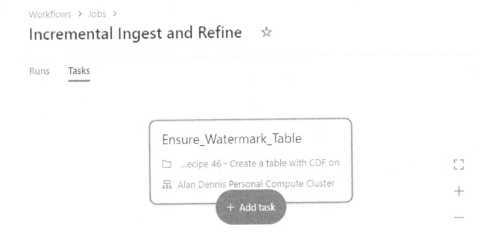

Figure 14.19: *Job overview after creating the first task*

Clicking **+ Add task** allows you to add another task to the job, as shown in *Figure 14.20*:

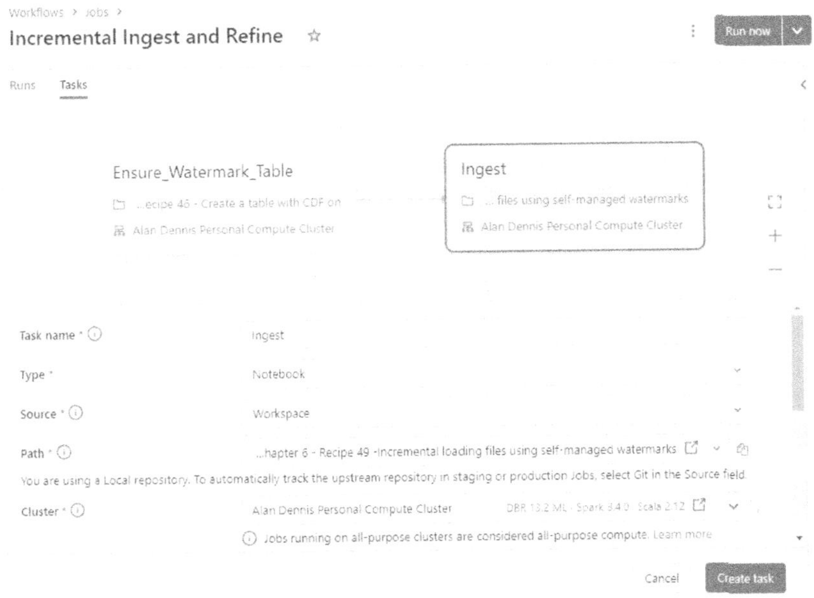

Figure 14.20: *Adding an ingestion task*

This task will invoke the ingestion notebook from *Recipe 49*. The task is prepopulated with values from the previous task, such as the Cluster information. As these notebooks do not expect parameters, there are no parameters required.

Now that we have ingested data to the bronze layer, the next step is to refine it to silver. In *Recipe 62*, we incrementally refined the data loaded by *Recipe 49*. Since the next task depends on the Ingest task we just added, we ensure it is selected and **Click + Add task**. If we selected **Ensure_Watermark_Table** and then added the task, the new task would be dependent on the completion of that task. Ensuring that the proper dependency graph is constructed is essential when constructing a job of tasks. After creating the final task, we can examine the overall flow, as shown in *Figure 14.21*:

Figure 14.21: *Job with a task to ensure required items, then ingest and refine*

The next step is to run the job by selecting **Run now** in the upper right-hand corner. This causes a run to be added to the list of runs and starts the process, as shown in *Figure 14.22*:

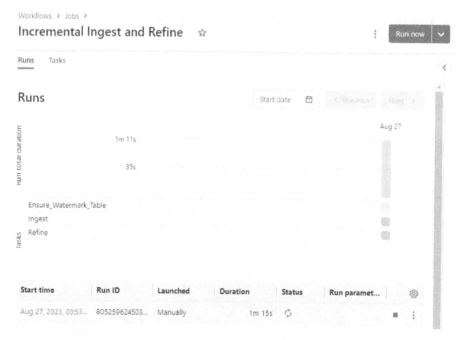

Figure 14.22: *Runs page with newly started job*

The majority of your time will likely be spent waiting for the cluster to start. Once it has started, the first task should be very quick. Clicking on the value in the Start time column will take you to a detailed view of the job, as shown in *Figure 14.23*:

Figure 14.23: Detailed view of a job run

Notice the Fit to viewport option above the plus sign. This will rescale the graph to fit the current windows. Also, as a task runs, the spinning arrows show it is running. Lastly, notice that the Refine task is in the Blocked state. This is because it is dependent on a task that has not completed. We have successfully constructed a job with dependencies.

Recipe 130: Saving a Job JSON

While we cannot add a Job to source control directly, we can work around this limitation by exporting the job's JSON. Do this by navigating to the job's detail page and then click on the three dots to the left of the Run now button, as shown in *Figure 14.24*:

Figure 14.24: Job menu

Select **View JSON**, and then select **Create**, as shown in *Figure 14.25*:

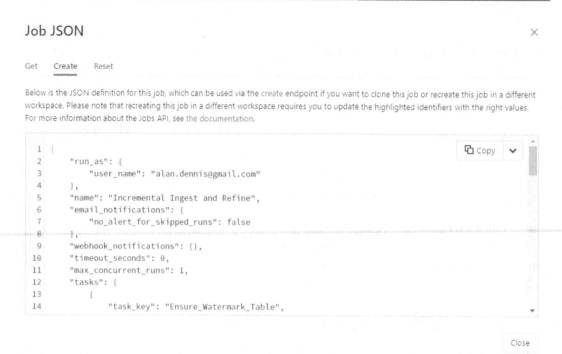

Figure 14.25: Viewing job create JSON

Selecting **Copy** from the upper right-hand corner gives you the JSON necessary to create your job. Note that if you attempt to do this in a different environment, you may need to change the job's JSON. For more on the job's JSON and associated jobs API see **https://docs.databricks.com/api/workspace/jobs**. You take the JSON placed in your clipboard and store it in a JSON file stored in a repository. In Databricks, you can create a new file in a folder (such as one within a repo) and then paste the JSON into that file, as shown in *Figure 14.26:*

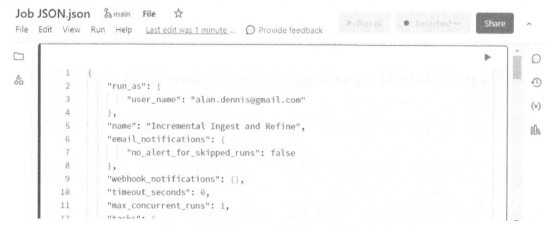

Figure 14.26: Job create JSON in a Databricks file

We have successfully exported a job's create JSON and added it to a repository. The next section will explore using Apache Airflow for cross-system orchestration.

Recipe 131: Use Airflow to coordinate processing

Apache Airflow, often referred to simply as Airflow, is a popular orchestration system. To learn more about Airflow, see **https://airflow.apache.org/docs/apache-airflow/stable**. When workloads span multiple systems, Airflow is a good choice. For a walkthrough of integrating Airflow with Databricks, see **https://docs.databricks.com/en/workflows/jobs/how-to/use-airflow-with-jobs.html**. We will loosely follow this approach in this example. There are two Databricks operators in Airflow. `DatabricksRunNowOperator` executes an existing Databricks job using the Databricks Jobs API's run-now method. We briefly discussed the Jobs API in the previous recipe. The other operator, `DatabricksSubmitRunOperator`, does not require an existing job. Instead, it creates and triggers a one-time job using the runs/submit method. To learn more about the Airflow Databricks operators, see **https://airflow.apache.org/docs/apache-airflow-providers-databricks/stable/**.

In this recipe, we will focus on the run-now operator.

We first need to create a simple job to test the run-now version of the operators. Before creating the job, we need to create something for the job to run, such as a notebook. In this case, we will create a simple Hello World job that runs a Hello World notebook, as shown in *Figure 14.27*:

Figure 14.27: Run of Hello World job running a simple notebook

We now have a job identifier to supply to the Airflow operation. Next, we need to create a Databricks personal access token, as we first did in Recipe 29. This token will be used by Airflow to connect to the Databricks workspace. We use this token by navigating to the connections of our instance of Airflow and locating the connection named `databricks_default`. The documentation in the Databricks article incorrectly states that you should supply the workspace instance name. Instead, supply the URL prefix for your workspace. This is the information before the `/?=o` in the URL. Additionally, rather than adding the personal access token into the Extras field, put it into the password field of the **`databricks_default`** connection, as shown in *Figure 14.28:*

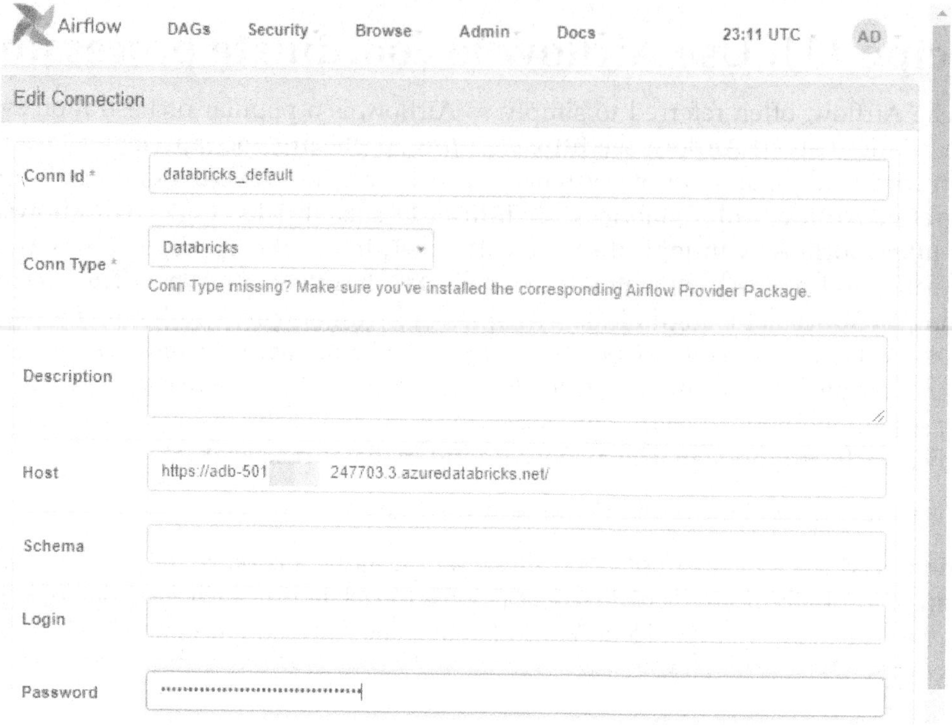

Figure 14.28: *Updating the default Databricks connection in Airflow*

Next, you need to create a new Airflow DAG. You do this by creating a Python file containing the job identifier to run, as shown in *Figure 14.29:*

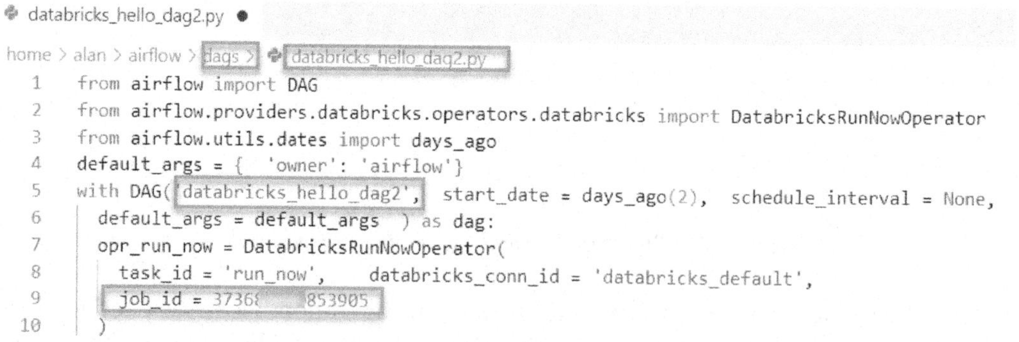

```
databricks_hello_dag2.py ●
home > alan > airflow > dags > databricks_hello_dag2.py
from airflow import DAG
from airflow.providers.databricks.operators.databricks import DatabricksRunNowOperator
from airflow.utils.dates import days_ago
default_args = {  'owner': 'airflow'}
with DAG('databricks_hello_dag2',  start_date = days_ago(2),  schedule_interval = None,
  default_args = default_args  ) as dag:
  opr_run_now = DatabricksRunNowOperator(
    task_id = 'run_now',    databricks_conn_id = 'databricks_default',
    job_id = 37368      853905
  )
```

Figure 14.29: *Python script to create a DAG*

This will result in a new DAG showing up in the list of DAGS in Airflow, as shown in *Figure 14.30:*

Figure 14.30: *Newly added DAG*

We have successfully created an Airflow DAG to invoke a Databricks job. In the next section, we will discuss the importance of ongoing maintenance for a well-running Databricks Lakehouse.

Scheduled and ongoing maintenance

Like most things, Lakehouses need ongoing maintenance to perform at peak levels. This section will revisit and extend some of the previously introduced concepts. In the next recipe, we will discuss repairing damaged tables.

Recipe 132: Repairing damaged tables

Ideally, tables would never become damaged. However, occasionally these incidents occur. To repair tables, we use the Delta FSCK command. The command syntax is:

```
FSCK REPAIR TABLE <catalog>.<schema>.<table> [DRY RUN]
```

DRY RUN is optional; as the name indicates, no changes are made when **DRY RUN** is supplied, making it useful for detecting tables needing to be repaired. If you are not using Unity Catalog, omit the catalog name and period. For the details on **FSCK**, see **https://docs.databricks.com/en/sql/language-manual/delta-fsck.html**.

Knowing how to repair tables is only part of the solution. We must first find those tables needing to be repaired. To do this, we will borrow from the ideas of *Recipe 42* and extend it to work with Unity Catalog. To make things a little easier to manage, we create a table to store the results of each operation's output. The idea is that the table can be monitored to determine when repair is required on a given table. Given the nature of FSCK, it is not typically automated. We ensure that the desired catalog, schema, and table are present before creating the table, as shown in *Figure 14.31:*

```
1   maintenanceCatalog = "LakehouseOperations"
2   maintenanceSchema = "Operations"
3   tableRepairTable = "TableRepair"
4   def EnsureTable():
5       spark.sql(f"CREATE CATALOG IF NOT EXISTS {maintenanceCatalog}")
6       spark.sql(f"CREATE SCHEMA IF NOT EXISTS {maintenanceCatalog}.{maintenanceSchema}
        ")
7       tableCreateString = f"CREATE TABLE IF NOT EXISTS {maintenanceCatalog}.
        {maintenanceSchema}.{tableRepairTable} (WhenChecked TIMESTAMP,catName string,
        schemaName string ,tableName string, results string)"
8       print(tableCreateString)
9       spark.sql(tableCreateString)
10  EnsureTable()
```

▸ (2) Spark Jobs

```
CREATE TABLE IF NOT EXISTS LakehouseOperations.Operations.TableRepair (WhenChecked TIMESTAMP,
catName string, schemaName string ,tableName string, results string)
```

Figure 14.31: *Python code to create a table to house results table inspections*

Notice that we print out the SQL that is used to create the table. This is done in part because dynamic SQL creation can be error prone. Next, we create a simple method to add records to this table, as shown in *Figure 14.32:*

```
1   def RecordRun(catalog,schema,table,result):
2       cleanedResult = result.replace('\n', ' ').replace('\r', '')
3       insertSQL = f"INSERT INTO {maintenanceCatalog}.{maintenanceSchema}.
        {tableRepairTable} VALUES (current_timestamp(), '{catalog}','{schema}','{table}',
        '{cleanedResult}')"
4       spark.sql(insertSQL)
```

Command took 0.09 seconds -- by alan.dennis@gmail.com at 8/28/2023, 7:42:59 PM on Alan Dennis's Cluster

Figure 14.32: *Recording function*

Notice that we pass four parameters to the function, as the highlighting shows. This lets us uniquely identify a given table and the inspection results. Now that we have a place for results to go, and a means to get them there, we need to create the code that traverses the catalog, schemas, and tables. We present this code in a different order than the actual execution. This is to ensure the purpose of each function is clear. We start by getting the catalogs in the workspace, as shown in *Figure 14.33:*

Cmd 6

```
1   catalogsDf = spark.sql("SHOW CATALOGS")
2   for catalogRow in catalogsDf.collect():
3       CatalogFunction(catalogRow)
```

▸ (30) Spark Jobs

▸ 🔲 catalogsDf: pyspark.sql.dataframe.DataFrame = [catalog: string]

Figure 14.33: *Retrieve all catalogs*

This code retrieves the catalogs in the workspace using the **SHOW CATALOGS** SQL statement. It then collects the DataFrame so that we can iterate across it, calling **CatalogFunction** with each row. We can highlight that this is command 6 because we will be working our way up the notebook.

CatalogFunction is defined in command 5. It extracts the name of the current catalog from the supplied row and prints it out. Next, it activates the catalog using the **USE CATALOG** command. Next, it retrieves the schemas in the activated catalog. Lastly, it collects the DataFrame returned by that command and iterates over it, invoking **SchemaFunction**, as shown in *Figure 14.34*:

```
Cmd 5

1    def CatalogFunction(row):
2        currentCatalog =row[0]
3        print(currentCatalog)
4        spark.sql("USE CATALOG " + currentCatalog)
5        currentSchemasDf = spark.sql("SHOW SCHEMAS")
6        for schemaRow in currentSchemasDf.collect():
7            SchemaFunction(schemaRow,currentCatalog)
```

Figure 14.34: Retrieve all schemas

Note that the function is defined in command 5. **SchemaFunction** is defined in command 4. It takes the supplied row and extracts the name of the schema. If the schema name is **information_schema** we return out of the function. This is because this is a system managed set of tables. Next, we activate the current schema using the **USE SCHEMA** command, retrieving all of the tables within that schema. Next, we collect the DataFrame and iterate across the rows, invoking **TableFunction** with each row, as shown in *Figure 14.35*:

```
Cmd 4
                                                                    Pyt

1    def SchemaFunction(row,currentCatalog):
2        currentSchemaName = row[0]
3        if currentSchemaName == "information_schema":
4            print("Skipping information_schema")
5            return
6        print("\t" + currentSchemaName)
7        spark.sql("USE SCHEMA " +currentSchemaName)
8        tablesDf = spark.sql("SHOW TABLES")
9        for tableRow in tablesDf.collect():
10           TableFunction(tableRow,currentCatalog,currentSchemaName)
```

Figure 14.35: Retrieve all tables

The final step is to determine if the table passed in to **TableFunction** is healthy. We will walk about this function in multiple parts, as it is fairly long. We start by defining the function and attempting to invoke the SQL **DESCRIBE DETAIL** statement, as shown in *Figure 14.36*:

Cmd 3

```
Python
1    def TableFunction(row,currentCatalog,currentSchemaName):
2        currentTable = row[1]
3        tableFullName = currentCatalog + "." + currentSchemaName + "." + currentTable
4        try:
5            detailCollected=spark.sql(f"describe detail {tableFullName}").collect()
6        except:
7            print("\t\t Unable to Describe - " + tableFullName)
8            RecordRun(currentCatalog,currentSchemaName,currentTable,"Unable to describe
             detail, Config issue or not Delta")
9            return
10       isDelta = detailCollected[0].asDict()['format'] == 'delta'
11       if not isDelta:
12           print("\t\t Skipping - Not Delta - " + tableFullName)
13           return
```

Figure 14.36: *Attempt to determine if the table is a Delta table*

Since we cannot fix non-Delta tables, when we detect one (in line 11), we exit the function. If we do not encounter any exceptions and the table reports to be a Delta table, we execute the **FSCK** command, as shown in *Figure 14.37*:

```
14       dryRunString = "FSCK REPAIR TABLE "+tableFullName+ " DRY RUN"
15       try:
16           dfTableDryRun = spark.sql(dryRunString).cache()
17           if dfTableDryRun.count() != 0:
18               print(dfTableDryRun.collect())
19               RecordRun(currentCatalog,currentSchemaName,currentTable,str
                 (dfTableDryRun.collect()))
20               print("\t\t NOT Healthy - " + currentTable)
21           else:
22               print("\t\t Healthy - " + tableFullName)
23       except Exception as ex:
24           print(dryRunString)
25           print("Problem with "+tableFullName)
26           print("\t\t Problem with - " + currentTable)
27
28           if hasattr(ex, 'message'):
29               RecordRun(currentCatalog,currentSchemaName,currentTable,ex.message)
30               print(ex.message)
31           else:
32               RecordRun(currentCatalog,currentSchemaName,currentTable,str(ex))
33               print(str(ex))
```

Figure 14.37: *Testing the Delta table*

In line 14, we construct the **FSCK** command for the current table. If there are no records returned, we know that the table is healthy. If records are returned or we encounter an exception, we know that the table should be investigated. In those cases, we invoke **RecordRun**, ensuring a record is added to the table. While there are many areas for improvement in this code, it does demonstrate a way to monitor the health of the tables in a Lakehouse. In the next section, we revisit using the VACUUM command to remove unwanted data.

Recipe 133: Vacuum unneeded data

As we discussed in *Recipe 79*, the vacuum command is one way to improve the performance of a Delta table. Recall that vacuum removes files from a table directory that are not managed or no longer needed based on the retention threshold. We can extend *Recipe 79*, using an approach similar to that in *Recipe 130*, to examine all tables in the catalog to see if they need to be vacuumed.

We start by extending the table in operations that capture the results of maintenance to be more generic. We do this by adding a column for maintenance type, as shown in *Figure 14.38*:

```
1    maintenanceCatalog = "LakehouseOperations"
2    maintenanceSchema = "Operations"
3    tableMaint = "Maintenance"
4    def EnsureTable():
5        spark.sql(f"CREATE CATALOG IF NOT EXISTS {maintenanceCatalog}")
6        spark.sql(f"CREATE SCHEMA IF NOT EXISTS {maintenanceCatalog}.{maintenanceSchema}")
7        tableCreateString = f"CREATE TABLE IF NOT EXISTS {maintenanceCatalog}.{maintenanceSchema}.
         {tableMaint} (WhenChecked TIMESTAMP,catName string, schemaName string ,tableName string,
         maintType string, results string)"
8        print(tableCreateString)
9        spark.sql(tableCreateString)
10   EnsureTable()
```

```
CREATE TABLE IF NOT EXISTS LakehouseOperations.Operations.Maintenance (WhenChecked TIMESTAMP,catName string, s
chemaName string ,tableName string, maintType string, results string)
```

Figure 14.38: Generic maintenance table

Next, we change the **RecordRun** method to supply the additional field and perform additional cleanup, as shown in *Figure 14.39*:

```
1    def RecordRun(catalog, schema, table, maintType, result):
2        cleanedResult = (
3            result.replace("\n", " ")
4            .replace("\r", "")
5            .replace(":", "")
6            .replace("'", "")
7            .replace('"', "")
8        )
9        insertSQL = f"INSERT INTO {maintenanceCatalog}.{maintenanceSchema}.{tableMaint} VALUES
         (current_timestamp(), '{catalog}','{schema}','{table}','{maintType}','{cleanedResult}')"
10       spark.sql(insertSQL)
```

Figure 14.39: Updated RecordRun method

We then update the **TableFunction** method to include a maintenance type parameter and generalize the **DRY RUN** portion of the command to be a generic string added after the command. We pass those values across each layer, allowing us to change the invocation to include the type of maintenance, the command, and any suffix, as shown in *Figure 14.40*:

```
1    catalogsDf = spark.sql("SHOW CATALOGS")
2    for catalogRow in catalogsDf.collect():
3        CatalogFunction(catalogRow,"Vacuum Dry Run","VACUUM","DRY RUN",False)
```

▶ (53) Spark Jobs

```
hive_metastore
        default
                    Healthy - hive_metastore.default.iris
                    Healthy - hive_metastore.default.wine_db_2cb40c
                    Healthy - hive_metastore.default.wine_db_c8478c
                    Healthy - hive_metastore.default.yellowtaxi_trips
```

Figure 14.40: Updated top-level maintenance function

The Boolean at the end of the statement controls if we treat a resulting DataFrame that contains records as an error. Recall that for **FSCK**, if there were any records returned, the table was in an error state. In the case of VACUUM, it means there will be files removed by the process. Once we are happy with the state of our tables, we can execute the command without **DRY RUN**. This will result in the removal of old or unused files, as shown in *Figure 14.41*:

```
1    catalogsDf = spark.sql("SHOW CATALOGS")
2    for catalogRow in catalogsDf.collect():
3        CatalogFunction(catalogRow,"Vacuum Actual","VACUUM","",False)
```

Cancel   Running command...

▶ (65) Spark Jobs ━━━━━━━━━━━━━━━━━━━━━━

```
hive_metastore
        default
                    Healthy - hive_metastore.default.iris
                    Healthy - hive_metastore.default.wine_db_2cb40c
```

Figure 14.41: Vacuum without DRY RUN

We have extended our maintenance support to include more generic solution. In the next section, we will use this approach with OPTIMIZE.

Recipe 134: Optimize Delta tables

We discussed the role of the OPTIMIZE command in *Recipe 78*. The idea is to handle common performance issues, such as the small or large file problem. To address these issues, the OPTIMIZE command may rewrite a table's files to improve performance. It can also filter the records that will be imported by supplying a predicate and ZORDER files by a set of columns. **ZORDER** arranges files so that related records are nearby but not necessarily sorted. To learn more about **OPTIMIZE**, see **https://docs.databricks.com/en/sql/language-manual/delta-optimize.html**. So that the recipe can stand by itself, we clone Recipe 131 and modify it to perform an OPTIMIZE, as shown in *Figure 14.42*:

```
1   catalogsDf = spark.sql("SHOW CATALOGS")
2   for catalogRow in catalogsDf.collect():
3   │   CatalogFunction(catalogRow,"Generic Optimize","OPTIMIZE","",False)

    Running command...

▶ (77) Spark Jobs ━━━━━━━━━━━━━━━━━━━━━━━━━━━━━

hive_metastore
        default
                    Healthy - hive_metastore.default.iris
                    Healthy - hive_metastore.default.wine_db_2cb40c
                    Healthy - hive_metastore.default.wine_db_c8478c
                    Healthy - hive_metastore.default.yellowtaxi_trips
        lakehousecookbook
                    Healthy - hive_metastore.lakehousecookbook.bronze_speedtest
                    Healthy - hive_metastore.lakehousecookbook.bronze_speedtestautoloader
```

Figure 14.42: Optimizing all tables

With minimal change, we can now optimize all of the tables in our catalog. In the next section, we will discuss ways to manage cost of a Databricks workspace.

Cost management

Cost management is an important aspect of any enterprise system. There are many best practices for managing costs, we will discuss two in this section. For more information on cost management, see **https://docs.databricks.com/en/lakehouse-architecture/cost-optimization/best-practices.html**.

Recipe 135: Use cluster policies

Everyone would know the best way to create and use clusters in an ideal world. However, since many do not, Databricks implemented cluster policies. Cluster policies allow administrators to establish limits on clusters. To learn more about cluster policies, see **https://docs.databricks.com/en/administration-guide/clusters/policies.html**. To create a cluster policy, navigate to the Compute section and select Policies. As shown in *Figure 14.43:*

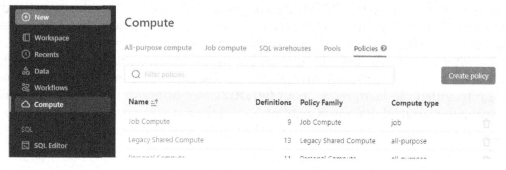

Figure 14.43: *Cluster Policies*

A workspace comes pre-populated with several policies, including job computer, legacy shared compute, personal compute, power user compute, and shared compute. Clicking the **Create policy** button brings up the Create policy form. The form allows for creation of a policy based on an existing policy, such as the Power User Computer. You make the changes to the policy by overriding existing values, as seen in *Figure 14.44:*

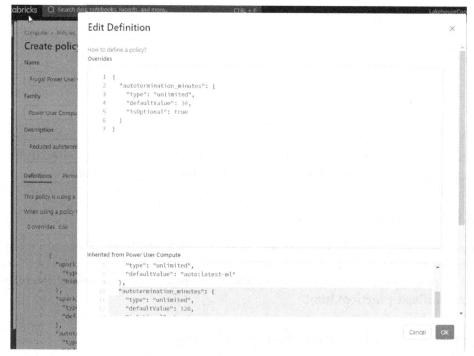

Figure 14.44: *Overriding a policy value*

Which is accessed from the Create Policy screen by clicking **Edit**, as shown in *Figure 14.45:*

Figure 14.45: Create policy screen

You can see that **autotermination_minutes** has been changed from the normal 120 to 30. You can also specify a node type, auto-scaling ranges, and if the nodes should be spot instances. Cluster policies allow you to restrict and control clusters with the aim of controlling cost. In the next section, we will discuss how to monitor costs using tags.

Recipe 136: Using tags to monitor costs

It is important for cost to be attributed to the appropriate cost center. One way that Databricks enables this is through the use of tags. Tags are name value pairs that can be associated with things such as jobs, clusters, jobs, and DLT clusters. For example, you can assign a tag to a cluster during its creation or by editing it, as shown in *Figure 14.46:*

Figure 14.46: Adding tags to a cluster

Notice that there are several automatically added tags. The idea of custom tags is to provide additional information, such as what department, organizational unit, or project costs should be associated with. Cloud providers off a mechanism of reporting from tags, such as using Azure's Cost analysis function as shown in *Figure 14.47*:

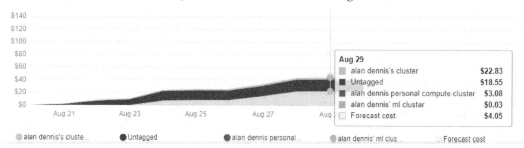

Figure 14.47: *Azure cost analysis with tag information*

This example is very crude, but shows that costs can be associated to tags, such as the ClusterName. For other best practices and approaches, see **https://docs.databricks.com/ en/lakehouse-architecture/operational-excellence/best-practices.html**. We have shown how tags can be associated with resources for reporting purposes. An organization needs to establish a tag organization and tagging approach to ensure that cost is attributed to the correct effort.

Conclusion

In this chapter, we talked about how to manage code. We discussed ways of orchestrating code internally to Databricks and across systems using Airflow. We discussed maintenance's importance and provided examples of how to perform it. We then concluded with a discussion of cost management and the importance of tags.

The next chapter is the conclusion of the book. In it we will discuss tips, tricks, troubleshooting, and best practices related to Databricks Lakehouses.

Join our book's Discord space

Join the book's Discord Workspace for Latest updates, Offers, Tech happenings around the world, New Release and Sessions with the Authors:

https://discord.bpbonline.com

CHAPTER 15

Tips, Tricks, Troubleshooting, and Best Practices

Introduction

Knowing the best way to accomplish a task when building a Lakehouse accelerates adoption. This chapter focuses on the tips and tricks to help build a successful Lakehouse. Additionally, finding out why things are not working as expected is an essential skill. Discussing and applying what we learn in this chapter will helps ensure the Lakehouse will stand the test of time and provide value for many years.

Structure

The chapter covers the following topics:

- Ingesting relational data with Databricks
- Performance optimization
- Programmatic deployment and interaction
- Reading a Kafka stream
- Notebook orchestration
- Best practices

Objectives

By the end of this chapter, you should be able to discuss relational data using Databricks and have a clear understanding of concurrency implications. You should also be able to investigate performance issues by examining a cluster's event log and the Spark UI. You should have a basic understanding of the role that pools play in reducing the time it takes to create clusters. You should be able to deploy a Databricks workspace using a template and interact with it using its API. You should have some understanding of interacting with Kafka, and how to do notebook-based orchestration. Lastly, will have a concise set of best practices.

Ingesting relational data with Databricks

We have used Databricks for both ingestion and refining. So far, we have focused on ingesting files or messages from an event stream. Another data source commonly ingested into a Lakehouse is from relational systems, such as an Azure SQL Database. This section will review the approaches to ingesting data from relational systems and highlight some risks.

Recipe 137: Loading data from MySQL

MySQL is a popular relational database system. Spark, Databricks' primary technology, has support to connect to many relational systems using **Java Database Connectivity (JDBC)**. We use JDBC by constructing a URL of a particular format and then pass it, along with the required information, to the **spark.read** method. In this example, we will also demonstrate the use of Python classes as a way to better structure code, as shown in *Figure 15.1*:

```
1   class MySqlReader:
2       def __init__(self, host, databasename, user, password, port=3306):       1
3           self.host = host
4           self.databasename = databasename
5           self.user = user
6           self.password = password
7           self.port = port
8           self.driver = "org.mariadb.jdbc.Driver"
9           self.url = f"jdbc:mysql://{self.host}:{self.port}/{self.databasename}?useSSL=true&requireSSL=true"
10      def Read(self,table):
11          df = (                                                2
12              spark.read.format("jdbc")
13              .option("driver", self.driver)
14              .option("url", self.url)
15              .option("dbtable", table)
16              .option("user", self.user)
17              .option("password", self.password)
18              .load()
19          )
20          return df
```

Figure 15.1: MySQL reading class

The class contains an initialization method along with a method named **Read**. The initialization function (callout 1) is similar to a constructor in object-oriented methods. To learn more about Python classes, see **https://docs.python.org/3/tutorial/classes.html**. By convention, class methods have a parameter named self. It is used to supply a reference to an instance of the class. You can think of it as being like **this** in C# or C++. Notice that we construct the URL with the information from the initialization method, adding a parameter requiring SSL use on line 9. The **Read** method (callout 2) invokes **spark.read** to return a DataFrame populated with the contents of the specified table. When we create an instance of the class, we supply information that will be used for the life of the class, as shown in *Figure 15.2*:

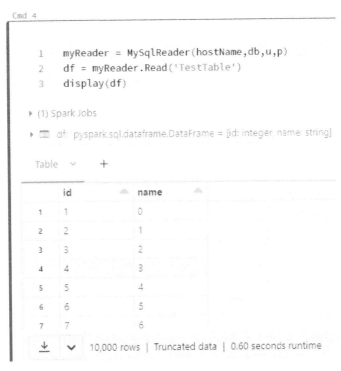

Figure 15.2: Creating an instance of the reader class

We create the instance of our class on line 1 of command 4. We pass in the hostname, database name, user identifier, and password parameters. We are not passing in the port number, causing the default value to be used. We then invoke the **Read** method to return the contents of **TestTable** and display the resulting DataFrame.

We have successfully read the contents of a MySQL table into a DataFrame.

> **Note: You may experience network and security challenges connecting to a database from Databricks. You may be required to use virtual network peering and injection to connect to a production database. In the next recipe, we will discuss extending a Python class with additional methods without following the traditional approach, as we did in Figure 15.1.**

Recipe 138: Extending a Python class and reading using Databricks runtime format

We created a Python class in the previous recipe to include MySQL table reading functions. We will extend this class using the **settattr** function and Databricks runtime formatting. Typically, we extend a class by creating a function definition in the class declaration. One challenge with this approach is that it can lead to long code blocks in a Databricks notebook cell. The **settattr** method allows you to set a value on an attribute at runtime, as shown in *Figure 15.3*:

```
Cmd 5

 1     def ReadDBRuntime(self, table):
 2         df = (
 3             spark.read.format("mysql")
 4             .option("dbtable", table)
 5             .option("host", self.host)
 6             .option("port", self.port)
 7             .option("database", self.databasename)
 8             .option("user", self.user)
 9             .option("password", self.password)
10             .option("useSSL",True)
11             .option("requireSSL",True)
12             .load()
13         )
14         return df
15     setattr(MySqlReader, "ReadDBRuntime", ReadDBRuntime)

Command took 0.09 seconds -- by alan.dennis@gmail.com at 9/6/2023, 5:5-
```

Figure 15.3: Setting a class method at runtime

We start by declaring a function named **ReadDBRuntime** (callout 1). It is like the **Read** method we defined earlier, where the key difference is that we specify the format as **mysql** instead of **jdbc** and includes the properties used to construct the URL (such as host, port, and database) rather than the URL itself. Also, this is just a function that we defined. It does not have a link to the class **MySqlReader** until the call to **setattr** (callout 4). Also, since we do not have a URL to manipulate, we must add the useSSL (callout 2) and requireSSL (callout 3) options. For more on **setattr** see **https://docs.python.org/3/library/functions.html#setattr**. We can verify that we did add the method by using the built-in **dir** function, as shown in *Figure 15.4*:

```
 1     methods = [method for method in dir(MySqlReader) if method.startswith("__") is False]
 2     print(methods)

['Read', 'ReadDBRuntime']

Command took 0.10 seconds -- by alan.dennis@gmail.com at 9/6/2023, 6:20:42 PM on Alan Dennis's Cluster
```

Figure 15.4: Listing methods in MySqlReader after using setattr

For more on the **dir** function, see **https://docs.python.org/3/library/functions.html#dir**. This code retrieves all of the methods of the class **MySqlReader** and filters out those which start with two underscores. This effectively removes internal methods, such as **__init__**. We can also test the method by invoking it, as shown in *Figure 15.5*:

```
1    df2 = myReader.ReadDBRuntime('TestTable')
2    display(df2)
3    print(df2.count())
```

▶ (3) Spark Jobs

▶ ▦ df2: pyspark.sql.dataframe.DataFrame = [id: integer, name: string]

Table ⌄   +

	id	name
1	1	0
2	2	1
3	3	2

Figure 15.5: *Using the new class method*

Using an alternative approach, we have added a new method to an existing class. That method also used the Databricks runtime format to read from a MySQL database. In the next recipe, we will discuss the importance of using the cache method of a DataFrame.

Recipe 139: Caching DataFrames

It is important to understand the fundamental nature of Spark, the supporting technology of Databricks, to process data efficiently. The two constructs are actions and transformations. A transformation creates a new DataFrame from an existing one. An example of a transformation is **withColumn**. An action causes a result to be computed. The count method of a DataFrame is a good example of an action. In Spark, all transformations are lazy. That means that they are only applied when an action is involved. For more on actions and transformations, see **https://spark.apache.org/docs/latest/rdd-programming-guide.html**.

With this background, we can see an example of an accidental inefficiency in *Figure 15.5*. The display statement is an action that causes transformations to be applied to produce a result. On line 3, we invoke the count method of the DataFrame, another action. This causes any operations to be performed again. We can see this by counting the number of rows in a table as it is being populated, as shown in *Figure 15.6*:

```
1    for i in range(1,10):
2    |    print(df2.count())
```

▸ (18) Spark Jobs

```
453312
453349
453386
453422
453458
453494
453533
453570
453607
```

Figure 15.6: *Counting rows of a table being populated without caching a DataFrame*

If we cache the DataFrame, we see a different result, as shown in *Figure 15.7*:

```
1    df2 = myReader.ReadDBRuntime('TestTable').cache()
2    for i in range(1,10):
3    |    print(df2.count())
```

▸ (19) Spark Jobs

▸ ▣ df2: pyspark.sql.dataframe.DataFrame = [id: integer, name: string]

```
453703
453703
453703
453703
453703
453703
453703
453703
453703
```

Figure 15.7: *Cached row count of a table being populated*

Notice that the same value for the row count is returned. When deciding to cache a DataFrame, you should ask yourself if you want to recompute the results with each action. It is important to understand this behavior, as a misunderstanding of Spark's behavior will result in an inefficient implementation.

So far, our implementation will execute code on a single node in our cluster. For small workloads, this may be acceptable. In the next section, we discuss how to increase the parallelism of queries when working with relational systems.

Recipe 140: Loading data from MySQL using workers

The default implementation of JDBC driver-based queries in Databricks is limited to a single thread. We often need more than a single node to retrieve information for larger data. To do this, we set additional options, as shown in *Figure 15.8*:

```
1   def ReadConcurrent(self, table):
2       df = (
3           spark.read.format("mysql")
4           .option("dbtable", table).option("host", self.host).option("port", self.port)
5           .option("database", self.databasename).option("user", self.user).option("password", self.password)
6           .option("useSSL",True).option("requireSSL",True)
7           .option("numPartitions",4)
8           .option("partitionColumn","modColumn")
9           .option("lowerBound",0)
10          .option("upperBound",5)
11          .load()
12      )
13      return df
14  setattr(MySqlReader, "ReadConcurrent", ReadConcurrent)
15  df3 = myReader.ReadConcurrent('TestTableModColumn')
16  display(df3)
17  print(df3.count())
```

▶ (3) Spark Jobs

▶ ▦ df3: pyspark.sql.dataframe.DataFrame = [id: integer, name: string ... 1 more field]

Table ∨ +

	id	name	modColumn
1	1	0	0
2	2	1	1
3	5	4	0
4	6	5	1

Figure 15.8: Setting options to increase parallelism

For more information on controlling query parallelism, see

https://docs.databricks.com/en/external-data/jdbc.html#control-parallelism-for-jdbc-queries. Based on experimentation, the only way to increase concurrency is to set **numPartitions**, **partitionColumn**, **lowerBound**, and **upperBound**. Examining the read details for a run where only **numPartitions** was set, we can see that the partition count was 1, as shown in *Figure 15.9*:

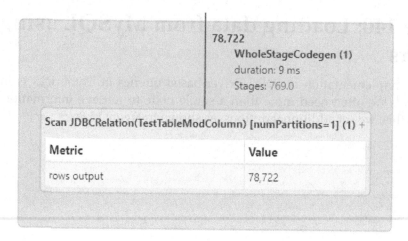

Figure 15.9: Execution details of partially set options

Notice that the **numPartitions** is 1. However, if we set all four options, we can see the **numPartitions** increases to 4, the number specified for **numPartitions**, as shown in *Figure 15.10:*

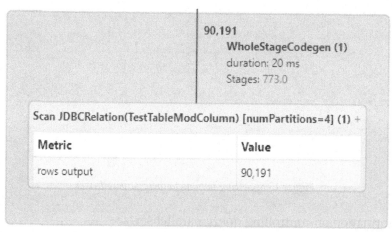

Figure 15.10: Partition count with all options set

In an upcoming recipe, we will discuss using the Spark UI to troubleshoot performance in depth. We will cover reading the SQL/DataFrame **Directed Acyclic Graph (DAG)** in detail. For now, understand that we have used the detailed information to verify that four threads were used to access the MySQL database. To increase the concurrency, we must specify the number of partitions we want, a column that has that many values (**modColumn** populated using the **MOD** function with the name column's values and four), and upper and lower bounds. The partition column must have an even distribution. For more on increasing parallelism in JDBC reads, see **https://luminousmen.com/post/spark-tips-optimizing-jdbc-data-source-reads**.

We have successfully controlled the concurrency while reading from a relational system. While we demonstrated it with MySQL, the approach is similar to other system types. In the next section, we will explore performance more, including examining the Spark UI mechanisms for examining execution, like that in *Figures 15.9* and *15.10*.

Performance optimization

Once an ingestion or refinement is working, the focus shifts to performance. Performance is usually a tradeoff between cost, time, and storage. This section explores ways to determine the performance of ingestions and refinements. We will start by exploring the cluster details page.

Using Databricks even log

When you look at a cluster's detail page, you see sections for **Configuration**, **Notebooks**, **Libraries**, and so on. One of the sections of note is the **Event log** section, as shown in *Figure 15.11:*

Figure 15.11: *Cluster's event log*

As the name implies, this section lets you see what events occurred related to your cluster. For example, we can see that Databricks could not allocate two **Virtual Machines (VM)** for the nodes in the cluster. While not explicitly performance-related, when trying to diagnose a performance-related issue, we often want to know what was going on when the issue occurred. For that, we can look at the event log. Clicking on one of the lines brings up a detailed description of the event, sometimes with help, as shown in *Figure 15.12:*

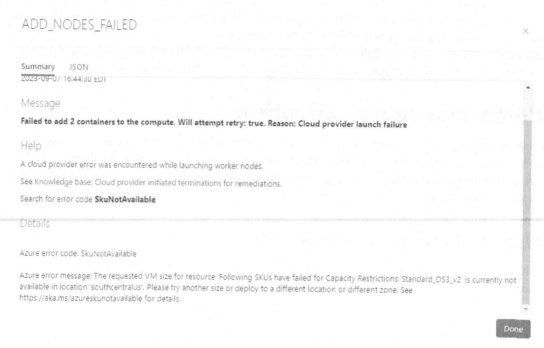

Figure 15.12: Detailed event page

In this case, the issue was related to the availability of a particular node type. The recommendation was to switch to a different type VM size. Located next to **Event log** is the **Spark UI**. In the next few sections, we will discuss the Spark UI within Databricks.

Exploring the Spark UI jobs tab

The Spark web **User Interface (UI)** is a place where you can monitor a Spark cluster using a web browser. It contains a set of tabs to organize the activities. The first tab is the **Jobs** tab, as shown in *Figure 15.13:*

Figure 15.13: Spark UI Jobs tab

Notice that in the upper right-hand corner there is a link to open the Spark UI in its own browsing tab. Also, in addition to the event timeline, you can scroll down to see the jobs which have completed. If you hover over one of the jobs, you can see information about it, as shown in *Figure 15.14:*

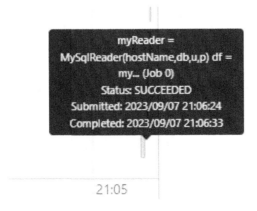

Figure 15.14: Job detail on the timeline

If you click on one of the jobs, you will be taken to the job's detail page. This page includes a description of the operations performed, metrics (such as duration), and if it was successful, as shown in *Figure 15.15:*

Figure 15.15: Job details page

From the details page, you can view the DAG visualization, by clicking the link above Completed Stages. The DAG visualization is a representation of the operations being performed during the job, as shown in *Figure 15.16:*

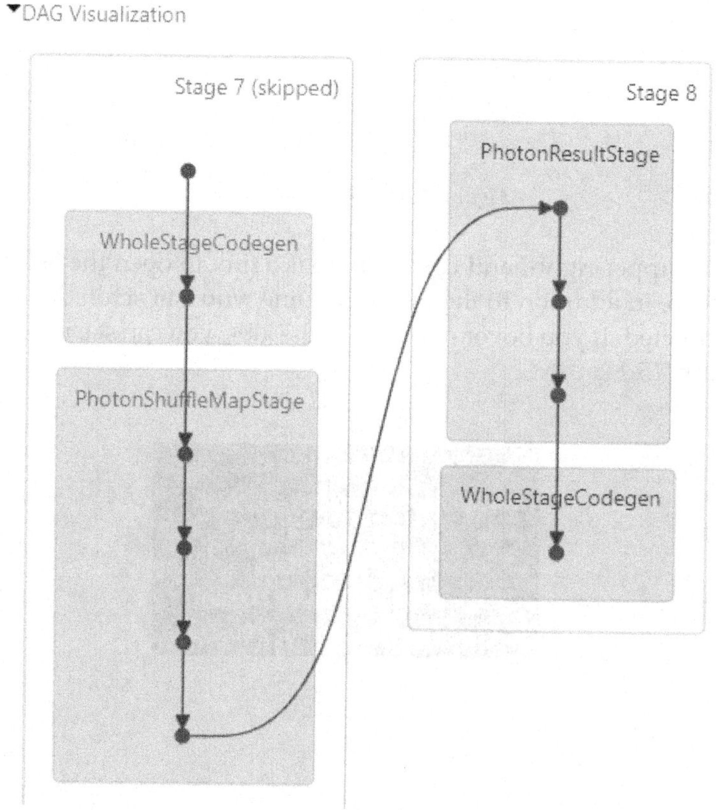

Figure 15.16: DAG of a simple job

Clicking on active areas will bring details about that stage. The stage detail page can also be access from the **Stages** tab, as shown in *Figure 15.17:*

Figure 15.17: Stages tab

The first line of the stages tab is for stage 8, the same as the stage in *Figure 15.16*. For more on the Stages tab see **https://spark.apache.org/docs/latest/web-ui.html#stages-tab**. We have briefly discussed the **Jobs** and **Stages** tab of the Spark UI. The other tabs are discussed in the previous link. In the next section we discuss the **SQL/DataFrame** tab.

Using the Spark UI SQL/DataFrame tab

The **SQL/DataFrame** tab allows you to view completed queries. These queries can be SQL-based or operations performed on a DataFrame. For example, in *Recipe 138*, we loaded a DataFrame with the contents of a MySQL database. We did so by using a DataFrame. The **SQL/DataFrame** tab organizes operations based on queries, as shown in *Figure 15.18*:

ID ▾	Description	Submitted	Duration	Job IDs
5	def ReadConcurrent(self, table): df = (... +details	2023/09/07 21:43:13	1 s	[5][6]
4	def ReadConcurrent(self, table): df = (... +details	2023/09/07 21:43:13	0.3 s	[4]

SQL / DataFrame

Completed Queries: 6

▼Completed Queries (6)

Page: 1   1 Pages. Jump to 1   . Show 100   items in a page.   Go

Figure 15.18: SQL/DataFrame tab

Clicking on a link in the **Description** column brings up a query detail page. The page contains a visual representation of the query's plan, metrics, text execution summary, details, and properties of the SQL/DataFrame, as shown in *Figure 15.19*:

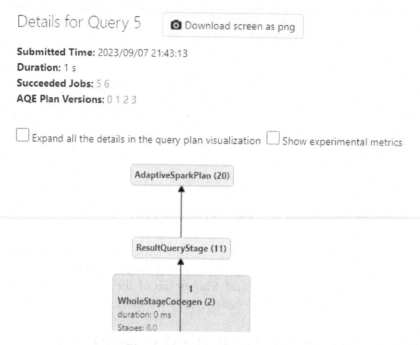

Figure 15.19: Query details page

Clicking the **Expand all the details in the query plan visualization** checkbox includes details for each step. Note that the order of execution is from bottom to top, as indicated by the arrows. That means the first thing you see (**AdaptiveSparkPlan** in this case) was the last thing to process. When doing optimization, we look for the element that is taking the longest to complete. This is because optimizing a short-running operation often results in little impact. An exception to that approach is if the short-running operation is frequently executed. In this case, reading from the MySQL database was the longest-running block, as shown in *Figure 15.20*:

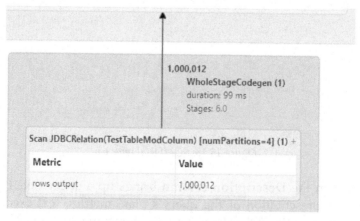

Figure 15.20: Block reading from MySQL

Notice that the block took 99 milliseconds and outputted a little over a million rows. Recall that this element the graph was used to demonstrate that the read was being performed using four threads. We can also see that fact by looking at one of the other blocks, as shown in *Figure 15.21*:

Metric	Value
PhotonAgg (3) +	
cumulative time total (min, med, max)	79 ms (1 ms, 23 ms, 32 ms)
exclusive time total (min, med, max) (experimental)	0 ms (0 ms, 0 ms, 0 ms)
num early close	0
number of output batches	4
permanent agg varlen pool size in bytes	0
rows output	4
tasks total	4

Figure 15.21: Details of a block

We have briefly discussed the **SQL/DataFrame** tab of the Spark UI. For more details, see **https://spark.apache.org/docs/latest/web-ui.html#sql-tab**. The key concept of using this tab is to look for the longer running queries and determine if they can be improved. To learn more about turning Spark, see **https://spark.apache.org/docs/latest/tuning.html**. In the next section we discuss a way of reducing the time it takes for a cluster to be available.

Recipe 141: Using pools to improve performance

If you have used Databricks for long, you have spent time waiting for a cluster to start. The same is true of scheduled jobs. The time to provision a job cluster can be as long as the execution time. One way to reduce the time to provision clusters is to use pools. Note that using pools may increase your Databricks consumption.

Pools are pre-allocated, ready-to-use instances. When a cluster is being provisioned, rather than creating instances from scratch, an instance in the pool is allocated to the cluster. If the pool does not have any available instances, more are allocated. Once the cluster no longer needs the instance, it is returned to the pool. As with clusters, you can control how long an unused instance is retained.

Pools can be configured to have a specified Databricks runtime version installed. If the version matches the pool uses, the time required to deploy the runtime will be saved. You have the option to use spot instances which is a way to save costs. Spot instances are unused computing resources; if they are needed, the spot instance is stopped. Next, you specify the idle minutes before auto termination, and if you wish to use Photon, as shown in *Figure 15.22:*

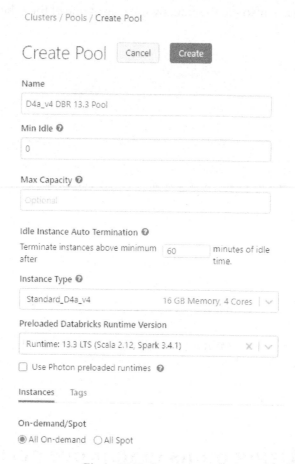

Figure 15.22: *Creating a pool*

Once you have created a pool you can use it in a cluster. When creating the cluster, ensure you select the pool from the Worker or Driver type combo, as shown in *Figure 15.23:*

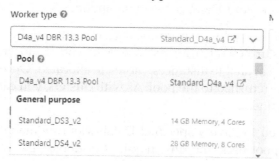

Figure 15.23: *Creating a pool-back cluster*

When creating a workflow, you can also specify to use a pool, as shown in *Figure 15.24*:

Figure 15.24: Specifying a pool when creating a job cluster in a workflow

To learn more about pools, see **https://docs.databricks.com/en/clusters/pools.html**. We have discussed ways of reducing the time it takes for a job to complete, determine bottlenecks, and being diagnosing problems. In the next section we will examine ways to programmatically deploy Databricks and an alternative to the web interface.

Programmatic deployment and interaction

When people perform operations, they often make mistakes. This includes people tasked with provisioning a Databricks workspace or moving items from place to place. In this section, we will discuss alternatives to manual interactions with Databricks. There are many other ways to programmatically interact with Databricks and in this section we will discuss using an **Azure Resource Manager** (**ARM**) template to create a workspace and interacting with Databricks via its API.

Recipe 142: Creating a workspace with ARM Template

In *Chapter 2, Setting up a Databricks Workspace*, we created a Databricks workspace using the portals of each cloud provider. While this approach is acceptable for certain situations, ideally, we utilize a more repeatable process. This is often referred to as **Infrastructure as Code (IaC)**.

Each cloud provider has a means of provisioning resources programmatically. In this recipe, we will explore **Azure Resource Manager (ARM)** templates. ARM templates are a JSON-based way of declaratively creating resources. The first step is to acquire a template. As we noted in *Chapter 2, Setting up a Databricks Workspace*, when you are viewing the preview screen during the manual Databricks provisioning process, you have the option to download the template, as shown in *Figure 15.25*:

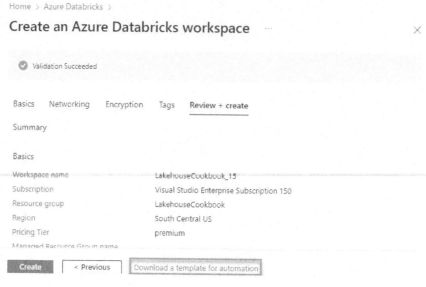

Figure 15.25: Databricks workspace review screen

Clicking **Download a template for automation** opens the Template detail page, as shown in *Figure 15.26*:

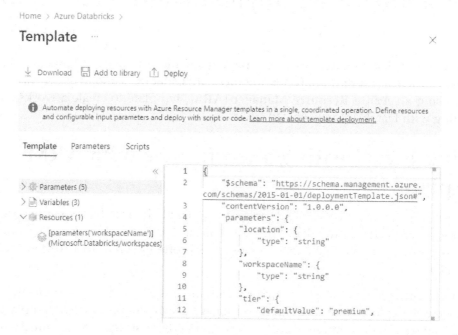

Figure 15.26: ARM template download form

After downloading the template and parameters in an archive, we can open the JSON files. You will notice that the parameters JSON file contains default values. Each parameter is also present in the template. The contents may seem familiar. This is because we deployed a custom template in Recipe 118, when we installed the Access connector for Databricks.

There are many ways to deploy ARM templates. For more details, visit **https://learn. microsoft.com/en-us/azure/azure-resource-manager/templates/overview**. For our example, we will follow an approach like we did in Recipe 118. We start by searching for **Deploy a custom template** in the Azure search bar, as shown in *Figure 15.27*:

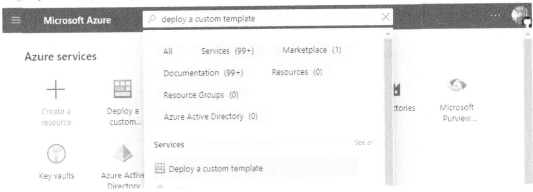

Figure 15.27: Searching for deploy a custom template

Once the **Custom deployment** screen comes up, select Build your own template in the editor, as shown in *Figure 15.28*:

Figure 15.28: Custom deployment

Next, you will see the **Edit template** screen. Select **Load file**, as shown in *Figure 15.29*:

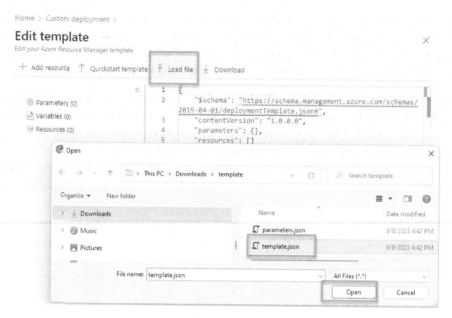

Figure 15.29: Loading a custom template

After loading the file, click Save. This will return you to the Custom deployment screen. Enter the desired values for the parameters, as shown in *Figure 15.30:*

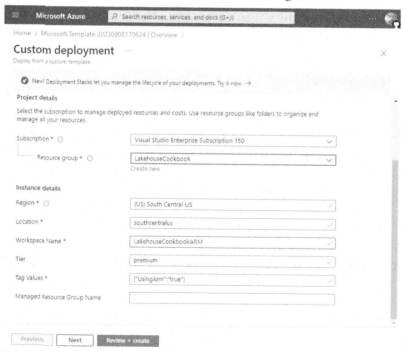

Figure 15.30: Populated parameters

As is the case with other Azure resources, clicking **Review + create** displays the captured values and offers the option to Create. This is a very simple example of using ARM templates. The idea is to reduce the human interactions, thus reducing the chance of error. In the next section, we will examine interacting with Databricks via its API.

Recipe 143: Using the Databricks API

Most modern system offer an **Application Programming Interface (API).** Databricks is no different. The API exposes most functionality available in the web interface. To learn more about the API, see **https://docs.databricks.com/api**. To make interaction with the API simpler, Databricks has created several **Software Development Kits (SDK)**. One of those SDKs is for Python, which we will use in this example. To learn more about the Databricks SDK for Python see **https://docs.databricks.com/en/dev-tools/sdk-python.html**.

To demonstrate some of the API's capabilities, we will create a simple Jupyter notebook that connects to a workspace and recursively extracts all the notebooks in a certain location, saving them to a local disk in HTML format.

We start by installing the Python SDK, as shown in *Figure 15.31:*

Install the Databricks Python SDK - https://docs.databricks.com/en/dev-tools/sdk-python.html

```
In [1]:  1 pip install databricks-sdk --upgrade
executed in 3.04s, finished 16:12:34 2023-09-08

Requirement already satisfied: databricks-sdk in c:\users\aland\anaconda3\envs\pyth
Requirement already satisfied: requests<3,>=2.28.1 in c:\users\aland\anaconda3\envs
ks-sdk) (2.31.0)
```

Figure 15.31: *Install the Databricks Python SDK*

You will likely see informational messages and possibly warnings. Next, we setup the logging and import necessary libraries. We use the Python logging library. To learn more about it, see **https://docs.python.org/3/howto/logging.html**. To test our configuration, we log an information message, as shown in *Figure 15.32:*

Imports and setting up the logger

For more on logging see https://docs.python.org/3/howto/logging.html

```
[2]:
import os
import io
import base64
import logging
from databricks.sdk import WorkspaceClient
from databricks.sdk.service import workspace

FORMAT = "[%(funcName)20s() ] %(message)s"
logging.basicConfig(format=FORMAT,level=logging.INFO)
logger = logging.getLogger('LakehouseCookbook')
logger.setLevel(logging.INFO)
logger.info("Staring Run of API Example")
executed in 659ms, finished 16:12:35 2023-09-08
[            <module>() ] Staring Run of API Example
```

Figure 15.32: *Imports and logging setup*

You may notice the use of Markdown in the Jupyter notebook. The idea is to make it so that if someone opened the notebook, they would be able to use it. Next, we assign variables that should be stored in a secure location, such as a Databricks user access token and the Databricks host URL, as shown in *Figure 15.33*:

```
Things that should be in a secret store

In [3]:   1  token = 'dapi38c            6070f1f0851e870'
          2  host = 'https://adb-9957774048    8.18.azuredatabricks.net'
          3  exportLocation = "C:\\LakehouseCookbook\\Export"
        executed in 13ms, finished 16:12:35 2023-09-08
```

Figure 15.33: *Configuration values*

Next, we create a **WorkspaceClient** to connect to the Databricks workspace. When we create it, we supply the token and host, as shown in *Figure 15.34*:

```
Create a workspace client using host and token

In [4]:   1  w = WorkspaceClient(
          2      host  = host,
          3      token = token
          4  )
        executed in 13ms, finished 16:12:35 2023-09-08
```

```
Check to see if the workspace client is working by pulling current user's name

In [5]:   1  logger.info(f'{w.current_user.me().user_name}')
        executed in 944ms, finished 16:12:36 2023-09-08

        [            <module>() ] alan.dennis@gmail.com
```

Figure 15.34: *Connecting to a Databricks workspace*

To ensure we are connecting, we use the **current_user** property of the workspace client to get the credentials associated with the token. Once we are processing the contents of the location in the workspace, we will need a means to save the notebooks to the local disk, as HTML files. To make things a little simpler, we use a Python function, as shown in *Figure 15.35*:

```
1   def ProcessFile(i,targetPath,dryRun):
2       targetFolder = os.path.dirname(targetPath)
3       logger.info(f"targetFolder = {targetFolder}")
4       if not os.path.exists(targetFolder):
5           os.makedirs(targetFolder)
6       logger.info(f"{i.object_type} - {i.path} ")
7       logger.info(f"targetpath = {targetPath} ")
8       if str(i.object_type) == "ObjectType.NOTEBOOK":
9           if dryRun == False:
10              logging.info(f"attempting export of {i.path}")
11              export_response = w.workspace.export(
12                  format=workspace.ExportFormat.HTML,
13                  path=i.path
14              )
15              decodedItem=base64.b64decode(export_response.content)
16              with open(targetPath, "wb") as f:
17                  f.write(decodedItem)
18              logger.info(f"wrote decoded notebook to {targetPath}")
19          else:
20              logger.info(f"Dry run, would have wrote notebook to {targetPath}")
```
executed in 18ms, finished 17:48:44 2023-09-08

Figure 15.35: Process file function

There are few interesting parts in this function. We pass three parameters to the function. The first is the object we get back from the SDK. The second is the path we want to write the file to. Last, we use the dry run concept we saw in Recipe 79. If true, the file will not be exported and saved. If false, we call the workspace's export function, asking for the HTML format, and supply the path to the item of interest. What we get back is a response object. We apply base 64 decoding to it to convert it to usable text. We write that text to a file at the target path.

Now that we have a method to write notebooks out to disk, we need a method of getting a list of those objects. To do this, we use another function, as shown in *Figure 15.36:*

```
1   def ExportPath(path,exportPath,dryRun):
2       logging.info(f"----------------------- ENTER -------------------------")
3       logging.info(f"path={path}")
4       logging.info(f"exportPath={exportPath}")
5       logging.info(f"dryRun={dryRun}")
6       if not os.path.exists(exportPath):
7           logging.info(f"creating path at {exportPath}")
8           os.makedirs(exportPath)
9       for i in w.workspace.list(path, recursive=False):
10          logger.info(f"=============== {i.path} {i.object_type} {str(i.object_type)}")
11          if str(i.object_type) == "ObjectType.DIRECTORY" or str(i.object_type) == "ObjectType.REPO":
12              directoryPortion= DetermineDirectoryPortion(path,i.path)
13              exportPathUpdate = os.path.join(exportPath, directoryPortion)
14              logger.info(f"exportPath {exportPath}")
15              logger.info(f"directoryPortion {directoryPortion} ")
16              logger.info(f"exportPathUpdate {exportPathUpdate} ")
17              print('recurse',i.path,i.object_type)
18              ExportPath(i.path,exportPathUpdate,dryRun)
19          else:
20              targetPath = i.path.replace(path,exportPath) + ".HTML"
21              ProcessFile(i,targetPath,dryRun)
```
executed in 5ms, finished 18:09:44 2023-09-08

Figure 15.36: Export path function

The function accepts a workspace and local path, along with a dry run flag. The function attempts to create the destination directory, on line 8. Then it asks the workspace for a list of items in the workspace path. It then iterates over the list, checking to see if the item is a repository or directory. If it is, the function determines the export folder, based on the workspace folder. It then calls itself, recusing into the folder or repository. If the item is a file, it calls the **ProcessFile** function we discussed.

The last step is to invoke the **ExportPath**, as shown in *Figure 15.37*:

```
1   ExportPath(pathInDB,pathLocal,False)
executed in 3m 48s, finished 18:13:34 2023-09-08
[          ExportPath() ] ------------------------ ENTER ---------------------------
[          ExportPath() ] path=/Repos/alan.dennis@gmail.com
[          ExportPath() ] exportPath-C:\LakehouseCookbook\Export
[          ExportPath() ] dryRun=False
[          ExportPath() ] =============== /Repos/alan.dennis@gmail.com/lakehousecookbook ObjectType
[          ExportPath() ] exportPath C:\LakehouseCookbook\Export
[          ExportPath() ] directoryPortion lakehousecookbook
[          ExportPath() ] exportPathUpdate C:\LakehouseCookbook\Export\lakehousecookbook
[          ExportPath() ] ------------------------ ENTER ---------------------------
[          ExportPath() ] path=/Repos/alan.dennis@gmail.com/lakehousecookbook
[          ExportPath() ] exportPath=C:\LakehouseCookbook\Export\lakehousecookbook
[          ExportPath() ] dryRun=False
[          ExportPath() ] =============== /Repos/alan.dennis@gmail.com/lakehousecookbook/Chapter 13
```

Figure 15.37: Invoke the ExportPath function

We have now created a process to extract all notebooks in a workspace. More importantly, we have demonstrated a process to interact with Databricks' REST API using the Python SDK. In the next section, we revisit ingesting stream data.

Reading a Kafka stream

In *Chapter 6, Extracting from Sourced and Loading to Bronze*, we discussed reading events from an Azure Event hub. In this section, we will revisit that concept using Confluent Cloud Kafka. You can sign up for a free account at **https://www.confluent.io/confluent-cloud/tryfree/**.

Recipe 144: Creating a Kafka cluster

When you sign up for a new Confluent Cloud account, you receive credits enabling you to use their service for free (for a limited time). Once you have an account, likely the first thing you will do is create a Kafka cluster. To do this, you first select the type of cluster, as shown in *Figure 15.38*:

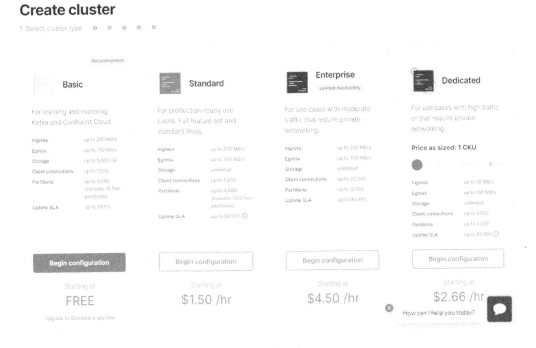

Figure 15.38: Select cluster type

For our purposes, the basic configuration is sufficient. Next, you select the cloud provider and associated region. For the basic tier, you are forced to use Google Cloud. If you wanted to use AWS or Azure, you would need to select a higher tier. You also need to select the level of availability, as shown in *Figure 15.39*:

Figure 15.39: Selecting cloud provider, region, and availability

Next, you are prompted for credit card information. You also have the choice of not adding payment information. Next, you are asked to supply a name for the cluster or use the default of cluster_0. You are presented with base cost, along with cluster details, as shown in *Figure 15.40*:

Figure 15.40: *Create cluster*

Once the cluster is created, you are presented with some options to make using the new cluster easier. You have the choice of using the cluster for data integration, or to build an event driven application. You also have the choice of bypassing the accelerators and exploring on your own. For our example, we will start by building an event-driven application.

The wizard lands you on the **Clients** section of the cluster, as shown in *Figure 15.41*:

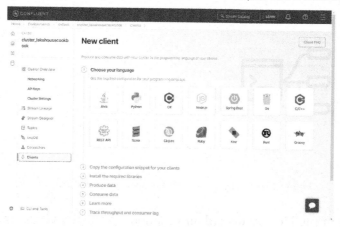

Figure 15.41: *Client selection*

Once your select your language, you are given detailed information for connecting to the cluster. We will use this information in the next section to produce and consume events.

Recipe 145: Using confluent cloud

In *Chapter 6, Extracting from Source and Loading into Bronze*, we used a Jupyter Notebook to create Event Hub traffic. In this section, we revisit that approach, targeting the Kafka cluster we created in Recipe 142. We start by creating a topic in Confluent Cloud. Topics are a way of organizing messages, similar to an Event Hub in an Event Hub Namespace. We create a topic by navigating to our environment, and then cluster, and select **Topics** from the left navigation, as shown in *Figure 15.42*:

Figure 15.42: Topics list

We can click **Add topic** from this page to begin the topic creation flow. You will be prompted to provide a name, and the number of partitions. As with other systems, partitioning is the mechanism for scaling Kafka. For our purposes, the default of six is overkill. The important thing to understand is that there is a mechanism to increase the number of messages that can be handled. By opening the advanced section, you can control things like message retention period and set a cleanup policy. Once you have created the topic, you will be provided with the option to create a schema for your messages. A schema is a way of detecting invalid messages before the consumer processes them. If your message is JSON-based, many free online tools exist to create a JSON schema from a JSON sample.

Once you have a topic, the next step is to create messages using it. We start by modifying the speed test Jupyter Notebook from *Recipe 62*. We update it to use the Confluent libraries, as shown in *Figure 15.43*:

```
In [2]:    1  # pip install confluent-kafka
           executed in 14ms, finished 17:04:55 2023-09-09

In [3]:    1  from configparser import ConfigParser
           2  from confluent_kafka import Producer
           3  import socket
           executed in 31ms, finished 17:04:56 2023-09-09

In [4]:    1  parser = ConfigParser()
           2  _ = parser.read("notebook.cfg")
           3  kakfaUsername = parser.get("my_Notebook", "sasl.username")
           4  kakfaPassword = parser.get("my_Notebook", "sasl.password")
           5  conf = {
           6      "bootstrap.servers": "pkc-419q3.us-east4.gcp.confluent.cloud:9092",
           7      "security.protocol": "SASL_SSL",
           8      "sasl.mechanism": "PLAIN",
           9      "sasl.username": kakfaUsername,
          10      "sasl.password": kakfaPassword,
          11      "client.id": socket.gethostname(),
          12  }
          13
          14  producer = Producer(conf)
          15  topics = producer.list_topics()
          16  print(topics)
           executed in 787ms, finished 17:04:56 2023-09-09
           lkc-7pxqnj
```

Figure 15.43: Installing Confluent Kafka library and initializing producer

We have commented out the **pip install confluent-kafka** command, as it has previously been installed. Next, we import the necessary libraries and then create a **ConfigParser** object. **ConfigParser** allows you to store configuration values in a file, in this case **notebook.cfg**. While it is not as secure as a secret store, it is better than having secrets in your notebook. To learn more about **ConfigParser** see **https://docs.python.org/3/library/configparser.html**. Once we have read the config file, we extract the Kafka username and password, and set them into a configuration dictionary. We pass that dictionary to the Producer constructor and then list out the topics. Interestingly, our cluster's identifier is returned instead of the defined topics.

The next few cells in the notebook are similar to that in Recipe 60. We update the method that sends messages to the cloud to use the producer object we created after reading the configuration, as shown in *Figure 15.44:*

```
 1  def acked(err, msg):
 2      print("Massage Acked")
 3      if err is not None:
 4          print("Failed to deliver message: %s: %s" % (str(msg), str(err)))
 5      else:
 6          print("Message produced: %s" % (str(msg)))
 7
 8
 9  def SendToStream(data):
10      try:
11          print("enter SendToStream", data)
12          result = producer.produce(topicName, key="reading", value=data, callback=acked)
13          producer.flush()
14          print("Sent data")
15      except Exception as e:
16          print("Unable to send data", e)
 executed in 31ms, finished 17:20:14 2023-09-09
```

Figure 15.44: Method to send to Kafka

The **SendToStream** method accepts a JSON object and sends it to Kafka. The flush statement on line 13 ensure the message is sent. We are notified if the message has been delivered by using a callback method. This is a common pattern in asynchronous programming. The remainder of the notebook has only minor changes. The next step is to create a consumer of the messages.

We can repurpose the Databricks notebook we used in Recipe 60 to consume from Confluence Cloud Kafka. We start by provisioning a new client to create a new username and password. You do this in Confluent cloud by navigating to your cluster and selecting Clients, and then New client. You then select a language, such as Python. The second step allows you to create a new cluster and schema registry API key. The remainder of the page is of marginal use, as it contains code that will not function or contains syntactical errors.

As in Recipe 60, we must install a library on our cluster. In this case, we install **confluent-ka fka[avro,json,protobuf]>=1.4.2**. You do this by navigating to the cluster's Libraries section, then select Install new, and switch the Library Source to PyPi, and then enter the library's name. We can now use the library in our notebooks.

As with previous examples, we use a Key Vault backed secrete scope. We need to add the Confluent APIs key and secret, essentially username and password, to the Key Vault. Once added, we can retrieve them using the **dbutils.secret.get** function, as shown in *Figure 15.45:*

```
1   confluentApiKey = dbutils.secrets.get(scope=secretScope, key="confluentApiKey")
2   confluentSecret = dbutils.secrets.get(scope=secretScope, key="confluentSecret")
3   confluentBootstrapServers = "pkc-419q3.us-east4.gcp.confluent.cloud:9092"
4   confluentTopicName = "speedtest"
5   configDict = {
6       "kafka.bootstrap.servers": confluentBootstrapServers,
7       "kafka.security.protocol": "SASL_SSL",
8       "kafka.sasl.jaas.config":
9           f"kafkashaded.org.apache.kafka.common.security.plain.PlainLoginModule required username='{confluentApiKey}' password='
            {confluentSecret}';",
10      "kafka.ssl.endpoint.identification.algorithm": "https",
11      "kafka.sasl.mechanism": "PLAIN",
12      "subscribe": confluentTopicName,
13      "startingOffsets": "earliest",
14      "failOnDataLoss": "false",
15  }
```

Figure 15.45: Retrieving secrets and setting up configuration dictionary

Now that we have our configuration dictionary, we can use that information to connect and retrieve records, as shown in *Figure 15.46:*

```
1    from datetime import datetime as dt
2    import json
3    import pyspark.sql.types as T
4    from pyspark.sql.functions import *
5
6    # Construct trans
7    payload_ddl = """utc LONG, download DOUBLE,ip STRING,ping DOUBLE, upload DOUBLE """
8    payload_schema = T._parse_datatype_string(payload_ddl)
9    df = (
10       spark.readStream.format("kafka")
11       .options(**configDict)
12       .load()
13       .withColumn("key", col("key").cast(StringType()))
14   )
15   df = df.withColumn("value", df["value"].cast("string"))
16   df = df.withColumn("parsed_records", from_json(col("value"), payload_schema))
17   df = df.where("parsed_records.utc is not null")
18   df = df.select("topic","partition","offset","timestamp","timestampType","key","parsed_records",
19   )
```

```
▼ ▣ df: pyspark.sql.dataframe.DataFrame
      topic: string
      partition: integer
      offset: long
      timestamp: timestamp
      timestampType: integer
      key: string
    ▼ parsed_records: struct
          utc: long
          download: double
          ip: string
          ping: double
          upload: double
```

Figure 15.46: Preparing to read records from Kafka

We can pass in our configuration dictionary using the **options** method, as shown on line 11. This cleans up the code, compared to chaining multiple **option** method calls. You can see that the schema of the DataFrame is returned. Since we applied the **payload_schema** to the string version of the value column we can see the structure of our internal payload.

The code from this point on is essentially same as that in Recipe 60, we specify a file location, establish a checkpoint directory, and then apply a once trigger invocation to the write stream of the streaming DataFrame, as shown in *Figure 15.47*:

```
1    # Setup checkpoint
2    filePath = "/mnt/lakehousecookbook/bronze/AlanDesktop/KakfaSource/SpeedTestStructuredStreaming/"
3    checkpointLocation = filePath.replace("/bronze/", "/checkpoints_bronze/")
4    dbutils.fs.mkdirs(checkpointLocation)
5    # Set table varaibles
6    schema = "lakehousecookbook"
7    tableName = "SpeedTestKafka"
8    spark.sql("set spark.databricks.delta.properties.defaults.enableChangeDataFeed = true;")
9    result = (
10       df.writeStream.trigger(once=True)
11       .format("delta").outputMode("append").option("checkpointLocation", checkpointLocation)
12       .option("mergeSchema", "true").option("path", filePath).toTable(schema + "." + tableName)
13   )
14   result.awaitTermination()
15   EnsureCDFIsOn(schema, tableName)
16   display(spark.sql(f"SELECT parsed_records.* FROM {schema}.{tableName}"))
```

▸ (3) Spark Jobs

```
lakehousecookbook SpeedTestKafka EnsureCDFIsOn: CDF already on
```

Table ⌄ +

	utc	download	ip	ping	upload
1	1694299372	4234475.9934586715	98.97.18.13	82.555	4832710.233016487
2	1694299601	15213020.346291725	98.97.18.13	44.424	9100218.905714631
3	1694299824	6952593.977875872	98.97.18.13	60.129	7153986.293889851
4	1694299146	4895469.25365155	98.97.18.13	89.731	13031447.584342629
5	1694300070	6495605.582977719	98.97.18.13	71.762	5297714.570500506

Figure 15.47: Writing the streaming DataFrame to an unmanaged Delta table

We have successfully read data from a Kafka topic and stored it in a Delta table. In the next section, will revisit orchestration and discuss Databricks notebook orchestration.

Notebook orchestration

In *Chapter 6, Extracting from Sourced and Loading to Bronze,* we discussed invoking one notebook from another. In this section we will expand on that discussion.

Recipe 146: Running a notebook with parameters

In *Chapter 6, Extracting from Sourced and Loading to Bronze,* we discussed using widgets to supply values to a notebook. In this recipe, we will use widgets as a way to pass values between notebooks, using **dbutils.notebook.run**. For this example, we will address a common problem. You will occasionally see folders in the **mnt** folder that are not valid mount points. Since mnt is a folder, you can create subfolders within it that are not linked to a storage system. In this recipe, we provide a simple way to detect this condition, as shown in *Figure 15.48:*

```
1    def CheckForFoldersInMnt():
2        mounts = dbutils.fs.mounts()
3        mountLookup = {}
4        for mount in mounts:
5            mountLookup[mount.mountPoint] = mount
6        mountContents = dbutils.fs.ls("/mnt/")
7        good = []
8        bad = []
9        for mountContent in mountContents:
10           mountContentPath = mountContent.path.replace("dbfs:", "").rstrip("/")
11           if mountContentPath in mountLookup:
12               good.append(mountContentPath)
13           else:
14               bad.append(mountContentPath)
15       if len(good) > 0:
16           print("---- Good ------")
17           for g in good:
18               print(f"Running notifcation notebook for {g}")
19               dbutils.notebook.run(notifcationNotebook,timeout_seconds,{"foldername": g, "IsMount": "True"},)
20       if len(bad) > 0:
21           print("----- Bad ------")
22           for b in bad:
23               print("Running notifcation notebook")
24               dbutils.notebook.run(notifcationNotebook,timeout_seconds,{"foldername": b, "IsMount": "False"},)
25   CheckForFoldersInMnt()
```

```
Notebook job #796522001870393
Notebook job #514501906869121
Notebook job #990287149171184

---- Good ------
Running notifcation notebook for /mnt/Lakehousecookbook
Running notifcation notebook for /mnt/sourceData
----- Bad ------
Running notifcation notebook
```

Figure 15.48: Detect non-mounts in mnt folder

Notice that we now have indication that Notebook jobs were created and executed. You also probably noticed that the process took a little longer than expected. The code constructs two lists, one of the folders that are not mount points and one of those that are. It then loops through those lists printing a message and invoking the notification notebook, setting the parameters. This process should be sub-second, however, it takes some time. This is because we are submitting a notebook job for execution. If you click one of the blue **Notebook job** links you will see the job's run page, as shown in *Figure 15.49*:

Figure 15.49: Notebook run page

On this page you can see the job's identifier, the values passed into it, and the results of its execution. The time it took to run was a produce of creating and submitting a notebook job for execution. In the next section, we will examine the results returned from a notebook's execution.

Recipe 147: Conditional execution of notebooks

In the previous recipe, we discussed invoking one notebook from another. In this section, we extend that flow by having the invoked notebook return a value that the caller examines. We clone the notebooks from Recipe 144 and use them as a starting point. In the invoked notebook, we add a call to **dbutils.notebook.exit**, as shown in *Figure 15.50:*

```
Cmd 3

1    if isMount:
2        print(f"{folderName} is a valid mountpoint ")
3        dbutils.notebook.exit(f"No notification, since mountpoint {folderName} is valid")
4    else:
5        print("We would replace with an process to send message to the right person.")
6        print(f"There is a folder in the mnt folder that is not a mount name=[{folderName}]")
7        dbutils.notebook.exit(f"Notification successful for {folderName}")

Notebook exited: Notification successful for Tesing
```

Figure 15.50: Returning a value from an invoked notebook

In our case, we return a simple string. Note that the string could be a JSON string created using **json.dumps**, as discussed here **https://docs.databricks.com/en/notebooks/notebook-workflows.html**. The only other changes required are to capture the return values from invoking **dbutils.notebook.run**, as shown in *Figure 15.51:*

```
15      if len(good) > 0:
16          print("---- Good ------")
17          for g in good:
18              print(f"Running notifcation notebook for {g}")
19              returncode = dbutils.notebook.run(notifcationNotebook,timeout_seconds,{"foldername": g, "IsMount": "True"},)
20              print(returncode)
21      if len(bad) > 0:
22          print("----- Bad ------")
23          for b in bad:
24              print("Running notifcation notebook")
25              returncode = dbutils.notebook.run(notifcationNotebook,timeout_seconds,{"foldername": b, "IsMount": "False"},)
26              print(returncode)
27  CheckForFoldersInMnt()
```

```
Notebook job #629310505511895
Notebook job #585233563408788
Notebook job #801456086921276

---- Good ------
Running notifcation notebook for /mnt/lakehousecookbook
No notification, since mountpoint /mnt/lakehousecookbook is valid
Running notifcation notebook for /mnt/sourceData
No notification, since mountpoint /mnt/sourceData is valid
----- Bad ------
Running notifcation notebook
Notification successful for /mnt/not a mount point

Command took 1.88 minutes -- by alan.dennis@gmail.com at 9/9/2023, 7:45:21 PM on Alan Dennis's Cluster
```

Figure 15.51: Capturing return values

You can see the string that was returned by the notification notebook is displayed after the notebook completes its execution. This is a brief introduction to workflow via notebook execution. It is best used for simple case. One tradeoff of this approach is the flow is not visible externally, as it is when using tasks in the workflow section, or an external tool such as Airflow. In the next section, we will discuss general best practices.

Best practices

Throughout this book, we have presented multiple best practices. With this section, we conclude the book by summarizing and possibly restating some guide best practices.

Organize data assets by source until silver

Throughout this book, we have advised that data elements should be organized by source system until they reach the silver zone. The motivation for this approach is to make the location of data elements guessable. This means that if a data engineer joins a team working on a Lakehouse, they should quickly be able to locate a particular silver table. Once tables need additional refinement, to produce intermediate or gold tables, diverging from this approach is appropriate.

The alternative to this approach is to organize tables around projects or units of work. When a data engineer is tasked with creating the tables to support a new dashboard, they may be tempted to organize bronze and silver tables based on that activity. The problems with this approach range from not being able to find the tables to data duplication and data inconsistencies. This built-for-task mindset leads to inefficiencies over time. While creating silver tables that are not currently being used might seem wasteful, in the long run it will reduce time to onboard additional use cases. It you have data assets not currently being consumed, set their incremental ingestion to infrequent, such as weekly. Advertise that they are available, by registering them in a data catalog. They will likely be used sooner than you anticipate.

Use automation as much as possibly

In *Recipe 141*, we discussed using the Databricks API. This allows developers to interact with an environment systematically. When you repeatedly do tasks, look for a way to automate them.

A good example of this is using CI/CD. We touched on this in recipe 126. It is worth the effort to automate the deployments to an environment based on a merge to a branch. This process depends on your version control system and its capabilities. The advice here is to invest the time to automate your deployments.

Also, ensure that your code does not have hard coded environmentally specific values. Poor configuration management often results in outages, defects, or improper processing. One approach is to leverage an environmentally specific secret store, having secrets with the same names but different values.

Ideally, develop automated unit and system tests. This is often challenging with data systems, but it is worth the investment. The idea is to have a set of tests to run automatically. These tests should ensure that the expected output is produced.

Use version control

As mentioned in Recipe 147, CI/CD is an important way to improve the quality of a Lakehouse. To perform CI/CD, you need a version control system in place. Entire books have been written on this topic, but the key point is that knowing who did what and when is essential. When something stops working, it is important to be able to identify what changes could have caused it. Additionally, knowing when the defect was introduced is necessary to fix the impacted data.

Generally, an individual or team does not get to pick their version control system. It is typically part of a larger DevOps effort. When starting a Lakehouse project, ensure you follow software development best practices because a data engineering project is a software engineering project.

Keep each step of the process simple

Before it was called the Databricks Lakehouse, Databricks introduced the same concepts under the name Delta Architecture. This was intended to address the challenges of the

Lambda architecture. For a good, but somewhat dated, discussion see **https://www. databricks.com/blog/2020/11/20/delta-vs-lambda-why-simplicity-trumps-complexity- for-data-pipelines.html**. One of the goals of the Lakehouse architecture is to break complex flows into simple elements. At its heart, you are reconstructing data elements as they existed in their source systems. Once that is done, and we call them silver items, you can focus on the process of combining them to answer business questions and generate value (we call them gold tables). This architectural approach directly opposes a point-to-point integration model, where flows are constructed for a certain business question from the source to the serving level. In general, simpler is better.

Do not be afraid to change

Throughout this book, we were introduced to many approaches and supplied some guidance. What we have captured is a point in time understanding of the architecture. The one constant in this industry is change. We must adapt our approaches and understandings to utilize technology as technology evolves. Keep a growth mindset, as you likely have as you have read this book.

Conclusion

This chapter discussed ways to ingest data from relational systems using Databricks. We touched on ways to diagnose performance challenges and reduce startup time. We explored ways to improve efficiencies and reduce quality issues by using automation. We examined reading a Kafka topic and orchestrating flow using native Databricks functionality. Lastly, we also supplied some high-level best practices.

We have covered a lot of material in this book, but it is only a brief introduction to many more important things. We started by going over the concepts of a Lakehouse, and why they are important to an organization. We then moved on to covering how to populate and then process data in a Lakehouse. Once data is in a Lakehouse, we can use different approaches to realize value from the data, such as graph processing and visualization. We also discussed the importance of Data governance using tools such as Purview or Unity Catalog. We hope you learned something from this book and will continue your journey towards the mastering the Databricks Lakehouse.

Index

Made in the USA
Columbia, SC
15 November 2024

46533150R00254